OXFORD WORLD'S CLASSICS

MEDITATIONS ON
FIRST PHILOSOPHY

RENÉ DESCARTES was born at La Haye near Tours on 31 March 1596. He was educated at the Jesuit Collège de la Flèche in Anjou, and at the University of Poitiers, where he took a Licenciate in Law in 1616. Two years later he entered the army of Prince Maurice of Nassau in Holland, and met a local schoolmaster, Isaac Beeckman, who fostered his interest in mathematics and physics. After further travels in Europe he settled in Paris in 1625, and came into contact with scientists, theologians, and philosophers in the circle of the Minim friar Marin Mersenne. At the end of 1628 Descartes left for Holland, which he made his home until 1648; he devoted himself to carrying forward the mathematical, scientific, and philosophical work he had begun in Paris. When he learned of the condemnation of Galileo for heresy in 1633, he abandoned his plans to publish a treatise on physics, and under pressure from his friends consented to have the *Discourse on the Method* printed, with three accompanying essays on topics in which he had made discoveries. In 1641 his *Meditations* appeared, setting out the metaphysical underpinnings of his physical theories; these were accompanied by objections written by contemporary philosophers, and Descartes's replies to them. His writings provoked controversy in both France and Holland, where his scientific ideas were banned in one university; his works, however (including the *Principles of Philosophy* of 1644) continued to be published, and to bring him notoriety and renown. In 1648 he accepted an invitation from Queen Christina of Sweden to settle in Stockholm; it was there he died of pneumonia on 11 February 1650.

MICHAEL MORIARTY is Drapers Professor of French at the University of Cambridge. Among his publications are *Early Modern French Thought: The Age of Suspicion* (2003) and *Fallen Nature, Fallen Selves: Early Modern French Thought II* (2006).

OXFORD WORLD'S CLASSICS

*For over 100 years Oxford World's Classics have brought
readers closer to the world's great literature. Now with over 700
titles—from the 4,000-year-old myths of Mesopotamia to the
twentieth century's greatest novels—the series makes available
lesser-known as well as celebrated writing.*

*The pocket-sized hardbacks of the early years contained
introductions by Virginia Woolf, T. S. Eliot, Graham Greene,
and other literary figures which enriched the experience of reading.
Today the series is recognized for its fine scholarship and
reliability in texts that span world literature, drama and poetry,
religion, philosophy and politics. Each edition includes perceptive
commentary and essential background information to meet the
changing needs of readers.*

OXFORD WORLD'S CLASSICS

RENÉ DESCARTES

Meditations on First Philosophy

With Selections from the Objections and Replies

Translated with an Introduction and Notes by
MICHAEL MORIARTY

OXFORD
UNIVERSITY PRESS

OXFORD
UNIVERSITY PRESS

Great Clarendon Street, Oxford ox2 6DP

Oxford University Press is a department of the University of Oxford.
It furthers the University's objective of excellence in research, scholarship,
and education by publishing worldwide in

Oxford New York

Auckland Cape Town Dar es Salaam Hong Kong Karachi
Kuala Lumpur Madrid Melbourne Mexico City Nairobi
New Delhi Shanghai Taipei Toronto

With offices in

Argentina Austria Brazil Chile Czech Republic France Greece
Guatemala Hungary Italy Japan Poland Portugal Singapore
South Korea Switzerland Thailand Turkey Ukraine Vietnam

Oxford is a registered trade mark of Oxford University Press
in the UK and in certain other countries

Published in the United States
by Oxford University Press Inc., New York

First published as an Oxford World's Classics paperback 2008

British Library Cataloguing in Publication Data

Data available

Library of Congress Cataloging in Publication Data

Descartes, René, 1596–1650.
[Meditationes de prima philosophia. English]
Meditations on first philosophy: with selections from the objections and replies/
René Descartes translated with an introduction and notes by Michael Moriarty.
p. cm.
Includes bibliographical references and index.

ISBN 978–0–19–280696–3
1. First philosophy. 2. God—Proof, Ontological. 3. Methodology. 4. Knowledge,
Theory of. I. Moriarty, Mike. II. Title.
B1853.E5M67 2008
194—dc22
2007044519

Typeset by Cepha Imaging Private Ltd., Bangalore, India
Printed in Great Britain by
Clays Ltd, Elcograf S.p.A.

ISBN 978–0–19–280696–3

18

CONTENTS

ACKNOWLEDGEMENTS

I have many people to thank for assistance with this edition. In particular, I would like to thank Terence Cave, Hannah Dawson, Susan James, Ian Maclean, and Morag Shiach for their generous assistance and support. I am most grateful to the anonymous readers for Oxford University Press for their valuable comments and suggestions. As series editor, Judith Luna has been an unfailing source of guidance and encouragement. Thanks also to Jeff New for his painstaking and vigilant copy-editing. As always, my colleagues at Queen Mary, University of London, have been a pleasure to work with and alongside. This work was begun in the last stages of a research leave jointly funded by Queen Mary and the Arts and Humanities Research Council. I am most grateful for this support.

Anyone working on Descartes knows how much he or she owes to the generations of scholars in various disciplines and from many countries whose work has illuminated the life, background, and above all the texts of this author. I hope that my own debts are, however imperfectly, acknowledged in the notes.

LIST OF ABBREVIATIONS

AT   *Œuvres de Descartes,* ed. Charles Adam and Paul Tannery,
            11 vols., rev. edn. (Paris: Vrin, 1996)
BGDM   Stephen Gaukroger (ed.), *The Blackwell Guide to Descartes'*
            'Meditations' (Oxford: Blackwell, 2006)
CCD   John Cottingham (ed.), *The Cambridge Companion to*
            Descartes (Cambridge: Cambridge University Press, 1992)
CHSCP   Daniel Garber and Michael Ayers (eds.), *The Cambridge*
            History of Seventeenth-Century Philosophy, 2 vols.
            (Cambridge: Cambridge University Press, 1998)
Discourse   Descartes, *A Discourse on the Method,* ed. and trans.
            Ian Maclean, Oxford World's Classics (Oxford:
            Oxford University Press, 2006)
F   Descartes, *Meditations,* French text
JHI   *Journal of the History of Ideas*
L   Descartes, *Meditations,* Latin text
OP   Descartes, *Œuvres philosophiques,* ed. Ferdinand Alquié,
            3 vols., Classiques Garnier (Paris: Garnier, 1963–73)
PL   *Patrologiæ cursus completus, Series latina,* ed. J. P. Migne
            (Paris: Migne, 1844–55)
VS   Montaigne, *Les Essais,* ed. Pierre Villey and V.-L. Saulnier,
            3 vols. paginated as one (Paris: Quadrige/Presses
            Universitaires de France, 1992 [1st publ. 1924])

INTRODUCTION

Descartes's *Meditations* is among the most influential texts in the history of Western philosophy. Many thinkers have challenged or rejected his thought, some of them almost totally, but his rigorous questioning of traditional certainties is at the source of most subsequent philosophical developments. The criticism he has received and continues to receive is a backhanded compliment he would not have appreciated, but an index, nonetheless, of the power of his philosophy.

Descartes's Life

Descartes was born in 1596, in La Haye, a town in Touraine (central-western France): the family home was in Châtellerault, in the neighbouring province of Poitou.[1] France was emerging from a civil war between Catholics and Protestants that had lasted for over thirty years. His family's background was in the legal profession and the royal administration. The office held by his father conferred noble rank, but such office-holding nobles had far less prestige than the military nobility. Yet Descartes, as Ian Maclean observes, derived a sense of status from this background, borne out in his later attitudes, including a tendency to refuse to be identified as a professional scholar.[2] In 1607 he entered the Jesuit college of La Flèche, near Le Mans, where he received an excellent education, which he describes

---

[1] For biographical material I have drawn on Stephen Gaukroger, *Descartes: An Intellectual Biography* (Oxford: Oxford University Press, 1995); Geneviève Rodis-Lewis, *Descartes: biographie* (Paris: Calmann-Lévy, 1995: in English as *Descartes: His Life and Thought*, trans. Jane Marie Todd (Ithaca, NY: Cornell University Press, 1998)); A. C. Grayling, *Descartes: The Life of René Descartes and its Place in his Times* (London: The Free Press, 2005); Desmond M. Clarke, *Descartes: A Biography* (Cambridge: Cambridge University Press, 2006). I am particularly grateful to Ian Maclean for his comments on a draft of this Introduction as well as on the draft Explanatory Notes.

[2] Descartes, *A Discourse on the Method of Correctly Conducting One's Reason and Seeking Truth in the Sciences*, ed. and trans. Ian Maclean, Oxford World's Classics (Oxford: Oxford University Press, 2006), pp. viii, xli, xliii. All references to the *Discourse* are to this edition, which gives a very full account of the context and significance of the text. (I give first the Part of the text referred to, and then the page number, so that ii. 15 refers to Part II of the *Discourse*, the passage in question being found on p. 15.)

in Part I of *A Discourse on the Method*. After leaving school in 1615 he
attended the University of Poitiers for a year, emerging with a degree
in law. But he did not follow a legal career: instead, in 1618 he did
what many young gentlemen did, namely volunteer for military
service. He enlisted first in the army of the United Provinces (the
Netherlands) under Prince Maurice of Nassau. During his stay in
the Netherlands he met the mathematician and scientist Isaac
Beeckman, who became an intellectual inspiration for him. In
January 1619 he left Maurice's army, and travelled to Germany,
where he joined the army of the Catholic Maximilian, duke of
Bavaria. While billeted at Neuburg in November 1619, sheltering
from the winter in a stove-heated room, he began, he tells us in
Part II of the *Discourse*, his search for a new method of seeking truth.
On the night of 10 November he had a series of dreams which he
associated with intellectual inspiration. He may have been present at
the Battle of the White Mountain near Prague in November 1620,
the first engagement in what became the horrific Thirty Years War.
He returned to France in 1622, travelled to Italy in 1623, returned to
France in 1625, and in 1628 left for the Netherlands, where he would
spend the next twenty years in various places. He seems to have
relished the isolation of being a foreigner, and the United Provinces
was a more tolerant society than most. In 1635 he had a child,
Francine, by a servant called Helena: Francine's death in 1640
seems to have been a source of great grief. For much of the 1640s
he was engaged in controversy, with Dutch Protestant theologians
and with his former disciple Regius. He also conducted a sustained
correspondence with Princess Elisabeth of Bohemia, whose intelligent and critical engagement with his philosophy encouraged him
to develop the psychological and ethical aspects of his thought. In
1649 he travelled to Sweden to take up a position at the court of
Queen Christina. He died in Stockholm of pneumonia in February
1650.

Throughout the 1620s and the early 1630s Descartes was develop-
ing his scientific work, without publishing it. He was committed to
the mechanistic conception of the physical world, which has been
excellently defined as follows: 'All natural phenomena . . . can be
explained in terms of the arrangement and motion (or rest) of
minute, insensible particles of matter (corpuscles), each of which is
characterized exclusively by certain fundamental and irreducible

properties—shape, size, and impenetrability.'[3] His plans to publish *Le Monde*, a treatise explaining the universe on mechanistic principles, had to be shelved when, in 1633, the Roman Catholic Church condemned Galileo for supporting the heliocentric view of the universe, to which Descartes himself was committed.[4] In 1637 he published *Discours de la méthode pour bien conduire sa raison et chercher la vérité dans les sciences* (*A Discourse on the Method of Correctly Conducting One's Reason and Seeking Truth in the Sciences*), accompanied by three essays on optics, geometry, and meteorology. True to its title, the *Discourse* sets out a programme and method for scientific research, but does so in the unusual form of an intellectual autobiography designed to justify the apparently strange project of approaching the search for knowledge by rejecting what currently passes for knowledge. Four years later Descartes published the *Meditationes de prima philosophia* (*Meditations on First Philosophy, in which the existence of God and the distinction of the human soul from the body are demonstrated*). This was followed in 1644 by the *Principia Philosophiæ* (*Principles of Philosophy*), which expounded his metaphysical and scientific theories in textbook form, and in 1649 by *Les Passions de l'âme* (*The Passions of the Soul*), which examines mind–body interaction with particular reference to the emotions.

The Genesis of the Meditations

In a letter of 1629 Descartes refers to 'a little treatise' he is working on (to Gibieuf, 18 July 1629, AT 1. 17);[5] this is normally identified with the unfinished 'little treatise on metaphysics', dedicated to proving the existence of God and the soul (to Mersenne, 25 November 1630, AT 1. 182). This work has been lost or destroyed. In any case, he explains to Mersenne that he wished to postpone publishing his

[3] Steven Nadler, 'Doctrines of Explanation in Late Scholasticism and in the Mechanical Philosophy', in Daniel Garber and Michael Ayers (eds.), *The Cambridge History of Seventeenth-Century Philosophy*, 2 vols. (Cambridge: Cambridge University Press, 1998 [hereafter *CHSCP*]), i. 513–52, at p. 520. Nadler cites Mersenne, Gassendi, and Boyle as other partisans of this approach.

[4] *Le Monde* was published posthumously, first in 1662 in a Latin translation, then in 1664 in the original French. See Gaukroger, *Descartes*, 225–92.

[5] The letters AT refer to the standard edition of Descartes's works, *Œuvres de Descartes*, ed. Charles Adam and Paul Tannery, 11 vols., rev. edn. (Paris: Vrin, 1996). The AT page numbers are given in many other editions, including this one, and are the standard method of referring to Descartes's work.

metaphysical discoveries until he had some idea of how his work in physics would be received (15 April 1630, AT 1. 145).

Part IV of the *Discourse on the Method* describes the author's attempt to find metaphysical positions solid enough to serve as foundations for the edifice of the new science. Here Descartes narrates his project of rejecting all those beliefs in the slightest degree open to doubt; his discovery of the Cogito ('I think, therefore I am', or 'I am thinking, therefore I exist') as a first principle for his new philosophy; the conclusion from the Cogito that he is, essentially, a thinking thing, a soul entirely distinct from the body; and the generalization, from the experience of certainty afforded by the Cogito, a truth clearly and distinctly conceived, that whatever we clearly and distinctly conceive is true.[6] The experience of doubt is an experience of imperfection: but this presupposes the idea of a being more perfect than oneself. Such an idea, Descartes argues, can only come from outside ourselves—from an actually existing perfect being, God. In fact, as an imperfect being, he himself cannot be independent; he could not even exist, were there not a perfect being on which he, and indeed all other finite beings, depended. Subsequent investigations in geometry reinforce the lesson that certainty depends on clear and distinct conception, and suggest a further argument for the existence of God: the concept of a perfect being involves existence, just as the concept of a triangle involves having three angles the sum of which is equal to two right angles. From the concept itself, we can thus infer God's actual existence. Descartes goes on to argue that all knowledge depends on that of God. If we do not know of his existence, we cannot ward off sceptical doubts about the reality of our bodies and the physical world: indeed, it is only because he exists, and is a perfect being, from whom all our properties derive, that we can be sure that whatever we clearly and distinctly conceive is true. Once, however, we know he exists, veracity being one of his perfections, all sceptical doubts fade away.[7]

Stated thus baldly, these arguments may seem unconvincing. And certainly Descartes himself was not satisfied with the formulation of

---

[6] Descartes, writing the *Discourse* in French, uses the verb 'concevoir' (to conceive intellectually) in his formulation of this rule. In Latin he tends to use 'percipere' (to perceive). These terminological issues are discussed below.

[7] *Discourse*, iv. 28–34, AT 6. 31–40.

them in the *Discourse*. He explains to a correspondent that he only decided at the last minute to include this section at all, implying that he wrote it under pressure; more importantly, he says he had toned down the sceptical arguments he there considers, as being unsuitable for a general readership, and had not sufficiently explained some of his principles.[8] The sceptical case—an indispensable preliminary to his own reconstruction of knowledge—is given its full force only in the *Meditations*—written in Latin for the learned.[9] But the *Meditations* are more than an expanded version of Part IV of the *Discourse*. The substance of the argument is very similar: but its ordering is altered, in ways that are philosophically significant.

The *Meditations on First Philosophy* are as original in philosophical form as in content. 'First philosophy' would have been recognized by Descartes's readers as synonymous with 'metaphysics', the study of being in general, rather than particular kinds of being: but although he speaks of the work as his 'metaphysics', he prefers the title 'Meditations on First Philosophy', because the book deals 'not specifically with God and the soul, but in general with all the first things we can know by philosophizing'.[10] And indeed, Descartes's 'metaphysics' or 'first philosophy' foregrounds questions of what we can know (what would nowadays be classed as 'epistemology' rather than 'metaphysics') as a prelude to discussion of what exists. But the word 'Meditations' itself suggests a radically new approach to philosophizing, affecting the whole form of the work. A typical scholastic treatise would have been composed in forms based on scholastic pedagogical techniques, in which debate or 'disputation' on opposite sides of the question played a key role. The subject-matter would have been divided into a series of 'questions', or debates, which might themselves be subdivided. Arguments on both sides of the question would be given, supported by accepted definitions and principles, and quotations from authoritative sources, especially Aristotle. The author's eventual resolution of the problem would thus be

---

[8] Descartes to Vatier, 22 Feb. 1638, AT 1. 560–1.

[9] *Meditations on First Philosophy*, Preface to the Reader, AT 7. 7; Fourth Replies, AT 7. 247.

[10] To Mersenne, 11 Nov. 1640, AT 3. 235: see John Cottingham, 'Introduction', in John Cottingham (ed.), *Descartes* (Oxford: Oxford University Press, 1998), 6. In early modern terminology 'philosophy' in the broader sense (as in Descartes's *Principles of Philosophy*) includes the study of the physical world (what we would call 'science').

situated explicitly in relation to the views of other scholars, from the recent or remote past: he would be seen, and would have seen himself, as contributing to an ongoing debate.

Descartes's approach is utterly different. He makes no reference in the body of the text to other thinkers' views, in accordance with his opinion that everyone is entitled to write what they think true, without worrying about whether they are disagreeing or agreeing with others.[11] Moreover, the title 'Meditations' presents the work as something other than a chain of philosophical argumentation, and links it, rather, to religious exercises.[12] In the Second Replies, Descartes explains the importance of his distinctive approach: 'I wrote Meditations, rather than Disputations, as philosophers normally do, or Theorems and Problems, in the manner of geometers, so that by this fact alone I might make clear that I have no business except with those who are prepared to make the effort to meditate along with me and to consider the subject attentively' (p. 101). Thus, in the First Meditation Descartes is not simply putting forward abstract arguments in favour of distrusting the senses. In the Second Replies, he suggests that 'readers [should] dwell on the matters contained in it, not simply for the short period of time required to read it, but for several months, or at least weeks, before they go on to the rest of the work' (AT 7. 130). The temporal dimension is marked in the text itself by such expressions as 'yesterday' (p. 17), 'these last few days' (p. 38), 'these past days' (p. 63), suggesting that each Meditation is the work of a day (even though the reader may need to extend these 'days' in order to assimilate the material properly). The 'withdrawal of the mind from the senses' Descartes

[11] To Huygens, 13 [it should be 10] Oct. 1642, AT 3. 579.

[12] See *Discourse*, 71 n., and Gary Hatfield, 'The Senses and the Fleshless Eye: The *Meditations* as Cognitive Exercises', in Amelie Oksenberg Rorty (ed.), *Essays on Descartes' Meditations* (Berkeley: University of California Press, 1986), 45–79. Hatfield stresses the different aims of Christian and Cartesian meditation (see p. 54), as does Fernand Hallyn, who pronounces the resemblance to religious meditation superficial (*Descartes: dissimulation et ironie* (Geneva: Droz, 2006), 110–15). See also Ferdinand Alquié, *La Découverte métaphysique de l'homme chez Descartes*, 6th edn. (Paris: Presses Universitaires de France, 2000 [1950]), 162–4; but also, for a different approach, Peter Dear, 'Mersenne's Suggestion: Cartesian Meditation and the Mathematical Model of Knowledge in the Seventeenth Century', in Roger Ariew and Marjorie Grene (eds.), *Descartes and his Contemporaries: Meditations, Objections, and Replies* (Chicago and London: University of Chicago, Press, 1995), 44–62.

recommends as a precondition of the search for truth may well seem more reminiscent of spiritual techniques than of scientific enquiry:[13] yet it is essential, he thinks, if our search for truth is not to be vitiated at the start by the long-held habits of thought, in which what we know by the senses is the most accessible and most solid reality.

Descartes was well aware that the novelty of this approach would be liable to arouse suspicion in a learned readership for whom what we might value as originality might well appear mere eccentricity and arrogance. He adopted various strategies aimed at overcoming this resistance. He hoped to receive the endorsement of the Sorbonne, the highly influential Theology Faculty of the University of Paris (for his letter to the Faculty see p. 3 below), and the first edition claims the work was so approved.[14] Another strategy bore more abundant fruit. The *Meditations* eschew the scholastic practice of formally setting out objections to one's position and replies to these objections. Instead, Descartes prevailed upon his friend the theologian, philosopher, and scientist Marin Mersenne, one of the great intellectual networkers of his age, to solicit objections from a variety of competent readers. The objections and Descartes's replies to these would be printed along with the main text of the Meditations.[15] Descartes's hope, repeatedly expressed in the Replies, was that the objections would be sufficiently comprehensive and searching to convince readers that his text had been as rigorously examined as possible, while his replies would convince them that it was invulnerable. The Objectors were, indeed, a varied and mostly distinguished

[13] The phrase 'abducere mentem a sensibus' (to withdraw one's mind from the senses) appears in letters to Mersenne (Mar. 1637) [probably, in fact, late April], AT 1. 351; and to Vatier (22 Feb. 1638, AT 1. 560). See Henri Gouhier, *La Pensée métaphysique de Descartes* (Paris: Vrin, 1962), 51–5; Stephen Menn, *Descartes and Augustine* (Cambridge: Cambridge University Press, 1998), 220–4.

[14] Jean-Robert Armogathe explains what happened in terms of the workings of the Sorbonne's system of censorship. In accordance with standard practice, a committee of censors was appointed to examine the *Méditations*. If the censors did not condemn a text, it was regarded as having the Faculty's approval. On this showing, the *Meditations* could be claimed to have been approved ('L'Approbation des *Meditationes* par la Faculté de Théologie de Paris (1641)', *Bulletin Cartésien*, 21: 1–3, in *Archives de philosophie*, 57: 1 (1994)).

[15] On the link between the Objections and Replies and the scholastic practice of disputation see Gary Hatfield, *Descartes and the 'Meditations'* (Abingdon: Routledge, 2003), 43.

group, including Mersenne himself, Pierre Gassendi, the English philosopher Thomas Hobbes, and Antoine Arnauld, who would soon win fame as a powerful and controversial theologian.[16] The Objections and Replies are of vital assistance to the understanding of the Meditations. They are therefore summarized, and the most important passages quoted, in this edition. Two sets, the Third and the Fourth (Hobbes's and Arnauld's respectively), are included unabridged, Hobbes's because of his standing as a philosopher, and Arnauld's because Descartes thought him the most penetrating of his readers (to Mersenne, 4 March 1641, AT 3. 331).

The first edition of the *Meditations*, including six sets of Objections and Replies, was published by Michel Soly in Paris in late August 1641. Descartes seems to have been dissatisfied with it (it contained many printer's errors), and started work on a second edition, to be printed in Amsterdam by the famous firm of Elzevier. It appeared in January 1642, and contained a seventh set of objections from the Jesuit priest Bourdin, with Descartes's replies, and a letter to Dinet, a former teacher of Descartes at La Flèche, who was now head of the French province of the Society of Jesus.[17] In 1647 a French translation (*Méditations métaphysiques touchant la première philosophie*) was published: the Meditations themselves were translated by a great nobleman, the duc de Luynes, a sympathizer of the Jansenist religious movement, and the Objections and Replies by Claude Clerselier.[18]

---

[16] More information on the Objectors is given in the Introduction to the Objections and Replies. The first set of Objections was solicited without the intervention of Mersenne (Clarke, *Descartes*, 202).

[17] The title of the first edition reads as *Meditations on First Philosophy in Which the Existence of God and the Immortality of the Soul are Demonstrated*. The title of the second edition claims (more accurately) proof not for the immortality of the soul but for its real distinction from the body (see the Synopsis, pp. 10–12, and Descartes to Mersenne, 24 Dec. 1640, AT 3. 265–6).

[18] 'Jansenism' is a term, originally hostile, applied to followers of the Flemish Roman Catholic theologian Cornelius Jansenius (1585–1638), who offered a rigorous restatement of St Augustine's doctrines on grace and predestination that, to his critics, seemed very close to Calvinism. It has often been noted that in France followers of Augustine's theology were sympathetic to Descartes: but not all of these were 'Jansenists'—Malebranche, for instance, was not. Antoine Arnauld is the most obvious example of a Jansenist whose philosophy was Cartesian. See Geneviève Rodis-Lewis, 'Augustinisme et cartésianisme', in *L'Anthropologie cartésienne* (Paris: Presses Universitaires de France, 1995 [1955]), 101–25; Henri Gouhier, *Cartésianisme et augustinisme au XVII*ᵉ *siècle* (Paris: Vrin, 1978); Tad M. Schmaltz, 'What Has Cartesianism To Do With Jansenism?', *Journal of the History of Ideas*, 60 (1999), 37–56.

Descartes himself, according to the publisher's preface to the French edition, checked the translations (AT 9. 2–3). But there are two exceptions here. This 1647 translation did not contain the Seventh Objections or the letter to Dinet. Clerselier's translation of these was published in the second French-language edition in 1661, but this was not revised by Descartes. Besides, Descartes did not initially wish the 1647 translation to include the exchange with Gassendi (the Fifth Objections and Replies). He consented, eventually, to its inclusion, but did not revise the translation. This edition also contained a letter by Descartes to Clerselier addressing a number of points ('instances') extracted from Gassendi's *Disquisitio metaphysica*, published in 1641, containing his original objections, and criticisms of Descartes's replies.[19]

The Rationale of the Meditations

Descartes's approach to the problem of truth was strikingly innovative. Truth was not to be sought by mastering a range of authoritative texts, and analysing the questions to which the reading of these might give rise, with full attention to the variety of views that might be taken. What was required was an individual search, conducted along the correct methodical lines, and the correct method involved divorcing oneself from one's inveterate tendency to turn to the senses for information about the world in which one lives. More particularly, it involved a wholesale repudiation of one's former beliefs: not merely casual opinions but deep convictions.

It is some years now since I realized how many false opinions I had accepted as true from childhood onwards, and that, whatever I had since built on such shaky foundations, could only be highly doubtful. Hence I saw that at some stage in my life the whole structure would have to be utterly demolished, and that I should have to begin again from the bottom up if I wished to construct something lasting and unshakable in the sciences. . . . I have withdrawn into seclusion and shall at last be able to devote myself seriously and without encumbrance to the task of destroying all my former opinions. (p. 17)

---

[19] On the publication history of the various editions in French and Latin see AT 7. v–xviii (Latin) and AT 9. v–x (French). On the translation of the Fifth Objections, see Clerselier's note at AT 9. 200–1. On Gassendi's *Disquisitio metaphysica*, see AT 7. 391–412.

But what need for such an unconventional approach? It puzzled many of Descartes's contemporaries, who would have been content, where certain knowledge was unavailable, with probabilities. But Descartes was urging them to put the probable on a level with the absolutely false.[20] Now, it is perfectly possible to offer a purely philosophical rationale for his approach.[21] It is equally possible to seek to focus on 'the *specific* question to which Descartes may have intended his doctrine of certainty as a solution', and thus to read the *Meditations* more in their historical context.[22] Some have read it as a response to the revival of ancient scepticism, to which Montaigne's essay 'Apologie de Raimond Sebond', first published in 1580, had given a powerful expression. Montaigne's challenge to all claims to achieve knowledge by purely human means was inspired by the 'Pyrrhonist' strand of scepticism represented by Sextus Empiricus (*c*.AD 160–210). Pyrrhonism challenges any attempt to achieve knowledge of a reality behind appearance. Snow looks white: but whether it *is* white or not we cannot know. Pyrrhonism makes no truth-claims itself: it does not even say: 'We cannot achieve knowledge.' It merely undermines everyone else's truth-claims. Any argument can be matched by an equally convincing counter-argument. We have no criterion or mark that guarantees a perception or a proposition as true. In particular, Montaigne draws on the Pyrrhonist argument that all our knowledge is unreliable, because it is ultimately based on sense-perception, which is untrustworthy.[23]

[20] That is, for the purposes of scientific knowledge. From the point of view of practical conduct, Descartes not only admits but insists that we must normally be content with probability. See *Discourse* iii. 22–3, AT 6. 24–5.

[21] See Bernard Williams, *Descartes: The Project of Pure Enquiry* (Harmondsworth: Pelican, 1978), esp. ch. 2. In a work aimed at introducing the reader both to the *Meditations* and to analytical philosophy, Catherine Wilson likewise offers an account of the project in terms of an ideal scientist's quest for non-obvious truths about things: *Descartes's 'Meditations': An Introduction* (Cambridge: Cambridge University Press, 2003), 1, 13–31. But she supplements this with a contextual account (pp. 230–8).

[22] Quentin Skinner, 'Meaning and Understanding in the History of Ideas', in *Visions of Politics*, vol. 1, *Regarding Method* (Cambridge: Cambridge University Press, 2002), 83 (my italics). The study of philosophy in France does not make the same sharp distinction between philosophy itself and the history of philosophy, or even of ideas, as is current in the English-speaking world. Moreover, much recent English-language Descartes scholarship bridges these distinctions very effectively.

[23] Montaigne, 'Apologie de Raimond Sebond', *Essais*, ed. Pierre Villey and V.-L. Saulnier, 3 vols. paginated as one (Paris: Quadrige/Presses Universitaires de France, 1992), II. 12, 438–604 (on Pyrrhonism, see esp. pp. 502–6, on the senses

(Scepticism of this kind did not necessarily imply rejection of religious belief: Montaigne presented it, rather, as a justification for religious faith.) Descartes's presentation of sceptical arguments certainly owes much to Montaigne.[24] But his ultimate aim is quite different: to use scepticism to root out not all claims to knowledge, but invalid ones, in particular the established Aristotelian philosophy for which he aimed to substitute his own mechanistic theories. (Descartes asserts that the *Meditations* contain all the principles of his physics (to Mersenne, 11 November 1640, AT 3. 233), but asks Mersenne to keep this quiet, to avoid alienating Aristotelian readers, who he hopes will assimilate his principles before they have realized that they make Aristotle's untenable (28 January 1641, AT 3. 297–8).) The use of scepticism, then, is a demolition exercise designed to clear a space for the laying of new and solid foundations, not only in metaphysics but in science.[25]

Although Descartes retains some key Aristotelian concepts (the difference, for example, explained below, between substance and accident), he rejects the Aristotelian heritage in more ways than can even be summarized here. I shall focus on merely two aspects in this section: others will emerge in the Explanatory Notes.

First, Descartes rejects the Aristotelian conception in which bodies are seen as combinations of fundamental elements (fire, air, water, earth), themselves understood as combinations of fundamental qualities (hot, cold, wet, dry), and in which their movements are ascribed to a tendency or 'inclination' of the different elements to return to their place of origin (a flame moves upwards, because the element of fire belongs in the upper regions of the universe; a stone downwards, because the earth of which it is composed seeks its

---

pp. 587–601). All references to Montaigne are to this edition (hereafter abbreviated to VS). The classic statement of Pyrrhonism is Sextus Empiricus, *Outlines of Pyrrhonism* [*Hypotyposes*]: see the edition by R. G. Bury, Loeb Classical Library (Cambridge, Mass. and London, 1933).

[24] Descartes's use of Montaigne is succinctly treated by Clarke, *Descartes*, 191, and in more detail by Gaukroger, *Descartes*, 314–19.

[25] The interpretation of Descartes's work as a response to scepticism is set out in Richard Popkin, *The History of Scepticism from Savonarola to Bayle*, rev. and expanded edn. (Oxford: Oxford University Press, 2003), first published as *The History of Scepticism from Erasmus to Descartes* (1960), and in more detail by E. M. Curley, *Descartes against the Skeptics* (Oxford: Blackwell, 1978). Curley, however, also stresses the anti-Aristotelian thrust of Descartes's philosophy (pp. 1–9, 207–36). This latter dimension is stressed in Gaukroger's biography, and by many recent writers.

resting-place at the centre of the universe).[26] He argues in *Le Monde* that a world exactly similar to the world we experience today could in theory have been formed out of homogeneous matter, credited with no qualities beyond extension (possession of length, breadth, and depth) and divisibility into parts: if different movements were produced by God in the different parts of matter, the ultimate result would be the formation of an ordered cosmos, such as the one we inhabit. (Descartes states the theory as a fiction so as to avoid the appearance of clashing with the biblical account of creation.)[27] The later *Principles of Philosophy* restate it, but in a less polemical fashion, so as not to provoke Aristotelian ire.

Now the philosophical strategy of the *Meditations* enables Descartes to conclude that matter has, in fact, no basic properties but those (extension, divisibility, etc.) presupposed by the mechanistic conception.[28] This strategy—this is the second point—involves showing that what we think we know through the senses is in fact unreliable, and that true knowledge must be sought independently of the senses through the understanding alone. Here Descartes clashes with a key Aristotelian thesis, summed up in the scholastic axiom (which he quotes in Part IV of the *Discourse*) that 'there is nothing in the intellect which has not previously been in the senses':[29] that is, that all our concepts, even those of immaterial entities, are formed, by means of abstraction, out of sense-perceptions. (In rejecting this

---

[26] W. D. Ross, *Aristotle*, 3rd edn. revd. (London: Methuen, 1937), 105–8, 99; Roger Ariew, 'Descartes and Scholasticism', in John Cottingham (ed.), *The Cambridge Companion to Descartes* (Cambridge: Cambridge University Press, 1992 [hereafter *CCD*]), 58–90, at p. 82, n. 14. The key Aristotelian text is *De caelo*, III. 2–IV (300ᵃ–313ᵇ), trans. *On the Heavens*, ed. and trans. W. K. C. Guthrie, Loeb Classical Library (London: Heinemann and Cambridge, Mass.: Harvard University Press, 1953).

[27] *Le Monde ou Traité de la lumière*, AT 11. 1–118; see esp. chs. 2, 5–7 (AT 11. 7–10, 23–48). On Descartes's natural philosophy see Daniel Garber, 'Descartes's Physics', in *CCD* 286–334, and *Descartes Embodied: Reading Cartesian Philosophy Through Cartesian Science* (Cambridge: Cambridge University Press, 2001); Gary C. Hatfield, 'Force (God) in Descartes' Physics', in John Cottingham (ed.), *Descartes*, 281–310. On the *Principles* in particular, see Gaukroger, *Descartes's System of Natural Philosophy* (Cambridge: Cambridge University Press, 2002).

[28] In a sense, this conception of body corresponds to Aristotle's basic definition of it, in terms of three-dimensional extension and divisibility, *De caelo*, I.i (268ᵃ). It discards the more specific theories Aristotle advances as to the actual constitution and properties of bodies.

[29] *Discourse*, iv. 32, AT 6. 37 and see p. li. A specific source is Aquinas, *De veritate*, II.3, *ad* 19 (see Jorge Secada, *Cartesian Metaphysics: The Late Scholastic Origins of Modern Philosophy* (Cambridge: Cambridge University Press, 2000), 10).

Aristotelian epistemology, Descartes has been seen as reviving the metaphysical approach of St Augustine.)[30] Alternatively, Descartes's break with Aristotelian scholasticism has been seen as powered by a metaphysical rather than (or as well as) a scientific programme: as a rejection of the generally accepted view that knowledge that a substance exists must precede knowledge of its essence or nature.[31]

There is a third possible contextual factor: the existence in 1620s Paris, perhaps amplified by the anxiety of the religious, of unbelievers, denying the existence of God and the life after death.[32] (Not all unbelievers were Pyrrhonists, nor all Pyrrhonists unbelievers.) In producing a philosophy that made the existence of God and the immateriality of the soul certain, Descartes was not simply laying foundations for science: he could claim, as he does in his letter to the Sorbonne, and quite sincerely, to be serving religion by depriving unbelief of any claim to rational justification.[33]

All of these arguments have historical relevance and plausibility; and we can continue to seek for ever-deeper knowledge of the context of Descartes's thought while agreeing with Jorge Secada that there is no 'single key to the interpretation of the Cartesian philosophy'.[34]

Reading the Meditations

It has been stressed above that the form of the 'meditation' is essential to Descartes's philosophical enterprise. Descartes eschews the impersonal discourse of scholastic philosophy or of mathematics: instead, the text narrates a series of discoveries made by a figure who refers to himself in the first person—an example of what Charles Taylor has called 'radical reflexivity', in which one focuses not on the objects of one's experience, but on oneself as experiencing it.[35]

---

[30] See Menn, *Descartes and Augustine*.

[31] Secada, *Cartesian Metaphysics*, 1–4.

[32] Gaukroger, *Descartes*, 135–8. The contemporary term was 'libertins': it often implied an immoral and debauched lifestyle as well as rejection of religion.

[33] Margaret Dauler Wilson, *Descartes* (London: Routledge & Kegan Paul, 1978), 3; Rodis-Lewis, *Descartes*, 10. She offers a broader discussion of Descartes's religious views on pp. 284–97.

[34] Secada, *Cartesian Metaphysics*, 2.

[35] Charles Taylor, *Sources of the Self: The Making of the Modern Identity* (Cambridge: Cambridge University Press, 1989), 130. He sees St Augustine as the source of this way of thinking, and Montaigne as another early modern practitioner (pp. 177–84). On Descartes, see pp. 143–58.

It would be a mistake to identify this figure with the individual Descartes: when Descartes wrote the *Meditations* he knew already what he thought about many issues about which the 'I' in the text appears initially to be ignorant or in error or confused. Hence it has become conventional to refer to the 'I' of the text as the Meditator, and I follow this usage here.[36]

The reader's task, then, is in a sense to identify with, to think along with, the Meditator.[37] But Descartes knows that there must be many resistances to such an identification, to the call to abandon spontaneous attitudes. The work of breaking down this resistance devolves partly on the writing, the style. Descartes scorns one of the objectors, Gassendi, for resorting to rhetorical shifts instead of philosophical argument (Fifth Replies, p. 183). But in fact he himself resorts to rhetoric: it is an integral part of his strategy. This is not to say that he uses rhetoric where he should be using philosophical argument, or to plug gaps in his arguments; or to assert, in deconstructionist fashion, that his discourse is controlled, unbeknownst to himself, by the play of rhetorical structures, which undermine the attempts to operate with pure concepts. (Hobbes, to be sure, accuses Descartes of substituting metaphors for proof: but Descartes replies, quite fairly, that he is using metaphor to clarify not to prove (Third Objections, XIII, p. 121).) Rhetoric has a specific function in the *Meditations*, which is not dissimilar to its function in the *Discourse*. There, the metaphors of the journey, the building, the city, and so forth were used to justify the apparently eccentric or arrogant project of rejecting the existing structure of knowledge in order to erect a new one.[38] Here metaphors and other rhetorical devices are used to unsettle the reader, to disturb his or her spontaneous convictions, first, about the world and his or her own relation in it, and secondly, about his or her own fundamental nature or self.

[36] Some recent commentators speak of the Meditator as 'she', in order to emphasize the distinction between the 'I' of the text and the historical Descartes (Hatfield, *Descartes and the 'Meditations'*, 51; and cf. C. Wilson, *Descartes's 'Meditations'*, 7). I do not follow this reasonable practice only because the original Latin puts the Meditator in the masculine gender.

[37] M. D. Wilson, *Descartes*, 4–5; C. Wilson, *Descartes's 'Meditations'*, 7; Hatfield, *Descartes and the 'Meditations'*, 50–1.

[38] Michèle Le Dœuff points out that philosophers have often treated metaphor as a device connecting the space of philosophy and the space outside (*L'Imaginaire philosophique* (Paris: Payot, 1980), 16), though she argues that its relationship with philosophical discourse is in fact more complex.

Thus, in the First Meditation Descartes is not simply giving a set of arguments for doubting the evidence of the senses. He is trying to induce a state of confusion and anxiety in the reader. In the unfinished dialogue *La Recherche de la vérité par la lumière naturelle* (*The Search for Truth by Means of the Natural Light*), Descartes's spokesman says that his arguments for doubting the senses will have been successful if they appeal sufficiently to the listener's imagination to make him afraid of them (AT 10. 513). This appeal to the passions is traditionally one of the functions of rhetoric. One of Descartes's rhetorical devices is to incorporate an element of dialogue into the structure of the Meditation. Especially, but not only, in the First Meditation it is not always clear at once who is speaking, or how we are supposed to take what is being said. It is important, then, to sort out the different voices in the text: one, sometimes rather bluff and blustering, which offers a defence of common-sense beliefs; the other, sometimes mordantly ironic, which corrodes them with sceptical arguments. But it is also important to recognize that we cannot securely distribute them between clearly identified figures, as we can in his *The Search for Truth*, where Poliandre represents the average gentleman, better acquainted with life than with books, Epistémon the scholar, and Eudoxe the correct thinker. In the First Meditation the speaker has confidently prepared himself for the wholesale and fearless demolition of all his opinions. But when he comes to assess the evidence of his senses, he cannot quite rest content with the prudent maxim of never wholly trusting those who have once cheated you, as the senses have sometimes done by giving us false information. The hammer is already uplifted to smash his belief in the senses, when he suddenly loses heart and lowers it. Surely, he tells himself, there are some things I can take for granted, on the basis of sensory evidence; but then he argues himself into rejecting this reassurance. Throughout this Meditation a debate, an argumentative duel, is going on within the Meditator, between the voice of doubt and the voice of common sense: again and again, he tries to resist the assaults of doubt and remain secure in a fall-back position; again and again, this security is denied him.

Descartes's sceptical arguments, like those of his proxy Eudoxe in *The Search for Truth*, appeal to the imagination. We are invited to imagine (ourselves as) the Meditator sitting by the fire in his gown; and then to consider that he might be dreaming, and imagine him in

bed, dreaming he is sitting by the fire. The difference between the
two states is artfully suggested by a series of antitheses. I think I am
sitting: I am in fact lying down; I think I am by the fire: I am between
the sheets; I think I am wrapped in my gown: I have taken off my
clothes. The speaker's nakedness (real or imagined) associates him
with the poor naked wretches of madmen he has just been thinking
of. The writing blurs the distinction between sleeping and waking,
madness and sanity. When I am stupefied by my inability to find reliable grounds for distinguishing sleeping from waking, maybe this
stupor is real, and I am in fact asleep. I try to reassure myself: look,
I can move my head, I am in control, therefore awake. But the movement of the head is rendered by the Latin verb *commoveo*, which
tends to denote a violent or agitated movement. We might imagine it
as the kind of jerky, exaggerated movement one makes when one is
gesturing to make a point: 'Look, I am not asleep: I can move my
head.' But such jerky movements are also characteristic of the person
struggling against sleep, 'nodding off', in fact, and this casts doubt
on the Meditator's subsequent claim that he is knowingly and deliberately stretching out his hand, which a sleeper could not do. The
appeal to the imagination, and the ambiguities of the writing, thus
help to convey the strictly philosophical point that all of us are liable
to vivid illusions of presence that in fact have no objective foundations: that we cannot settle a philosophical doubt by simply appealing to a supposedly self-evident division between the sane and the
mad, and that, if such a division exists, we cannot know, from our
subjective experience, on which side of it we should fall.[39]

This antithetical structure can be found on a larger scale in the use
of metaphors. The end of the First Meditation juxtaposes images of
sleeping and waking, darkness and light. But perhaps the key
metaphor here, as in the *Discourse*, is that of building, solidity being
contrasted with precariousness. The Meditator realizes that existing
knowledge is unreliable: it must be demolished, and rebuilt from the
bottom up.[40] Yet his search for solid ground on which to build seems

[39] On Descartes's attitude to madness, see Michel Foucault, *Histoire de la folie à l'âge classique* (Paris: Gallimard, 1972 [1961]), 56–9, and the reply by Jacques Derrida, 'Cogito et histoire de la folie', in *L'Écriture et la différence* (Paris: Seuil, 1967), 51–97.

[40] The metaphor of knowledge as a building and the basic principles of a science as its foundations is central to the *Discourse on Method*. But it was already used by Montaigne (*Les Essais*, II. 12, 'Apologie de Raimond Sebond', VS ii. 587–8).

doomed: doubt has pushed him into a deep whirlpool, so that he can neither touch bottom nor swim to the surface. Eventually, he finds a stable if narrow footing on the discovery of his own existence. At this point the building can commence.

Summary of the Text

At the start of the First Meditation the Meditator is setting out to fulfil a long-held ambition: to achieve certainty in the sciences.[41] To this end, he decides he must abandon all his former opinions. To disprove each and every one of them would perhaps be impossible: but he decides to reject any he can find some reason for doubting. It would take for ever to examine them one by one, but he could demolish them all at once, by unsettling their foundations. Up to now, he believes, all his beliefs were founded on sense experience. What is meant here is that they involve either specific perceptions (e.g. the sun is yellow) or concepts that (according to the prevailing Aristotelian-Thomist theory of knowledge) ultimately derive, by abstraction, from such perceptions.[42] But the senses are sometimes unreliable: therefore, if we reject what is open to doubt, we must reject what they seem to teach us. Various attempts to vindicate the senses' reliability, at least to a certain extent, are tested out. These founder on the dream hypothesis: that is, given that in dreams we have vivid perceptual 'experiences' of non-existent objects, how can we know that our so-called waking experience is not an illusion?[43] If the senses are unreliable, the Meditator wonders whether mathematical truths, at least, are immune to doubt. But two sceptical hypotheses invalidate

[41] In what follows, 'the Meditator' refers to the 'I' in the text, Descartes to the author of the text.

[42] The critique of the senses as the foundation of knowledge can be found, as noted above, in Montaigne, 'Apologie de Raimond Sebond', VS ii. 587–601. The hypothesis that our experience might be all a dream appears there also (p. 596).

[43] There is disagreement as to whether Descartes is claiming that we may be dreaming all the time, or rather that, on any given occasion, we cannot know whether or not we are dreaming. The latter possibility, in any case, is enough for his purpose: it makes it impossible to point to an unquestionably reliable sense-experience. See Harry G. Frankfurt, *Demons, Dreamers, and Madmen: The Defense of Reason in Descartes's 'Meditations'* (Indianapolis and New York: Bobbs-Merrill, 1970), 49–53; M. D. Wilson, *Descartes*, 12–13, 17–31; Curley, *Descartes Against the Skeptics*, 46–69; Georges Dicker, *Descartes: An Analytical and Historical Introduction* (New York and Oxford: Oxford University Press, 1993), 27–9; Hatfield, *Descartes and the 'Meditations'*, 76–7.

any attempt either to rehabilitate sense-perception or to fall back on mathematical propositions as the sole field of certainty. First, the Meditator might be being deceived by God into wholesale error; secondly, if there is no God, and he himself has come into being purely by blind fate or chance, he may be so intrinsically defective as to be perpetually in error. The deep-rooted beliefs of a lifetime make these ideas hard to entertain: but in order to combat the pressure of these beliefs, the Meditator imagines an all-powerful evil spirit systematically deceiving him. The thought that this deceiver might be at work will protect the Meditator against mistakenly assenting to any false beliefs.

Not all Descartes's initial readers saw the benefits of such a strategy. Gassendi wondered why he had to reject all his former beliefs as false: why could he not pronounce them merely uncertain, and subsequently pick out those he found to be true? Besides, he cannot really believe, as he pretends to, that his former opinions are all false, and that he is being systematically deluded by dreams or a demon. Bourdin argued that if he takes doubt to such extreme limits, he denies himself any future possibility of certainty.

This position seems hard to challenge, as the Meditator flounders in the waters of doubt at the beginning of the Second Meditation. But he then realizes that the ultra-sceptical hypothesis of the deceiving spirit paradoxically offers him one piece of certain knowledge. In order to be being deceived, he must exist. Thus, scepticism can be turned against itself. [44] The thinker's discovery of his own existence, known traditionally as the Cogito, is one of the most debated moments in Western philosophy. How exactly does the Meditator acquire knowledge of his existence? In *A Discourse on the Method*, it appeared to be by an inference: 'je pense, donc je suis' (I am thinking, therefore I exist) (*Discourse*, 28, AT 6. 32). Here the inferential structure seems to be replaced by a direct intuition: 'I can finally decide that this proposition, "I am, I exist", whenever it is uttered by me, or conceived in the mind, is necessarily true' (p. 18). [45] But does this not

---

[44] See Charles Larmore, 'Descartes and Skepticism', in Stephen Gaukroger (ed.), *The Blackwell Guide to Descartes' 'Meditations'* (Oxford: Blackwell, 2006 [hereafter *BGDM*]), 17–29 (esp. pp. 23–6) on this turning of scepticism against itself.

[45] Alquié argues that the Cogito of the *Meditations* and that of the *Discourse* are different: the *Meditations* draws on an ontological experience of the I as existing, the *Discourse* focuses on the relationship between 'I am thinking' and 'I exist' (*OP*, i. 603, n. 2, 604, n. 1; ii. 416; cf. *La Découverte*, 180–200).

require prior knowledge of a general principle, 'Whatever thinks, exists', which is not alluded to here? What is the relationship of the knowledge of one's own existence to this general principle? If the former is inferred from the latter, what right has Descartes to presuppose the general principle? Descartes himself discusses the point in the Second Replies (§3, p. 92). Further clarification is provided by the 'Conversation with Burman' (AT 5. 147). What complicates the matter is that Descartes's own conception of intuition includes not only truths grasped immediately, but propositions directly inferred from these (*Rules for the Direction of the Mind*, III, AT 10. 368–70). If the knowledge of one's own existence is intuitive, into which of these categories of intuition does it fall? Do I grasp immediately that I exist or do I infer it from the primary intuition that I think?[46]

The second objection to the Cogito to be mentioned here does not, unlike the first, date back to the original Objections. It was first, apparently, put forward by the eighteenth-century German thinker Lichtenberg, who argued that Descartes had no right to assert 'I am thinking': at most he could say 'there is thinking going on'.[47] The objection is vigorously urged by Nietzsche.[48] Descartes himself makes it quite clear that he believes he has an irreducible experience of thought as his own thought: 'For that it is I that am doubting, understanding, wishing, is so obvious that nothing further is needed in order to explain it more clearly' (p. 21).[49] An alternative critique, developed by Kant, and restated by Husserl, holds that

[46] Peter Markie, 'The Cogito and its Importance' (*CCD* 140–73) explains how the Cogito can be interpreted as a combination of primary intuition ('I think') and immediate inference therefrom ('I exist'), while pointing to various passages that seem to contradict this view, and that therefore, he thinks, require the interpretation to be modified. For an alternative analysis, staying closer to Descartes's text, see Hatfield, *Descartes and the 'Meditations'*, 106–15. A quite different interpretation holds that the Cogito is to be understood in terms of performance: I grasp my existence in the *act* of attempting to doubt it: Jaako Hintikka, '*Cogito, Ergo Sum*: Inference or Performance?', in Willis Doney (ed.), *Descartes: A Collection of Critical Essays* (London and Basingstoke: Macmillan, 1970), 108–39.

[47] Hatfield, *Descartes and the 'Meditations'*, 103–5.

[48] Nietzsche, *Beyond Good and Evil*, trans. and ed. Marion Faber, introduction by Robert C. Holub, Oxford World's Classics (Oxford: Oxford University Press, 1998), §16.

[49] For a closely argued discussion of the point, see Bernard Williams, *Descartes*, 95–101.

Descartes failed to distinguish the ego we encounter in experience and the ego presupposed as subject of knowledge but inaccessible to experience.[50]

The Meditator, at any rate, believes that through his thinking he has gained knowledge not only of his existence but of his nature. He compares what he now knows of himself with his former beliefs about himself, which happen, though Descartes cannily refrains from pointing this out, to be those of the orthodox Aristotelian philosophy of his time. According to these beliefs, all the functions of life (nourishment, motion, sensation, and thinking) pertain to the soul, which is imagined as a mysterious air or fire diffused through the solid body. But the deceiver hypothesis leads the Meditator to eliminate both the body and those functions ascribed to the soul (like motion and sensation) that depend on the body. Thought is all he is left with that cannot be separated from him. He can say, then, that he knows himself to be (nothing other than) a thinking thing (in other words, a mind or soul, using this last term in what he now knows to be the proper sense), and his knowledge of himself comes purely and simply from his thinking, not from sense-experience which might, for all he knows, be illusory. (As is pointed out later, this is simply a provisional state of knowledge. The Meditator will later know himself also as, in another sense, a composite of soul and body.)

During the First Meditation the Meditator became aware of the pressure of custom, that is, of lifelong beliefs. He has the same realization now: he cannot quite convince himself that he does not, after all, know bodies better than he knows himself. Hence he conducts an experiment with a piece of wax. It possesses various sensible qualities: but these are completely altered when it is heated. That he knows it is the same wax is therefore an intellectual judgement, not one based in sensation. Likewise, he realizes, recognizing

[50] Immanuel Kant, *Critique of Pure Reason*, trans. Norman Kemp Smith, intro. by Howard Caygill, revd. 2nd edn. (Basingstoke: Palgrave Macmillan, 2003), 246 (B 277), 334 (A 350); Edmund Husserl, *The Crisis of European Sciences and Transcendental Phenomenology: An Introduction to Phenomenological Philosophy*, trans. and intro. David Carr (Evanston: Northwestern University Press, 1970), 81–2; *Cartesian Meditations: An Introduction to Phenomenology*, trans. Dorion Cairns (The Hague: Nijhoff, 1960), 23–5. For an account of Descartes drawing on this critique, see Dalia Judowitz, *Subjectivity and Representation in Descartes: The Origins of Modernity* (Cambridge: Cambridge University Press, 1988).

moving shapes as people walking down the street is an intellectual, not a purely visual, act. In fact, exploring varieties of perceptual experience, he is getting to know not so much bodies, which after all may not exist, as his mind, which is doing the perceiving.

One result, then, the knowledge of his own existence, seems definitely acquired at the start of the Third Meditation. What distinguishes this experience of certainty is that it is a very clear and distinct perception.[51] This seems to suggest that the Meditator could formulate a general rule: whatever I very clearly and distinctly perceive is true. Sense perceptions do not have this kind of clarity and distinctness (we tend to confuse 'seeing the sun' as a thought ('I seem to see the sun') with an actual perception of a hot yellow body outside us): those of mathematics do. But suppose a deceitful God is at work on him: might he not be in error even about mathematical propositions? He can know nothing until he has come to a decision on the deceitful God hypothesis.[52]

Descartes follows an apparently roundabout route to the existence of God. He distinguishes three categories of ideas: innate, adventitious (deriving from things outside himself), and factitious (invented by himself). Concepts like 'thing', 'truth', 'thought' must be innate, that is, must derive from his own nature: he did not encounter them, that is, in sense-experience, which for all he knows still is illusory. Sensations, he has always thought, are caused by bodies outside him: but these may not exist. Other ideas, like 'siren' or 'hippogriff', are invented. Essentially, he first decides that his ideas (representative thoughts) of material things might conceivably have been produced by himself. If they were in fact produced by external things, this does not prove they resemble those things.

But the Meditator finds he can distinguish different levels of reality contained in his ideas. This section needs some explanation. First, Descartes draws on the traditional Aristotelian metaphysics of substance and accident. To put it as simply as possible, accidents

---

[51] These terms are defied by Descartes as follows: 'I call a clear [perception] one that is present and manifest to a mind paying attention [. . .]; and a distinct one, one that, as well as being clear, is so separate and marked off from all others that it contains nothing at all but what is clear' (*Principles*, I. 45, and cf. I. 46).

[52] 'Know' here is ambiguous; and in fact scholars are divided as to whether or in what sense Descartes holds that *all* our knowledge depends on the knowledge of God. See the notes to the Third Meditation (AT 7. 36).

(e.g. 'white') are predicated of a subject (e.g. a jacket). That of which they are predicated, and which cannot be predicated of something else, is a substance.[53] Being a jacket is not being a property of some other thing: the jacket is a thing, or substance, in its own right. In this perspective, the accident, or as Descartes prefers to call it, the 'mode', is less real than the substance without which it cannot exist.[54] And likewise, finite and dependent substances are less real than is an infinite independent substance (supposing one exists) (Third Objections, IX, p. 117). There are, thus, degrees of reality. By the same token, our ideas must contain greater or lesser degrees of reality corresponding to those of their objects—whether or not these objects actually exist. Thus my idea of Odysseus 'contains' more reality than my idea of his scar or his cunning; but also more reality than my idea of, say, Stalin's cunning. The kind of reality contained in an idea is called 'objective', in a sense, obviously, quite different from the modern sense.

The Meditator proceeds to argue that the principle that a cause must contain at least as much reality as its effects must apply to objective as well as to actual (what he calls 'formal' reality). That there is a stone here requires an explanation (someone put it there). But my idea of a stone (my seeing, or seeming to see it, say) also requires an explanation: that is, its objective reality must be accounted for by some formal reality. In this case, a good explanation for my seeing a stone (a finite substance) would be that there is a stone there (put there by someone). Or it might be that what I am seeing is not a stone but a cricket-ball: perhaps it is too dark or I am too short-sighted to perceive the shape and colour clearly. But the cricket-ball has the same degree of reality as the stone: they are both finite substances. So the causal principle still applies. On the other hand, a mode like 'short-sightedness' could not explain the

---

[53] Aristotle, *Metaphysics*, V.viii.1 (1017ᵇ), VII.iii.3 (1029ᵉ).

[54] Descartes's definition of substance is given in *Principles*, I. 51, and those of mode, quality, and attribute in I. 56. Descartes's equation (p. 29) of 'modes' and 'accidents' elides a scholastic distinction between these two concepts: an accident has an aptitude or propensity for existing in a subject, a mode is actually inhering in one. On the differences between Descartes's concept of substance and that of the scholastics, see Jorge Secada, 'The Doctrine of Substance', in *BGDM* 67–85 (esp. pp. 74–6). On the notion of 'real' in Descartes, see Stephen Menn, 'The Greatest Stumbling Block: Descartes's Denial of Real Qualities', in Ariew and Grene (eds.), *Descartes and his Contemporaries*, 182–207.

misperception of a specific substance: it does not contain enough reality to account for the reality 'contained' in the perception. (Whether the substantial reality of the short-sighted person would suffice is another question: Descartes entertains the possibility that, as a finite substance, I might myself have generated all my ideas of bodies, being finite substances.) The Meditator argues, then, that the objective reality contained in his idea of God, an infinite substance, can be accounted for only by the actual ('formal') reality of an existing infinite substance. (The idea could not, Descartes argues repeatedly, be generated by amplification of an idea of finite substance. I have knowledge: I can conceive a being whose knowledge is without limit. But how could I form the idea of greater knowledge than I actually possess from my own limited knowledge, if that were all the knowledge in existence?)

Descartes was well aware that this was an unusual kind of argument for the existence of God. The proofs put forward by St Thomas Aquinas, say, are based for the most part on our experience of change, causation, coming to be and passing away in the physical world. But he did make the concession of offering a variant form of the causal argument, to the effect that the existence of the thinker cannot be explained save by the existence of an infinite being who created him, and indeed sustains him in being from one instant to the next. Now if an infinite being, that is, God, exists, possessing all perfections (for this is part of what Descartes understands by infinite), it is clear he must be no deceiver: for deception involves malice, an imperfection.[55]

In the Fourth Meditation the Meditator pursues this insight, analysing the nature of error. Error must arise not by the action of God, but from some deficiency in the creature: not an intrinsic flaw, but a misuse of the God-given powers of intellect and will. It occurs, that is, when we choose to make a judgement, which Descartes takes to be an act of will, a choice to affirm or deny that something is the case, when our understanding has no clear and distinct idea on which such a judgement can be based. If, on the other hand, the Meditator makes no affirmation or denial except where he has a clear and distinct idea, he will not fall into error. He can thus rely on the rule he

[55] The proof of an infinitely perfect God excludes the hypothesis of the all-powerful demon.

formulated at the start of the Third Meditation: whatever I clearly and distinctly perceive is true.

In the Fifth Meditation he decides that he cannot conclude whether bodies exist or not before he has a clear and distinct idea of what body is. The clear and distinct idea he discovers is of continuous quantity, occupying three-dimensional space, containing various parts, of varying magnitudes, shapes, positions, moving in space over varying periods of time. In addition to this general idea, he has various particular ideas of geometrical entities. Whether or not there are any triangles in the world, he has a certain determinate idea of a triangle's nature or essence (e.g. the sum of its angles is 180°), which he cannot, as he can with ideas he has invented, alter at will.

Now this furnishes him with another argument for the existence of God. For, since necessary existence belongs to the very concept of the supremely perfect being, he realizes that the concept itself involves the existence of the being that is its object. Thus, from the very idea of the supremely perfect being, we can reliably infer its existence. This argument, known since Kant as the 'ontological' proof, was invented by St Anselm (1033–1109), though Descartes seeks to distinguish his argument from Anselm's. It is one of the most striking and perplexing arguments in the history of philosophy: various criticisms of it are discussed in the notes on the Fifth Meditation and the Objections.

In the Sixth Meditation the Meditator infers, from his clear and distinct idea of material things, that it is possible for them to exist, in the sense that God is capable of creating them. But in order to find out whether they in fact exist, he needs to review his past attitudes to the senses by which he once thought he perceived them. He thus re-traverses the ground he traversed in the Second Meditation, surveying again and in more detail his former beliefs about himself, not simply describing them, but attempting to understand their origin.

He had the sensation of having a body, which he considered as part of himself, if not his whole self; and also the sensation that this body was involved with and affected by other bodies. He registered their effect on himself by pain and pleasure. He was also aware in himself of appetites and passions, and of sensible qualities (besides extension, shape, and motion), such as hardness or heat, light and colour, smells, tastes, and sounds. By means of these he distinguished various bodies such as the sky, earth, and sea. The ideas of these qualities seemed to derive from the presence of bodies outside himself: for the ideas were not under his control and were more vivid than ideas put together by his imagination or found in his memory. Finally, he had a particular relationship to the body he called his own.

Later, he came to doubt the senses, since experience and the reasons set out in the First Meditation seemed to show they were unreliable. Now, however, he does not think they should be treated as altogether doubtful.

However, he knows that whatever he clearly and distinctly understands can be produced by God as he understands it. So if he can clearly and distinctly understand one thing without another, they must be distinct.[56] And since he knows his existence purely from thought, he knows himself purely as a thinking thing. So, if he has a body, he must be distinct from it, and capable of existing without it.

But he has certain faculties (e.g. changing place), which must inhere in a substance, and cannot inhere in a thinking substance, because they have no intellectual dimension. So they must exist in a bodily substance. And the ideas he has of sensible things must be produced by a material substance. For his strong inclination to believe they are produced by actually existing physical bodies would be deceptive, if they are merely appearances produced in the absence of such bodies, and God would be responsible for the deception, which is impossible. Therefore bodies exist, even if they are not in reality exactly as our senses confusedly represent them. And he is so constituted as to believe he has a body, to which he is closely linked, because otherwise he, as a thinking substance, could not have a sensation of pain, when there is something wrong with it: he would merely be intellectually aware of the trouble. And his sensations must relate to some properties that really exist in bodies, even if they do not resemble them.[57] Sensations, in fact, have the function of indicating what is beneficial or harmful to the body, and from this point

---

[56] This argument may seem fragile (how do I know my concepts of mind and body are adequate?), and was shrewdly criticized in particular by Arnauld in the Fourth Objections (pp. 126–30). But, while not fully endorsing Descartes's argument, Margaret D. Wilson clarifies it in such a way as to elude this line of attack: 'The Epistemological Argument for Mind–Body Distinctness', in Cottingham (ed.), *Descartes*, 186–96.

[57] The denial that bodies must possess qualities that resemble those we experience in our sensations of them is more fully explained in *Le Monde*, ch. 1, AT 11. 3–6.

of view they are generally reliable: the error is to think that they give information about the essence of bodies in themselves. The process of mind–body interaction is explained. The soul is affected not by all parts of the body, but by a particular part of the brain: whenever this part is affected in the same way by motions in the nerves it presents the same idea to the mind. Thus, an injury to the foot affects the nerves in the foot, and they transmit this experience to the brain, causing the mind to experience pain, and thus initiate action to remove the cause of the injury. When the body is out of order, this process may go wrong, but in general it works to preserve our body in being. We can thus, on the whole, rely on the senses and discard the doubts about them raised in the First Meditation. The difference between dreams and waking experience now appears very clear: waking experience has a kind of continuity, attested by the memory, very different from the disconnected experiences we have in dreams. God's veracity enables us to rely on this distinction, and thus distinguish waking experience from the illusions of dreams.

Key Issues

It is impossible in an introduction like this to discuss with any adequacy the problems that over the centuries have been detected in Descartes's argumentation, or the objections that have been raised to his very enterprise of seeking certainty through doubt. Some of them are touched on in the Explanatory Notes. However, I shall mention two here: the circle, and the relation between mind and body.

The most powerful objection to Descartes's achievement comes in two sentences, almost casually uttered by Antoine Arnauld, author of the Fourth Objections:

I have only one final reservation: how can the author avoid arguing in a circle, when he says we know for certain that the things we clearly and distinctly perceive are true, only because God exists?

   But we can only be certain God exists, because this is clearly and distinctly perceived by us. Therefore before we can be certain God exists, we must be certain, that whatever is clearly and distinctly perceived by us is true. (p. 137)

Immense efforts have been devoted both to defending Descartes against this accusation, and to refuting his defence. As Gary Hatfield very well observes, 'we may [. . .] arrive at different conclusions depending on whether we ask what Descartes intended to argue, as opposed to what he needed to argue to achieve his results (which is what Arnauld asked, and ultimately what we should ask as well)'.[58] Many philosophers, especially analytic philosophers, agree with Hatfield that we should work out what Descartes needed to argue, or could and should have argued, because there is a widespread perception that his actual reply is inadequate.

That reply runs as follows:

That I did not argue in a circle when I said that we can be certain that what we clearly and distinctly perceive is true, only if God exists, and we can be certain that God exists, only because we clearly perceive it, is already made sufficiently clear in the Second Replies, §§3–4, where I distinguished between what we clearly perceive in actual fact and what we remember we once clearly perceived. For first of all, we are certain that God exists, since we reflect on the reasons by which his existence is proved; but subsequently it is sufficient for us to remember that we have clearly perceived something, in order to be certain it is true; and this would not be sufficient, unless we knew that God exists and does not deceive us. (p. 158)

Descartes had already replied along the same lines to a similar, but more limited, objection in the second set (Second Replies, §3, p. 92). Following Ferdinand Alquié, we can summarize the two major problems with this reply as follows:

1. Descartes seems to imply that the guarantee of the divine veracity is required only for remembered perceptions, not current ones—but elsewhere he seems to require current perceptions also to be validated in this way;

2. The memory of past perceptions is only a memory like other memories, so how can it be validated by the appeal to the divine veracity, any more than any other kind of memory?[59]

Many efforts have been made to find a more satisfactory answer.[60] The debate will doubtless continue.

---

[58] Hatfield, *Descartes and the 'Meditations'*, 172.

[59] See Alquié, *OP* ii. 563, n. 3. For a more extended and influential critique of the 'memory answer' or 'memory defence', see Frankfurt, *Demons, Dreamers, and Madmen*, 156–69. Louis E. Loeb, 'The Cartesian Circle', in *CCD* 200–35 pronounces the 'memory defence' defunct, in the light of Frankfurt's critique (p. 225, n. 2), as does Hatfield, *Descartes and the 'Meditations'*, 181.

[60] See e.g. Anthony Kenny, *Descartes: A Study of his Philosophy* (New York: Random House, 1968), 172–99; Frankfurt, *Demons, Dreamers, and Madmen*, 170–80; Williams, *Descartes*, 189–210; Dicker, *Descartes*, 119–41; Loeb, 'The Cartesian Circle';

As it will on the nature of 'Cartesian dualism'. First, it looks as if Descartes has to explain how two utterly different substances, one thinking and non-extended, the other extended and non-thinking, can interact, as his theory seems to require. Descartes does not seem to have been greatly worried by this: he was content to observe that experience shows it takes place, that we have a basic notion of our soul and body as interacting.[61] Other philosophers were less easily satisfied, and propounded alternative solutions. Malebranche and others developed what is commonly called an 'occasionalist' theory: this holds that, say, a physical event, like the collision between one's foot and a stone, does not, properly speaking, cause an event in the mind (the sensation of pain); nor does a mental event, my decision to stand up, cause movements in my limbs. Rather, God has established laws, according to which when, for example, contact between bodies takes place, certain sensations occur in the mind, and when a given volition occurs in the mind, certain processes occur in the nerves and the muscles by which the volition is accomplished. The causal efficacy is thus in the laws, and hence ultimately God's will, rather than the physical or mental events as such. Leibniz formulated an alternative theory of 'pre-established harmony'. Just as two clocks can be set up so as always to keep time together, likewise God has ordained that a certain sequence of bodily events takes place in parallel with a certain sequence of events in the mind. Spinoza adopted a more radical solution: soul and body are not two distinct substances, but two attributes of the one infinite substance that is all that exists. What we call distinguish as bodily and mental processes are two aspects of the movement of this single substance: a thought-process can be thought of as the expression of a process going on in the body, but no interaction between the two attributes takes place.[62]

Whether or not Descartes was arguing in a circle is a vital question for students of his philosophy, but it does not engage our deepest convictions about the kind of creatures we are. But the relation

James Van Cleve, 'Foundationalism, Epistemic Principles, and the Cartesian Circle', in Cottingham (ed.), *Descartes*, 101–31; Edwin Curley, 'The Cogito', in *BGDM* 39–44. Gary Hatfield, 'The Cartesian Circle', *BGDM* 122–41, is an acute analysis of different approaches: he discusses the problem at length also in *Descartes and the 'Meditations'*, 169–80, 200–1, 226–34.

[61] See the letters to Elisabeth of 21 May and 28 June 1643, AT 3. 663–8, 690–5.

[62] See Daniel Garber and Margaret Wilson, 'Mind–Body Problems', *CHSCP* i. 833–67, for an account of this debate.

between mind and body does. Among philosophers, the view that the mind is an immaterial substance distinct from the body, and capable of existing without it, is, to put it mildly, unfashionable. But in the larger intellectual community, and indeed among some philosophers, it is often perceived as objectionable: as complicit with a pernicious and ultimately repressive devaluation of our physical and this-worldly existence (and perhaps, if it is accepted that the hierarchical distinction between mind and body has, historically, been mapped onto the hierarchical distinction male–female, with the maintenance of gender inequality).[63] His denial of souls to animals has been viewed as legitimating a purely instrumental attitude to them, indifferent to the suffering it fails to recognize.[64]

Be that as it may, the clarification of Descartes's doctrine remains an enduring interest, and recent analyses have been effectively directed against an oversimplified understanding of it.[65] Descartes's reduction of the 'self' to a thinking thing has to be understood as tactical and provisional: it is geared specifically to the discovery of epistemological certitude. Human life in general, however, involves experiences and actions in which soul and body function in unison. It is fair to say, though, that for a full understanding of Descartes's conception of mind–body relationships we must go beyond the *Meditations* to later works, the letters to Princess Elisabeth and the treatise on *The Passions of the Soul*.[66] As regards the ideological implications of Descartes's doctrine, it is difficult to read them off from

[63] See e.g. Francis Barker, *The Tremulous Private Body: Essays on Subjection*, 2nd edn. (Ann Arbor: University of Michigan Press, 1995), and, for the feminist critique, Genevieve Lloyd, *The Man of Reason: 'Male' and 'Female' in Western Philosophy*, 2nd edn. (London: Routledge, 1993), 39–50.

[64] For a clarification of Descartes's position see John Cottingham, 'Descartes' Treatment of Animals', in Cottingham (ed.), *Descartes*, 225–33, and Tom Sorell, *Descartes Reinvented* (Cambridge: Cambridge University Press, 2005), 149–60. Sorell's book is in part a rehabilitation of Descartes in the face of what one might call ideological critiques.

[65] See e.g. John Cottingham, 'Cartesian Dualism: Theology, Metaphysics, and Science', in *CCD* 236–57, and 'The Mind–Body Relation', in *BGDM* 179–92; Gordon Baker and Katherine J. Morris, *Descartes' Dualism* (London: Routledge, 1996); Marleen Rozemond, *Descartes's Dualism* (Cambridge, Mass.: Harvard University Press, 1998); Desmond M. Clarke, *Descartes's Theory of Mind* (Oxford: Oxford University Press, 2003).

[66] See Amelie Oksenberg Rorty, 'Descartes on Thinking with the Body', *CCD* 371–92; Susan James, *Passion and Action: The Emotions in Seventeenth-Century Philosophy* (Oxford: Clarendon Press, 1997); Michael Moriarty, *Early Modern French Thought: The Age of Suspicion* (Oxford: Oxford University Press, 2003), 50–99.

specific philosophical positions, or to map doctrines onto ideological tendencies, as if materialism were inherently progressive and dualism intrinsically reactionary. These are matters requiring contextual and historical analysis. But one of the surprises that may lie in wait for readers of the Objections, if they are not already acquainted with the medieval Aristotelian tradition, is the realization that Descartes's distinction between mind and body was perceived by contemporaries, not as reassuring or uplifting, but as downright strange. The physical dimension of thought and experience was not something scholastic philosophers and theologians needed to have revealed by audacious and heterodox innovators like Spinoza. They took it for granted.

Descartes's Legacy

They might have been surprised, however, by a new way of doing philosophy: one that respected no authorities beyond the thinker's own cognitive powers, that dispensed, in particular, with the reading of canonical texts. But, in fact, though sometimes puzzled by the content of Descartes's arguments, and sometimes convinced his whole approach is wrong, the Objectors do not appear especially scandalized by it. Yet Descartes has often been seen as inaugurating a 'completely new manner of philosophizing which seeks its ultimate foundations in the subjective'.[67] Along with Husserl, Martin Heidegger has influentially propounded this view: Descartes, he contends, is chiefly responsible for the development of a new concept of the subject as coextensive with the human I, and as driven by the quest for power over the entire earth.[68] This view of the 'Cartesian subject' has also helped to reinforce some of the ideological objections noted above in connection with dualism. Or, again, the 'Cartesian subject' has been targeted by exponents of psychoanalysis, who challenge the conception of an ego identifying itself with consciousness. But it is, arguably, misleading to read Descartes

---

[67] Husserl, *Crisis of the European Sciences*, 81.

[68] Martin Heidegger, *Nietzsche*, 4 vols., trans. Frank A. Capuzzi, ed. David Farrell Krell (San Francisco: Harper & Row, 1979–87), vol. 4, *Nihilism* (1982), 96–9. Jerrold Seigel offers a useful corrective to this view: *The Idea of the Self: Thought and Experience in Western Europe Since the Seventeenth Century* (Cambridge: Cambridge University Press, 2005), 40–4, 55–74.

retrospectively through a concept of 'subject' projected onto rather than discovered in his work.[69]

Certainly, in philosophy Descartes helped to set the agenda for at least the following century: the work of Spinoza, Malebranche, and Leibniz offered quite diverse solutions to problems deemed to be unresolved in his conception of mind and matter as separate substances, capable of interaction; Locke reasserted the claims of empiricism against him; Hume those of scepticism. Hume in turn provoked Kant into seeking his own solution to the problem addressed by Descartes of justifying scientific knowledge while allowing room for the human free will on which Descartes laid so much stress. One key effect of his philosophy was to undermine the Aristotelian view that in knowledge the mind, so to speak, becomes one with its object, assimilating its 'form' or nature without its matter. On this showing truth consists in a match or conformity between the intellect and the thing ('adæquatio rei et intellectus'). This conception of truth survives even in a philosopher like Gassendi, who was no Aristotelian (see Fifth Objections, IV. 3, p. 176). Descartes's theory of truth as correspondence is apparently identical: it consists in the conformity of thought to the object (to Mersenne, 16 October 1639, AT 2. 597). But he holds that we have no knowledge of what is outside ourselves except via the ideas we have in ourselves: and therefore our judgements cannot be immediately matched against things. The conformity of the idea to its object is evaluated not in relation to the thing to which the idea relates, but by means of a clarification of the idea itself (to Gibieuf, 19 January 1642, AT 3. 474). How we know our ideas correspond to reality became a major problem for those subsequent philosophers who accepted Descartes's formulation of the problem of knowledge, but not his solution.

If, perhaps, the influence of Kant or Hegel helped to diminish the presence of Descartes in nineteenth-century thought, he certainly made a comeback in European philosophy of the twentieth century. Though criticizing him in detail, Husserl claims Descartes as an

---

[69] There is some discussion of approaches to Descartes that invoke the 'subject' in my *Early Modern French Thought*, 53–4, 93–9. That Descartes's conception of the thinking self excludes (and is vitiated by its failure to include) the possibility of unconscious thoughts is not to be taken for granted. The subject is magisterially treated in Geneviève Lewis, *Le Problème de l'inconscient et le cartésianisme* (Paris: Presses Universitaires de France, 1950).

inspiration for his phenomenology, as the very title of his *Cartesian Meditations* makes clear.[70] In *Being and Nothingness* Sartre adapts the notion of the Cogito to the purposes of his own phenomenology.[71] Emmanuel Levinas, whose work has been profoundly influential on contemporary philosophy in the 'continental' tradition, shows a profound engagement with the *Meditations*.[72] Philosophy, like every other activity, has its fashions, but, to judge by the history of the three-and-a-half centuries since their appearance, the *Meditations* are unlikely to lose their position in the front rank of European philosophical texts.

[70] See Husserl, *Cartesian Meditations*, 1–6.
[71] Jean-Paul Sartre, *L'Être et le néant: essai d'ontologie phénoménologique* (Paris: Gallimard, 1943), 16–23.
[72] Emmanuel Levinas, *Totalité et infini: essai sur l'extériorité* (The Hague: Nijhoff, 1971).

NOTE ON THE TEXT AND TRANSLATION

The Text

This volume contains the full text of the *Meditations*, based on that
of the Adam–Tannery edition (see the Select Bibliography). It contains Descartes's letter to the Sorbonne, his Preface to the Reader,
and his own Synopsis, and extracts from the Objections and Replies.
It omits the letter to Father Dinet, head of the French branch, or
'province', of the Society of Jesus, which was published in the second
Latin edition along with the Seventh Objections, since this is of more
biographical than philosophical importance.[1] As is noted in the
Introduction, the Third and Fourth Objections and Replies are
reproduced in full. The others are summarized, with verbatim quotations of the more important passages. The convention is followed
of printing the Objections in italic and Descartes's Replies in roman.
Editorial summaries are printed in smaller type.

Throughout the text, both of the Meditations and the Objections
and Replies, AT page numbers are given in the margin. This enables
the reader both to compare this edition with the original texts and to
use it with works of secondary literature that give references using
AT pagination. Where one passage refers to another that is contained
in this volume (e.g. when one of the Objections makes reference to
the text of the Meditations) the reference given is to the page number
in this volume. Otherwise, all references to Descartes's works and
correspondence are to AT, with the exception of *Principia philosophiae*
(*Principles of Philosophy*) and *Les Passions de l'âme* (*The Passions of
the Soul*). Here the subdivisions of the text—into part and section
(*Principles*) or into articles (*Passions*)—are sufficient for the reader to
locate any passage.

The Translation

I have tried to produce a reading experience in English as close as
possible to the experience of reading Descartes's original text. I have

---

[1] A full summary placing the letter in context is given in Clarke, *Descartes*, 226–9.

xlii   *Note on the Text and Translation*

worked from the Latin text (here referred to as L), cross-checking against the French version (F). Where there is some discrepancy between them, this is mentioned in the notes.

Ian Maclean has given an excellent characterization of Descartes's style, which applies to his Latin as well as his French: alluding to Descartes's 'clear but complex syntax', he goes on: 'He has a predilection for subordinate clauses and qualifications; he shows great care in expressing preconditions and causal relations . . . , and he is very adept in the use of negation, double negation, and even on occasion triple negation' (*Discourse*, p. lxiv). This does not make him straightforward to read: but part of the experience of reading the *Meditations* is the challenge (and the pleasure) of following the intricacies of Descartes's syntax; intricacies paralleled at the higher level of the plan of each Meditation. He leads us on a path that winds, that sometimes appears to be taking us nowhere, or nowhere very clear, but that, all the time, conveys us inexorably towards our destination. As regards his vocabulary, Descartes is sometimes technical (though in the French version these technical terms are often glossed) and always precise. For this reason, there is much to be said for the practice of attempting to match one term in the original to one English term.[2] But this is not always possible. What follows is a list of a few difficulties faced by the translator, and the solutions adopted here. It is not a general glossary of Descartes's vocabulary: his technical terms are defined in the Notes, where they first occur. The definitions he himself gives of certain key terms in the Second Replies are included in the extracts from the Second Replies below (pp. 102–3).

Cognoscere / cognitio; nosse / notitia; scire / scientia. All these words could in principle be translated as 'know' / 'knowledge'. But in fact they apply to different kinds of knowing or knowledge, and perform different functions in Descartes's text.[3] It could be misleading to

---

[2] There is a valuable discussion of methodological issues of translating Descartes by John Carriero and Paul Hoffman in *Philosophical Review*, 99: 1 (Jan. 1990), 93–104. I am grateful to one of the readers for OUP for drawing my attention to this.

[3] The distinction between *cognoscere* and *scire* roughly corresponds to that in French between *connaître* and *savoir*. The distinction itself is a feature of the Latin language, but Descartes is also appealing to common technical usage: for he says, 'the knowledge of principles is not normally referred to as "science" by logicians' (Second Replies, §3, p. 92), implying that they reserve the term for what can be deduced from principles. The importance of the distinction in Descartes is stressed in Menn, *Descartes and Augustine*,

translate them all as 'know': nor can one find different one-to-one English equivalents for each. So I have often indicated in parentheses which of them occurs in the original.

Cognoscere, first of all, means to get to know, to discover, or realize. *Cognitio*, then, is, first, the action by which this takes place; secondly, the result of this action (I translate it sometimes as 'act of knowledge'). In the Second Meditation it is used of the Meditator's knowledge of his own existence (p. 18). In the Third Meditation Descartes writes, again of the Meditator's knowledge of his own existence: 'In this first act of knowledge (*cognitione*) there is nothing other than a clear and distinct perception of what I affirm to be the case' (p. 25). We can understand *cognitio* here as both the act of clear and distinct perception and the piece of knowledge to which it gives rise. *Cognoscere* can readily take a direct object, in which case it means to know something by being acquainted with it. To refer to what 'I know' by virtue of 'cognition' or by direct acquaintance, Descartes sometimes uses *novi*, and the resultant knowledge is *notitia*.[4] These words appear in a cluster in this passage from the Second Meditation: 'I know [*novi*] that I exist; I am trying to find out what this "I" is, whom I know [*novi*]. It is absolutely certain that this knowledge [*notitia*], in the precise sense in question here, does not depend on things of which I do not yet know [*novi*] whether they exist' (p. 20). And indeed the Second Meditation involves a twofold process: realizing (*cognoscere*) that he exists; and getting to know himself (*nosse*) as a thinking thing.

Scire and *scientia* refer to: (i) a piece of knowledge, a cognitive result, that we can take for granted as acquired, and on which we can build; (ii) a *body* of knowledge, an accumulation and ordering of cognitive results; (iii) the kind of knowledge we have of (i) or (ii). It is this kind of knowledge that, Descartes says, depends on the knowledge that God exists and is no deceiver (Fifth Meditation, pp. 49–51): an atheist can have cognition of geometrical truths, but no scientific

---

311–12, and Sorell, *Descartes Reinvented*, 60–4. It has been argued to be present in Aquinas: Scott MacDonald, 'Theory of Knowledge', in Norman Kretzmann and Eleonore Stump (eds.), *The Cambridge Companion to Aquinas* (Cambridge: Cambridge University Press, 1993), 160–95.

[4] *Novi* is, grammatically, the perfect form (I have got to know) of the root verb *nosco* (I begin to know) from which the more common *cognosco* is formed. The infinitive form is *nosse*.

knowledge of them (Second Replies, §3, pp. 92–3), because he cannot explain his entitlement to this cognition.[5] A key aspect of the distinction between *cognitio* and *scientia* seems to be that to possess *scientia* of a certain truth we do not need to be attending to it, as we are when *cognitio*, linked as it is to an experience of knowledge, is involved. This arguably throws light on the problem of the circle: but there is no room to discuss this here.[6]

Per se notum: literally, 'known through itself'. In scholastic parlance *per se notum* is applied to truths that are directly intuited or apprehended, rather than being grasped as the conclusion of a process of reasoning. 'Self-evident', a possible translation, might be misleading (as is shown by Edwin Curley, in *BGDM* 34): the principle of contradiction, 'a thing cannot be both A and not-A', is self-evident given the meaning of its constituent terms. But 'I exist' (or even, 'I think, therefore I exist') is not self-evident in this way: its evidence depends not simply on the constituent terms, but on a concrete act of thought, and the becoming aware of this act. Nor does Descartes think that, in order to be *per se notum*, a proposition must be clearly and obviously true to everybody: see below, Postulate 5, pp. 104–5. The usual rendering here is 'directly known'.

Percipere: 'perceive'; *perceptio*: 'perception'. 'Perception' in modern philosophical English is defined as 'the extraction and use of information about one's environment . . . and one's own body':[7] as far as external objects go, it relates to information accessed through the senses. Descartes uses *percipere* in a far broader sense to denote all forms of apprehension, including the operations of the pure intellect, which deal with concepts of objects that may be inaccessible to the senses, for example, God. Even bodies, in fact, he says, are perceived by the mind (p. 23). It is true that F frequently uses *concevoir* (to conceive)/*conception* (conception) to refer to the operations of the

---

[5] Descartes's use of *scientia* is similar in this respect to Aristotle's concept of scientific knowledge (*episteme*): 'the man who cannot give an account of the reason for a fact, although there is a proof available, is not possessed of scientific knowledge': *Posterior Analytics*, I.6 (74ᵇ).

[6] 'Cognition', it might be argued, corresponds to 'intuition', as used by Anthony Kenny in his vindication of Descartes against the accusation of circularity: *Descartes: A Study of His Philosophy* (New York: Random House, 1968), 172–99.

[7] Fred Dretske, 'Perception', in Ted Honderich (ed.), *The Oxford Companion to Philosophy* (Oxford: Oxford University Press, 1995), 652.

intellect: cf. AT 7. 31/9. 24. But to impose this distinction on Descartes might risk obscuring his basic insistence that all thinking involves the *perception* of an idea, p. 102 (Definition II).

Sentire: 'perceive by the senses'. In many cases, the translation 'feel' will do. 'Ignem sentiam' (AT 7. 38) means, literally, 'I feel the fire', and is rendered 'I feel the heat of the fire'. Elsewhere, 'perceive by the senses' will sometimes do: but that tends to imply that what is perceived is real. In the Sixth Meditation the Meditator uses *sentire* repeatedly when recapitulating the former convictions about his body and the physical world that (he thought) derived from his sense-experience, which, later, he realized might be unreliable. Here, therefore, I have used some form of the construction 'have the sensation of'. In any case, whenever Descartes uses *sentire*, and 'feel' will not do, I make it clear that sense-perception or sensation is being dealt with, as distinct from perception, in the broad sense, in general.

SELECT BIBLIOGRAPHY

Editions of the Meditations

The standard edition of Descartes's works is: *Œuvres de Descartes*, ed. Charles Adam and Paul Tannery, 11 vols., rev. edn. (Paris: Vrin, 1996). The Latin text of the *Meditations* and of the *Objections* and *Replies* is in volume 7, the French in volume 9.

The standard edition in English is *The Philosophical Writings of Descartes*, trans. John Cottingham, Robert Stoothoff, Dugald Murdoch, and Anthony Kenny (Cambridge: Cambridge University Press, 1985–91). Stephen Gaukroger (ed.), *The Blackwell Guide to Descartes' 'Meditations'* (see below), reproduces the only early modern English translation of the *Meditations*, by William Molyneux (1680), in an appendix.

There is an excellent selected edition by Ferdinand Alquié: Descartes, *Œuvres philosophiques*, 3 vols., Classiques Garnier (Paris: Garnier, 1963–73). Both Latin and French texts of the Meditations appear in vol. 2; the text of the Objections and Replies is in French only. The annotation is excellent.

An online version of the *Meditations*, ed. David B. Manley and Charles S. Taylor, with Latin, French, and English texts can be found at: http://www.wright.edu/cola/descartes/

A very useful and easily accessible edition of the *Meditations*, giving the Meditations in parallel Latin and French texts and the Objections and Replies in French, is: Descartes, *Méditations métaphysiques, Objections et Réponses, suivies de quatre lettres*, ed. Jean-Marie Beyssade and Michelle Beyssade, GF Flammarion (Paris: Flammarion, 1992 [1979]).

Other Works

Descartes, *A Discourse on the Method of Correctly Conducting one's Reason and Seeking Truth in the Sciences*, ed. and trans. Ian Maclean, Oxford World's Classics (Oxford: Oxford University Press, 2006).

Discours de la méthode, ed. Étienne Gilson, 6th edn. (Paris: Vrin, 1987 [1925]).

What follows is merely a selection from the vast range of Descartes scholarship. In an English-language edition it seemed natural to give precedence to English-language sources: however, some valuable French-language works are included.

Biographical Studies

Clarke, Desmond M., *Descartes: A Biography* (Cambridge: Cambridge University Press, 2006).

Gaukroger, Stephen, *Descartes: An Intellectual Biography* (Oxford: Oxford University Press, 1995).

Grayling, A. C., *Descartes: The Life of René Descartes and its Place in his Times* (London: The Free Press, 2005).

Rodis-Lewis, Geneviève, *Descartes: Biographie* (Paris: Calmann-Lévy, 1995); in English as *Descartes: His Life and Thought*, trans. Jane Marie Todd (Ithaca, NY: Cornell University Press, 1998).

General

Garber, Daniel, and Michael Ayers (eds.), *The Cambridge History of Seventeenth-Century Philosophy*, 2 vols. (Cambridge: Cambridge University Press, 1998).

Collections of Essays

Ariew, Roger, and Marjorie Grene (eds.), *Descartes and His Contemporaries: Meditations, Objections, and Replies* (Chicago and London: University of Chicago, Press, 1995).

Cottingham, John (ed.), *The Cambridge Companion to Descartes* (Cambridge: Cambridge University Press, 1992).

—— *Descartes* (Oxford: Oxford University Press, 1998).

Doney, Willis (ed.), *Descartes: A Collection of Critical Essays* (London and Basingstoke: Macmillan, 1970).

Gaukroger, Stephen (ed.), *The Blackwell Guide to Descartes' 'Meditations'* (Oxford: Blackwell, 2006).

Rorty, Amélie Oksenberg, *Essays on Descartes' Meditations* (Berkeley: University of California Press, 1986).

Individual Studies

Alquié, Ferdinand, *La Découverte métaphysique de l'homme chez Descartes*, 6th edn. (Paris: Presses Universitaires de France, 2000 [1950]).

Baker, Gordon, and Katherine J. Morris, *Descartes' Dualism* (London: Routledge, 1996).

Cave, Terence, *Pré-Histoires: textes troublés au seuil de la modernité* (Geneva: Droz, 1999).

Clarke, Desmond M., *Descartes's Theory of Mind* (Oxford: Oxford University Press, 2003).

Cottingham, John, *A Descartes Dictionary* (Oxford: Blackwell, 1993).

Curley, E. M., *Descartes Against the Skeptics* (Oxford: Blackwell, 1978).

Dicker, Georges, *Descartes: An Analytical and Historical Introduction* (New York and Oxford: Oxford University Press, 1993).

Frankfurt, Harry G., *Demons, Dreamers, and Madmen: The Defense of Reason in Descartes's 'Meditations'* (Indianapolis and New York: Bobbs-Merrill, 1970).

Gouhier, Henri, *La Pensée métaphysique de Descartes* (Paris: Vrin, 1962).

Hatfield, Gary, *Descartes and the 'Meditations'* (Abingdon: Routledge, 2003).

James, Susan, *Passion and Action: The Emotions in Seventeenth-Century Philosophy* (Oxford: Clarendon Press, 1997).

Kenny, Anthony, *Descartes: A Study of His Philosophy* (New York: Random House, 1968).

Marion, Jean-Luc, *Sur le prisme métaphysique de Descartes: constitution et limites de l'onto-théologie dans la pensée cartésienne* (Paris: Presses Universitaires de France, 1986).

—— *Questions cartésiennes: méthode et métaphysique* (Paris: Presses Universitaires de France, 1991).

Menn, Stephen, *Descartes and Augustine* (Cambridge: Cambridge University Press, 1998).

Popkin, Richard, *The History of Scepticism from Savonarola to Bayle*, rev. and expanded ed. (Oxford: Oxford University Press, 2003); first published as *The History of Scepticism from Erasmus to Descartes* (1960).

Rozemond, Marleen, *Descartes's Dualism* (Cambridge, Mass.: Harvard University Press, 1998).

Secada, Jorge, *Cartesian Metaphysics: The Late Scholastic Origins of Modern Philosophy* (Cambridge: Cambridge University Press, 2000).

Sorell, Tom, *Descartes: A Very Short Introduction* (Oxford: Oxford University Press, 2000).

—— *Descartes Reinvented* (Cambridge: Cambridge University Press, 2005).

Williams, Bernard, *Descartes: The Project of Pure Enquiry* (Harmondsworth: Pelican, 1978).

Wilson, Catherine, *Descartes's 'Meditations': An Introduction* (Cambridge: Cambridge University Press, 2003).

Wilson, Margaret Dauler, *Descartes* (London: Routledge & Kegan Paul, 1978).

Further Reading in Oxford World's Classics

Berkeley, George, *Principles of Human Knowledge and Three Dialogues*, ed. Howard Robinson.

Hobbes, Thomas, *The Elements of Law Natural and Politic*, ed. J. C. A. Gaskin.

—— *Leviathan*, ed. J. C. A. Gaskin.

A CHRONOLOGY OF RENÉ DESCARTES

1596   31 March: born at La Haye near Tours.

1607–15 Attends the Jesuit college of La Flèche.

1610   Galileo's observation of the four moons of Jupiter.

1616   Licenciate of Law, University of Poitiers.

1618   Joins the army of Prince Maurice of Nassau in Holland.

1619   Moves to the army of Elector Maximilian, duke of Bavaria, in Germany.

1619   10 November: dream of a 'wonderful science'.

1620   Publication of Bacon's *Novum Organum*.

1622–5 Travels in Europe.

1623–5 Imprisonment of Théophile de Viau as ringleader of the Parisian free-thinkers.

1625–8 Based in Paris, in the circle of Mersenne.

1628   Publication of Harvey's *Circulation of the Blood*.

1628 (or 1629) Completion of *Rules For the Direction of Our Native Intelligence*.

1628 (end) Move to Holland.

1629   Work on *The Universe*.

1633   Publication of Galileo's *Dialogue Concerning the Two Chief World Systems*.

1633   Condemnation of Galileo by the Roman Inquisition; Descartes abandons plans to publish *The Universe*.

1635   Birth of Descartes's natural daughter, named Francine, baptized 7 August (died 1640).

1637   Publication of *A Discourse on the Method*, with three essays: *Dioptrics*, *Meteorology*, and *Geometry*.

1641   Publication of *Meditations*, with the first six sets of Objections and Replies.

1642   Publication of second edition of *Meditations*, with all seven sets of Objections and Replies. First contact with Princess Elisabeth of Bohemia.

1643   Cartesian philosophy condemned at the University of Utrecht.

1644   Visit to France; publication of the Latin version of *The Principles of Philosophy* (French translation 1647), and the Latin version of the *Discourse* and the *Essays*.

1647   Award of a pension by the king of France; return to France to arrange its receipt. Publication of *Comments on a Certain Broadsheet*.

1648   16 April: interview with Frans Burman at Egmond-Binnen.

1648   Beginning of the civil war known as 'La Fronde' in France.

1649   Journey to Sweden on invitation of Queen Christina; publication of the *Passions of the Soul*.

1650   11 February: death in Stockholm from pneumonia.

1666   Descartes's remains returned to France, to rest eventually in Saint-Germain des Prés.

MEDITATIONS ON
FIRST PHILOSOPHY

IN WHICH THE EXISTENCE OF GOD
AND THE DISTINCTION OF THE
HUMAN SOUL FROM THE BODY
ARE DEMONSTRATED

LETTER

To these wisest and most distinguished men,
the Dean and Doctors of the holy Faculty of Theology
at the University of Paris

I have such good reason for offering this work to you, and I trust 1
that you will have such good reason for taking it under your protec-
tion, once you understand my intention in writing it, that I could
recommend it here in no better way than by saying briefly what my
aim was.

I have always thought that the two issues of God and the soul
were the most important of those that should be resolved by philosophical rather than theological means. For although it is sufficient
for us Christians to believe by faith that the human soul does not
perish with the body and that God exists, yet it seems certain that 2
unbelievers cannot be convinced of the truth of religion, and scarcely
even of any moral values, unless these first two truths are proved to
them by natural reason. And since often in this life there are greater
rewards for the vices than for the virtues, few will prefer what is right
to what is useful, if they neither fear God nor expect an afterlife. And
although it is completely true that we should believe in the existence
of God because it is taught in the holy scriptures, and by the same
token that we should believe the holy scriptures because we have
them from God—since, faith being a gift of God, he who gives us
the grace to believe the rest of religion can also give us the grace to
believe he exists—there is no point in asserting this to unbelievers,
because they would call it arguing in a circle. And indeed I have
observed that not only do you and all other theologians affirm that
God's existence can be proved by natural reason, but that also the
holy scriptures imply that the knowledge of him is much easier to
attain than that of many created things: so easy, in fact, that those
who lack it do so by their own fault. This is clear from this passage
of Wisdom 13: 'They have no excuse. For if they are capable of
acquiring enough knowledge to be able to investigate the world, how
have they been so slow to find its Master?'* And in Romans 1: [20]
they are said to 'have no excuse'. In the same chapter [1: 19], the
words 'What can be known about God is perfectly plain in them,'*

seem to be pointing out that all that can be known of God can be shown by reasons derived from no other source than our own mind. How this comes to be true, and by what means God may be known more easily and with more certainty than the things of this world, I thought it would be appropriate to investigate.

3 And as regards the soul, even though many authors have judged that it is very difficult to discover its nature, and some have even dared to say that human reasoning convinces us that it perishes along with the body, and that we believe the contrary by faith alone, nonetheless because the Council of the Lateran* held in the reign of Leo X condemns these people (session 8), and explicitly enjoins Christian philosophers to refute their arguments, and to make every effort to prove the truth, I did not hesitate to tackle this issue as well. Besides, I know that most of the impious refuse to believe that God exists and that the human mind is distinct from the body, for no other reason than that they say that these two points have never been proved by anybody up to now. I do not agree with them at all in this: on the contrary, I think that nearly all the reasons adduced by great thinkers in this debate, when they are sufficiently grasped, have the status of demonstrations;* and I can scarcely persuade myself that any proofs might be found that have not been already discovered by someone else. Nonetheless I think that I could achieve nothing more useful in philosophy than to perform a careful search, once and for all, for the best arguments put forward by anyone, and to arrange them in so clear and precise an order* that from now on everyone will accept them as having the status of demonstrations. And finally, since there are several people who know that I have developed a particular method for resolving all difficulties in the sciences—not indeed a new one, for nothing is older than truth, but one they have seen me use with some success in other areas—they have insistently urged me to do this; and therefore I decided it was my duty to make an effort in this area as well.

4 Whatever I have been able to achieve is all in this treatise. It is not that I have sought in it to bring together all the different arguments that can be adduced to prove these two points, since this does not seem worth while, except where there is no argument considered sufficiently certain. But I have gone into the primary and most important arguments in such a way that I now dare to offer them as demonstrations that are as certain and evident as possible. I will add

[margin, handwritten: "TRUTH" actively implies options]

[margin, handwritten: → to find]

that they are such, that I do not think there is any path open to
human intelligence along which better ones can ever be found: for
the importance of the issues and the glory of God, for the sake of
which this whole book was written, compel me here to speak a little
more freely about my own work than is my custom. Yet, however
certain and evident I think them, I do not for that reason convince
myself that they are capable of being grasped by all. In geometry
there are many arguments by Archimedes, Apollonius, Pappus, and
others that are regarded as evident and also as certain by everyone,
because everything they contain, considered separately, is very easy
to know, and the later sections are fully coherent with the earlier
ones; yet because they are on the long side and demand a very attentive reader, they are grasped by very few people indeed. In the same
way, although I think the arguments I use here are no less certain and
evident than the geometrical ones, indeed more so, I am afraid that
many people will not be able to grasp them sufficiently clearly, both
because they too are on the long side, and one part depends on
another, and above all because they require a mind completely free of
prejudices, and which can readily withdraw itself from the company
of the senses. And it is certain that the capacity for metaphysics is
not more widespread than that for geometry. And there is another 5
difference between the two. In geometry everyone is convinced that
nothing is written down, as a rule, without a rigorous demonstration,
and so the unskilful more often err in approving what is false, since
they want to be thought to understand it, than in challenging what is
true. On the other hand, in philosophy, since it is believed that one
can argue on both sides of any question,* few search for the truth,
and many more seek a reputation for intelligence on account of their
daring to challenge the soundest views.

And therefore, whatever my reasons are worth, because they
deal with philosophical issues, I do not think they will have a great
impact, unless you help me with your patronage. But since everyone
holds your faculty in such high and deep-rooted esteem, and since
the name of the Sorbonne has such authority that not only in matters
of faith there is no group of men, after the holy councils, that has
greater influence than yours, but also in human philosophy no one
can think of anywhere where there is greater perspicacity and seriousness, and a greater integrity and wisdom in passing judgement,
than among yourselves, I do not doubt that if you deign to take an

interest in this work—first, by correcting it (for mindful of my own
humanity and above all of my own ignorance, I do not claim that it
contains no errors); secondly, where there are gaps, or imperfections,
or parts that need further explanation, by adding to it, improving it,
and clarifying it, or at least, pointing out these defects to me so that
I can undertake the task; and finally, once the arguments contained
in it, by which the existence of God and the distinction between
mind and body are proved, have been brought to the degree of clar-
6   ity to which I trust they can be brought, so that they can be considered as absolutely rigorous demonstrations, by agreeing to declare
this and bear public witness to it—I do not doubt, I say, that if this
takes place, all the erroneous views that have ever been held on these
questions will swiftly be erased from people's minds. For the truth
itself will readily bring other intelligent and learned men to subscribe
to your judgement; and your authority will bring atheists, who are
generally pretenders to knowledge rather than genuinely intelligent
and learned, to lay aside their urge to contradict, and perhaps even to
give their support to reasons that they know are regarded as demonstrative by all people of intelligence, in case they might seem incapable of understanding them. And finally everyone else will readily
believe so many testimonies, and there will be no one else in the
world who dares to question the existence of God or the real distinction between the human soul and the body. How useful this would
be, you yourselves, with your outstanding wisdom, will judge better
than anybody; nor would it be seemly for me to recommend the
cause of God and religion any further to you, who have always been
the staunchest support of the Catholic Church.

I have already touched on questions concerning God and the human mind a few years ago in the *Discourse on the Method of Rightly Conducting One's Reason and of Seeking for Truth in the Sciences*, published in French in 1637. But I was not intending to treat such matters thoroughly there, but merely offering a foretaste of them, so that I could learn from readers' responses how they should subsequently be properly dealt with. For they seemed to me of such importance that I judged I should deal with them more than once; and I follow a path in their investigation that is so untrodden, and so remote from common experience, that I thought it would not be useful to expound it more fully in a work written in French for all to read, in case those of rather feeble intellect should think that they too should set out on that path.

Although, however, I had requested in that text that everyone who found something deserving of criticism in my writings should be so kind as to point it out to me,* no objection worthy of note was put forward with regard to my discussion of these matters, except for two, to which I shall briefly reply here, before embarking on a more thorough explanation of the same issues.

The first is that although the human mind, when it turns in on 8 itself, does not perceive itself to be anything apart from a thinking thing, it does not follow that its nature or 'essence' consists purely in its being a thinking thing, 'purely', that is, in a sense that would exclude everything else that might perhaps be said to belong to its nature. To this objection I reply that at this point I did not wish to exclude these other things from the point of view of the actual truth of the matter (with which in fact I was not then concerned), but solely from the point of view of my own perception, so that my meaning was that I was aware of nothing at all that I knew to belong to my essence, except the fact that I was a thinking thing, or a thing possessing the faculty of thinking. However, in the present work I shall show how, from the fact that I know nothing else as belonging to my essence, it follows that nothing else in fact belongs to it.

The second objection is, that it does not follow from the fact that I have in myself the idea of a more perfect thing than myself, that the idea itself is more perfect than me. Still less does it follow that the thing represented by this idea exists. I answer that the term 'idea' here is ambiguous. It can be taken either in the material sense, as an operation of the understanding, in which case it cannot be said to be more perfect than myself, or objectively, for the thing represented by this operation; and this thing, even if it is not supposed to exist outside my understanding, can nonetheless be more perfect than me in virtue of its essence. How in fact it follows, from the mere fact that the idea of a more perfect thing is within me, that the thing itself actually exists, I shall show at length in the present work.

I have in fact also seen two quite long writings* in which, however, it is not so much my proofs as my conclusions that are attacked, by arguments borrowed from the stock of atheists' commonplaces. And since arguments of this kind can have no credibility for those who understand my proofs, and, besides, the judgements of many people are so perverse and feeble that they are convinced more readily by the opinions they first encounter, however false and repugnant to reason these are, than by a true and unshakeable refutation of these opinions that they encounter subsequently, I have no intention of responding to them here, since I should first have to set them out. I shall only remark in general that all the common objections to the existence of God that atheists so smugly put forward, always depend on one of two things: either they imagine human emotions in God, or they claim so much power and wisdom for our own minds, that we should try to decide and understand whatever God can or ought to do. So much is this the case that, as long as we simply remember that our minds have to be considered as finite, and God as incomprehensible and infinite, these arguments will never cause us any difficulty.

But now, since I have once and for all made trial of people's responses, I will again tackle these same questions about God and the human mind, and at the same time deal with the foundations of the whole of first philosophy. But I shall do so in such a way that I must expect no popular approval, and no great crowds of readers. Indeed, I shall go so far as to say that I seek to be read by none, except those who will be able and willing to meditate seriously alongside me, and to withdraw their minds from the senses, and at the same time from all their preconceptions. Of these I well know already that there are very few. But as for those who do not trouble to grasp the chain and connection of my arguments, and who busy themselves in quibbling over isolated propositions (and there are many people whose habit 10 this is), they will derive very little benefit from reading this work; and although perhaps they will find frequent opportunities to carp, it is unlikely that they will be able to put forward any objection that causes real difficulty or deserves a reply.

But because I do not promise even the other kind of readers that I will satisfy them throughout on first reading, nor am I so arrogant as to be sure that I can foresee everything that will seem difficult to anybody, I shall first explain in these Meditations the particular thought-processes by the help of which I think I have attained the certain and evident knowledge of truth, so that I may test whether, perhaps, I can convince other people by the same arguments as I have convinced myself. Afterwards, however, I shall reply to the objections of several people outstanding for their intelligence and learning to whom these Meditations were sent for examination before publication. Their objections are so many and so various that I dare to hope that it will be difficult for anyone else to think of anything (anything significant, at least) that they have not already put forward. Hence I would very strongly urge my readers not to pass judgement upon these Meditations before they have taken the trouble to read through all these objections and my replies to them.

SYNOPSIS OF THE FOLLOWING
SIX MEDITATIONS

In the First Meditation the reasons are set out why we can doubt of all things, especially material things: that is, as long as we have no foundations for the sciences other than those we have had up to now. Now, although the benefits of such far-reaching doubt do not appear at first sight, it has this very great benefit, that it liberates us from all prejudices, and opens up a very easy pathway to the withdrawal of our mind from the senses. Finally, it means that we can doubt no further of whatever we subsequently discover to be true.

In the Second, the mind that, using its own freedom, supposes that all the things of the existence of which it can entertain even the slightest doubt, do not exist, becomes aware that this cannot happen unless it itself exists at the same time. This also is very useful, since by this means the mind can easily distinguish what belongs to it, that is, to an intellectual nature, and what to the body. But because some people will perhaps expect some proofs of the soul's immortality here, I think I
should warn them right away that I have tried to put nothing in this treatise that I do not rigorously demonstrate. Therefore I could follow no other order than the one geometers use, that is, I deal with everything on which the proposition we are investigating depends, before drawing any conclusion about the proposition itself. The first and most important prerequisite to discovering the soul's immortality is to form a concept of the soul that is as clear as possible, and entirely distinct from any concept of the body. This I have done here. But further, we also need to know that whatever we clearly and distinctly understand is true, in the way in which we understand it. This could not have been proved before the Fourth Meditation. We also need to have a distinct concept of bodily nature, which is formed partly in this Second Meditation, partly in the Fifth and Sixth. From these points we must conclude that all things we clearly and distinctly conceive as different substances, as mind and body are conceived, are indeed substances really distinct from each other; and I drew this conclusion in the Sixth Meditation. The same point is proved there from the fact that we can understand no body except as divisible, but on the other hand no mind except as indivisible: for we cannot conceive a half of

any mind, as we can with any body, however small it is. The upshot of
this is that their natures are recognized not only as different, but also
in a sense contrary. But I have treated no further of this matter in the
present work. For one thing, because these points are sufficient to show
that the corruption of the body does not cause the mind to perish, and
thus that mortals may have hope of another life. For another, because
the premises from which this immortality of the mind may be deduced
depend on an explanation of the whole of physics, which would show, 14
first, that all substances whatever—things, that is, that have to be created by God in order to exist—are of their own nature incorruptible,
and can never cease to exist, unless they are reduced to nothing by the
same God's denying them his support; and, secondly, that body in a
general sense is a substance, and never perishes; but that the human
body, in so far as it differs from the rest of bodies, is constituted purely
by a certain arrangement of parts and by other accidents of the same
kind; whereas the mind is not composed of any accidents in this way,
but is a pure substance. For even if all its accidents were to change,
for instance, if it understood, or wished, or perceived via the senses
a different set of things, it would still be the same mind. On the other
hand, the human body becomes something different from the very
fact that the shape of some of its parts is changed. From this it follows
that the body can very easily perish, but that the mind is of its nature
immortal.

In the Third Meditation I have explained my principal proof of
the existence of God at, I think, considerable length. However, because,
in order to withdraw my readers' minds as far as possible from the
senses, I decided to make use of no comparisons derived from bodily
things, perhaps many obscurities have remained. These, I hope, will
be fully cleared up later on, in my Replies to the Objections: for
instance, how the idea we possess of a supremely perfect being has so
much objective reality that it can derive only from a supremely perfect cause. This is illustrated in the Replies by the comparison with
a very perfect machine, the idea of which is in the mind of some
artificer. For just as the objective artifice of this idea must have some
cause, namely the knowledge of the artisan, or of someone else from
whom he derived his knowledge, so the idea we possess of God can 15
have only God as its cause.*

In the Fourth Meditation it is proved that all those things we
clearly and distinctly perceive are true, and at the same time it is

explained in what falsity consists. Both these points are necessary, in order to set the seal on what goes before, as well as for the understanding of what comes after. (But I should point out that at this point I am not at all dealing with sin,* that is, the error that is committed in the pursuit of good and evil, but only of error that affects the discernment of true from false.) Nor do I examine matters to do with faith or with the conduct of one's life, but only speculative truths known by the help of the natural light.

In the Fifth, besides the explanation of the nature of bodies in general, the existence of God is also demonstrated by a new argument. In this, however, perhaps several difficulties will crop up again, which will be settled in the Reply to Objections. Finally, it will be shown how it comes to be true that the certainty of geometrical demonstrations themselves depends on the knowledge of God.

Finally, in the Sixth the distinction is made between intellection and imagination; the distinctive features of each are described; it is proved that the mind is really distinct from the body; and yet so closely conjoined to it that it forms a single entity with it; a full list is given of all the errors that typically arise from the senses and the means by which these may be avoided are explained. Finally, all the reasons are put forward that lead us to conclude in the existence of material things: not that I think these are very useful when it comes to proving what they do prove, namely that a world really exists, and that human beings have bodies, and so forth, things which no one in their right mind has ever seriously doubted; they are useful because, by considering them, we come to recognize that they are not as solid and clear as those by which we come to the knowledge of our mind and of God; indeed, those latter are the most certain and evident of all reasons that can be grasped by human intelligence. And this is all I was intending to prove in these Meditations. This is why I do not here mention several questions that are also treated incidentally in the course of the work.

I like the concept of evil because it
implies this need for growth —
as though humans have divine power to fill

FIRST MEDITATION   17

OF THOSE THINGS THAT MAY BE CALLED INTO DOUBT

It is some years now since I realized how many false opinions I had
accepted as true from childhood onwards,* and that, whatever I had
since built on such shaky foundations, could only be highly doubtful.
Hence I saw that at some stage in my life the whole structure would
have to be utterly demolished, and that I should have to begin again
from the bottom up if I wished to construct something lasting and
unshakeable in the sciences. But this seemed to be a massive task, and
so I postponed it until I had reached the age when one is as fit as one
will ever be to master the various disciplines. Hence I have delayed
so long that now I should be at fault if I used up in deliberating the
time that is left for acting. The moment has come, and so today I have
discharged my mind from all its cares, and have carved out a space of   18
untroubled leisure. I have withdrawn into seclusion and shall at last
be able to devote myself seriously and without encumbrance to the
task of destroying all my former opinions.

To this end, however, it will not be necessary to prove them all
false—a thing I should perhaps never be able to achieve. But since
reason already persuades me that I should no less scrupulously
withhold my assent from what is not fully certain and indubitable
than from what is blatantly false, then, in order to reject them all, it
will be sufficient to find some reason for doubting each one. Nor shall
I therefore have to go through them each individually, which would
be an endless task: but since, once the foundations are undermined,
the building will collapse of its own accord, I shall straight away
attack the very principles that form the basis of all my former beliefs.

Certainly, up to now whatever I have accepted as fully true I have
learned either from or by means of the senses: but I have discovered
that they sometimes deceive us, and prudence dictates that we
should never fully trust those who have deceived us even once.

But perhaps, although they sometimes deceive us about things
that are little, or rather a long way away, there are plenty of other
things of which there is clearly no doubt, although it was from the
senses that we learned them: for instance, that I am now here, sitting
by the fire, wrapped in a warm winter gown, handling this paper,

and suchlike. Indeed, that these hands themselves, and this whole body are mine—what reason could there be for doubting this? Unless

19 perhaps I were to compare myself to one of those madmen, whose little brains have been so befuddled by a pestilential vapour arising from the black bile,* that they swear blind that they are kings, though they are beggars, or that they are clad in purple, when they are naked, or that their head is made of clay, or that their whole body is a jug, or made entirely of glass. But they are lunatics, and I should seem no less of a madman myself if I should follow their example in any way.

This is all very well, to be sure. But am I not a human being, and therefore in the habit of sleeping at night, when in my dreams I have all the same experiences as these madmen do when they are awake—or sometimes even stranger ones? How often my sleep at night has convinced me of all these familiar things—that I was here, wrapped in my gown, sitting by the fire—when in fact I was lying naked under the bedclothes.—All the same, I am now perceiving this paper with eyes that are certainly awake; the head I am nodding is not drowsy; I stretch out my hand and feel it knowingly and deliberately; a sleeper would not have these experiences so distinctly.—But have I then forgotten those other occasions on which I have been deceived by similar thoughts in my dreams? When I think this over more carefully I see so clearly that waking can never be distinguished from sleep by any conclusive indications that I am stupefied; and this very stupor comes close to persuading me that I am asleep after all.

Let us then suppose* that we are dreaming, and that these particular things (that we have our eyes open, are moving our head, stretching out our hands) are not true; and that perhaps we do not even have hands or the rest of a body like what we see. It must nonetheless be admitted that the things we see in sleep are, so to speak, painted images, which could not be formed except on the basis of a resemblance with real things; and that for this reason these general things at least (such as eyes, head, hands, and the rest of the body) are not imaginary things, but real and existing. For the fact is that when

20 painters desire to represent sirens and little satyrs with utterly unfamiliar shapes, they cannot devise altogether new natures for them, but simply combine parts from different animals; or if perhaps they do think up something so new that nothing at all like it has ever been seen, which is thus altogether fictitious and false, it is certain that at

least the colours which they combine to form images must be real. By the same token, even though these general things—eyes, head, hands, and so forth—might be imaginary, it must necessarily be admitted that at least some other still more simple and universal realities must exist, from which (as the painter's image is produced from real colours) all these images of things—be they true or false—that occur in our thoughts are produced.

In this category it seems we should include bodily nature in general, and its extension; likewise the shape of extended things and their quantity (magnitude and number); likewise the place in which they exist, the time during which they exist, and suchlike.

From all this, perhaps, we may safely conclude that physics, astronomy, medicine, and all the other disciplines which involve the study of composite things are indeed doubtful; but that arithmetic, geometry, and other disciplines of the same kind, which deal only with the very simplest and most general things, and care little whether they exist in nature or not, contain something certain and indubitable. For whether I am waking or sleeping, two plus three equals five, and a square has no more than four sides; nor does it seem possible that such obvious truths could be affected by any suspicion that they are false.

However, there is a certain opinion long fixed in my mind, that 21 there is a God who is all-powerful, and by whom I was created such as I am now. Now how do I know that he has not brought it about NOTHING— that there is no earth at all, no heavens, no extended things, no shape, to build no magnitude, no place—and yet that all these things appear to me up to exist just as they do now?* Or even—just as I judge now and again that other people are mistaken about things they believe they know with the greatest certitude—that I too should be similarly deceived whenever I add two and three, or count the sides of a square, or make a judgement about something even simpler, if anything simpler can be imagined?

But perhaps God has not willed that I should be so cheated, for he is said to be supremely good.—But if it were incompatible with his goodness to have created me such that I am perpetually deceived, it would seem equally inconsistent with that quality to permit me to be sometimes deceived. Nonetheless, I cannot doubt that he does permit it.

Perhaps, indeed, there might be some people who would prefer to deny the existence of any God so powerful, rather than believing that all other things are uncertain. But let us not quarrel with them, and let us grant that all this we have said of God is only a fiction; and let them suppose that it is by fate or chance or a continuous sequence of things that I have come to be what I am. Since, though, to be deceived and to err appear to be some kind of imperfection, the less powerful the source they invoke to explain my being, the more probable it will be that I am so imperfect that I am perpetually deceived. To all these arguments, indeed, I have no answer, but at length I am forced to admit that there is nothing of all those things I once thought true, of which it is not legitimate to doubt—and not out of any thoughtlessness or irresponsibility, but for sound and well-weighed reasons; and therefore that, from these things as well, no less than from what is blatantly false, I must now carefully withhold my assent if I wish to discover any thing that is certain.*

But it is not enough to have realized all this, I must take care to remember it: for my accustomed opinions continually creep back into my mind, and take possession of my belief, which has, so to speak, been enslaved to them by long experience and familiarity, for the most part against my will. Nor shall I ever break the habit of assenting to them and relying on them, as long as I go on supposing them to be such as they are in truth, that is to say, doubtful indeed in some respect, as has been shown just now, and yet nonetheless highly probable, so that it is much more rational to believe than to deny them. Hence, it seems to me, I shall not be acting unwisely if, willing myself to believe the contrary, I deceive myself, and make believe, for some considerable time, that they are altogether false and imaginary, until, once the prior judgements on each side have been evenly balanced in the scales, no evil custom can any longer twist my judgement away from the correct perception of things. For I know for sure that no danger or error will ensue as a result of this, and that there is no risk that I shall be giving too free a rein to my distrustfulness, since my concern at the moment is not with action but only with the attainment of knowledge.*

I will therefore suppose that, not God, who is perfectly good and the source of truth, but some evil spirit, supremely powerful and cunning, has devoted all his efforts to deceiving me.* I will think that the sky, the air, the earth, colours, shapes, sounds, and all external things are no different from the illusions of our dreams, and that they are traps he has laid for my credulity; I will consider myself as having no hands, no eyes, no flesh, no blood, and no senses, but yet as falsely believing that I have all these;* I will obstinately cling to these thoughts, and in this way, if indeed it is not in my power to discover any truth,* yet certainly to the best of my ability and determination I will take care not to give my assent to anything false, or to allow this deceiver, however powerful and cunning he may be, to impose upon me in any way.

But to carry out this plan requires great effort, and there is a kind of indolence that drags me back to my customary way of life. Just as a prisoner, who was perhaps enjoying an imaginary freedom in his dreams, when he then begins to suspect that he is asleep is afraid of being woken up, and lets himself sink back into his soothing illusions; so I of my own accord slip back into my former opinions, and am scared to awake, for fear that tranquil sleep will give way to laborious hours of waking, which from now on I shall have to spend not in any kind of light, but in the unrelenting darkness of the difficulties just stirred up.

SECOND MEDITATION

OF THE NATURE OF THE HUMAN MIND; THAT IT IS MORE EASILY KNOWN THAN THE BODY

Yesterday's meditation has plunged me into so many doubts that I still cannot put them out of my mind, nor, on the other hand, can I see any way to resolve them; but, as if I had suddenly slipped into 24 a deep whirlpool, I am in such difficulties that I can neither touch bottom with my foot nor swim back to the surface. Yet I will struggle on, and I will try the same path again as the one I set out on yesterday, that is to say, eliminating everything in which there is the smallest element of doubt, exactly as if I had found it to be false through and through; and I shall pursue my way until I discover something certain; or, failing that, discover that it is certain only that nothing is certain. Archimedes* claimed, that if only he had a point that was firm and immovable, he would move the whole earth; and great things are likewise to be hoped, if I can find just one little thing that is certain and unshakeable.

I therefore suppose that all I see is false; I believe that none of those things* represented by my deceitful memory has ever existed; in fact I have no senses at all; body, shape, extension in space, motion, and place itself are all illusions. What truth then is left? Perhaps this alone, that nothing is certain.

But how do I know that there is not something different from all those things I have just listed, about which there is not the slightest room for doubt? Is there not, after all, some God, or whatever he should be called, that puts these thoughts into my mind? But why should I think that, when perhaps I myself could be the source of these thoughts? But am I at least not something, after all? But I have already denied that I have any senses or any body. Now I am at a loss,
25   because what follows from this? Am I so bound up with my body and senses that I cannot exist without them? But I convinced myself that there was nothing at all in the world, no sky, no earth, no minds, no bodies. Did I therefore not also convince myself that I did not exist either? No: certainly I did exist, if I convinced myself of something.—But there is some deceiver or other, supremely powerful and cunning, who is deliberately deceiving me all the time.— Beyond doubt then, I also exist, if he is deceiving me; and he can deceive me all he likes, but he will never bring it about that I should be nothing as long as I think I am something. So that, having weighed all these considerations sufficiently and more than sufficiently, I can finally decide* that this proposition, 'I am, I exist', whenever it is uttered by me, or conceived in the mind, is necessarily true.

But indeed I do not yet sufficiently understand what in fact this 'I' is that now necessarily exists;* so that from now on I must take care in case I should happen imprudently to take something else to be me that is not me, and thus go astray in the very knowledge [*cognitione*] that I claim to be the most certain and evident of all. Hence I shall now meditate afresh on what I once believed myself to be, before I fell into this train of thought. From this I shall then subtract whatever it has been possible to cast doubt on, even in the slightest degree, by the reasons put forward above, so that in the end there shall remain exactly and only that which is certain and unshakeable.

So what in fact did I think I was before all this? A human being, of course. But what is a human being? Shall I say, 'a rational animal'?* No, for then I should have to examine what exactly an animal is, and what 'rational' is, and hence, starting with one question, I should stumble into more and more difficult ones. Nor do I now have so much leisure that I can afford to fritter it away on subtleties of this kind. But here I shall rather direct my attention to the thoughts that

spontaneously and by nature's prompting came to my mind before- 26
hand, whenever I considered what I was. The first was that I have a
face, hands, arms, and this whole mechanism of limbs, such as we see
even in corpses; this I referred to as the body. Next, that I took nourishment, moved, perceived with my senses, and thought: these
actions indeed I attributed to the soul.* What this soul was, however,
either I never considered, or I imagined it as something very rarefied
and subtle, like a wind, or fire, or thin air, infused into my coarser
parts. But about the body itself, on the other hand, I had no doubts,
but I thought I distinctly knew its nature, which, if I had attempted
to describe how I conceived it in my mind, I would have explained as
follows: by body I mean everything that is capable of being bounded
by some shape, of existing in a definite place, of filling a space in such
a way as to exclude the presence of any other body within it; of being
perceived by touch, sight, hearing, taste, or smell, and also of being
moved in various ways, not indeed by itself, but by some other thing
by which it is touched; for to have the power of moving itself, and
also of perceiving by the senses or thinking, I judged could in no way
belong to the nature of body; rather, I was puzzled by the fact that
such capacities were found in certain bodies.

But what about now, when I am supposing that some deceiver,
who is supremely powerful and, if I may venture to say so, evil, has
been exerting all his efforts to delude me in every way? Can I affirm
that I possess the slightest thing of all those that I have just said
belong to the nature of body? I consider, I think, I go over it all in my 27
mind: nothing comes up. It would be a waste of effort to go through
the list again. But what about the attributes I used to ascribe to the
soul? What about taking nourishment or moving? But since I now
have no body, these also are nothing but illusions. What about sense-
perception? But certainly this does not take place without a body,
and I have seemed to perceive very many things when asleep that
I later realized I had not perceived. What about thinking? Here I do
find something: it is thought; this alone cannot be stripped from me.
I am, I exist, this is certain. But for how long? Certainly only for as
long as I am thinking; for perhaps if I were to cease from all thinking
it might also come to pass that I might immediately cease altogether
to exist. I am now admitting nothing except what is necessarily true:
I am therefore, speaking precisely, only a thinking thing, that is,
a mind, or a soul, or an intellect, or a reason—words the meaning of

which was previously unknown to me. I am therefore a true thing, and one that truly exists; but what kind of thing? I have said it already: one that thinks.

What comes next? I will imagine: I am not that framework of limbs that is called a human body; I am not some thin air infused into these limbs, or a wind, or a fire, or a vapour, or a breath, or whatever I can picture myself as: for I have supposed that these things do not exist. But even if I keep to this supposition, nonetheless I am still something.*—But all the same, it is perhaps still the case that these very things I am supposing to be nothing, are nevertheless not distinct from this 'me' that I know* [*novi*].—Perhaps: I don't know. But this is not the point at issue at present. I can pass judgement only on those things that are known to me. I know [*novi*] that I exist; I am trying to find out what this 'I' is, whom I know [*novi*]. It is absolutely certain that this knowledge [*notitia*], in the precise sense in question here, does not depend on things of which I do not yet know [*novi*] whether they exist; and therefore it depends on none of those things I picture in my imagination. This very word 'imagination' shows where I am going wrong. For I should certainly be 'imagining things' if I *imagined* myself to be anything, since imagining is nothing other than contemplating the shape or image of a bodily thing. Now, however, I know [*scio*] for certain that I exist; and that, at the same time, it could be the case that all these images, and in general everything that pertains to the nature of body, are nothing but illusions. Now this is clear to me, it would seem as foolish of me to say: 'I shall use my imagination, in order to recognize more clearly what I am', as it would be to say: 'Now I am awake, and I see something true; but because I cannot yet see it clearly enough, I shall do my best to get back to sleep again so that my dreams can show it to me more truly and more clearly.' And so I realize [*cognosco*] that nothing that I can grasp by means of the imagination has to do with this knowledge [*notitiam*] I have of myself, and that I need to withdraw my mind from such things as thoroughly as possible, if it is to perceive its own nature as distinctly as possible.

But what therefore am I? A thinking thing. What is that? I mean a thing that doubts, that understands, that affirms, that denies, that wishes to do this and does not wish to do that, and also that imagines and perceives by the senses.

Well, indeed, there is quite a lot there, if all these things really do belong to me. But why should they not belong to me? Is it not me who currently doubts virtually everything, who nonetheless understands something, who affirms this alone to be true, and denies the rest, who wishes to know more, and wishes not to be deceived, who imagines many things, even against his will, and is aware of many things that appear to come via the senses? Is there any of these things 29 that is not equally true as the fact that I exist—even if I am always asleep, and even if my creator is deceiving me to the best of his ability? Is there any of them that can be distinguished from my thinking? Is there any that can be said to be separate from me? For that it is I that am doubting, understanding, wishing, is so obvious that nothing further is needed in order to explain it more clearly. But indeed it is also this same I that is imagining; for although it might be the case, as I have been supposing, that none of these imagined things is true, yet the actual power of imagining certainly does exist, and is part of my thinking. And finally it is the same I that perceives by means of the senses, or who is aware of corporeal things as if by means of the senses: for example, I am seeing a light, hearing a noise, feeling heat.— But these things are false, since I am asleep!—But certainly I *seem to* be seeing, hearing, getting hot. This cannot be false. This is what is properly meant by speaking of myself as having sensations; and, understood in this precise sense, it is nothing other than thinking.

From all of this, I am indeed beginning to know [*nosse*] rather better what I in fact am. But it still seems (and I cannot help thinking this) that the bodily things of which the images are formed in our thought, and which the senses themselves investigate, are much more distinctly recognized than that part of myself, whatever it is, that cannot be represented by the imagination. Although, indeed, it is strange that things that I realize are doubtful, unknown, unrelated to me should be more distinctly grasped by me than what is true and what is known—more distinctly grasped even than myself. But I see what is happening. My mind enjoys wandering off the track, and will not yet allow itself to be confined within the boundaries of truth. Very well, then: let us, once again, slacken its reins as far as possible— 30 then, before too long, a tug on them at the right moment will bring it more easily back to obedience.*

Let us consider those things which are commonly thought to be more distinctly grasped than anything else: I mean the bodies we

touch and see; but not bodies in general, for these general perceptions are usually considerably more confused, but one body in particular. Let us, for example, take this wax: it has only just been
removed from the honeycomb; it has not yet lost all the flavour of its
honey; it retains some of the scent of the flowers among which it was
gathered; its colour, shape, and size are clearly visible; it is hard,
cold, easy to touch, and if you tap it with your knuckle, it makes a
sound. In short, it has all the properties that seem to be required for
a given body to be known as distinctly as possible. But wait—while
I am speaking, it is brought close to the fire. The remains of its
flavour evaporate; the smell fades; the colour is changed, the shape is
taken away, it grows in size, becomes liquid, becomes warm, it can
hardly be touched, and now, if you strike it, it will give off no sound.
Does the same wax still remain? We must admit it does remain: no
one would say or think it does not. So what was there in it that was
so distinctly grasped? Certainly, none of those qualities I apprehended by the senses: for whatever came under taste, or smell, or
sight, or touch, or hearing, has now changed: but the wax remains.

Perhaps the truth of the matter was what I now think it is: namely,
that the wax itself was not in fact this sweetness of the honey, or the
fragrance of the flowers, or the whiteness, shape, or sonority, but the
body which not long ago appeared to me as perceptible in these
modes,* but now appears in others. But what exactly is this that I am
imagining in this way? Let us consider the matter, and, thinking
away those things that do not belong to the wax, let us see what
remains. Something extended, flexible, mutable: certainly, that is all.
But in what do this flexibility and mutability consist? Is it in the fact
that I can imagine this wax being changed in shape, from a circle to
a square, and from a square into a triangle? That cannot be right: for
I understand that it is capable of innumerable changes of this sort,
yet I cannot keep track of all these by using my imagination. Therefore
my understanding of these properties is not achieved by using the
faculty of imagination. What about 'extended'? Surely I know something about the nature of its extension. For it is greater when the wax
is melting, greater still when it is boiling, and greater still when the
heat is further increased. And I would not be correctly judging
what the wax is if I failed to see that it is capable of receiving
more varieties, as regards extension, than I have ever grasped in my
imagination. So I am left with no alternative, but to accept that I am

not at all *imagining* what this wax is, I am perceiving it with my mind alone: I say 'this wax' in particular, for the point is even clearer about wax in general. So then, what is this wax, which is only perceived by the mind? Certainly it is the same wax I see, touch, and imagine, and in short it is the same wax I judged it to be from the beginning. But yet—and this is important—the perception of it is not sight, touch, or imagination, and never was, although it seemed to be so at first: it is an inspection by the mind alone, which can be either imperfect and confused, as it was before in this case, or clear and distinct, as it now is, depending on the greater or lesser degree of attention I pay to what it consists of.

But in the meantime I am amazed by the proneness of my mind to error. For although I am considering all this in myself silently and without speech, yet I am still ensnared by words themselves, and all but deceived by the very ways in which we usually put things. For we say that we 'see' the wax itself, if it is present, not that we judge it to be there on the basis of its colour or shape. From this I would have immediately concluded that I therefore knew the wax by the sight of my eyes, not by the inspection of the mind alone—if I had not happened to glance out of the window at people walking along the street. Using the customary expression, I say that I 'see' them, just as I 'see' the wax. But what do I actually see other than hats and coats, which could be covering automata?* But I judge that they are people. And therefore what I thought I saw with my eyes, I in fact grasp only by the faculty of judging that is in my mind.

But one who desires to know more than the common herd might be ashamed to have gone to the speech of the common herd to find a reason for doubting. Let us then go on where we left off by considering whether I perceived more perfectly and more evidently what the wax was, when I first encountered it, and believed that I knew [*cognoscere*] it by these external senses, or at least by what they call the 'common sense',* that is, the imaginative power; or whether I perceive it better now, after I have more carefully investigated both what it is and how it is known [*cognoscatur*]. Certainly it would be foolish to doubt that I have a much better grasp of it now. For what, if anything, was distinct in my original perception? What was there, if anything, that seemed to go beyond the perception of the lowest animals?* But on the other hand, when I distinguish the wax from its external forms, and, as if I had stripped off its garments, consider it in all its

nakedness, then, indeed, although there may still be error in my judgements, I cannot perceive it in this way except by the human mind.

33   But what, then, shall I say about this mind, or about myself? For
I do not yet accept that there is anything in me but a mind. What,
I say, am I who seem to perceive this wax so distinctly? Do I not
know [*cognosco*] myself not only much more truly, much more certainly, but also much more distinctly and evidently than the wax?
For, if I judge that the wax exists, for the reason that I see it, it is certainly much more evident that I myself also exist, from the very fact
that I am seeing it. For it could be the case that what I am seeing is
not really wax; it could be the case that I do not even have eyes with
which to see anything; but it certainly cannot be the case, when I see
something, or when I think I am seeing something (the difference is
irrelevant for the moment), that I myself who think should not be
something. By the same token, if I judge that the wax exists, for the
reason that I am touching it, the same consequence follows: namely,
that I exist. If I judge it exists, for the reason I am imagining it, or for
any other reason, again, the same certainly applies. But what I have
realized in the case of the wax, I can apply to anything that exists outside myself. Moreover, if the perception of the wax appeared more
distinct after it became known to me from many sources, and not
from sight or touch alone, how much more distinctly—it must be
admitted—I now know [*cognosci*] myself. For there are no reasons
that can enhance the perception either of the wax or of any other
body at all that do not at the same time prove better to me the nature
of my own mind. But there are so many things besides in the mind
itself that can serve to make the knowledge [*notitia*] of it more distinct, that there seems scarcely any point in listing all the perceptions
that flow into it from the body.

34   But I see now that, without realizing it, I have ended up back
where I wanted to be. For since I have now learned that bodies themselves are perceived not, strictly speaking, by the senses or by the
imaginative faculty, but by the intellect alone, and that they are not
perceived because they are touched or seen, but only because they
are understood, I clearly realize [*cognosco*] that nothing can be perceived by me more easily or more clearly than my own mind. But
since a long-held opinion is a habit that cannot so readily be laid
aside, I intend to stop here for a while, in order to fix this newly
acquired knowledge more deeply in my memory by long meditation.

THIRD MEDITATION

OF GOD, THAT HE EXISTS

I shall now close my eyes, I shall block up my ears, I shall divert all my senses, and I shall even delete all bodily images from my thought or, since this is virtually impossible to achieve, at least count them as empty and worthless; and I shall try, by conversing only with myself and looking deep within myself, to make myself gradually better known and more familiar to myself. I am a thinking thing, that is, one that doubts, affirms, denies, understands a few things, is ignorant of many others, wills this and not that, and also imagines and perceives by the senses; for as I have already remarked, although the things I perceive or imagine outside myself do not perhaps exist, yet I am certain that the modes of thinking that I call sensations and imaginations, considered purely and simply as modes of thinking, do exist inside me. 35

And this, short as it is, is a complete list of what I truly know [*scio*], or at least of what, up to now, I have realized that I know. Now I shall examine more carefully whether perhaps there are any further items of knowledge in my possession to which I have not yet paid attention. I am certain that I am a thinking thing. But do I not therefore also know what is required in order for me to be certain of something? For in this first act of knowledge [*cognitione*] there is nothing other than a clear and distinct perception of what I affirm to be the case; and this certainly would be insufficient to make me certain of the truth of the matter, if it could ever come to pass that something I perceived so clearly and distinctly was false. And therefore I seem already to be able to lay down, as a general rule, that everything I very clearly and distinctly perceive is true.

And yet there are many things that I once accepted as completely certain and obvious, that I have since realized were doubtful. What kind of things were these? The earth, the sky, the stars, and everything else I became aware of through the senses. But what did I clearly perceive here? Certainly, that the ideas or thoughts of such things were present to my mind. And even now I do not deny that these ideas exist in me. But there was something else that I was affirming, and that, because I was used to believing it, I thought

I perceived clearly, although in fact I was not really perceiving it; namely, that there were certain things existing outside me from which these ideas derived and that the ideas perfectly resembled. This was my mistake; or at least, if I was after all right in thinking this, the rightness was not due to my perception.

36　　But when in arithmetic or geometry I considered something very simple and easy—for instance, two plus three equals five—surely I intuited this kind of thing at least clearly enough to declare it true? In fact, when I later judged that such things should be doubted, this was only because the thought had come to me, that perhaps some God might have endowed me with such a nature that I could be deceived even about those things that appeared supremely obvious. But whenever this preconceived opinion of God's supreme power occurs to me, I cannot help admitting, that, if indeed he wishes to, he can easily bring it about that I should be mistaken, even about matters that I think I intuit with the eye of the mind as evidently as possible. On the other hand, whenever I turn my attention to the things themselves that I think I perceive very clearly, I am so thoroughly convinced by them, that I cannot help exclaiming: 'Let whoever can, deceive me as much as he likes: still he can never bring it about that I am nothing, as long as I think I am something; or that one day it will be true that I have never existed, when it is true now that I exist; or that perhaps two plus three added together are more or less than five; or that other such things should be true in which I recognize an obvious contradiction.' And certainly, since I have no grounds for thinking that any deceitful God exists—in fact, I do not yet sufficiently know whether there is any God at all—then a reason for doubting that depends wholly on the belief in a deceitful God is very slight, and, so to speak, metaphysical. In order to remove it, then, at the first opportunity, I must examine whether there is a God, and, if there is, whether he can be a deceiver; since, as long as I remain ignorant of this matter, I seem unable ever to be certain of any other at all.*

　　But now it seems that, to proceed in an orderly fashion, I should
37　first divide up all my thoughts into definite categories, and examine to which of these truth and falsity can properly be said to pertain. Some of these thoughts are apparently images of things,* and to these alone the name 'idea' is properly applied: for instance, when I think of a human being, or a chimera, or the heavens, or an angel,

or God. But others have certain other forms as well; thus, when I will, or fear, or affirm, or deny, I am always in fact apprehending some thing as the subject of this thought,* but I am including something further within the thought than the mere likeness of the thing; and of thoughts of this kind some are called volitions, or affects, whereas others are called judgements.

Now, as far as ideas are concerned, if they are considered purely in themselves, and if I do not connect them with anything outside themselves, they cannot, strictly speaking, be false; for whether I am imagining a goat or a chimera, it is no less true that I am imagining one than that I am imagining the other. Again, there is no fear of falsehood in the will itself, or in the affects: for although I can desire something wicked, and even something that does not exist at all, this does not mean that it is not true that I desire it. This leaves only judgements: in these alone I must take care not to be deceived. The most glaring and widespread error that can be found in them consists in my judging that the ideas that are in me are similar to or in accordance with some things existing outside me. For certainly, if I conceived the ideas themselves purely and simply as modifications of my thinking, and did not connect them with anything else, they could scarcely give me any occasion to err.

Of these ideas, some seem to me to be innate, others adventitious,* others produced by myself. For understanding what a thing is, what 38 truth is, what thought is, is something I seem to possess purely in virtue of my nature itself. But if I am now hearing a noise, seeing the sun, feeling the heat of a fire,* up to now I have judged that such sensations derive from things existing outside myself. Finally, sirens, hippogriffs, and suchlike creatures are inventions of my own imagination. But perhaps I can think that all my ideas are adventitious, or all innate, or all produced by me: for I have not yet clearly discovered their true source.

About those ideas that I consider as proceeding from things existing outside myself, the key question to ask here is: What reason do I have for thinking the ideas are like the things? Well, certainly, nature itself seems to teach me to think so. Besides, experience shows me that they do not depend on my own will, and therefore do not depend on myself. For they often intrude upon me against my will. Now, for instance, I am feeling heat, whether I want to or not, and this is why I think that this sensation, or idea, of heat is coming to me from a thing distinct from myself, in this case from the heat of the fire by which I am sitting. And by far the most obvious judgement to make is that what the thing is transmitting to me is its own likeness rather than anything else.

But I shall now see whether these reasons are sufficiently solid. When I say here that 'I am taught by nature' to think so, I mean only that I am prompted to believe this by some spontaneous inclination, not that it is shown to me to be true by some natural light.* The two things are very different: for whatever is shown to me by the natural light (for instance, that, from the fact that I am doubting, it follows that I exist, and suchlike) can in no way be doubtful, because there can be no other faculty that I could trust as much as this light, and that could teach me that such things are not, after all, true. But when it comes to natural inclinations, I have before now often judged in the past that I have been led by these in the wrong direction, when it was a matter of choosing the good,* nor do I see why I should trust them more in any other domain.

Then again, although these ideas do not depend on my own will, it does not necessarily follow that they derive from things existing outside me. For just as those inclinations of which I was speaking a moment ago, although they are inside me, seem, however, to be distinct from my will, so perhaps there is some other faculty within me, as yet insufficiently known to me, that produces such ideas—just as up to now it has always seemed to me that they form themselves in me while I am asleep without any assistance from external things.*

And finally, even if they did derive from things distinct from myself, it does not follow that they have to be like those things. Indeed, in many of them I seem to have discovered major discrepancies between the idea and the object. For instance, I find within me two different ideas of the sun. One appears to be derived from the senses, and it would absolutely have to be placed in the category of ideas I class as 'adventitious'. This idea represents the sun as very small. The other, however, derives from astronomical reasoning—that is to say, it is derived from some notions innate within me, or has been produced by me in some other way. This idea represents the sun as several times larger than the earth. But certainly, both cannot be like one and the same sun existing outside me; and reason persuades me that the one that seems to have flowed directly from the sun itself* is in fact the one that is most unlike it.

All these considerations are sufficient proof that, up to now, it is as a result not of a certain judgement, but only of some blind inclin- 40 ation, that I have believed in the existence of various things distinct from myself, and conveying ideas or images of themselves to me through the sense-organs or in some other manner.

But there is yet another way that occurs to me by which I could investigate whether any of those things of which the ideas are in me exist outside me. Certainly, in so far as these ideas are only various modifications of my thinking, I acknowledge that they are all on the same footing, and they all seem to derive from me in the same way. But, in so far as one represents one thing, another another, it is plain that they differ widely among themselves. For beyond doubt those ideas that represent substances to me are something greater, and contain, if I may use the term, more 'objective reality' in themselves, than those that represent merely modes or accidents. And by the same token, the idea by which I conceive a supreme God, eternal, infinite, omniscient, all-powerful, and the creator of all things that exist beside himself, certainly has more objective reality in itself than those by which finite substances are represented.

But now it is manifest by the natural light that there must be at least as much reality in the total and efficient cause as in its effect. For, I ask, from where could the effect derive its reality, if not from the cause? And how could the cause give it reality, if it did not also possess it? Hence it follows, both that nothing can come from nothing, and that what is more perfect (that is, what contains more reality within itself) cannot derive from what is less perfect. And this 41 is not only plainly true of those effects whose reality is actual or formal, but also of ideas, in which only the objective reality is considered. For instance, a stone that did not previously exist, cannot now begin to be, unless it is produced by some thing in which everything exists, either formally or eminently,* that enters into the composition of the stone. Nor can heat be brought about in a subject that was not hot before, unless by a thing that belongs to at least the same order of perfection as heat; and the same is true elsewhere. But, by the same token, the *idea* of heat, or of the stone, cannot exist in me, unless it is produced in me by some cause in which there is at least as much reality as I conceive to be in the heat or in the stone. For although this cause transmits none of its actual or formal reality to my idea, we must not therefore think that it (the cause) must be less real; rather, the nature of the idea itself is such that it requires no other formal reality outside itself,* except what it borrows from my thought, of which it is a mode. But the fact that this idea contains this or that objective reality, and not some other kind—this must certainly be due to some other cause, in which there is at least as much formal reality as the idea contains objective reality. For if we suppose that something is found in the idea that is not in its cause, it would have this something from nothing; and however imperfect the kind of being by which a thing exists objectively in the understanding in the form of an idea, it is certainly not nothing, and therefore cannot come from nothing.

42   Nor should I suppose that since the reality I am considering in my ideas is purely objective, there is no need for the same reality to exist formally in the causes of these ideas, but that it is enough for it also to exist in them objectively. For just as this objective mode of being pertains to ideas from their very nature, so the formal mode of being pertains to the causes of the ideas—at least the first and dominant causes—from their nature also. And although perhaps one idea can be born from another, we cannot here have an infinite regress, but in the end we have to arrive at some first idea, the cause of which takes the form of an archetype, which formally contains all the reality that is only objectively in the idea. So that it is clear to me by the natural light that the ideas in me are of the nature of images, which can easily fall short of the perfection of the things from which they derive, but cannot, however, contain anything greater or more perfect.

And the longer and more carefully I examine all these things, the more clearly and distinctly I realize [*cognosco*] they are true. But what conclusion am I to draw from them? Certainly, if the objective reality of some one of my ideas is so great that I am certain that that reality does not exist in me either formally or eminently, and therefore that I myself cannot be the cause of this idea, it necessarily follows that I am not alone in the world, but that some other thing also exists that is the cause of this idea. But if in fact no such idea is found in me, I shall certainly have no argument that can convince me with certainty of the existence of any thing distinct from myself; for I have examined all these things very closely, and up to now I have found no other such argument.

Of these ideas I have—apart from the one that represents me to
43   myself, about which there can be no difficulty here*— one represents

God, others bodily and inanimate things, others angels, others animals, and others, finally, other human beings like myself.

As regards the ideas that represent other human beings, or animals, or angels, I can easily see that they might have been put together from the ideas I have of myself, and bodily things, and God, even if there were no other human beings, or animals, or angels in the world.

As regards ideas of bodily things, they contain nothing that is so great that it cannot apparently derive from myself: for if I inspect them more closely, and examine them one by one in the same way as I yesterday examined the idea of the wax, I realize that there is very little in them that I clearly and distinctly perceive: there is only magnitude, or extension in length, breadth, and depth; shape, which results from the limitation of this extension; place, the situation differently shaped bodies occupy relative to one another; and motion, that is, change of place. To these substance, duration, and number can be added. But the rest, such as light and colours, sounds, smells, tastes, heat and cold, and the other tactile qualities are thought by me only in very confused and obscure fashion—so much so that I do not even know whether they are true or false, that is, whether the ideas I have concerning them, are ideas of actual things or of non-things. For although I remarked not long ago that falsity in the proper ('formal') sense can be found only in judgements, there is nonetheless certainly another ('material') kind of falsity in ideas, when they represent what is nothing as if it were something. For example, the ideas I have of heat and cold are so unclear and so indistinct that 44 I cannot tell from them whether cold is nothing but a privation of heat, or heat a privation of cold, or whether both are real qualities, or neither. But there can be no ideas that do not seem to represent something to us. And therefore, if indeed it is true that cold is nothing other than the privation of heat, the idea that represents it to me as something real and positive can very properly be called false. The same applies to all other such ideas.

Certainly, I do not need to ascribe any author to these ideas apart from myself. For if indeed they are false—that is, if there is nothing they actually represent—it is known to me by the natural light that they derive from nothing: that is, they exist in me purely on account of some shortcoming in my nature, which indeed is far from perfect. But if, on the other hand, they are true, the degree of reality they represent to me is so scanty that I cannot even distinguish between it and unreality; and therefore I cannot see why they might not derive from myself.*

But of the clear and distinct elements in my ideas of bodily things, there are some that it seems possible I borrowed from the idea of myself, namely substance, duration, number, and any other things there may be of that sort. For when I think that a stone is a substance, that is to say, a thing capable of existing by itself, and likewise that I am myself a substance, then although I conceive myself to be a thinking and not an extended thing, and the stone, on the other hand, to be an extended and not a thinking thing, so that there is a very great difference between the two concepts, they seem, however, to have this in common: they both represent a substance. Again, when I perceive that I exist now, and also remember that I existed at some time before now, and when I have various thoughts of which 45 I know the number, I acquire the ideas of duration and number, which then I can transfer to other things, of whatever kind they are. On the other hand, all the other elements from which the ideas of bodily things are put together, namely extension, shape, place, and motion, are not contained formally in myself, since I am nothing other than a thinking thing. But because they are only various modes of substance, and I moreover am a substance, it seems they could be contained in me eminently.

And so there remains only the idea of God, in which I must consider whether there is anything that could not derive from myself. By the name 'God' I understand an infinite, independent, supremely intelligent, supremely powerful substance, by which I myself and whatever else exists (if anything else does exist) was created. But certainly, all these properties are such that, the more carefully I consider them, the less it seems possible that they can be derived from me alone.* And so I must conclude that it necessarily follows from all that has been said up to now that God exists.

For indeed, even if the idea of substance is in me as a result of the very fact that I am a substance, the idea of an infinite substance would not therefore be in me, since I am finite, unless it derived from some substance that is really infinite.

Nor should I think that I perceive the infinite not by a true idea but only by negation of the finite, as I perceive rest and darkness by the negation of motion and light; for on the contrary, I manifestly understand that there is more reality in infinite than in finite substance, and that therefore the perception of the infinite in me must be in some way prior to that of the finite: the perception of God, in other words, prior to that of myself. For how could I possibly understand that I doubt, and that I desire, that is, that there is something lacking in me, and that I am not completely perfect, if there were no idea in me of a more perfect being, by comparison with which I could recognize my own shortcomings?*

46

Nor can it be said that perhaps this idea of God is materially false, and could therefore derive from nothing, as I remarked not long ago apropos of the ideas of heat and cold and suchlike. For on the contrary, since it is supremely clear and distinct, and contains more objective reality than any other, there is no idea that is truer in itself and in which less suspicion of falsity can be found. This idea of a supremely perfect and infinite being is, I say, supremely true; for although it perhaps might be imagined that no such being actually exists, it cannot be imagined that the idea of it represents nothing real to me, as I previously said of the idea of cold. It is also supremely clear and distinct; for whatever I clearly and distinctly perceive that is real and true and that contains some perfection is all included within it. And this remains no less true even though I do not comprehend the infinite, or even if there are innumerable other attributes in God that I can neither comprehend, nor even perhaps apprehend* in the slightest by my thought; for it is of the nature of the infinite that it should be incomprehensible to me, who am finite. Provided that I understand this and judge that everything I clearly perceive, and that I know [*scio*] to involve some perfection, as well, perhaps, as innumerable other attributes I do not know, exists in God either formally or eminently, the idea I have of him will be the truest and most clear and distinct of all my ideas.

And yet perhaps I am something greater than I understand myself to be, and all the perfections I attribute to God, are in some sense in me potentially, even if they have not yet revealed themselves, or been brought into actuality.* For I am already experiencing a gradual increase in my knowledge [*cognitio*]; and I cannot see any reason why it should not be increased in this way further and further to infinity; nor why, if my knowledge were so increased, I could not by means of

47

Our human difference is that we don't experience infinitely ? Augustine?

it obtain all the other perfections of God; nor finally why the potentiality of these perfections, if it exists in me already, should not be enough actually to produce the idea of them.

But none of this can be true. For, first of all, even granting it to be true that my knowledge [*cognitio*] is gradually increasing and that there are many things in me in potentiality that are not yet so in actuality, nothing of this is relevant to the idea of God, in which indeed there is absolutely no potentiality: for this very fact of gradual increase is an infallible index of imperfection. Besides, even if my knowledge did continually increase, nonetheless I understand that it would still never be actually infinite, since it will never get to the point of being incapable of further increase; but I judge God to be infinite in actuality in such a way that nothing can be added to his perfection. And finally I perceive that the objective being of an idea cannot be produced from purely potential being, which properly speaking is nothing, but only from actual or formal being.

And indeed there is nothing in all this that is not manifest by the natural light to one who considers it carefully; but because, when my attention wavers, and the images of sensible things blind the eye of the mind, I do not remember so easily why the idea of a being more perfect than myself necessarily proceeds from some being that is truly perfect, I wish to investigate further whether I, who have this idea, could exist if no such being existed.*

From what indeed could I derive my being? From myself, perhaps, or from my parents, or from some other beings less perfect than God: for nothing more perfect than him, or even equally perfect, can be conceived or imagined.

But if I existed of myself, I would not doubt, or wish, or lack anything at all: for I would have given myself all the perfections of which there is some idea in me, and thus I should myself be God. Nor should I suppose that what is lacking in me is perhaps more difficult to acquire than what is already in me, since on the contrary, it is plain that it was far more difficult for me, that is, a thinking thing or substance, to emerge from nothing than to acquire knowledge of the many things I do not know, since such knowledge is only an accident of this substance. But certainly, if I had this greater thing [existence] from myself, I should not have denied myself at least the things that can more easily be obtained; what is more, I should not have denied myself any of those things I perceive to be contained in the idea of

God; for indeed none of them seems to me more difficult to achieve. But if any were in fact more difficult to achieve, certainly they would appear to me to be so, if I did indeed derive my other properties from myself, since I would experience the limits of my power with respect to them.

And I cannot elude the force of these reasons by supposing that perhaps I have always been as I now am, as if it followed from that that there is no need to seek an author of my existence. For since all the time of a life can be divided into innumerable parts, of which 49 each particular one in no way depends on the rest, it does not follow from the fact that I existed not long ago that I have to exist now, unless some cause, so to speak, creates me again at this moment, or in other words, conserves me in being. For it is clear, if one considers the nature of time, that the same power and action is required to conserve any thing, whatever it may be, in being during the individual moments in which it continues to exist, as would be needed to create the same thing from the start if it did not yet exist. So clear is this in fact that we may add to the list of things manifest by the natural light that the distinction between conservation and creation exists purely in our thought.*

So therefore I need now to inquire of myself, whether I have some power, by means of which I can bring it to pass that this 'I'* that now exists shall still exist at some time in the near future. For since I am nothing other than a thinking thing, or at least, to speak precisely, since I am now dealing only with that part of myself that is a thinking thing, if any power of this sort were in me, I should beyond doubt be conscious of it. But I can find no such power, and from this I very clearly realize [*cognosco*] that I depend upon some being distinct from myself.

But perhaps this being is not God, and I was and am produced either by my parents or by some other causes less perfect than God, whatever they might be. No: for, as I have already said, it is plain that there must be at least as much in the cause as there is in the effect; and therefore, since I am a thinking thing, and one that has the idea of God in myself, it must be admitted that whatever cause is finally assigned to me must also itself be a thinking thing and one that has the idea of all the perfections I ascribe to God. And then of this thing too we can ask whether it exists of itself or by virtue of some other thing. For if it exists of itself, it is clear from the above that it must

50 itself be God, because since it has from itself the power to exist, it undoubtedly has the power to possess in reality all the perfections of which it has the idea in itself, that is, all the perfections I conceive to be in God. But if, on the other hand, it exists in virtue of some other thing, then we shall ask whether this thing too exists of itself, or in virtue of some other thing, until finally we come to an ultimate cause: and this will be God.

For it is sufficiently plain that here there is no possibility of an infinite regress,* especially because I am not dealing so much with the cause that produced me at some time in the past, as, above all, with the one that conserves me in the present time.

Nor can it be imagined that perhaps many partial causes have come together to produce me, and that from one of them I received the idea of one of the perfections I attribute to God, and from another the idea of another perfection, so that all these perfections are found, indeed, somewhere in the universe, but not all combined together in any one being that would be God. For on the contrary, the unity, simplicity, or inseparability of all those things that are in God is one of the principal perfections that I understand to inhere in him. Nor, certainly, could the idea of this unity of all his perfections have been implanted in me by any cause from which I did not also derive the ideas of the other perfections: for such a cause could not have brought it about that I should understand them as simultaneously combined and inseparable, unless it had at the same time enabled me to know what they all were.

Finally, as far as my parents are concerned, even if everything is true of them that I have ever thought to be so, certainly they do not conserve me in being, nor did they in any way produce me insofar as I am a thinking thing; they only implanted certain dispositions in the matter that I judged myself (that is, my mind, which for the moment 51 I take to be identical with my self) to inhabit. And so there can be no difficulty here about them; but we must necessarily conclude that, from the bare fact that I exist, and that in me there is an idea of a supremely perfect being, that is, God, it is proved beyond question that God also exists.

It remains for me only to examine in what manner I received this idea from God. For I did not derive it from the senses, nor did it ever thrust itself spontaneously on my attention, as do the ideas of sensible things, when the things themselves make an impression on the external sense-organs (or appear to do so). Nor is it a fiction, a creation of my own, for I cannot subtract anything from it, or add anything at all to it. It must therefore be that the idea is innate within me, in the same way as the idea of myself is innate within me.

And certainly it is no wonder if God, when he created me, inscribed this idea within me, to serve, so to speak, as the mark by which the craftsman makes himself known in his handiwork. This mark does not have to be something distinct from the object itself. But, given this one basic fact that God created me, it is highly credible that I was in some way created in his image and likeness,* and that the likeness, in which the idea of God is contained, is perceived by me by the same faculty by which I myself am perceived by myself. That is, when I turn the eye of my mind on myself, I do not only understand myself to be an entity that is incomplete and that depends on another, and that is endowed with an indefinite aspiration to greater and greater or better things; but at the same time I understand that the being on whom I depend possesses all these greater things not only indefinitely and in potentiality but in actuality and infinitely, and is thus God. The whole force of the argument comes down to this, that I recognize that it cannot be that I should 52 exist, with the nature I possess (that is, having the idea of God within myself), unless in reality God also exists—the same God whose idea is within me, that is, the one who possesses all the perfections that I cannot comprehend but can to some extent apprehend in my thinking, and who is subject to no kind of deficiency. From this it is sufficiently clear that he cannot be a deceiver: for all cunning and deception presuppose some shortcoming, as is plain by the natural light.

But before I go more thoroughly into this, and at the same time investigate the other truths that can be deduced from it, I wish to remain here for some time in the contemplation of God himself, to ponder on his attributes, and to gaze on, wonder at, and worship the beauty of this immense light, as much as the eye of my understanding, shrouded as it is in darkness, is capable of doing. For, just as we believe by faith that the supreme happiness of the other life consists purely in the contemplation of the divine greatness, so we find also by experience that this contemplation, though far less perfect, affords us the greatest pleasure of which we are capable in this life.

FOURTH MEDITATION
OF TRUTH AND FALSITY

Over these last few days I have grown so accustomed to withdrawing
my mind from the senses, and have so thoroughly grasped that true
perceptions of bodily things are very rare, but that more can be
known [*cognosci*] about the human mind, and still more about God,
that I can now direct my thought without any difficulty away from
things that can be imagined and towards those that are purely intelligible, and detached from all matter. And certainly the idea I have of
the human mind, in so far as it is a thinking thing, not extended in
length, breadth, and depth, or having any other bodily properties, is
much more distinct than the idea of any bodily thing. And when
I consider that I doubt, or that I am an incomplete and dependent
thing, so clear and distinct an idea of an independent and complete
being (that is, God) comes to my mind, and from this single fact that
such an idea is in me, or that I exist possessing this idea, I so manifestly conclude that God also exists, and that all my existence, from
one moment to the next, depends on him, that I can confidently
assert that nothing can be more evidently or certainly discovered
[*cognosci*] by human intelligence. And now I seem to glimpse a path
by which, from this contemplation of the true God, in whom indeed
all the treasures of the sciences and wisdom lie hidden, we can pass
to the knowledge of other things.

First of all, I recognize that it cannot happen that he should ever
deceive me; for in all deceit and trickery some element of imperfection is to be found; and although to be able to deceive seems to be some
indication of intelligence or power, nonetheless to wish to deceive is
beyond doubt a proof of malice or feeble-mindedness, to which God
cannot be liable.

Besides, I know by experience that there is within me a faculty of
judging, which I certainly received from God, along with everything
else that is in me; and since he does not wish to deceive me, this
God-given faculty must be such that I shall never go astray, as long
as I use it correctly.

It would seem that there is no room left for doubt on this matter,
except that it would apparently follow from what has just been said,

that I can therefore never be mistaken at all. For if whatever is in me, I have from God, and if he has not given me any faculty of making mistakes, it seems I can never be mistaken. And indeed, as long as I am thinking only of God, and directing my attention wholly to him, I cannot detect any cause of error or falsity; but when presently I turn back to myself, I find by experience that I am, on the contrary, subject to innumerable errors. When I investigate the cause of these, I observe that, besides the real and positive idea of God, or the supremely perfect being, there is also, so to speak, a certain negative idea of nothingness, or of that which is infinitely remote from all perfections, that presents itself to me; and I see also that I am so constituted as a medium term between God and nothingness, or between the supreme being and non-being, that, in so far as I was created by the supreme being, there is indeed nothing within me by which I can be deceived or led into error; but that, in so far as I have, in a way, a share of nothingness or non-being (in so far, in other words, as I am not myself the supreme being), and very many things are lacking to me, it does not seem so strange that I should be deceived. And thus I can understand, quite certainly, that error, in so far as it is error, is not something real dependent on God, but purely and simply a deficiency; and therefore that, in order to make mistakes I do not need a special mistake-making faculty given me by God for this purpose, but that it happens that I make mistakes, for the reason that the faculty of judging the truth, which he did give me, is not infinite in me.

And yet this does not satisfy me completely. For error is not a pure negation but a privation,* a lack of some knowledge [*cognitio*] that ought to be in me in some way; and when I consider God's nature, it does not seem possible that he should have endowed me with some faculty that is not perfect of its kind, or that is deprived of some perfection due to it. For if, the more skilful the craftsman, the more perfect the works he produces, what can have been produced by this supreme creator of everything that is not perfect in all its components? Nor is there any doubt that God could have created me incapable of being deceived; besides, there is no doubt that he wishes always what is best—but could it be better for me to be deceived than not?

When I go into this more closely, it first occurs to me that I should not be surprised if God does some things the reasons for which I do not understand. Nor would there be any reason to doubt his existence if perhaps I discovered other things of which I cannot understand how or why he produced them. For since I already know [*sciam*] that my nature is very weak and limited, while on the other hand God's is immense, incomprehensible, and infinite, it follows that I know [*scio*] quite clearly that he can do innumerable things of the causes of which I am ignorant; and for this reason alone, I judge that the whole category of causes that people are in the habit of seeking by considering the purposes of things* is of no use in the study of physics; for I think that it could only be rash of me to investigate God's purposes.

My next reflection is that we should not look at any one single creature in isolation, but at the whole universe of things, whenever we are inquiring whether God's works are perfect. For what would perhaps appear (and not without reason) very imperfect if it were taken in isolation, is completely perfect if considered as a part of the universe; and although, since I have decided to doubt everything, I have not yet discovered [*cognovi*] for certain whether anything else exists besides God and myself, I cannot however deny, since I have become aware of the immense power of God, that many other things have been created by him, or at least could be created by him, in which case I too would exist as a part of the universe.

Finally, coming closer to myself and investigating the nature of my errors (which are sufficient proof by themselves that there is some imperfection in me), I realize that they depend on two simultaneously operative causes, namely, the faculty I possess of acquiring knowledge [*cognoscendi*] and the faculty of choosing, or free will; that is, they depend on the intellect and the will simultaneously. For through the intellect alone I only perceive ideas on which I can pass judgement, nor can any error in the strict sense be found in it when considered from this precise viewpoint. For although, perhaps, there are innumerable things in existence of which the ideas are not in me, I cannot be said, strictly speaking, to be deprived of these ideas, but only, in a negative sense, to be without them; since, certainly, I can adduce no reason to prove that God should have given me a greater faculty of acquiring knowledge [*cognoscendi*] than the one he has given me; and although I understand him to be the most skilful craftsman possible, I do not therefore think that he should have endowed each individual piece of his handiwork with all the perfections with which he may endow some. Nor indeed can I complain that I have received from him an insufficiently wide-ranging and perfect will, or freedom of choice; for I experience it as unbounded by any limits. And it seems to me particularly important to note that there is no other property in me, apart from this one, that is so 57 perfect or so great that I cannot understand how it could be more perfect or greater. For if, for example, I consider the faculty of understanding, I immediately recognize that in me it is very small and seriously limited; and at the same time I form the idea of another faculty that is far greater, one indeed that is supremely great and infinite, and, from the very fact that I can form the idea of it, I perceive that it belongs to the nature of God. By the same token, if I examine the faculty of remembering or imagining, or any other, I realize they are all very inadequate and restricted in me, but that in God they are boundless. It is only the will, or freedom of choice, that I experience in myself as so great that I can form the idea of none greater; so much so that it is chiefly on account of the will that I understand that I bear a certain image and likeness of God. For although the will is incomparably greater in God than in me, first, in virtue of the knowledge and power that are combined with it in him, and that make it stronger and more effective, and secondly, in virtue of its object, since its range is far greater, nonetheless, when it is considered strictly as it is essentially in itself, it does not seem to be greater in him than in me. This is because it consists purely in our ability to do or not to do a given thing (that is, to affirm or deny something, pursue something or avoid it); or rather, it consists purely in this: that we are moved in relation to that which the intellect presents to us as to be affirmed or denied, pursued or avoided, in such a way that we feel we are not being determined in that direction by any external force.* For, in order to be free, I do not have to be able to be moved in either direction.* On the contrary, the more I incline to one alternative, whether because I clearly understand that 58 the good and the true are on that side, or because God so disposes my innermost thoughts,* the more freely I choose it. Certainly, neither divine grace nor natural knowledge [*cognitio*] ever diminishes freedom; on the contrary, they increase and reinforce it. On the other hand, the indifference I experience, when no reason impels me towards one alternative rather than the other, is the lowest degree of freedom, and is not a mark of perfection but only of a shortfall in my knowledge, or a certain negation;* for if I always clearly saw what is true and good, I would never need to deliberate about a judgement to be made or a course of action to be chosen; and in that case, although I would be fully free, I could never be indifferent.

From all this, I perceive that the cause of my errors is neither the God-given power of willing, considered in itself, for it is extremely extensive and perfect of its kind; nor the power of understanding, for whatever I understand, since my understanding is a gift of God, most certainly I understand it correctly, nor is there any possibility of my being deceived in this. So what is the origin of my errors? It can only be this: that, since the range of the will is greater than that of the intellect, I do not confine it within the same limits, but extend it even to matters I do not understand;* and since it is indifferent to these, it easily falls away from the true and the good, and this is both how I come to be deceived and how I come to sin.*

For example, when I was examining, over these last few days, whether anything existed in the world, and realized that, from the very fact that I was examining this point, it clearly followed that I existed, I could not indeed refrain from judging that what I so clearly understood was true. It was not that I was compelled to this by some external force, but that a great illumination of the intellect was followed by a great inclination of the will; and in this way my belief was all the freer and more spontaneous for my being less indifferent. But now, however, I not only know that I, in so far as I am a thinking thing, exist: a certain idea of bodily nature also presents itself to me, as a result of which I doubt whether the thinking nature that is within me, or rather that I myself am,* is distinct from this bodily nature, or whether they are both one and the same. (I am supposing here that no reason has yet occurred to my intellect to convince me in favour of one view or the other.) And from this fact alone, I am certainly indifferent as regards affirming or denying one view or the other, and indeed as regards making no judgement at all about the matter.

But indeed, this indifference does not extend only to those matters about which the intellect has no knowledge at all, but also to all things in general that are not sufficiently clearly known by the intellect at the time when the will is deliberating about them. For however strongly probable conjectures may draw me to one alternative, the mere fact of knowing that they are only conjectures, and not certain and indubitable reasons, is sufficient to impel me to assent to the contrary view. This has been fully borne out in my own experience during these last few days, when, considering all the beliefs I had once very firmly held as true, I decided, simply because I had realized that it was possible to doubt them in some respect, to suppose them to be altogether false.

Now, if indeed, whenever I do not sufficiently clearly and distinctly perceive where the truth lies, I refrain from passing judgement, it is clear that I am acting rightly and not being deceived. But if I either affirm or deny, then I am not making the right use of my freedom of choice; and if I adopt the view that is false, I shall be altogether deceived. Yet if I adopt the other view, although it happens to be the true one, I shall still be at fault, because it is manifest by the natural light that a decision on the part of the will should always be preceded by a perception on the part of the intellect. The privation in which the essence of error consists lies in this wrong use of free choice. The privation, that is, lies in the operation itself, in so far as it derives from me, but not in the faculty given to me by God, or in the operation in so far as that depends on him.*

Nor do I have any grounds for complaining that God has not given me a more powerful intellectual capacity, or a greater natural light, than he actually has, since it is of the essence of a finite intellect that it is unable to understand many things, and to be finite is of the essence of a created intellect. Rather, I should be grateful to him, who has never owed me anything, for what he has bestowed on me. But I have no cause to think that I have been deprived by him of those things he has not given me, or that he has robbed me of them.

I have no more reason to complain at his giving me a will that is more wide-ranging than my understanding; for since the will consists purely in a single property that is, so to speak, indivisible, its very nature seems to make it impossible that anything should be taken away from it. Indeed, the more extensive it is, the more grateful I should be to him who has given it to me.

And finally, I have no right to complain that God cooperates with me in the production of those acts of the will, or those judgements, in which I am deceived; for these acts are altogether true and good, in so far as they depend on God, and it is in some ways a greater perfection in me to be able to perform them than not. For the privation in which alone the essence of falsity and guilt consists requires no cooperation on God's part, since it is not a thing, nor a privation related to him as to its cause: it should be classed, purely and simply, as a negation.* For it is certainly no imperfection on God's part that he has given me the freedom to assent or not to assent to some things of which he has implanted no clear and distinct perception in my intellect; but it is undoubtedly an imperfection on my part not to use this freedom properly, and to pass judgement on things I do not rightly understand. I see, however, that God could have easily brought it about that, while remaining free and endowed only with finite knowledge, I should never err: for instance, if he had implanted in my intellect a clear and distinct perception of everything upon which I would ever have to make up my mind; or if he had simply engraved on my memory, so deeply that I could never forget it, the resolution never to pass judgement about anything I do not clearly and distinctly understand. And I can easily grasp that, in so far as I consider myself as a totality, I would have been more perfect than I am now, if I had been so created by God. But, for all that, I cannot deny that in a way the universe as a whole is more perfect as a result of the fact that some of its parts are not immune from error, while others are, than it would have been if all its parts were entirely similar. And I have no right to complain that the part God has given me to play in the world is not the most prominent and perfect of all.

Besides, even though I cannot refrain from error in the first of the ways just mentioned, which would involve my having an evident perception of everything about which I would ever need to make up my mind, I can in the second way, which simply involves my remembering that, whenever the truth of a matter is not clear, I should abstain from passing judgement. For although I find by experience that there is a weakness in my nature that means that I cannot always concentrate attentively on one and the same piece of knowledge [*cognitioni*], I can nonetheless, by careful and frequently repeated meditation, ensure that I remember this maxim whenever I need to, and thus I can acquire a certain habit of not making mistakes.

And since the greatest and most distinctive perfection of a human being consists in this, I think I have derived no little profit from today's meditation, since I have tracked down the cause of error and falsity. And indeed, this cause can be no other than I have explained. For whenever in passing judgement I so keep my will under control that it confines itself to items clearly and distinctly represented to it by the intellect, it certainly cannot come about that I should make a mistake; since every clear and distinct perception is something, and therefore cannot come from nothing, but necessarily derives from God—God, the supremely perfect being, whose nature is incompatible with deception. It is therefore undoubtedly true. And I have learned today not only what I should avoid in order not to be deceived, but at the same time what I must do in order to attain truth; for I certainly shall attain it, provided I pay sufficient attention to everything I perfectly understand, and keep it quite separate from everything else that I apprehend more confusedly and obscurely. And I shall take particular care to do this in future.

FIFTH MEDITATION 63

OF THE ESSENCE OF MATERIAL THINGS; AND AGAIN OF GOD, THAT HE EXISTS

There remain many attributes of God, and many aspects of the nature of myself, or my mind, for me to investigate. But perhaps I shall return to these another time, and for the moment nothing appears more urgent (now that I have realized what to avoid and what to do in order to attain truth) than to attempt to extricate myself from the doubts I have fallen into during these past days, and to see whether any certainty is possible with respect to material things.

And indeed, before investigating whether any such things exist outside me, I should first consider the ideas of them, in so far as these ideas exist in my thought, and see which of them are distinct, and which confused.

I can certainly distinctly imagine the quantity that philosophers commonly call 'continuous': that is, the extension of this quantity (or rather, of the thing to which the quantity is attributed) in length, breadth, and depth. I can count various parts within it. To each of these parts I ascribe various magnitudes, shapes, positions, and local motions, and to the motions I ascribe various durations.

Not only are these things, considered in these general terms, clearly known and grasped by me: I also, if I pay close attention, perceive innumerable particular facts involving shape, number, motion, and suchlike—facts so plainly true, and so much in conformity with 64 my nature, that when I first discover them I do not seem to be learning anything new, but rather to be remembering something I knew before, or to be noticing for the first time something that was in me already, although I had not previously turned the gaze of my mind in its direction.

And what I think particularly needs to be considered here is this: that I find in myself innumerable ideas of certain things, that, even if, perhaps, they do not exist anywhere outside me, cannot yet be said to be nothing. And although, in a sense, whether I think of them or not is up to me, yet they are not inventions of my own mind, but they have true and immutable natures of their own. For instance, when I imagine a triangle, even if perhaps such a figure does not exist, and has never existed, anywhere at all outside my thought, it nonetheless certainly has a determinate nature, or essence, or form, that is immutable and eternal, which was not invented by me, and does not depend on my mind. This is clear from the fact that it is possible to demonstrate various properties of the triangle (for instance, that its three angles are equal to two right angles, and that the hypotenuse subtends the greatest angle, and so forth) which, whether I like it or not, I now clearly recognize to hold good, even if up to now I have never thought of them in any way when imagining a triangle. And therefore these properties were not invented by me.

It would make no difference if I were to say that perhaps this idea of a triangle has come to me from things outside myself via the sense-organs, because, that is, I have occasionally seen bodies of a triangular shape. For I can think up innumerable other shapes that it 65 is impossible to suspect ever reached me via the senses; and yet I can demonstrate several of their properties, just as I can with the triangle. And all of these properties are certainly true, since they are clearly known [*cognoscuntur*] by me, and therefore they are something, and not a pure nothing. For it is clear that everything that is true, is something; and I have already abundantly demonstrated that everything I clearly know [*cognosco*], is true. And even if I had not demonstrated this, the nature of my mind is such that I cannot in any case help assenting to the things I clearly perceive, at least, for as long as I clearly* perceive them; and I remember that even in past times, when I was as closely attached to the objects of the senses as it is possible to be, I always considered that truths of this kind that I clearly recognized, concerning shapes, or numbers, or other matters belonging to arithmetic or geometry or, in general, pure and abstract mathematics, were the most certain of all.

But now, if, from the fact alone that I can produce the idea of a given thing from my thought, it follows that everything I clearly and distinctly perceive to belong to the thing does in fact belong to it, cannot I also find here a further proof of the existence of God? Certainly, I find the idea of him, that is, of a supremely perfect being, in myself, just as much as I find the idea of any shape or number. And I clearly and distinctly understand that eternal existence belongs to his nature—just as clearly and distinctly as I understand that the properties I can demonstrate of some shape or number belong in fact to the nature of that shape or number. So that, even if not all the con- clusions I have come to in my meditations over the past few days were true, I would still have to ascribe the same degree of certainty to the existence of God that I up to now have ascribed to mathematical truths. 66

To be sure, this is not altogether evident at first sight: it appears to be something of a sophism. For since I am accustomed in all other things to distinguish existence from essence, I can easily convince myself that existence can be separated from the essence of God, and thus that God can be thought of as not existing. But if one considers the matter more closely, it becomes plain that existence can no more be separated from the essence of God than we can separate from the essence of a triangle that the sum of its three angles adds up to two right angles, or than we can separate the idea of a mountain from the idea of a valley.* So true is this that the thought of a God (that is, a supremely perfect being) who lacks existence (that is, who lacks a certain perfection) is no less contradictory than the thought of a mountain without a valley.

However, even if I can no more think of God without existence than I can think of a mountain without a valley, yet certainly, it does not follow from my thinking of a mountain as having a valley that any mountain exists in the world; similarly, from my thinking of God as existing, it does not seem to follow that God exists. For my thought imposes no necessity on things; and just as I am free to imagine a winged horse, even if no horse actually does have wings, so perhaps I can imagine the existence of a God, even though no God in fact exists.

No: this is where the sophism is lurking here. The point is not that, from my inability to think of a mountain except with a valley, it

follows that a mountain and a valley exist somewhere, but only that
67 the mountain and the valley, whether they exist or not, cannot be
separated from each other. Whereas from the fact that I cannot think
of God except as existing, it follows that existence is inseparable from
God, and therefore that he exists in reality. It is not that my thought
brings his existence about, or that it imposes any necessity on anything, but, on the contrary, that the necessity of the thing itself, namely
the existence of God, determines me to think it. Nor am I free to
think of God without existence (that is, to think of the supremely
perfect being without the supreme perfection), in the way I am free
to imagine a horse with or without wings.

Nor can it be maintained that, although it is necessary to admit
that God exists, once I have supposed him to possess all perfections,
since existence is one of these perfections, the original supposition
was not itself necessary* (just as it is not necessary for me to think
that all quadrilateral shapes can be inscribed in a circle, but, supposing I do think this, I must admit that a rhombus can be inscribed
in a circle, which, however, is patently impossible). For although it
is not necessary that I should ever find myself thinking of God,
nonetheless, whenever I choose to think about the first and supreme
being, and bring forth the idea of him, so to speak, from the treasury
of my mind, I must necessarily credit him with all perfections, even
if at the time I neither list them all nor consider them individually.
And this necessity is quite sufficient for me subsequently, when
I recognize that existence is a perfection, to conclude, quite rightly,
that the first and supreme being exists. In the same way, it is not
necessary that I should ever imagine any triangle: but whenever I want
to consider a straight-sided shape having only three angles, I must
68 necessarily credit it with properties from which it can be correctly
inferred that the sum of its three angles does not exceed that of two
right angles, even if I do not at the time realize this. On the other
hand, when I am examining what shapes can be inscribed in a circle,
there is absolutely no necessity for me to think that all quadrilaterals
fall into this category: indeed, I cannot even imagine this to be true,
as long as I am intending to accept only what I clearly and distinctly
understand. Hence there is a great difference between false suppositions, such as this one, and true ideas innate within me, the first and
most important of which is the idea of God. For indeed, I understand in many ways that this idea is not something fictitious that

depends on my own thinking, but the image of a true and immutable nature: first, because no other thing can be conceived by me to the essence of which existence belongs, besides God himself; secondly, because I cannot conceive of two or more such Gods, and because, granted that one exists now, I plainly see that it is necessary both that he should have existed for all eternity up to now, and that he will continue to exist for an eternity in the future; and finally, because I perceive many other properties in God of which none can be subtracted or altered by me.

But indeed, whatever kind of proof I use, the issue always comes down to this: that nothing convinces me fully but what I clearly and distinctly perceive. It is true that, of the things I so perceive, although there are several that are obvious to anyone, there are others that can be discovered only by those who look into the matter more closely and examine it carefully. Once, however, these latter have been discovered, they are counted as no less certain than the former. Just as, if we are dealing with a right-angled triangle, it does not so readily appear that that the square of the base is equal to the square of the sides as it does that the base is subtended by its greatest angle, nonetheless, once the first proposition has been grasped, it is as firmly believed as the second. But as far as God is concerned, certainly, if I were not overwhelmed by prejudices and if the images of sensible things were not pressing in on my thoughts from all directions, I should recognize nothing sooner and more readily than him. For what is more obvious in itself than that the supreme being exists, that is to say, that God, to whose essence alone existence belongs, exists?

And although careful consideration was required before I was capable of perceiving this truth, now, however, not only am I equally certain of it as I am of anything else that seems completely certain, but, moreover, I also observe that the certitude of all these other things depends on it so completely that without it nothing can ever be perfectly known [*sciri*].

For although my nature is such that, as long as I perceive something very clearly and distinctly, I cannot not believe that it is true, nonetheless, because my nature is also such that I cannot continuously fix the gaze of the mind on the same thing in order to perceive it clearly, and what often happens is that I *remember* judging something to be true, then, when I am no longer concentrating on the reasons for which I made that judgement, other reasons can be adduced that would easily (were I ignorant of God) shake me out of my opinion. And thus I should never have true and certain knowledge [*scientia*] of anything, but only vague and shifting opinions. Thus, for example, when I am considering the nature of a triangle, it certainly appears utterly evident to me (being, as I am, well versed in the principles of geometry) that its three angles are equal to two right angles; and I cannot not believe this is true, as long as I am concentrating on the proof; but, as soon as I have turned the eye of the mind in a different direction, then however well I remember that I grasped the proof very clearly, I can still easily find myself doubting its truth, if I am ignorant of God. For I can persuade myself that I was so made by nature that I am sometimes deceived in matters which I think I perceive entirely clearly, especially since I remember counting many things as true and certain that later, when guided by other reasons, I judged to be false.

But once I have perceived that God exists, then because I grasped at the same time that everything else depends on him, and that he is no deceiver, and from this deduced that everything I clearly and distinctly perceive is necessarily true, then, even if I am no longer concentrating on the reasons why I judged this to be true, provided I remember that I did see it clearly and distinctly, no contrary reason can be adduced that can induce me to doubt it; and thus I have true and certain knowledge [*scientia*] of it. And not only of it, but of all the other propositions I remember demonstrating at some stage, such as the truths of geometry and others of the same kind. For what objections can now be raised against me? That I am so constituted as often to be deceived? But I know now [*scio*] that in matters I clearly understand, I cannot be deceived. That I once counted many things as true and certain that I later realized to be false? But I had perceived none of these clearly and distinctly, but, unaware as I was of this criterion of truth, perhaps I believed them for other reasons, which I later discovered to be less sound than I had thought. So what further objection can be raised? Perhaps (an objection I put to myself not long ago) I am sleeping, or all the things I am now thinking are no more true than the thoughts that occur to one who is asleep. But this makes no difference. For certainly, even if I were sleeping, if something is evident to my understanding, then it is altogether true.

And so I plainly see that the certitude and truth of all knowledge [*scientiae*] depends on the knowledge [*cognitione*] of the true God alone: so much so, that before I had discovered this knowledge, I could have no perfect knowledge [*scire*] of anything else at all. But now innumerable truths, concerning both, on the one hand, God himself and other intellectual things and, on the other, the whole of this bodily nature which is the object of pure mathematics,* can be plainly known to me with certainty.

SIXTH MEDITATION

OF THE EXISTENCE OF MATERIAL THINGS, AND THE REAL DISTINCTION BETWEEN MIND AND BODY

It remains for me to examine whether material things exist. And indeed, I now know [*scio*] at least that, in so far as they are the object of pure mathematics, they can exist, since I perceive them clearly and distinctly. For there is no doubt that God is capable of producing everything I am capable of perceiving in this way; and I have never judged that anything was impossible for him to do, except when, in attempting to perceive it distinctly, I ran up against a contradiction. Besides, it seems to follow from the existence of the imaginative faculty, of which I experience myself as making use when dealing with these material things, that they exist. For if I consider more closely what kind of thing the imagination is, it appears to be nothing other than a certain application of the knowing faculty to a body intimately present to that faculty, and therefore existing. 72

To make this plain, I shall first examine the difference that exists between imagination and pure intellection. For example, when I imagine a triangle, not only do I understand it to be a shape enclosed by three lines, but at the same time, with the eye of the mind, I contemplate the three lines as present, and this is what I call imagining. But if, on the other hand, I wish to think of a chiliogon, I do indeed understand that this is a shape consisting of a thousand sides, no less clearly than I understand that the triangle consists of three: but I do not imagine the thousand sides in the same way, that is, contemplate them as present. And although at the time, because I am accustomed always to imagine something whenever I am thinking of bodily things, I may perhaps picture some figure to myself in a confused fashion, it is quite clear that this is not a chiliogon, because it is not at all different from the picture I would also form in my mind if I were thinking about a myriogon,* or some other many-sided figure. Nor is it of any assistance in recognizing the properties by which the chiliogon differs from other polygons. But if I am dealing with a pentagon, I can certainly understand its shape, like that of the chiliogon, without the help of the imagination: but I can also imagine it, that is, by applying the eye of the mind to its five sides, and at the same time to the area contained within them; and here I observe very plainly that I need to make a particular

73 mental effort in order to imagine, that I do not make when understanding. This further effort of the mind clearly indicates the difference between imagination and pure intellection.

At this point, I consider that this power of imagining I possess, in so far as it differs from the power of understanding, is not integral to my essence, that is, to the essence of my mind; for even if I lacked it, I should nonetheless certainly remain the same person as I now am. From this it seems to follow that the imagination depends on something distinct from me.* And I can easily understand that if some body exists to which the mind is so closely joined that it may, whenever it chooses, apply itself, so to speak, to looking into it, it could be the case that this is exactly how I imagine corporeal things. So that this mode of thinking would differ from pure intellection in the following respect alone: that the mind, while it understands, turns itself in some way towards itself, and gazes on one of the ideas that are contained within itself; but, while it imagines, it turns itself towards the body, and considers something in it that corresponds either to an idea it understands itself* or to an idea perceived by the senses. I can readily understand, I say, how the imagination may function in this way, provided, that is, the body exists. And because no other equally convenient way of explaining it occurs to me, I therefore conclude with great probability that the body exists. But this is only a probability, and although I am investigating the whole matter with great care, I do not yet see that, from this distinct idea of bodily nature that I find in my imagination, any argument can be derived that will lead necessarily to the conclusion that some body exists.

74 But I am accustomed to imagining many other things, besides this bodily nature that is the object of pure mathematics,* such as colours, sounds, pain, and suchlike: but none of these with equal distinctness.

And because I perceive these things better by the senses, from which they seem to have made their way, with the help of memory, to the imagination, in order to examine them more conveniently, I should examine sensation at the same time, and see whether, from those things that are perceived by the form of thinking I call 'sensation', I can derive some decisive argument in favour of the existence of bodily things.

And first of all, I will here go over in my memory what those things were that I previously thought were true, because they were perceived by the senses, and the reasons I had for thinking this. Then I shall weigh the reasons for which I later called these things into question. Finally, I shall consider what view I should now take.

First of all, then, I had the sensation of having a head, hands, feet, and all the other parts comprising this body I used to consider as part of myself, or perhaps even as the whole of myself. Then I had the sensation of this body as situated among many other bodies by which it could be affected—harmed or benefited: and I measured the benefits by a certain feeling of pleasure and the harm by a feeling of pain. And besides pain and pleasure, I also had the sensation of hunger, thirst, and other such appetites in myself, not to mention various bodily propensities, to joy, to sadness, to anger, and other such passions. Outside myself, besides the extension, shapes, and motions of bodies, I had sensations of hardness, heat, and other tactile qualities in them; light, as well, and colours, and smells, and tastes, and sounds, the variety of which enabled me to distinguish the sky, the earth, the sea, and other bodies one from another. And surely it was not without reason that, on account of the ideas of all these qualities that presented themselves to my thought, and of which alone I had personal and immediate sensations, I believed I was sensing certain things quite distinct from my thought, that is to say, bodies from which these ideas proceeded. For I experienced these ideas as coming to me without any consent of mine: so much so, that neither could I have a sensation of any object, however much I wanted to, unless the object itself were present to a sense-organ, nor could I help having the sensation of it when it was present. And since the ideas perceived by the senses were much more vivid and emphatic,* and in their own way more distinct, than any of the ideas that I deliberately and knowingly formed* by myself in my meditations, or that I found engraved upon my memory, it seemed impossible that they should proceed from myself.* And so it had to be the case that they derived from some other things. But since I had no knowledge of these other things except from these ideas themselves, I could only suppose that the things were like the ideas. And also because I remembered that I had made use of my senses before I made use of my reason, and saw, as well, that the ideas I formed myself were not as emphatic as those I perceived by the senses, and were mostly put together from those ideas, I readily convinced myself that I had nothing at all in the intellect, that I had not previously had in the senses.* Nor was it without reason that I judged that the par-

76 ticular body I seemed specially entitled to call my own belonged more closely to me than any other body. For I could not ever be separated from it, as I could from the other bodies; I felt all my appetites and passions in it and for it; and finally I was aware of pain and pleasure in parts of it, but not in any other body existing outside it. But why this mysterious feeling of pain is followed by a feeling of sadness in the soul, and why the awareness of pleasure is followed by joy, or why the mysterious pangs in the stomach I call hunger prompt me to take food, while a dryness in the throat prompts me to drink, and so on, I certainly could not explain except by saying that nature teaches me that it is so. For there is plainly no affinity (at least, none that I understand) between the pangs in the stomach and the will to eat, or between the sensation of a thing that is causing pain and a thought of sadness arising from this feeling. And all the other things I judged concerning the objects of the senses, I thought I had also learned from nature. For I had persuaded myself that this was the way things were before I had considered any reasons by which this could be proved.

But afterwards many experiences gradually undermined all the faith I had placed in the senses. For sometimes towers that from a distance had seemed round appeared from close up as square;* and giant statues perched on the top of those towers did not look particularly large to one gazing up from below; and by innumerable other such experiences I came to realize that in matters of the external senses our judgements are at fault. Not only the internal senses,

77 moreover; the internal ones as well. For what can be more intimate than pain? Yet I had often heard from people whose arm or leg had been amputated, that they still occasionally seemed to feel pain in the part of the body they were missing; and therefore even in myself it did not seem to be wholly certain that one of my limbs was hurting, even though I was feeling pain in it. To these points I recently added

two very general reasons for doubting. The first was that everything I have ever believed I was having a sensation of while awake, I can sometimes think I am having a sensation of while asleep; and since I do not believe that what I seem to see when asleep comes from anything existing outside me, I could not see any reason why I should believe this of the sensations I seem to have when awake. The second reason was that, since I was still ignorant of the author of my existence (or at least was pretending to be so),* I could see no reason why I could not be so constituted by nature as to be deceived, even in things that appeared to me entirely true. And as for the reasons by which I had previously convinced myself of the truth of sensible things, I could answer them without difficulty. For since I saw that I was impelled by nature to many things from which reason dissuaded me, I thought I should not place much faith in the teachings of nature. And although sense-perceptions do not depend on my will, I thought that I should not therefore conclude that they derived from things distinct from myself, because perhaps there might be some faculty within me, although yet unknown to me, that produces them.

Now, however, that I begin to know myself and the author of my existence rather better, although I do not think that all that the senses seem to teach me is to be rashly accepted, I do not think that it 78 should all be called in doubt.

First, since I know that whatever I clearly and distinctly understand can be produced by God such as I understand it to be, then if I can clearly and distinctly understand one thing without another, this is sufficient for me to be certain that the one is distinct from the other, since they can at least be produced separately by God. By what power this separation comes about makes no difference to the judgement that the things are distinct. Next, from the very fact that I know [*sciam*] I exist, and that for the moment I am aware of nothing else at all as belonging to my nature or essence, apart from the single fact that I am a thinking thing, I rightly conclude that my essence consists in this alone, that I am a thinking thing. And although perhaps (or rather certainly, as I shall shortly claim) I have a body, which is very closely conjoined to me, yet because, on the one hand, I have a clear and distinct idea of myself, in so far as I am a thinking and not an extended thing, and, on the other, a distinct idea of the body, in so far as it is only an extended and not a thinking thing, it is certain that I am really distinct from my body,* and can exist without it.

Moreover, I find in myself faculties of thinking in various specific ways—namely, the faculties of imagination and sensation—without which I can understand myself clearly and distinctly as a whole. But the converse is not true—I cannot understand them apart from an intelligent substance in which they inhere (for they contain a certain degree of intellection in their formal concept).* Hence I perceive that they are to be distinguished from me as modes are from a thing.* I also recognize various other faculties, such as those of changing place, and assuming various postures, that cannot be understood (any more than those just mentioned) without some substance in which to inhere, and that therefore cannot exist without it. But it is plain that, if indeed these exist, they must inhere in a bodily or extended substance—but not, however, an intelligent one; for the clear and distinct concept of them includes some measure of extension, but does not at all include intellection. Moreover, there is in me a certain passive faculty of sensation, that is, of receiving and knowing [*cognoscendi*] ideas of sensible things. But I could make no use of it at all, if there did not exist, either in me or in another being, some active faculty of producing or generating these ideas. Now this faculty cannot, certainly, exist in myself,* because it presupposes no intellection at all, and because these ideas are produced not only without my cooperation but often even against my will.* It therefore follows that it must exist in some substance distinct from me, which substance must contain, either formally or eminently, all the reality that exists objectively in the ideas produced by the faculty (as I have already pointed out above).* This substance is either a body, or a bodily nature, that formally contains all that is contained objectively in the ideas; or else it has to be God, or some other creature nobler than a body, in which this is contained eminently. But because God is no deceiver, it is altogether plain that he does not transmit these ideas to me immediately, or by the intermediary of some creature, in whom their objective reality is contained not formally but only eminently. For since he has certainly given me no faculty by which I might realize this to be true, but has, on the contrary, endowed me with a strong propensity to believe that these ideas are conveyed by bodily things, I cannot see how, if they were in fact from some other source, it would be possible to think of him except as a deceiver. And therefore bodily things exist. Perhaps, however, they do not all exist exactly as I apprehend them by the senses, since this sensory apprehension is very obscure and confused in many respects. But at least all those properties are in them that I clearly and distinctly understand: that is, all those, generally considered, that are included in the object of pure mathematics.*

As to the remaining properties that are either purely particular (for instance, the sun's being of a certain magnitude or shape) or less clearly understood (for instance, light, sound, pain, and suchlike), although they are very doubtful and uncertain, yet this basic fact, that God is no deceiver, and that therefore it cannot be the case that any falsity should be found in my opinions, unless there is also some God-given faculty in me for correcting it, offers me a firm hope of discovering the truth with respect to them as well. And certainly, there is no doubt that everything I am taught by nature contains some element of truth: for by nature, in a general sense, I now mean nothing other than either God himself, or the system of created things established by God; and by my own nature in particular, I mean nothing other than the combination of all the properties bestowed on me by God.

Now there is nothing I am more emphatically taught by this nature of mine than that I have a body, with which there is something wrong when I feel pain, which needs food or drink, when I experience hunger or thirst, and so on and so forth. Hence I cannot doubt that there is some truth in all this.

Nature likewise teaches me, through these very feelings of pain, 81 hunger, thirst, and so forth, that I am not present in my body only as a pilot is present in a ship,* but that I am very closely conjoined to it and, so to speak, fused with it, so as to form a single entity with it. For otherwise, when the body is injured, I, who am nothing other than a thinking thing, would not feel pain as a result, but would perceive the injury purely intellectually, as the pilot perceives by sight any damage occurring to his ship; and when the body lacks food or drink, I would understand this explicitly, instead of having confused feelings of hunger and thirst. For certainly, these feelings of thirst, hunger, pain, and so forth are nothing other than certain confused modes of thinking, arising from the union and, so to speak, fusion of the mind with the body.

Besides, I am further taught by nature that various other bodies exist around mine: of these, some are to be pursued by me, others avoided. And certainly, from the fact that I perceive very different

colours, sounds, smells, tastes, degrees of heat, of hardness, and suchlike, I can validly conclude that in the bodies from which these varied
sensory perceptions arise there are variations that correspond to
them, even if, perhaps, they do not resemble them. And from the fact
that some of these perceptions are pleasing to me, others displeasing,
it is quite certain that my body, or rather myself as a whole, in so far
as I am composed of a body and a mind, can be benefited or harmed
by the surrounding bodies.

82   But there are many other beliefs that, although I seem to be taught
them by nature, I have in fact derived not from nature itself, but
from a certain habit of judging without due consideration, and so
these can easily turn out to be false. For instance, that every space in
which nothing at all is happening that has an impact on my senses is
a vacuum;* or that in a body that is hot, say, there is something altogether similar to the idea of heat in me; that in a white or green body,
there is the same whiteness or greenness of which I have the sensation, in one that is bitter or sweet the same taste, and so on and so
forth;* that stars and towers and whatever other distant bodies one
can think of are only of the same size and shape as they appear to be
to my senses, and so on. But there is a risk I may fail to perceive this
matter sufficiently clearly if I do not first define more precisely what
exactly I mean when I say that I am taught something by nature.
Here I am taking 'nature' in a more restricted sense than when I use
the term to denote the combination of all the properties bestowed on
me by God. For in this combination there are many things that
belong to the mind alone, such as my perception that what has happened cannot not have happened, and all the other things that I know
by the natural light. These are not my concern here. There are also
many that relate to the body alone, as that it has a tendency to fall
downwards,* and suchlike. But I am not here concerned with these
either, only with those things bestowed by God on me, as a composite of mind and body. Now nature in this sense teaches us to avoid
those things that cause a sensation of pain, and pursue those that produce a sensation of pleasure, and so forth. But it does not appear that
nature teaches us anything else that would enable us to reach any
conclusion, on the basis of these sensory perceptions, about things
existing outside ourselves, without a prior examination by the intel-
83   lect; because it seems that a true knowledge [*scire*] of these belongs
to the mind alone, but not to the composite entity. Thus, although a

star affects my eye no more than the gleam of a small torch, there is no real or positive inclination here to believe that the star is no bigger than the torch:* but I formed this belief in childhood without any reason to support it. And although when I come close to the fire I feel heat, and in fact I feel pain when I come too close to it, there is certainly no reason that should persuade me that there is something in the fire like the heat, any more than there is something in it like the pain—only that there is something in the fire, whatever in fact it is, that produces these feelings of heat or pain. Again, although in a given space there may be nothing that affects the senses, it does not therefore follow that there is no body in it. But I see that in these, and in very many other things, I have grown accustomed to perverting the order of nature, because I use sensory perceptions, which were specifically given by nature for signifying to the mind* what things are beneficial or harmful to the composite of which the mind is part—for which purpose they are sufficiently clear and distinct—as if they were reliable criteria for immediately discerning the essence of bodies existing outside us. Of this, however, they signify nothing, except in very obscure and confused fashion.

But I have already sufficiently examined how it can come to pass that, notwithstanding the goodness of God, my judgements are false. A further difficulty, however, arises here concerning these very things that are represented to me by nature as to be pursued or avoided, and concerning also the internal senses in which I seem to have discovered errors: as when someone, tricked by the pleasant taste of some food, absorbs a poison concealed in it. But in this case 84 he is prompted by nature to desire only the source of the pleasant taste, not the poison of which he knows nothing. And nothing more is to be inferred from this than that this nature is not omniscient; which is not surprising, since, man being a limited creature, the only nature he can be endowed with is one of limited perfection.

But yet we do quite frequently go astray even in things to which we are impelled by nature: as when sick people desire drink or food that will shortly do them harm. Someone might say here that they are led astray only because their nature has been corrupted:* but this does not remove the difficulty, because in truth, a sick human being is just as much a creature of God as a healthy one. And so it seems just as contrary to the goodness of God that his nature should be deceptive. Now a clock, an assembly of wheels and weights, obeys all the laws of

nature just as strictly when it has been badly manufactured and does not tell the time accurately as when it fulfils the clockmaker's wishes in every respect. And I can likewise consider the body of a human being as a kind of machine made up of bones, nerves, muscles, veins, blood, and skin so fitted together that, even if there were no mind within it, it would still have all the movements it currently has that do not result from the command of the will (and hence the mind). I can easily see that it would be natural, if, for example, the body were suffering from dropsy, for it to experience the dryness of the throat that usually communicates the sensation of thirst to the mind, so that, as a result, its nerves and other parts would be so disposed that it would have something to drink, thus making the disease worse; just as natural as it would be for a perfectly healthy body to be prompted
85 by a similar dryness in the throat to take a drink that would do it good. And although, if we take into account the intended function of the clock, we can say that, when it fails to indicate the time correctly, it has fallen away from its nature; and likewise, if we consider the machine of the human body as designed so as to enable the movements that usually take place in it, I may think that it has gone astray from its own nature if its throat is dry at a time when drink will not conduce to its preservation, yet I can see perfectly clearly that this latter meaning of 'nature' is quite different from the former. For the latter meaning is nothing more than a denomination* dependent on my thinking, when I compare a sick human being and a badly made clock with my idea of a healthy human being and a well-made clock, and it tells us nothing about the actual things in question; whereas by the former I mean something that is actually found in the things themselves, and therefore contains a degree of truth.

But certainly, even though, when considering the body suffering from dropsy, to speak of its nature being corrupted, on the grounds that its throat is dry and yet it does not need to drink, is merely an extrinsic denomination; yet if we consider the composite entity, that is, the mind as united to a body in this state (thirsty when drink would be harmful to it), this is not a pure denomination, but a genuine error of nature.* And so the question refuses to go away, how it is that the goodness of God does not prevent nature in this precise sense from being deceptive.

Now, first of all, I observe here that there is a great difference between the mind and the body, in this respect, that the body of its

nature is endlessly divisible, but the mind completely indivisible: for 86
certainly, when I consider the mind, or myself in so far as I am purely
a thinking thing, I can distinguish no parts in myself but understand
myself to be a thing that is entirely one and complete. And although
the whole mind appears to be united with the whole body, if the foot
is cut off, or the arm, or any other part of the body, I know [*cognosco*]
that nothing is therefore subtracted from the mind. Nor can the faculties of willing, perceiving by the senses, understanding, and so
forth be said to be parts of the mind, since it is one and the same
mind that wills, that senses, and that understands. On the other
hand, however, no bodily or extended thing can be thought by me
that I cannot mentally divide into parts, without any difficulty; and
I therefore understand it is divisible. This point alone would suffice
to show me that the mind is altogether distinct from the body, if I did
not yet sufficiently know [*scirem*] this for other reasons.

Next, I observe that the mind is not affected immediately by all the
parts of the body, but only by the brain, or perhaps only by one very
small part of the brain, namely that in which the 'common sense' is
said to reside.* Whenever this part is affected in the same way, it represents the same thing to the mind, even if the other parts of the body
happen to be differently affected at the same time. This is proved by
innumerable observations* [*experimenta*] that there is no need to go
into here.

Moreover, I observe that it is of the nature of a body that none of
its parts can be moved by another part somewhat distant from it,
without its being able to be moved in the same way by any of the
parts that lie between them, even when the more distant part is not
involved in the movement. For instance, take a piece of string, with
points A, B, C, and D. If the last part, D, is pulled, the first part, A, 87
will be moved in exactly the same way as it would be moved if one of
the intermediate points, B or C, were pulled, while the final point, D,
remained immobile. By the same token, when I feel a pain in the foot,
physics* teaches me that this sensation is produced by means of the
nerves dispersed through the foot, which, since they extend upwards
like strings as far as the brain, when plucked in the foot also pluck the
inmost parts of the brain in which they terminate, thus stimulating a
particular motion in these parts of the brain, which is so ordained by
nature that it affects the mind with a feeling of pain apparently
located in the foot. But because these nerves have to pass up the leg,

the thigh, the loins, the back, and the neck in order to connect the foot and the brain, it can come about that, even if the part of the nerve that is in the foot is not affected, but only one of the intermediate parts, exactly the same movement will take place in the brain as takes place when the foot is injured, so that the mind will necessarily experience the same pain. And the same must apply to all our other sensations.

Finally, I observe that, since each one of the motions that take place in the part of the brain that directly affects the mind produces only one sensation in the mind, no better explanation of this can be conceived than that the particular movement produces, of all the possible sensations it could produce, the sensation that most effectively and most frequently conduces to the preservation of the human being in good health. And experience bears witness that this applies to all the sensations with which nature has endowed us, and that therefore nothing at all can be found in them that does not bear 88 witness to God's immense power and goodness. Thus, for instance, when the nerves in the foot are violently and unusually stimulated, their movement, transmitted through the spinal cord to the inner parts of the brain, there gives a signal to the mind to experience a certain sensation, namely a pain experienced as being in the foot. By this the mind is stimulated to do its best to remove the cause of the pain, as being damaging to the foot. To be sure, the nature of man could have been so established by God that this same motion in the brain could have represented something different to the mind: it could have represented itself, in so far as it takes place in the brain, or in so far as it takes place in the foot, or in any of the places in between, or it could have represented something else altogether;* but nothing else would have been so conducive to the body's preservation. In the same way, when we need to drink, a certain dryness originates in the throat, setting in motion the nerves there, and by their means the inner parts of the brain; and this motion affects the mind with the sensation of thirst, because in this situation there is nothing more useful to us to know than that we need a drink for the sake of preserving our health. And the same applies with all our other sensations.

From all this, it is entirely plain that, notwithstanding God's immense goodness, the nature of man, as a composite of mind and body, cannot but be liable to error at times. For if some cause not in the foot, but in some one of the other parts through which the nerves run on their way from the foot to the brain, or indeed in the brain itself, stimulates the very same motion as is usually stimulated by some injury to the foot, a pain will be felt as if in the foot, and our sense will be naturally deceived. This is because, since one and the same movement in the brain can only produce one and the same sensation in the mind, and since it is much more usually produced by some cause injuring the foot than by any other cause located somewhere else, it is in accordance with reason that it should always 89 represent to the mind a pain in the foot rather than in any other part. And if sometimes a dryness in the throat arises, not from its usual cause, which is that the body's health would be benefited by drinking, but from some other, contrary cause, as happens with those suffering from dropsy, it is better that it should deceive us in this latter case, than that, on the contrary, it should always deceive us when the body is healthy. And the same applies elsewhere.

And this consideration will assist me greatly, not only to be aware of all the errors to which my nature is liable, but also to correct or avoid them easily. For certainly, since I know [*sciam*] that all our sensations indicate the truth far more frequently than the contrary, as far as the well-being of the body is concerned, and since in examining a particular case I can almost always draw on several of them, as well as on my memory, which connects present with past, and on my understanding, which has already discovered all the causes of error, I need no longer fear that the things the senses represent to me in ordinary life are false: on the contrary, the hyperbolic doubts of these past days can be dismissed as ridiculous. Especially the ultimate doubts concerning sleeping, which I could not distinguish from waking; for now I realize that there is a massive difference between them, inasmuch as dreams are never combined by my memory with the rest of the actions of my life, as happens with my waking experiences. For certainly if, while I was awake, someone suddenly appeared before me, and then immediately disappeared, as happens in dreams, in such a way, I mean, that I could not see where he was coming from or where he was going, I would not unreasonably judge it to 90 be an apparition or a delusion produced by my brain, rather than a real person. But when things happen to me in such a way that I am distinctly aware of whence, where, and when they have come, and I connect the perception of them to the rest of my life, without any gaps, then I am well and truly certain that they are happening not in my sleep but when I am awake. Nor should I doubt even in the slightest degree of their truth, if after I have summoned all the senses, the memory, and the understanding to join in their examination, none of these reports anything that clashes with the report of the rest. For, from the fact that God is not a deceiver, it follows inescapably that in such cases I am not deceived. But because the necessities of action do not always allow us the opportunity for such a thorough examination, we must admit that human life is subject to frequent error in connection with particular things, and we must acknowledge the frailties of our nature.*

THE OBJECTIONS
AND REPLIES

INTRODUCTION

The Objections and Replies[1]

Descartes sent the text of the Meditations to two Dutch acquaint-
ances, Bannius and Bloemart, and they submitted the text for com-
ment to Johann de Kater—Caterus, to give the Latin form of his
name—a Roman Catholic priest living in Alkmaar. His reply, the
First Objections, is addressed to them rather than to Descartes. His
comments bear chiefly on the proofs of the existence of God.
Although Caterus refers to St Thomas Aquinas, and his reactions
bear the marks of his scholastic training, Jean-Robert Armogathe
suggests that his own point of view was neither thoroughly Thomist
nor coherently independent.[2] But his objections are shrewd, and
required Descartes to clarify his notion of objective reality, his conception of God as cause of himself, and the nature of the distinction
between mind and body. Both the first and the last points are represented in the extracts: to avoid repetition, the second is held over till
the fuller discussion in the Fourth Objections and Replies, which
relates back to the text of the First Objections.

The Second Objections and Replies were collected by Mersenne.
But it has been argued by Daniel Garber[3] that the mathematician and
astrologer Jean-Baptiste Morin was among the contributors, and that
Descartes's reply was targeting a work of Morin's, *Quod Deus sit*
(*That God Exists*). The Objectors raise some significant points: they
cannot see how Descartes has proved that thinking is not a bodily
operation; they cast doubt on both the causal and ontological proofs of
God; query whether Descartes's argumentation is self-undermining,
and whether all knowledge does depend on the knowledge of God.
They ask Descartes for a presentation of his argument along geometrical lines: his reply contains some interesting discussion of method,
and shows his sense of the limitations of a purely mathematical approach
to knowledge.

---

[1] An indispensable study of the Objections and Replies is Roger Ariew and Marjorie
Grene (eds.), *Descartes and His Contemporaries: Meditations, Objections and Replies*
(Chicago: University of Chicago Press, 1995). I have drawn on it frequently in what fol-
lows, but mention the individual chapters only as regards particular points.

[2] Jean-Robert Armogathe, 'Caterus' Objections to God', in ibid. 34–43.

[3] Ibid. 63–82.

Thomas Hobbes (1588–1679), author of the Third Objections (there are no separate replies: the text gives Descartes's reply to each of Hobbes's objections as it comes up), is undoubtedly the greatest thinker among the Objectors. He was living in Paris when the *Meditations* were published, since he feared being targeted by the parliamentary opponents of the king, and got to know Mersenne. His first major work, *De cive*, appeared in the year after the *Meditations*. His objections and Descartes's replies hardly indicate a meeting of minds, but they are philosophically interesting for Hobbes's attempt to substitute a materialist ontology and method for Descartes's own approach.

Antoine Arnauld (1612–94), who submitted the Fourth Objections, was the most remarkable member of a remarkable family, which was closely linked to the convents of Port-Royal that were the centre of the movement in theology and spirituality known as Jansenism. His learning, acumen, logic, and sheer doggedness made him the foremost defender of the version of Augustine's theology upheld by the 'Jansenists'.[4] But his interests were not confined to theology. He and Pierre Nicole drew up one of the classic textbooks of logic, *La Logique ou l'art de penser* (1662). Later he engaged in philosophical controversy with Malebranche, and in correspondence with Leibniz. When Louis XIV set about extirpating the Jansenist movement, Arnauld went into exile. The Objections show his critical engagement with Descartes, but he seems to have been satisfied with Descartes's replies, though there was a further exchange of views in 1648. At any rate, he thereafter maintained Cartesian positions in philosophy, albeit in a critical and independent fashion.[5] At the time of the Objections, however, he was very much an up-and-coming scholar, preparing for the doctorate in theology, and his sympathies, it has been argued, were with the theology of William of Ockham rather than that of St Thomas: which may have prepared him to accept certain Cartesian positions.[6]

[4] Blaise Pascal (1623–62), the mathematician and scientist, was also a follower of the Jansenist movement, and a more original thinker than Arnauld. But Arnauld's theology is more systematic.
[5] Steven Nadler argues for the innovative and specific character of Arnauld's Cartesianism: *Descartes and His Contemporaries*, 'Occasionalism and the Question of Arnauld's Cartesianism', in Ariew and Grene, 129–44.
[6] Vincent Carraud, 'Arnauld: From Ockhamism to Cartesianism', in ibid. 110–28.

The Fifth Objections come from Pierre Gassendi (1592–1655), who was, like Descartes, an anti-Aristotelian: but his opposition took a very different form, which hardly predisposed him to espouse Descartes's philosophy. His own philosophical interests were in scepticism and Epicureanism, and commentators have laboured to reconcile this with his status as an apparently conscientious Catholic priest.[7] His objections are sometimes prolix, which is why they have been largely summarized rather than translated here, but contain some significant points: in particular, he can be said to anticipate Kant's critique of the ontological argument. As with Hobbes, the interest is partly in the clash of opposing, and indeed irreconcilable, philosophical perspectives; and, as with Hobbes, the tone of Descartes's replies is often far from amicable. Gassendi pursued the debate, and Descartes replied again (see above, p. xvii). In 1648 Descartes and Gassendi were publicly reconciled.[8]

The Sixth Objections were put forward by a group of philosophers, theologians, and geometers, and collected by Mersenne. Most of the points they raise had already been urged by others. The most significant relate to dualism: the real distinction between soul and body and the denial of souls to animals. Descartes's replies are often of interest, especially the last section, where he describes his own intellectual evolution.

The Seventh Objections, by the Jesuit Pierre Bourdin, are the longest set of all. They are difficult, and would be unrewarding, to summarize in great detail. This is principally because Bourdin misunderstands Descartes more seriously than any of the other objectors, to the point where the latter accuses him of dishonesty. Moreover, the intercutting of Bourdin's dissertation and Descartes's comments makes for difficult reading. (The structure is not identical to that of the Third Objections and Replies: Hobbes is working his way through Descartes's actual text, and raising difficulties as they come up, whereas Bourdin offers a dissertation, based on his own arrangement of Descartes's material.) But the difficulty also derives

---

[7] A thorough and judicious analysis is provided by Olivier René Bloch, *La Philosophie de Gassendi: nominalisme, matérialisme, métaphysique* (The Hague: Nijhoff, 1971). Detailed analyses in relation to his Objections are given by Margaret J. Osler and Thomas M. Lennon, in Ariew and Grene, *Descartes and His Contemporaries*, 145–58, 159–81.

[8] Clarke, *Descartes*, 377.

from Bourdin's style, which is elaborately metaphorical and dialogical. His attempts at humour are painfully laboured, and his tone is often irritatingly smug and snide, with its affectation of submission and respect giving way to schoolmasterly diatribes addressed as if to a cocky pupil who needs taking down a peg or two: Descartes understandably objects to it (AT 7. 526). In other ways Bourdin's style is rhetorically interesting, especially in the sections of dialogue, rapid-fire exchanges of succinct utterances, systematically sustaining a set of core metaphors: a far cry from the complex syntax and technical vocabulary of most contemporary scholastic philosophy. Provoked by Bourdin's needling, and despising his philosophical critique, Descartes responds in a far more rhetorical vein than is usual in his writings, playing with metaphors to ridicule his opponent. Seizing on the military imagery used by Bourdin, Descartes depicts him as a sort of rhetorical Don Quixote, battling with enemies spawned by his own imagination.

The Objections cover only the first two Meditations, though, to be fair, Bourdin clearly believes that his critique of Descartes's fundamental positions is so destructive that there is no point in discussing the subsequent arguments based on them. But the institutional context may be relevant here. Descartes was planning, as he explains to Dinet, head of the French branch, or 'province', of the Society of Jesus, a presentation of his philosophy suitable for use in educational establishments (this was eventually published as the *Principles of Philosophy*, AT 7. 577–8). Had the Jesuits themselves adopted it as a textbook, the success of his philosophy would have been assured. If Bourdin was, as has been suggested, expressing the view of the Society of Jesus, it is natural that he should concentrate on the supposed flaws of the Method, in order to show its unsuitability as a basis for teaching.[9]

Although on the whole less philosophically significant than any of the earlier sets, the Seventh Objections are of great interest from the point of view of intellectual and cultural history. Generally, the other Objectors at least make an effort to engage with Descartes's arguments, even when their own approach, as with Hobbes and Gassendi, is quite antithetical to his. But the Seventh Objections

---

[9] See Roger Ariew, 'Pierre Bourdin and the Seventh Objections' in Ariew and Grene, *Descartes and His Contemporaries*, 208–25.

show why an intelligent reader, not hidebound by traditional views, could either find his effort to understand completely fruitless or perhaps simply fail to see why the effort was worth making. Precisely because they do not closely engage with the particular arguments, they throw light on what Bourdin sees as baffling in Descartes's general approach. Essentially, Bourdin cannot see that Descartes is constructing and regulating a philosophical *experience* in the course of which truth is discovered, in which propositions that may initially have appeared false or doubtful emerge as true, and some we initially took as true are revealed as needing to be rejected or corrected. As Descartes points out, Bourdin treats 'true', 'false', 'doubtful' as if they were inherent properties of propositions, irrespective of the thinker's relationship to them as it develops over time. (This is not an individual quirk, but reflects a general scholastic habit of thought, whereby to become learned in a discipline involves assimilating the general consensus of scholars as to what propositions are true, false, or doubtful.) He tries to put Descartes's arguments into a traditional logical framework, e.g. as follows:

> I am either a mind or a body.
> But I am not a body.
> ∴ I am a mind;

and then points out that they do not work. But this way of putting the argument is foreign to Descartes, whose concern is with the discovery of knowledge in experience.[10] Moreover, Bourdin fails to distinguish between beliefs Descartes once held, and those he currently upholds. He thus supposes that the former beliefs about soul and body recalled by Descartes in the Second Meditations are being reasserted as his current position, when of course they are being drastically corrected. The following summary does not contain all the many instances where Descartes objects to Bourdin's misunderstandings or misrepresentations of his views, or where he imputes unworthy motives to his critic.

In one area, though, Bourdin's criticism is distinctive, and sharper than Descartes acknowledges. Scholars have sometimes noted that

---

[10] The fundamental clash between Bourdin's logical approach and Descartes's experiential method is well brought out by Alquié (*OP* II, 1052, n. 1, 1053, nn. 1-2).

Descartes's sceptical critique really bears on the unreliability of sense-perception: clear and distinct intellectual perception is left out of account.[11] Bourdin urges that Descartes's doubt ought logically to extend further: that the dream-hypothesis destabilizes not only sense-perceptions but supposedly clear and distinct perceptions of intellectual truths.

Bourdin's dissertation consists essentially of two Questions (a scholastic way of organizing the material), each of which is sub-divided into a number of sections, in which Descartes's positions are expounded and criticized. (He represents the Questions as being put to him by Descartes, who objects to this version of the relationship between them.) Each Question is followed by an Answer, in which Bourdin delivers his overall judgement on the issue.[12] The core of Bourdin's dissertation (his Question 2) consists of a series of attempts to get inside Descartes's method (he takes up the image of thinking as a journey found in the *Discourse on Method*, and sustains the metaphor throughout this section). He represents himself as a nervous fellow-traveller seeking guidance from the philosopher, and reconstructs the dialogue between them, in a set of rapid-fire exchanges. But every time they attempt to get moving they are confronted by a new impassable obstacle, some previously unsuspected crying defect in the method. Finally, the would-be traveller gives up, and conducts, as he puts it, an orderly retreat. That is, he sets out what he takes to be Descartes's key argument in syllogistic form, in such a way as to expose its invalidity. The Answer to Question 2 contains a twelve-part condemnation of Descartes's method.

Descartes's comments are slotted in between the sections of Bourdin's text (a detailed account is given below). His comments on the Answer to Question 2 involves a sustained development of the building metaphor which he also used in the *Discourse* and which Bourdin occasionally invokes here. Descartes compares himself to an architect, methodically clearing and excavating the ground before laying the foundations for a temple. He is persecuted by a common

---

[11] See Louis E. Loeb, 'The Cartesian Circle', in *CCD* 200–35 (p. 228, n. 21). Jean-Luc Marion, 'Cartesian Metaphysics and the Role of the Simple Natures', *CCD* 115–39 (p. 129) makes a similar point in different terms.

[12] It is important to recognize that the Answers are Bourdin's replies to his own Questions: they are not replies to Descartes's critique of those Questions, which is printed before them.

mason (Bourdin), who ignorantly criticizes the architect's whole procedure in public. The metaphor is historically interesting in that it
draws on a very general reconfiguration of productive practices in the
early modern period, the emergence of a distinction between 'arts',
with an intellectual and conceptual content that renders them more
socially prestigious, and 'crafts', inferior because (supposedly) reliant on
mere manual knowhow. Bourdin's criticisms are restated by Descartes
in keeping with this allegory, so as to exhibit their irrelevance.

   The summary given is selective, not exhaustive. Bourdin addresses
Descartes in the second person: Descartes's comments usually refer
to Bourdin in the third, and I follow this pattern here. Descartes's
replies are sometimes addressed to points explicitly made by Bourdin,
sometimes to implications (perhaps unsuspected) or flaws in the Jesuit's
text. In the latter case, I have not troubled to summarize the original
statement of Bourdin's to which Descartes takes exception or on
which he comments. Bourdin's text was printed with marginal letters
indicating the points to which Descartes replies. To find Descartes's
reply to a particular point, the reader looks for the corresponding
letter in his section of the text. I shall include these letters here,
where possible and helpful.

In what follows, the Objections are printed in italic, Descartes's Replies
in roman type. My summaries and comments are given in smaller
type. As before, numbers in the margin or in square brackets refer to
page numbers in AT.

FIRST OBJECTIONS

BY A LEARNED THEOLOGIAN
FROM THE NETHERLANDS

Descartes's proof of God by means of the concept of 'objective reality'

Here I am forced to linger a little, lest I become exhausted. For my mind is seething like the turbulent straits of Euripus.* I accept, I deny, I approve, I refute again, I do not wish to disagree with him, I cannot agree. For I ask what cause does an idea require? Or tell me what an idea is. It is the thing itself that is thought, insofar as it exists objectively in the intellect.* But what does it mean, to 'exist objectively in the intellect'? As I was taught, it means determining the act of the intellect in the manner of an object.* But this is purely an extrinsic denomination,* and no part of the thing.* For just as for me to be seen is nothing other than an act of vision's being directed at me, so for a thing's to be thought, or to exist objectively in the intellect means that it determines and arrests the mind's thought in itself. This can happen without any movement and change in the thing, indeed even if the thing does not exist. Why therefore should I seek a cause for something that does not exist in actuality, which is a bare denomination, a nothing?

And yet, this great mind asserts, the fact that this idea contains one objective reality rather than another—this must certainly be due to some cause (p. 30). But it has no cause at all. For objective reality is a pure denomination, it has no existence in actuality. A cause, however, exerts a *real and actual influence; but what does not exist in actuality cannot receive anything, and therefore it cannot even receive an actual causal influence, let alone require it. Therefore, I have ideas, but I do not have a cause for my ideas, let alone one greater than myself and infinite.*

'But if you will not concede a cause for ideas, at least give some reason why this idea contains this objective reality rather than that one.' Very willingly: for I am not in the habit of acting meanly with my friends, but I deal with them as generously as possible. I say in general, as applicable to all ideas, what M. Descartes says of the triangle: Even if perhaps such a figure does not exist, and has never existed, anywhere at all outside my thought, it nonetheless has a certain determinate nature, or essence, or form, that is immutable and eternal (p. 46). *For a truth is eternal that*

does not require a cause, e.g. that a boat is a boat, and not something else;
that Davus is Davus and not Oedipus. But if you insist on demanding a
reason, it is the imperfection of our understanding, which is not infinite.
For since it cannot encompass the universal good, which exists all at the
same time and once and for all, in a single act of understanding, it divides
it all up into parts. And thus what it cannot realize as a whole, it con-
ceives bit by bit, or, as they say, inadequately.

   But the great man goes on to say: However imperfect the kind of
being by which a thing exists objectively in the understanding in the
form of an idea, it is certainly not nothing, and therefore cannot come
from nothing (p. 30). *There is an ambiguity here. For if 'nothing' means*
the same as not existing in actuality, this 'kind of being' is certainly noth-
ing, because it does not exist in actuality, and therefore it comes from
nothing, that is, it comes from no cause. But if 'nothing' means 'something 94
imagined', what is commonly called an 'ens rationis',* that is not nothing,
but something real that is distinctly conceived. And yet because it is simply
conceived and does not exist in actuality, it can indeed be conceived, but
cannot possibly be caused.

[94–5] The proof of God from the Meditator's own existence

Caterus goes on to suggest that when Descartes argues that he could not
exist, unless God existed, he is putting forward the same argument, based
on efficient causality, as Aquinas's 'second way' of proving the existence of
God, an argument ultimately derived from Aristotle.

He then criticizes Descartes's argument that if he existed of himself, he
would have given himself all the perfections of which he has the idea in
himself, and would therefore in effect be God (p. 34). This depends on the
ambiguous phrase 'to exist of oneself', which can mean 'to exist of oneself
as if in virtue of a cause' or simply 'not to exist on account of anything
else'. But it is impossible for something to be the cause of itself: and speaking of a thing's 'giving itself all perfections' makes it sound as if an entity
could, prior to its existence, foresee what it could be, so as to choose in
advance what it is going to be. But if something exists of itself in the sense
of 'not existing on account of anything else', then it might still have limitations intrinsic to its nature: so that existing of oneself in this sense is no
proof of having an infinite nature.

[95–7] The knowledge of God

Caterus accepts that everything we clearly and distinctly know is true, and
that error is due to judgement and will, but he doubts that we can claim

any clear and distinct knowledge of the infinite being, any more than we can clearly picture a chiliogon. He cites St Thomas in support.

[97–100] The proof of God's existence from his essence

Caterus points out that St Thomas had already quoted an argument (derived from St Anselm) identical to Descartes's, and goes on to cite St Thomas's reply to this argument: 'Granted that everyone understands that the word "God" means what has been said, i.e. a being than which nothing greater can be thought, it does not therefore follow that everyone understands that what is signified by the name exists in reality, but only that it exists in the apprehension of the intellect. Nor can it be argued that it exists in reality, unless it is conceded that there exists in reality something than which nothing greater can be thought: but this is not conceded by those who hold that God does not exist' (*Summa theologiæ*, Ia, q. 2, a. 1, *ad* 2). Caterus endorses this objection.

100   **The distinction between soul and body**

Of the essence of the soul, and of its distinction with the body, I shall say little. For I admit that this great mind has so exhausted me that I can barely do anything more. The distinction between mind and body, if it exists, seems to be being proved from the fact that they can be conceived distinctly and separately. Here I would refer this most learned man to Duns Scotus. Scotus says that in order for something to be conceived distinctly and separately from something else, what he calls a formal and objective distinction is sufficient. He posits this as a halfway house between real distinction and abstract distinction. This is the kind of distinction he says exists between the divine justice and the divine mercy: for they have, he says, prior to any operation by the intellect, distinct essences* [rationes formales], inasmuch as one is not the other; yet it does not follow that the justice can be conceived separately from the mercy, or hence that they can exist separately.*

101   FIRST REPLIES

The proof of God by means of the concept of 'objective reality'

102   ... I wrote *The idea is the thing itself that is thought about, in so far as it exists objectively in the intellect.** These words the theologian represents himself as understanding* in a completely different sense from

that in which I meant them, so that he may give me a fuller opportunity to explain the matter. He says that *existing objectively in the intellect means determining the act of the intellect in the manner of an object. But this is purely an extrinsic denomination, and adds nothing to the thing itself.* Here I should point out that he is considering the thing itself as existing outside the intellect, from which point of view its objective existence in the intellect is indeed an extrinsic denomination. But I was talking of the idea that does not exist at any time outside the intellect, from which point of view 'objective existence' means nothing other than 'existing in the intellect, in the way that objects normally exist within it'. So, supposing someone asks, for example, how it affects the sun that it exists objectively in my intellect, we can very well answer that it is not at all affected, except that an extrinsic denomination is applied to it, that is, it does indeed determine the operation of the intellect in the manner of an object. But if the question is 'What is the idea of the sun?' and the answer is given that it is the thing itself that is being thought of, in so far as it exists objectively in the intellect, no one will think that the idea is the sun itself, in so far as this extrinsic denomination is being applied to it. Nor does 'to exist objectively in the intellect' here mean 'to determine the operation of the intellect, in the manner of an object'. What it means is 'to exist in the intellect, in the way that its objects normally exist within it': so that the idea of the sun is the sun itself existing in the intellect, not indeed formally (as the sun exists in the sky), but objectively, that is, in the way that objects normally exist within the intellect; and this mode of being is far more imperfect than that in which things exist outside the understanding, but, as I have previously written, this does not mean it is nothing.

And when the most learned theologian says that there is an *ambiguity* in these words, he seems to have been wishing to draw my attention to the misunderstanding I remarked on just now, in case I had missed it. For he says, first of all, that the thing thus existing in the intellect by means of an idea does not exist in actuality, that is, it is not something existing outside the intellect. Which is true. Then he goes on to say that it is *not something imagined, or an 'ens rationis', but something real that is distinctly conceived*: in these words he concedes everything I have affirmed. However, he goes on to add that *because it is simply conceived and does not exist in actuality* (that is, because it is only an idea, and not a thing existing outside the intellect) *it can indeed be conceived, but cannot possibly be caused*, that is to say, it does not need a cause for its existing outside the intellect. This I admit, but it certainly needs a cause in order for it to be conceived, and this alone is what we are talking about. For instance, if someone has in their intellect the idea of some machine devised with extraordinary complexity,* we are certainly quite justified in asking what is the cause of this idea. Nor shall we be satisfied if someone says that the idea does not exist outside the intellect, and therefore cannot be caused, but only conceived, because the point at issue here is precisely this: what is the cause of its being conceived? And we shall not be satisfied either by someone's saying that the intellect itself is the cause of it, that is, inasmuch as the idea is an operation of the intellect. For that is not the point at issue: what we are asking about is the cause of the objective complexity that exists in the idea.

104   For the fact that this idea of the machine contains one kind of objective complexity rather than another must derive from some cause. And objective complexity stands in the same relation to this idea as objective reality to the idea of God. Now we could find different causes for this complexity: for perhaps the cause is a real machine of this kind that the person has already seen, and on which the idea was patterned; or the person possesses in his understanding a profound knowledge of mechanics, or perhaps great subtlety of intelligence, by the help of which he was able to discover the idea even without prior knowledge. And we should note that all the complexity that exists purely objectively in this idea, must necessarily exist in its cause, whatever that may be, whether formally or eminently. And the same applies to the objective reality contained in the idea of God. For in what can this exist in this way, except in a God that really exists? But my perspicacious reader has seen all this very clearly, and therefore admits that we can ask *why this idea contains more objective reality than that one.* His first answer to this question is this: *I say in general, as applicable to all ideas, what M. Descartes says of the triangle: Even if perhaps such a figure does not exist, and has never existed, anywhere at all outside my thought, it nonetheless has a certain determinate nature, or essence, or form, that is immutable and eternal.* And this, he says, *does not require a cause.* But he has seen clearly enough that this will not quite do. For even if the nature of a triangle is immutable and eternal, this does not make it any less legitimate to ask why we have an idea of it in us. Therefore he adds: *But if you insist on demanding a*

reason, it is the imperfection of our understanding. By this answer it
seems he meant to show* purely that those who wish to disagree with
me on this point cannot give any plausible answer. For it is certainly 105
no more probable that the cause of our having an idea of God in us is
the imperfection of our intellect, than that ignorance of the mechanical art is the cause of our imagining some machine of extremely complex ingeniousness rather than another and more imperfect machine.
The contrary is patently true: if someone has the idea of a machine in
which every conceivable kind of workmanship is displayed, this is a
very good reason for thinking that this idea derives from some cause
in which every conceivable kind of workmanship actually exists, even
though it exists in the idea in purely objective fashion. And by the
same token, since we have in ourselves the idea of God, in which all
conceivable perfection is contained, it follows beyond question that
this idea depends on some cause in which all this perfection also
exists, namely in God himself, who actually exists. For surely no
greater difficulty would appear in one case than in the other if, just as
not everyone is skilled in mechanics, and therefore not everyone can
have ideas of machines of very complex workmanship, similarly not
everyone has the same faculty of conceiving the idea of God; but
because it is imprinted in the same way on all of our minds, and we
are never aware of it as coming to us from somewhere other than ourselves, we suppose it belongs to the nature of our intellect. And this
in itself is not wrong, but we overlook something else of great importance, on which the whole force and clarity of the argument depends,
namely that this faculty of having the idea of God within ourselves
could not exist in our intellect, if this intellect were only a finite
being, as indeed it is, and did not have God to cause it. Therefore 106
I pursued the investigation by asking *whether I could exist, if God did
not exist*, not so much to put forward a different argument from the
preceding one, as to explain one and the same argument more fully.

[106–7] The proof of God from the Meditator's own existence

Descartes goes on to explain how his causal argument differs from that of
St Thomas. He does not base his argument on causal relations between
sensible things, both because he thinks that God's existence is much more
evident than that of any sensible things, and because he sees that his
inability to conceive an infinite succession of causes unfolding from all

eternity, without a first cause, does not necessarily prove that there is in fact a first cause, only that his finite intellect cannot embrace infinity. Therefore, he concentrates on the fact of his existence in the present, of which he is in any case most certain, thus eliminating the aspect of temporal succession.

107 Moreover, I did not investigate what is the cause of myself, in so far as I consist of mind and body, but only in so far as I am a thinking thing. I think this is far from insignificant: for in this way I was far better able to rid myself of prejudice, to concentrate on the natural light, to question myself, and to assert for certain that there can be nothing in me of which I am in no way aware* [*conscius*]. [. . .]

Besides, I did not ask only what is the cause of myself, in so far as I am a thinking thing, but especially and above all, in so far as I am aware within myself, among other thoughts, of the idea of a supremely perfect being. For on this one thing the whole force of my demonstration depends: first, because this idea contains what God is, at least, to the extent that he can be understood by me; and, according to the rules of true logic, before we ask of anything *whether it*
108 *exists* we must first understand *what it is;** secondly, because it is this very idea that gives me an opportunity to investigate whether I exist of myself or by another and to acknowledge my own deficiencies; and finally, it is this idea that teaches me that not only there is some cause of my existence, but besides that in that cause all perfections are contained, and therefore that it is God.*

[108–12] Descartes's analysis of the sense in which a being may be said to be cause of itself is taken up again in the Fourth Replies, with reference back to the present discussion: hence it is omitted here.

[112–15] The knowledge of God

Descartes holds that although we cannot comprehend the infinite, we can understand it, in the sense that if we clearly and distinctly understand that a thing is such that no limits can be found within it, we clearly understand that it is infinite. He distinguishes infinity, the absence of all limits, which pertains only to God, from indefiniteness, the absence of limits from a certain point of view: thus space, extending without limit, is indefinite, but not infinite, because its absence of limits applies only to its limited range of attributes. We must distinguish between infinity as a concept and an infinite thing. We grasp the concept only negatively, that is, as the absence of limits: but we understand the thing positively, although not adequately: that is, we do not understand everything in it that is understandable.

We cannot fully comprehend God, but we can have a clear and distinct knowledge of his perfections.

[115–20] The proof of God's existence from his essence

Descartes argues that he agrees with St Thomas that the knowledge of God is not so plain as to make proof unnecessary. He accepts St Thomas's refutation of St Anselm's proof of God (that, if 'God' means a being than which no greater can be thought, and if it is greater to exist in reality than only in the intellect, then God must exist in reality). But he contends that his own argument is quite different: it runs as follows:

Whatever we clearly and distinctly understand to belong to the true 115 and immutable nature, or essence, or form, of some thing, can be truly asserted of that thing; but after we have carefully examined 116 what God is, we clearly and distinctly understand that it belongs to his true and immutable nature to exist; therefore we can truly assert of God, that he exists. Here the conclusion at least is clearly valid. But nor can we deny the major premise, because it has been granted already that *all we clearly and distinctly understand is true.* This leaves only the minor, and here I admit that there is a significant difficulty. First, we are so accustomed in the case of all other things to distinguish existence from essence that we do not sufficiently realize how existence belongs to the essence of God as distinct from other things; secondly, because we fail to distinguish between what belongs to the true and immutable essence of some thing and what is merely attributed to it by a fiction of our intellect, and therefore, even if we are quite aware that existence belongs to God's essence, we fail to conclude that God exists, because we do not know whether his essence is immutable and true or merely a fiction created by ourselves.

But, to remove the first part of this difficulty, we have to distinguish between possible and necessary existence,* and to note that possible existence is contained in the concept or idea of all things that are clearly and distinctly understood, but that necessary existence is contained only in the idea of God. For I have no doubt that those who pay careful attention to the difference between the idea of God and all other ideas will perceive that, even if we never understand 117 other things except as if they existed, it does not follow that they do exist, only that they can exist. This is because we do not understand it to be necessary that actual existence should be conjoined with their other properties. But from the fact that we understand actual existence necessarily and always to be conjoined with the rest of God's attributes, it follows beyond doubt that God exists.

Next, to remove the second part of this difficulty, we need to realize that those ideas that contain not true and immutable natures, but only fictitious natures put together by the intellect, can be broken down by this same intellect not only by abstraction, but by a clear and distinct operation—so much so, that whatever cannot be thus broken down by the intellect must certainly not have been put together by it. For example, when I think of a winged horse or a lion actually existing, or a triangle inscribed in a square, I readily understand that I can on the contrary think of a horse without wings, or a non-existent lion, or a triangle without a square, and so forth: I understand, therefore, that such things do not possess true and immutable natures. But if I think of a triangle or a square (I shall say nothing here of the lion or the horse, because their natures are not entirely known to us), then, certainly, whatever I grasp as being contained in the idea of the triangle (for instance, that the sum of its three angles equals two right angles) I shall affirm of the triangle, and with truth; and whatever I find in the idea of the square, I shall affirm of the square. For even if I can understand a triangle, in abstraction from the fact that the sum of its three angles equals two right angles, I cannot deny
118 this of it, by means of a clear and distinct operation, that is, I cannot do so if I properly understand what I am saying. [. . .]

If I consider existence as being contained in the idea of a supremely perfect body, because it is a greater perfection to exist both in reality and in the intellect than in the intellect alone, I cannot therefore conclude that this supremely perfect body exists, only that it can exist; for I clearly realize that this idea was put together by my own intellect combining all bodily perfections; and that existence does not result from the other bodily perfections, because we can equally well say that they exist or that they do not. And indeed, because, examining the idea of body, I can perceive within it no power of producing or conserving itself, I rightly conclude that necessary existence (which alone is in question here) does not belong to the nature of a body, however perfect, any more than it belongs to the nature of a mountain that it does not have a valley, or to the idea of a triangle that the sum of its angles is greater than two right angles. But now, if we enquire, not of a body, but of a thing, whatever it may be, that
119 has all perfections that can simultaneously coexist, whether existence

should be counted among these, we shall at first sight be uncertain: because, since our mind, which is finite, is unused to considering these perfections except in isolation, it perhaps does not immediately realize how necessarily they are interrelated. However, if we carefully examine whether existence belongs to a supremely powerful being, and, if so, what type of existence, we shall clearly and distinctly perceive, first of all, that possible existence at least belongs to it, as it does to all other things of which there is a distinct idea in ourselves, and even those put together by a fiction of our intellect. Then, because we cannot think that its existence is possible, without immediately recognizing, when we consider its immense power,* that it can exist in virtue of that, we shall therefore conclude that it does exist in reality, and has existed from all eternity. For it is very obvious to the natural light that what can exist by its own power has always existed. And thus we shall understand that necessary existence is contained in the idea of the supremely powerful being, not in virtue of any fiction of the intellect, but because it belongs to the true and immutable nature of such a being to exist. And we shall also readily perceive that this supremely powerful being cannot not possess in itself all the other perfections contained in the idea of God, so that, without any fiction of the intellect being involved, and in virtue of their own nature, they are simultaneously combined together, and exist in God.

All this is clearly obvious to anyone who will consider it attentively. 120 Nor does it differ from what I had written previously, except in the form in which I have explained it, which I have deliberately modified in order to cater for the diversity of people's minds. Nor shall I deny here that this argument is such that those who do not bear in mind everything that contributes to the proof of it, will readily take it for a sophism. Therefore at the outset I was quite doubtful whether to use it, for fear of giving occasion to those who failed to grasp it to disagree with other proofs. But because there are only two ways of proving the existence of God,* one, that is, by arguing from his effects, and the other by considering his very essence or nature, I explained the first of these, to the best of my ability, but I thought I should not fail to include the other at a later stage.

The distinction between soul and body

As for the formal distinction, which our most learned theologian finds in Scotus, I shall say here briefly that it does not differ from the modal distinction,* and applies only to incomplete entities, which I have carefully distinguished from complete ones. For the formal distinction to apply, it is sufficient that one thing can be conceived as distinct and separate from the other by an act of abstraction on the part of the intellect, but not as distinct and separate in the sense that we understand each of them individually as a being by itself and distinct from every other being: for that to be the case, there has to be a real distinction between them. Thus, for example, between the motion and the shape of one and the same body, there is a formal distinction, and I can perfectly well understand the motion without the shape, and the shape without the motion, and both of them in abstraction from the body: but I cannot, however, completely understand motion apart from the thing in which it takes place, nor shape without a thing in which the shape exists; nor, finally, can I imagine that motion exists in a thing that can exist without shape, or that shape exists in a thing incapable of motion. And in the same way, I cannot understand justice apart from one who is just, or mercy apart from one who is merciful; nor can we imagine that one and the same person, who is just, cannot be merciful. But I have a complete understanding of what body is, by thinking of it purely as having extension, shape, motion, and so forth, and by denying that it has any of the properties that belong to the nature of mind. And on the other hand, I understand the mind to be a complete thing, which doubts, understands, wills, and so forth, although I deny that there is anything in it that is contained in the idea of body. And this could not possibly be the case, if there were not a real distinction between the mind and the body.

1. You concluded in the Second Meditation that you are a thinking thing, but you do not know what a thinking thing is: how do you know thinking is not a bodily operation?

2. The idea of a supreme being does not need to derive from an actually existing supreme being:

(i) It could have been formed by ourselves. We possess some degree of perfection: can we not form the idea of a supreme being by adding more and more degrees of perfection to this, just as we can go on adding number to number?

(ii) It is not necessarily true that there must be as much reality in the cause as in the effect. Flies and plants are produced by the sun, the rain, and the earth, which are lifeless.*

(iii) The idea of God is a purely intellectual entity [ens rationis] having no greater reality [lit. 'being no more noble than'] than the human mind [and could therefore have been produced by it].

(iv) The idea has probably been derived from other people: would you have formed it if you had been raised in isolation? Savages such as the Canadians and the Hurons do not possess it.*

(v) The idea might have been formed from the knowledge of bodily things: but this would only prove the existence of a very perfect corporeal being.

(vi) Would not the same argument apply to the idea of an angel, which is more perfect than you? On your showing, this would have to have been produced by an actual angel.

(vii) You have in fact no idea of God, any more than you have that of an infinite number or an infinite line; and if you had such an idea, this would not imply that an infinite number exists, which is impossible.

(viii) The idea of a unitary perfection encompassing all the others is a production by the intellect, of the same kind as universal ideas such as generic unity,* which correspond to nothing in reality.

3. (i) You say that you can be certain of nothing unless you know for certain that God exists. But when you concluded that you are a thinking thing, you had not proved God's existence: therefore your conclusion was not certain.*

(ii) An atheist knows for certain that the sum of the three angles of a triangle is equal to two right angles.

(iii) He might support his disbelief in God by arguing that an infinitely perfect being would exclude all other forms of being and good, on the one hand, and of non-being and evil, on the other: but in fact there are many beings and many goods, and many non-beings and many evils.

4. (i) You deny that God can deceive: but there are biblical texts to the contrary:* he might deceive us for our own good, like a doctor with his patients or a father with his children.

(ii) We might be so constituted as to be deceived even in things we think we know clearly and distinctly, even in the absence of a deceiving deity.

(iii) Clear and distinct perception is no guarantee of certainty: we often see people in error about things they believe they perceive in this way.

5. You say that the will is safe from error or sin when it is governed by clear and distinct knowledge, and is in danger only when it pursues obscure and confused intellectual conceptions. If this were so, then Turks and other infidels would be wrong to espouse the Christian and Catholic religion, since they do not have a clear and distinct knowledge of its truth.* Besides, we know so few things clearly and distinctly that if such knowledge were requisite to all our decisions, there are very few decisions we could ever take.

6. You argue that what we know to belong to the essence of a thing can be safely asserted of that thing and then that, having considered the essence of God, we see that existence belongs to it. You thus conclude that he exists. You should have concluded only that it belongs to his nature to exist. For his actual existence follows only if we know his nature is intrinsically possible: that is, if we know that the idea of a supremely perfect being is not self-contradictory. Besides, since all God's attributes are infinite, how can we understand them except imperfectly? In other words, how can we have the clear knowledge of his essence to which you lay claim?

7. You say nothing of the soul's immortality, although you claimed you would be proving this.* You have not sufficiently proved the distinction between mind and body (as suggested above), and even if the soul is distinct from the body, this does not make it incorruptible. For all we know, it may expire along with the body.

In general, it would be a good idea to present your argument in geometrical form, beginning with definitions, postulates, and axioms.

SECOND REPLIES

1. How do you know a body cannot think?

129 1. [. . .] [In the second Meditation] I was not yet investigating whether the mind was distinct from the body, only examining those of its properties of which I could have certain and evident knowledge.

And because I became aware of several of these at this point, I cannot unreservedly accept what you go on to say, *that I do not know what a thinking thing is*. For even if I admit that at that stage I did not know whether this thinking thing was identical with the body or distinct from it, I do not therefore admit that I had no knowledge of it. For who has ever known anything in such a way that he knew that there was absolutely nothing in it except what he knew?* But the more we perceive of some thing, the better we are said to know it. In this way, we know the people we live with every day better than those of whom we have only seen the face or heard the name, even if these latter would not be said to be completely unknown to us. In this sense, I think I have demonstrated that the mind, considered without those properties that are normally ascribed to the body, is better known than the body considered without the mind, and this is all I meant to establish here.

Descartes goes on to suggest that what the Objectors are getting at is that the first two Meditations yield very little beyond the above conclusion. He thus justifies his method:

Since therefore nothing is so conducive to the acquisition of reliable knowledge, as to accustom ourselves beforehand to doubt of all things and especially bodily things, even though I had long ago seen several books on this subject composed by Academics* and Sceptics, and therefore it was with some distaste that I found myself rehashing all this stuff, I could not dispense myself from devoting a whole Meditation to it; and I would wish readers to dwell on the matters contained in it, not simply for the short period of time required to read it, but for several months, or at least weeks, before they go on to the rest of the work. For by doing so they would beyond doubt derive much greater benefit from what follows.

Then, because previously we did not have any ideas of those things that belong to the mind, except very confused ones, muddled up with the ideas of sensible things, and this was the first and most important reason why none of what people said about the soul and God could be sufficiently clearly understood, I thought I would be doing something of considerable value if I showed how the properties or qualities of the mind are to be distinguished from the qualities of the body. For although many had previously said that in order to understand metaphysical matters, the mind must be withdrawn from the senses, no one up to now, to the best of my knowledge, had shown by what method this was to be achieved. But the true and, to my mind, the only way to achieve it is contained in my Second Meditation. However, it is of such a nature that it is not enough to have glanced over it once only: it must be studied for a long time and examined again and again, so that the lifelong habit of confusing the things of the intellect with those of the body can be erased by a habit of distinguishing them built up at least over a few days. And this seemed to be a very good reason why I should not attempt to deal with any other subject in the Second Meditation.

Besides you inquire here *how I demonstrate that the body cannot think?* But excuse me if I answer that I have not yet given any occasion for this question, since I first engaged with it only in the Sixth
132 Meditation. [. . .]. To this we can readily add the following: *Whatever can think is a mind, or is called a mind; but since mind and body are really distinct, no body is a mind; therefore no body can think.*

And I certainly cannot see what you can disagree with here: or can you deny that it is sufficient for us to clearly understand one thing without another, in order to recognize that they are really distinct? If so, give us some more certain sign of a real distinction; for I am confident that none can be given. What can you say instead? That two things are really distinct if either of them can exist without the other? But again, I shall ask how you know that one thing can exist without the other? For this has to be known, if it is to be the sign of a distinction. Perhaps you will say you have learned this from the senses, because you see or touch one thing in the absence of the other. But the senses are less reliable than the intellect; and it can happen in many ways that one and the same thing can appear in various forms or in several places or modes, and thus be mistaken for two things. And, finally, if you remember what was said about the wax at the end of the Second Meditation, you will realize that bodies themselves are not even perceived, properly speaking, by the senses, but by the intellect; so that there is no difference between, on the one hand, having a sensation of one thing in the absence of another thing and, on the other, having the idea of one thing, and understanding that this idea is not the same as the idea of another thing. And this
133 can be understood only if one thing is perceived without the other; and it can be understood with certainty only if the idea of each thing is clear and distinct; so that if this sign of a real distinction is to be a certain one, it has to be equated with mine.

But if there are any people who deny that they have distinct ideas of the mind and the body, I can do no more than request them to consider carefully the points I make in this Second Meditation; and they should realize that the opinion they have (if they do in fact have it) that the parts of the brain play a role in the formation of thoughts derives from no positive reason, but simply from the fact that they have never experienced themselves in the absence of body, and have not infrequently been impeded by the body in their operations; they are like someone who, having been continually in fetters ever since his childhood, thinks that the fetters are part of his body and that he needs them in order to walk.

[133–5] 2. The proof of God from the objective reality of the idea of God

Descartes replies systematically to this set of objections (the roman numbers have been added to guide the reader):

i. In a sense, the Objectors are quite right to say that the foundation of the idea of God is in ourselves; Descartes holds it to be an innate idea. But we could not have the faculty of forming it, his argument establishes, if God did not exist.

ii. The point about flies and plants does not prove that something can exist in the effect that does not exist in the cause. Our ignorance of their causes is no reason to doubt a principle evident by the natural light. Besides an objection based on the assumption material things exist will not occur to one following the method of withdrawing his thoughts from sensible things.

iii. The idea of God is not an *ens rationis*, a purely intellectual construct, if by this is meant something non-existent in reality. Descartes's concern is with the *objective reality* of the idea, as requiring a really existent cause.*

And indeed I cannot see what more could be added to make it clearer 135 that this idea could not be present in me, unless a supreme being existed, except on the part of the reader—I mean, that, by very carefully considering what I have already written, he should free himself from the prejudices by which, perhaps, his natural light is clouded, and accustom himself to believe in primary notions than which there can be nothing more evident or more true, rather than obscure and false opinions rooted in the mind by inveterate custom.

For that *there is nothing in the effect that was not previously in the cause, either in similar or in more eminent form*, is a primary notion, as clear as any we have; and it comes to the same thing as the common saying *of nothing, nothing will come*; because if it were granted that there was something in the effect that was not in the cause, one would also have to grant that this something was made by nothing; nor is it clear why nothing cannot be the cause of anything, except because in such a cause there would not be the same as there is in the effect.

It is also a primary notion that *all the reality or perfection that exists only objectively in ideas, must exist either formally or eminently in the cause of these ideas*; and this is the sole foundation for all our opinions we have had as to the existence of things outside our minds. For how did we come to suspect that they existed, except because the ideas of them were transmitted by the senses to our mind?

But that there is some idea in us of a being supremely powerful and perfect, and also that the objective reality of this idea is not to be found within us either formally or eminently—this will be clear to those who pay sufficiently close attention and meditate for a long
136 time along with me.* From all this, the manifest conclusion is that God exists. But for the sake of those whose natural light is so limited that they cannot see that *all the perfection that exists objectively in the idea must exist in reality in some cause of the idea*, I have given a still more palpable demonstration of the point, based on the fact that the mind that has this idea cannot exist of itself; and therefore I cannot see what you could further require of me in order to give your assent.

iv. Nor does it cause any difficulty, to think that perhaps I acquired the idea that represents God to me, *from preconceived ideas in the mind, from books, conversations with friends, etc., rather than from my own mind.* For it makes no difference to the progress of the argument, whether I am asking if those from whom I am said to have received it, have the idea from themselves, or from someone else, or whether I am asking the question of myself; and I shall always conclude that the one from whom it first derived is God.

[136–7] v. We can no more have formed the idea of God from that of bodily things than we could form the idea of sounds from the faculty of vision, if we had no sense of hearing. If you want to know how to arrive at the idea of incorporeal or spiritual being, reread the Second Meditation, where this is gone into as carefully as possible.

137 Nor is it a problem that in this Meditation I was dealing only with the human mind; for I freely and willingly admit that the idea we have, for instance, of the divine intellect does not differ from our idea of our own intellect, except in the same way as the idea of an infinite number differs from the idea of a finite number. The same applies to

the rest of God's individual attributes* of which we recognize there to be some trace in ourselves.

But, more than this, we understand there to be in God an absolute immensity, a simplicity, and a unity encompassing all his other attributes, of which there is no other example, but which is, as I said before, *the mark by which the craftsman makes himself known in his handiwork*, in virtue of which we recognize that nothing of those things that, on account of the shortcomings of our intellect, we consider in God separately, as we perceive them in ourselves, pertains to him and to us univocally; and so we also come to realize that, of many particulars without limit, of which we have ideas, such as knowledge without limit, and power, number, length, and so on, without limit, there are some that are contained formally in the idea of God, such as knowledge and power, others only eminently, such as number and length; and this could certainly not be the case, if this idea in ourselves were   138
nothing more than a fiction.*

Nor, [if it were], would it be so consistently conceived by everyone in the same way. For it is an extremely striking fact that all metaphysicians are unanimously agreed in their description of God's attributes (I mean those that can be known by human reason alone), whereas there is no physical or sensible thing, no thing of which we have an idea, however solid and palpable it may be, on the nature of which we do not find philosophers disagreeing far more extensively.

[138–9] The notion, invoked by the Objectors, of an extremely perfect bodily entity is self-contradictory (since divisibility is less perfect than indivisibility), and could never be confused with the notion of God.

vi. The idea of an angel, as Descartes himself acknowledges in the Third Meditation, could have been formed by combining the ideas of God and a human being.

But, as for those who deny they have an idea of God but instead of   139
him imagine some idol or something of the kind, they are denying the name and affirming the thing.*

vii. Descartes takes up the Objectors' analogy between the idea of God and the idea of an infinite number. That he cannot grasp the idea of an infinite number does not imply that such a number cannot exist. But it does show that his power of understanding that a number can exist that transcends his own ability to conceive it comes not from himself, but from a more perfect being.

[140] He discusses what is meant by calling God unthinkable (*incog-itabilis*) or inconceivable:

When God is said to be *unthinkable*, what this excludes is a conception of him that grasps him adequately: it does not rule out the inadequate idea of him that we possess and which is sufficient for a knowledge of his existence.

viii. The analogy between the idea of the unity of God's perfections and generic unity falls down. The unity of the genus is simply an intellectual construct: it adds nothing to the nature of the individuals within it. Whereas the unity of God's perfections is a distinctive and positive perfection in God: it makes him different from other beings.

3. Whether all knowledge depends on the knowledge of God's existence

Thirdly, when I said, *that we can know* [scire] *nothing for certain unless we first know that God exists*, I made it quite clear in so many words that I was speaking only of those conclusions *of which the memory may come back to us, when we are not particularly considering the reasons on the basis of which we deduced them.** For the knowledge [*notitia*] of principles is not usually called 'scientific knowledge'* by logicians. But when we realize we are thinking things, this is a first notion not derived from any syllogism. And, when someone says, *I am thinking, therefore I am, or exist*, he is not deducing existence from thought by means of a syllogism, but recognizes it as known directly [*per se notam*]* by a simple intuition of the mind. This is clear from the fact that, if he were deducing it by a syllogism, he would first have had to know the major premise, *Whatever thinks, is or exists*. Whereas in fact he actually learns this truth from what he experiences in himself, that it cannot be that he should think, unless he exists. For such is the nature of our mind that it forms general propositions on the basis of the knowledge of particulars.

141

But that *an atheist can clearly know* [cognoscere] that *the three angles of a triangle add up to two right angles*, I do not deny. All I say is that this knowledge [*cognitio*] is not true scientific knowledge [*scientia*], because it seems that no knowledge that can be rendered doubtful should be called scientific. And since he is supposed to be an atheist, he cannot be certain that he is not deceived even in things that appear to him completely evident, as has been sufficiently shown; and although perhaps this doubt has never occurred to him, it may occur to him, if he considers the matter, or if someone suggests it to him: nor will he ever be safe from it, unless he first recognizes a God.

And it makes no difference if he happens to think he has demonstrations proving that there is no God. For since these are not at all true, their faults can always be pointed out to him; and when this is done, he will be shaken out of his opinion.

This will not be difficult to achieve, if the only demonstration he can put forward is the one you add here, namely, that *the infinite in every kind of perfection excludes all other kinds of being.* For, first, if questioned how he knows that it belongs to the nature of the infinite to exclude all other beings in this way, he can make no reasonable reply, because the word *infinite* is not generally taken to mean something that excludes the existence of finite things and because he can know nothing of the nature of what he thinks is non-existent and therefore has no nature, except what consists in the bare meaning of 142 the name as it is understood by other people. Then, what would be produced by the infinite power of this imaginary infinite being, if it could never create anything? And finally, from the fact that we are aware of a certain power of thinking within ourselves, we can readily conceive that the power of thinking may exist in some other being, in a greater degree than in us; but although we can suppose that this power can be extended to infinity, we are not therefore afraid that our own will become less as a result. The same applies to all the other properties that are ascribed to God, including his power, as long as we do not suppose that there is any power in us not subject to the will of God; and therefore he can be understood to be absolutely infinite without any exclusion of created things.

4. Descartes sets aside appeals to the Bible by appealing to an established distinction between types of discourse:

Everyone is familiar with the distinction between ways of speaking of God (such as are common in the holy scriptures) adapted to the understanding of ordinary people, and containing a certain kind of truth, but one relative to human beings, and other ways of speaking of him, that instead express the naked truth, not in any relation to human beings. Everyone in philosophy should stick to these latter ways of speaking, and this applied particularly to me in my Meditations, since I did not at this stage even suppose that there were any human

143   beings known to me, nor did I consider myself as consisting of mind
and body, but as a mind pure and simple.

[143–4] Thus, when he says God cannot lie, what he means to exclude is
not literal falsity but the will to harm through deception. (In any case,
'Nineveh will be destroyed' was a threat, not a false statement about the
future; and God's hardening of Pharaoh's heart was not a positive
action, but a negative one, that of denying him the grace of conversion.)*
Descartes entertains the possibility, then, that God may, like a doctor,
occasionally make literally false statements for the listener's good, but this
would not apply to the wholesale deception involved in allowing us to
assent to clear and distinct ideas that are in fact false. The occasional existence of deceptive impulses, like the dropsical patient's desire to drink, has
been dealt with in the Sixth Meditation. The fact that we have ideas of
true and false shows we have a positive faculty for recognizing truth. If,
when we use this faculty correctly, by assenting only to clear and distinct
ideas, we may in fact be wrong, then God, the giver of the faculty, would
be not an occasional but a wholesale deceiver.

Descartes, perceiving that the Objectors seem not to have grasped his
solution to the doubts he put forward in the First Meditation, expands
upon the nature of human certainty:

144   First of all, immediately we think something has been rightly perceived by us, we spontaneously convince ourselves it is true. If this
conviction is so firm that we can never have any cause to doubt what
we convince ourselves of in this way, there is no need for further inves-
145   tigation; we have all we can rationally desire. For what difference does
it make to us if, say, someone imagines that the very thing of the truth
of which we are so firmly convinced, appears false to God or an angel,
and is therefore, absolutely speaking, false? Why should we bother
about this absolute falsity, since we simply do not believe in it in any
way, or even have the slightest suspicion of it? For we suppose there
to be a conviction so firm that it cannot in any way be uprooted; and
so this conviction is precisely the same as the most perfect certitude.

But it is possible to doubt whether we can have any such certitude,
or firm and unshakable conviction.

It is indeed perfectly clear that we do not have it as regards things
that we perceive with the slightest degree of confusion or obscurity:
for this obscurity, whatever form it takes, is sufficient reason for our
doubting them. Nor do we have it as regards things that are perceived by the senses alone, however clearly, because we have often

observed that errors may be found in sense-perception, as when a sufferer from dropsy is thirsty or one with jaundice sees snow as yellow: for he sees it no less clearly and distinctly as yellow than we see it as white. It therefore remains that, if we do have any such certainty, it applies only to things clearly perceived by the intellect.

Of these, there are some that are so clear and at the same time so simple, that we can never think of them without believing them to be true: for instance, that while I am thinking, I exist; that what has once happened, cannot not have happened, and suchlike. Of these it is obvious that we have such certitude. For we cannot doubt of them, without thinking of them; but we cannot think of them, without simultaneously believing them true, as I just said; therefore we cannot doubt of them, without simultaneously believing them to be true. That is, we cannot ever doubt of them. 146

And it is pointless to urge that *we have often found others to have been deceived in things they believed themselves to know more clearly than the sun.* For we have never observed, nor can anyone ever observe, that this has befallen those who sought the clarity of their perception from the intellect alone, only those who derived it either from the senses, or from some false prejudice.

It is likewise pointless for someone to imagine that these things appear to be false to God or to an angel, because the evidence of our perception does not allow us to pay any attention to someone imagining this.

There are other things that are indeed very clearly perceived by our intellect, when we pay sufficient attention to the reasons on which our knowledge of them depends, and therefore at the time we cannot doubt them. But because we can forget those reasons, and yet sometimes remember the conclusions deduced from them, it can be asked whether we also have a firm and unshakeable certitude of these conclusions, as long as we recall that they were deduced from evident principles. For we must suppose that there is this recall, for them to be called conclusions in the first place. I answer that such certitude is enjoyed by those who know God in such a way as to understand that it cannot be that the faculty of understanding he has granted them should not be directed to the truth. But others do not enjoy it. And I explained all this so clearly in the Fifth Meditation that nothing further needs to be said here.

[147] 5. Faith and understanding

Descartes insists that all philosophers and theologians, indeed all reasonable people, would agree that the danger of error is less when we clearly understand what it is we are giving our assent to. He expands on the issue of our assent to faith:

148 Then we must observe that the clarity or perspicuity by which our will can be moved to assent to something takes two forms: one derived from the natural light, and the other from divine grace. Now, even though faith is commonly said to deal with obscure matters, this, however, is understood to apply only to the thing, or the matter, in question; but it does not mean that the formal reason, in virtue of which we give our assent to the things of faith, is obscure. For this formal reason consists in a certain inner light, by means of which, supernaturally enlightened by God, we firmly believe that those things put forward for our belief have been revealed by God, and that it simply cannot be the case that he should lie—a light more certain than the whole light of nature,* and often also, on account of the light of grace, more evident.

And certainly, when Turks and other infidels fail to embrace the Christian religion, they are guilty of sin not because they refuse to assent to things that are obscure, in so far as they are obscure; only because they are fighting against an inner impulse of divine grace or because, on account of their other sins, they render themselves unworthy of grace. And I will boldly say that an infidel wholly deprived of supernatural grace and completely ignorant of those things we Christians believe have been revealed by God, who nonetheless, on the basis of some faulty arguments, gave his assent to these beliefs, although they were obscure to him, would not therefore count as having faith—rather, he would be sinning, inasmuch as he would not be using his reason correctly. And I do not think any orthodox theologian has ever had a different opinion about this. Nor can any of my readers think I have failed to acknowledge this supernatural light, when in the Fourth Meditation, in which I investigated
149 the cause of falsity, I quite explicitly said that *it disposes my innermost thoughts to willing, and yet does not diminish our freedom.**

Besides, I would urge you to remember here that, as regards those things that are fit objects for the will to embrace, I have distinguished most scrupulously between the conduct of life and the contemplation of the truth. For, as regards the conduct of life, I am so far from

thinking that we should give our assent only to what we clearly
perceive, that, on the contrary, I think we cannot always even wait
for probabilities: sometimes, we have to choose one of a number of
options that are completely unknown; and yet we must hold fast to
this choice, once it has been made, as long as no reasons to the
contrary emerge, just as much as if we had made it for very obvious
reasons (I explained this in the *Discourse on the Method* [III. 22–3,
AT 6. 25]). But when the issue is the contemplation of truth, who has
ever denied that we must withhold our assent from what is obscure
and not sufficiently distinctly perceived? And this alone is what I was
dealing with in my Meditations, as the subject-matter itself indicates,
and as I made clear in so many words at the end of the First
Meditation, when I said that *my concern there was not with action but
only with the attainment of knowledge* (p. 16).

6. The argument from the nature of God to his existence

When you criticize the conclusion of my syllogism, it seems that you
are in the wrong about it. For, given the conclusion you wish to
draw, the major premise should be formulated as follows: *Whatever
we clearly understand to belong to the nature of some thing, can be truly
affirmed to belong to that thing's nature.* And there would be nothing
in this beyond a pointless tautology. But my major premise is this: 150
*Whatever we clearly understand to belong to the nature of some thing, can
be truly affirmed of that thing.* Thus, if to be an animal belongs to
man's nature, we can affirm that man is an animal; if to have three
angles equal to two right angles belongs to the nature of a triangle,
we can say that a triangle has three angles equal to two right angles;
if existence belongs to the nature of God, we can affirm that God
exists; and so on. And the minor premise was this: *But it belongs to
the nature of God to exist.* From the major and the minor, it is clear
that we should draw the conclusion I drew: *Therefore we can truly
affirm of God, that he exists*; but not, as you would have it: *Therefore
we can truly affirm, that it belongs to God's nature to exist.*

Therefore, in order to make room for the qualification you make,
you should have denied the major premise, and said: *Whatever we
clearly understand to belong to the nature of some thing, cannot, however,
be affirmed of that thing, unless the thing's nature is possible, that is, not
self-contradictory.* But I urge you to recognize the pointlessness of
this qualification. For you are either using *possible* in its normal sense

to mean whatever is not repugnant to human understanding—in which sense it is obvious that God's nature, as I described it, is possible, since I have supposed it to contain nothing except what we clearly and distinctly perceive must belong to it, so that it cannot be repugnant to the understanding. Or you must be imagining some other kind of possibility pertaining to the object itself, and unless this coincides with the former kind, it can never be known by the human 151 intellect, and has therefore no more power to compel us to deny the nature or existence of God than to overthrow human knowledge about everything else. For if it were legitimate to deny that the nature of God is possible, even though no impossibility can be discovered on the conceptual level, but, on the contrary, all those attributes we include in this concept of the divine nature are so interconnected that it seems to us self-contradictory that any one of them should not belong to God, by the same token one could deny that it is possible for the three angles of a triangle to be equal to two right angles, or for one who is actually thinking to exist; and certainly one would be far more entitled to deny that any of those things we access by the senses is true; and thus the whole of human knowledge would be over-thrown—and yet without the slightest reason. [. . .]

152 Even if we conceive God only inadequately, or, if you like, only very inadequately, this does not prevent its being certain that his nature is possible, or not self-contradictory. Nor does it prevent us from truly asserting that we have investigated it sufficiently clearly (sufficiently, that is, in order to know this, and indeed to know that necessary exist-ence belongs to this same nature of God). For all impossibility (or 'implicancy'*) resides in our thought alone, when it incorrectly joins together ideas that clash with one another; and it cannot reside in anything existing outside the intellect, because, by the very fact that something exists outside the intellect, it is clear that it is not self-contradictory but possible. Now all self-contradictoriness arises in our concepts purely and simply because they are obscure and confused, and it cannot exist at all in concepts that are clear and distinct. And therefore it is sufficient for us to understand clearly and distinctly, although by no means adequately, the few things we perceive about God, and to realize, among other things, that necessary existence is contained in this concept we have of him, however inadequate it may be, in order for us to affirm that we have investigated his nature sufficiently clearly, and that it is not self-contradictory.

[153–4] 7. Immortality

Descartes has explained in the Synopsis why he says nothing of immortality. He has shown that mind is a substance distinct from the body, and therefore need not be affected by the disintegration of the body; nor is there any reason for thinking that a substance can perish by annihilation. Natural philosophy therefore concludes that the soul is immortal. Yet God could indeed have decreed, as the Objectors suggest, that human souls should cease to exist when the bodies to which they are coupled are destroyed. Only revelation assures us that this is not so, and that the soul is in fact immortal.

[154–5] Descartes thanks the Objectors for their frank and helpful statement of objections, and discusses the suggestion that he should set out his arguments in geometrical form:

Finally, as regards your suggestion that *I should put forward my* 155 *arguments in the geometrical manner, so that they can be grasped by the reader at a single glance*, it would be worth my while to explain how far I have followed it, and then how far I think it should be followed. I distinguish two things in the geometrical manner of writing, the order and the method of proof.

Order consists purely and simply in this, that the things that are put forward first have to be known without any help from those that come later, and all the rest then have to be arranged in such a way that they are demonstrated only from those that go before. And I have certainly tried to follow this order as rigorously as possible in my Meditations. It was in keeping with this that I dealt with the distinction between mind and body not in the second but only when I had got to the sixth; and I left out many other things knowingly and deliberately, because they presupposed my explaining several other things.

But the method of proof takes two forms, one by analysis, the other by synthesis.

Analysis shows the true path by which the thing was methodically discovered, as if *a priori*,* so that, if the reader is willing to follow it and to pay sufficient attention to every point, he will understand it and assimilate it as perfectly as if he had discovered it himself. But it has nothing that can compel the assent of a lazy or reluctant reader. 156 For if the slightest element in the argument is missed, the necessity of the resultant conclusions does not appear, and often this form of argument scarcely touches on many things, because they are quite obvious to one paying sufficient attention, that it is nonetheless crucial to realize.

Synthesis, on the other hand, works in the opposite direction,
retracing the path, so to speak, *a posteriori*.* It clearly demonstrates
whatever conclusions have been drawn, and makes use of a long
string of definitions, postulates, axioms, theorems, and problems; so
that if a reader should deny any of its consequences, it immediately
shows that the consequence is contained in the antecedents, and thus
forces him, however reluctant or recalcitrant, to yield his assent. But
it is not so satisfying as the other, nor so fulfilling for those who really
wish to learn, since it does not reveal the method by which the thing
was discovered.

The old geometers used only the second method in their writings,
not because they were altogether unaware of the other, but because,
to my mind, they thought of it so highly that they kept it to themselves as a valuable secret.

Now I have followed this analytic method alone, as the true and
best way of teaching, in my Meditations; but as for synthesis, which
is certainly what you are asking of me here, although it plays a most
valuable role in geometry, when placed after analysis, it cannot be
applied so conveniently to these metaphysical matters.

For this is the difference: that the primary notions that are presupposed in order to demonstrate geometrical truths are in accordance
with habitual sense-perception, and are readily accepted by everyone.
157 Therefore there is no difficulty here except in deducing the consequences properly; and this can be achieved by all kinds of people,
even the less attentive, provided only that they remember what has
gone before. And their memory is assisted by the formulation of
different propositions, each corresponding to a particular aspect of
the problem in question, so that readers can dwell separately on each
one, which can be subsequently referred to so as to refresh the
memory even of the reluctant.*

On the other hand, the major difficulty in metaphysics is with the
clear and distinct perception of the primary notions. For even if they
are intrinsically no less knowable, or even more knowable, than those
considered by geometers, because they are, nonetheless, at odds with
many prejudices of the senses to which we have grown accustomed
since childhood, they are not perfectly known except to those who pay
close attention, who meditate, and who withdraw their minds from
bodily things as far as possible. And thus, if they were baldly stated by
themselves, they could be easily denied by those inclined to contradict.

This is why I wrote Meditations, rather than Disputations,* as philosophers normally do, or Theorems and Problems, in the manner of geometers, so that by this fact alone I might make clear that I have no business except with those who are prepared to make the effort to meditate along with me and to consider the subject attentively. In fact, by setting himself to fight against truth, which is what someone is doing if he holds back from considering the reasons that establish it, so as to find others that tend against it, he makes himself less capable of perceiving it.*

Perhaps someone will object that there is admittedly no need to search for reasons to the contrary, when we know that the truth is 158 being offered us; but that, as long as there is any doubt on this point, it is proper for the reasons on both sides to be set out, so that we can discover which are more solid; and that I am therefore making unfair demands, if I require my arguments to be accepted as true, before they have been examined, and forbid other arguments to the contrary to be considered.

This would certainly be a fair point, if any of the reasons that I required the reader to be attentive and cooperative in order to grasp were such as to distract him from considering various other reasons, in which there was even the slightest hope of finding more truth than in mine. But since the reasons I put forward include a universal doubt taken to its limits, and I recommend nothing more strongly than very careful consideration of each particular point, and nothing, in short, is accepted except what has been viewed so clearly and distinctly that we cannot withhold our assent from it; and since, on the other hand, there are no other reasons from which I wish to convert my readers' minds, except those they have never examined properly, and that they derived not from any solid reason, but from the senses alone, I do not think anyone can believe that he will be in greater danger of erring, if he considers only the reasons I have to offer him, than if he turns aside his mind from them and turns it instead to other reasons that are opposed to these in some way and that merely darken the issue (I mean the prejudices of the senses).

Therefore, not only is it perfectly fair of me to require particular attention on the part of my readers, I chose the particular way of writing that I thought most capable of inspiring it, and from which I am convinced that my readers will receive more benefit than 159 they themselves will realize; whereas, on the other hand, from the synthetic way of writing they usually think they have learned more than in fact they have; but I also think myself entitled to reject out of hand and to regard as of no account whatever the judgements passed on my work by those who have refused to meditate along with me and who stick to their own prior opinions.

But because I know how difficult it will be, even for those who will pay attention and make a serious search for truth, to get an overall view of my Meditations, and at the same time to pick out the particular elements (both of which I think must be done at the same time, if one is to derive the fullest possible benefit from the work), I shall add a few points here in the synthetic style, which I hope will be of some assistance; provided that these readers will be good enough to bear in mind that I do not wish to cover as much material here as in the Meditations, because I would have to be much more prolix than I had to be in the original work, and also that what I do cover I shall not be explaining in detail, partly because I am concerned to be brief, and partly in case anyone thinks that this is sufficient, and therefore takes less trouble to examine the Meditations, from which I am convinced there is much more benefit to be gained.

160 REASONS PROVING THE EXISTENCE OF GOD AND THE
DISTINCTION BETWEEN THE SOUL AND THE BODY,
SET OUT IN GEOMETRICAL FASHION

Definitions

I. I use the term *thought* to cover everything that is in us in such a way that we are immediately conscious of it. Thus all operations of the will, the intellect, the imagination, and the senses are thoughts. But I added 'immediate', so as to exclude the consequences of these operations: for instance, voluntary motion certainly has thought at its origin, but is not itself a thought.

II. By the term *idea* I understand the form, of any thought whatever, by the immediate perception of which I am conscious of the same thought itself; so that I cannot express anything in words (understanding what I am saying), without its being certain, for this very reason, that there is in me the idea of the thing that is signified by those words. And therefore I do not confine the term 'ideas' only to the mental pictures depicted in the imagination; in fact, I do not here call these 'ideas' at all, in so far as they are depicted in the bodily imagination, that is, in some part of the brain, but only in so far as 161 they inform the mind itself, when it is directed towards that part of the brain.

III. By *the objective reality of an idea* I mean the being of the thing represented by the idea, in so far as it exists in the idea; along the same lines, one can say 'objective perfection', or 'objective complexity', and so forth. For whatever we perceive as being in the objects of our ideas, is in the ideas themselves objectively.

IV. The same properties are said to exist *formally* in the objects of ideas, when they are in them such as we perceive them; and *eminently*, when they are not in the object in this way, but instead there are properties so great as to take their place.

V. Every thing in which something we perceive—that is, some property, or quality, or attribute—exists immediately, as in its subject, or through which something we perceive exists, and of which we have a real idea in ourselves, is called a *substance*. Nor do we have any other idea of substance in this precise sense than this: it is a thing in which, either formally or eminently, the something exists that we perceive or that exists objectively in some one of our ideas; because it is known to the natural light that there can be no real attributes of nothing.

VI. The substance in which thought immediately exists is called *mind*: I say *mind* here, rather than soul, because the word 'soul' is equivocal, and is often used to refer to a bodily thing.

VII. The substance that is the immediate subject of local extension, and of the accidents that presuppose extension, such as shapes, places, local motions, and so forth, is called *body*. But whether there 162 is one and the same substance, called both *mind* and *body*, or two distinct substances, will be investigated later.

VIII. The substance we understand to be supremely perfect, and in which we conceive nothing at all that involves any defect or limitation of perfection, is called God.

IX. When we say that something is contained in the nature or concept of some thing, this is the same as saying that it is true of that thing, or that it can be affirmed of that thing.

X. Two substances are said to be really distinguished, when each of them can exist without the other.

Postulates*

FIRST, I request my readers to realize how feeble are the reasons for which, up to now, they have trusted to their senses, and how uncertain are all the judgements that they have founded on these; and to go over this so long and so often that they will finally acquire the habit of no longer trusting to them excessively. For I judge this necessary if one is to perceive certainty in metaphysical matters.

SECONDLY, that they should consider their own mind, and all its attributes, about which they will realize that they cannot doubt, even though they suppose that everything they have ever received from the senses is false; and they should pursue this consideration as long as it takes to acquire the habit of perceiving the mind clearly, and of believing it to be easier to know than all bodily things.

THIRDLY, that they should carefully weigh the directly known [*per se notas*] propositions that they discover within themselves, such
163 as *That a thing cannot both be and not be at one and the same time*; *that nothingness cannot be the efficient cause of any thing*, and suchlike; they will thus be putting into practice the perspicuity of the intellect that nature has implanted in us, purifying and liberating it from the powerful disturbing influence constantly exerted by the perceptions of the senses. By this method they will easily come to be aware of the truth of the Axioms that follow.

FOURTHLY, that they should examine the ideas of different natures in which a simultaneous combination of many different attributes is contained, such as the nature of a triangle, or of a square, or of any other shape; and also, the nature of mind, the nature of body, and above all the nature of God, or the supremely perfect being; and that they should realize that all that we perceive to be contained in these can be truly affirmed of them. For instance, because it is contained in the nature of a triangle that its three angles are equal to two right angles, and in the nature of a body, or an extended thing, that it should be divisible (for we can conceive of no extended thing, however small, that we cannot divide, at least in thought), it is true to say that the three angles of any triangle are equal to two right angles, and that every body is divisible.

FIFTHLY, that they should devote considerable time to serious contemplation of the nature of the supremely perfect being; and consider, among other things, that possible existence is contained in the ideas of all other natures whatsoever; but that in the idea of God not only possible but absolutely necessary existence is contained. From this alone, and without any process of reasoning, they will know God exists; and this will be as directly known to them as that the number two is even and the number three odd, and suchlike. For there are many truths directly known to some that are understood by others only by a process of reasoning.

SIXTHLY, that, by examining all the examples of clear and distinct perception, and also those of obscure and confused perception, that I have listed in my Meditations, they should accustom themselves to distinguishing things that are clearly known from those that are obscure; for this is learned more easily by examples than by rules, and I think that in the text I have either explained or at least touched on all the examples of this.

SEVENTHLY, and finally, that, realizing that they have never detected any falsity in things that they have clearly perceived, and on the other hand that they have never, except by chance, encountered the truth in things they have understood only obscurely, that they should consider that it is altogether contrary to reason that, purely on account of the prejudices of the senses, or on account of some hypothesis that contains an unknown element, they should call into question things that are clearly and distinctly perceived by the pure intellect. For in this way they will readily accept the following axioms as true and indubitable. Although indeed some of these could have been better explained, and put forward as theorems rather than axioms,* if I had wished to take the trouble.

AXIOMS

OR

COMMON NOTIONS

I. Nothing exists of which we cannot ask what is the cause of its existence. We can even ask this question of God himself, not that he requires some cause for his existence, but because the very immensity of his nature is the cause or reason why he needs no cause for his existence.

II. The present moment does not depend on the moment immediately preceding, and therefore the conservation of a thing requires a cause no less than its original bringing into being.

III. No thing, nor any actually existing perfection of a thing, can have *nothing*, or a non-existent thing, as the cause of its existence.

IV. Whatever reality or perfection there is in any thing exists formally or eminently in its first and adequate cause.

V. Hence it follows that the objective reality of our ideas requires a cause, in which this same reality is contained, not only objectively but formally or eminently. And it should be noted that this axiom is so necessary to accept because all knowledge, whether its object can be perceived by the senses or not, depends on it alone. For how, for example, do we know that the sky exists? Because we see it? But this sight does not affect the mind, except in so far as it is an idea: an idea, I say, inhering in the mind itself, not an image depicted in the imagination. Now on the basis of this idea we cannot judge that the sky exists, unless because every idea must have a really existing cause of its objective reality, a cause we judge to be the sky itself, and so on.

VI. There are different degrees of reality or being; for a substance has more reality than an accident or mode; and infinite substance more than finite. Therefore there is more objective reality in the idea 166 of a substance than in that of an accident; and in the idea of an infinite substance than in that of a finite substance.

VII. The will of a thinking thing is carried, but voluntarily and freely (for this is of the essence of will), and yet infallibly, towards a good it clearly knows; therefore, if it knows that there are some perfections it lacks, it will give them to itself immediately, if they are in its power.

VIII. What can bring about what is greater or more difficult, can also bring about what is less so.

IX. It is a greater thing to create or conserve a substance than to create or conserve the attributes or properties of a substance; nor is creating a greater thing than conserving, as has already been stated.

X. Existence is contained in the idea or concept of every thing, because we can conceive nothing except as existing; to be precise, possible or contingent existence is contained in the concept of a limited thing, but necessary and perfect existence in the concept of a supremely perfect being.

[166–70] There follow four propositions proved from these definitions and axioms: that God's existence is known from his nature; that it is known from the presence of his idea in us; that it is known from the fact that we, having this idea, exist (with the corollary that he created all things, and can produce all that we can clearly perceive, as we perceive it); that there is a real distinction between soul and body.

First Objection
On the First Meditation: Of those things that can be
called into doubt

It is clear from what is said in this Meditation, that there is no criterion*
by which our dreams may be distinguished from the waking state and from
true sensation; and, therefore, that the phantasms* we have when awake
and sentient are not accidents inhering in external objects, nor a proof that
such external objects exist at all. Hence if we go along with our senses
without any further reasoning-process, we shall rightly doubt whether
anything exists or not. Therefore we recognize the truth of this Meditation.
But since Plato and other ancient philosophers argued for the uncertainty
of sensible things, and the difficulty of distinguishing sleep from waking is
a matter of common observation, I would have wished this excellent
author of new speculations to refrain from publishing these old ones.

Reply

The reasons for doubting, which are here admitted to be true by the
Philosopher,* were put forward by me only as probable; and when
I made use of them, I was not intending to pass them off as new, but
partly to prepare readers' minds to consider intellectual things and to   172
distinguish them from those of the body, for which purpose they
seem to me to be altogether necessary; partly to answer them in the
succeeding Meditations; and partly also to show how firm are the
truths I later advance, since they cannot be shaken by these metaphysical doubts.* So in listing them here I was not seeking for praise;
but I think I could no more have omitted them here than a writer on
medicine can omit the description of the disease he aims to show us
the method of curing.

Objection II
On the Second Meditation: On the nature of the human mind

I am a thinking thing (p. 19): *all well and good. For from the fact that*
I think, or have a phantasm, whether I am asleep or awake, it can be

*inferred that I am thinking; for 'I think' and 'I am thinking' mean the
same. From the fact that I am thinking, it follows that I exist, since what
thinks is not nothing.* But where he goes on to say that is, I am a mind,
a soul, an understanding, a reason (p. 19), *this is where doubt creeps in.
For it does not seem a valid piece of reasoning to say, 'I am thinking,
therefore I am a thought'; or 'I am understanding, therefore I am an
understanding'. For I could similarly argue 'I am walking, therefore I am
a walk'. Therefore M. Descartes is running together the thing that understands and intellection, which is an act of the thing that understands; or at
least he is taking the thing that understands to be the same thing as the
understanding, which is a power of the intelligent thing. Yet all philosophers distinguish the subject from its faculties and acts, that is, from its
properties and essences; for the 'being' itself is one thing, and its 'essence' is
another. Therefore it may be the case that a thinking thing is the subject of
the mind, the reason, or the understanding, and therefore something bodily.
M. Descartes assumes the contrary without proof. But his inference is the
foundation of the conclusion he seems to be trying to establish here.*

In the same place, we find this: I know that I exist; I am trying to
find out what this 'I' is, whose existence I know. It is absolutely certain that this knowledge, in the precise sense in question here, does
not depend on things of which I do not yet know whether they exist
(p. 20).

*It is absolutely certain that the knowledge of this proposition 'I exist'
depends on this one 'I am thinking', as he himself has rightly shown. But
where does the knowledge that 'I am thinking' come from? Certainly from
nothing else than this: that we cannot conceive any action without its subject: we cannot conceive dancing without a dancer, knowledge without
one who knows, thinking without a thinker.*

*And it seems to follow from this that the thinking thing is something
bodily; for it seems that the subject of any act* can be understood only in
bodily or material terms. He shows this himself later by the example of the
wax, which, although its colour, hardness, shape, and other acts are
changed, is still understood to be the same thing all along, that is, the same
matter, subjected to all these transformations. For 'I am thinking' is not
inferred from another thought: someone may think that he has thought
(which is the same as remembering he has thought), but it is altogether
impossible to think that one is thinking, just as one cannot know one is
knowing. For there would then be an infinite string of questions: how do
you know that you know that you know that you are knowing?*

*Since, therefore, the knowledge of this proposition 'I exist' depends on
the knowledge of this one, 'I am thinking'; and the knowledge of the latter
on the fact that we cannot separate the act of thought from the matter that
thinks, it seems the inference should be that a thinking thing is material* 174
rather than immaterial.

Reply

When I said, 'that is, a mind, a soul, an understanding, a reason', I
did not use these words merely to denote the various faculties, but to
denote the things endowed with the faculty of thinking. The first two
are usually understood in this sense, and the other two are often used
in this way. And I have said this so explicitly and in so many places,
that there seems to be no room for doubt here.

Nor does the comparison between walking and thinking hold good
here. For the word 'walk' is normally understood only as denoting
the action; but 'thought' is sometimes taken to refer to the action,
sometimes to the faculty, and sometimes to the thing possessing the
faculty.

Nor am I saying that the thing that understands and the act of
intellection are one and the same, or that the thing that understands
is the same as the understanding, in the sense of the *faculty* of understanding; they are the same only when 'understanding' is taken to
refer to the thing that understands. I readily admit that I have used
the most abstract words possible when referring to a thing or a
substance, which I wanted to strip of everything that does not belong
to it; whereas, on the other hand, the Philosopher uses the most concrete words possible—'subject', 'matter', 'body'—when he refers to
the thinking thing, so as to prevent it being divested of its body.

Nor do I fear that a reader may think that his method of combining a number of things together* is better equipped for finding the
truth than mine, in which I distinguish things as much as possible.
But let us forget about words, and talk about things.

He says: 'It may be the case that the thinking thing is something 175
bodily. M. Descartes assumes the contrary without proof.' I certainly
did not assume the contrary, or treat it as a foundation. I left the issue
completely open, until the Sixth Meditation, in which I prove my
view.*

Then he says, rightly, that 'we cannot conceive any action without its subject', as thought without a thinker, because what thinks is

not nothing. But without any reason, and contrary to all our ordinary ways of talking and all logic, he adds: *It seems to follow from this that the thinking thing is something bodily; for indeed the subjects of all acts can be understood only in terms of substances* (or, if you prefer, *in terms of matter*, that is, metaphysical matter), but this does not mean they can be understood only in bodily terms.*

But all logicians and nearly all ordinary people as well are accustomed to say that some substances are spiritual, others bodily. And all I proved by the example of the wax was that colour, hardness, shape do not belong to the essence (*ratio formalis*) of the wax itself. And I said nothing here of the essence of the mind, or indeed of the essence of body.

Nor is what the Philosopher says here, that one thought cannot be the subject of another thought, at all relevant. Whoever, apart from himself, ever imagined this?* But—to explain the issue as briefly as possible—it is certain that thought cannot exist without a thinking 176 thing, nor can any act or any accident at all exist without a substance in which it inheres.

But since we do not know substance itself immediately by itself, but only inasmuch as it is the subject of certain acts,* it is entirely reasonable and in accordance with ordinary usage to call those substances we recognize to be the subjects of quite different acts or accidents by different names, examining at a later stage whether those different names refer to different things or to one and the same thing. Now there are some acts we call 'bodily', such as size, shape, movement, and all those other things that cannot be conceived without extension in space; and we call the substance in which they inhere a 'body'. Nor can we imagine that there is one substance that is the subject of shape, and another that is the subject of local motion, and so forth, because all these acts come together under a single common concept (*ratio*) of extension. Then there are other acts, which we call 'cogitative', such as understanding, willing, imagining, perceiving by the senses, and so on, which all come together under a common concept of thought, or perception, or consciousness; and the substance in which they inhere is called a 'thinking thing', or a 'mind', or any other name we choose, as long as we do not confuse this substance with bodily substance, since cogitative acts have no affinity with bodily acts, and thought, which is the common element in all of them, differs radically from extension, which is the common element

of the other kind. But after we have formed two distinct concepts of
these two substances, it is easy, from what is said in the Sixth
Meditation, to discover whether they are one and the same or two
different substances.

Objection III

What therefore is there that can be distinguished from my thinking?
What is there that can be said to be separate from me? (p. 21)*

*Someone might perhaps answer this question as follows: I myself, who
think, am to be distinguished from my thinking; and my thinking is not
separate from me, but different from me, just as dancing is distinguished
from the dancer (as was pointed out above). But if M. Descartes has shown
that the one who understands and the understanding are one and the same,
we shall fall back into the scholastic way of talking: 'the understanding
understands', 'the sight sees', 'the will wills', and, to use an exact analogy,
'the walk (or at least the faculty of walking) walks'. But all these expressions are obscure, inaccurate, and most unworthy of M. Descartes's usual
perspicuity.*

Reply

I do not deny that I, who think, am to be distinguished from my
thinking, as a thing from a mode; but when I ask 'Is there any of them
that can be distinguished from my thinking?', I am talking about the
various modes of thinking just listed, and not about my substance;
and, when I add 'Is there any of them that can be said to be separate
from me?', I mean only that all these modes of thinking are present
in me; and I cannot see what can be imagined to be doubtful or
obscure in any of this.

Objection IV

So I am left with no alternative, but to accept that I am not at all
imagining what this wax is, I am conceiving* it with my mind alone
(pp. 22–3).

There is a great difference between imagining, that is, having some 178
*idea, and conceiving with the mind, that is, inferring that something is, or
exists, by a process of reasoning. But M. Descartes has not explained to
us in what the difference consists. The Peripatetics* of old also showed
quite clearly that substance is not perceived by the senses, but inferred by
reasoning.*

But what if reasoning is nothing other than a coupling and attachment of names or labels, by means of the word 'is'?* *It would follow that by rea-soning we infer nothing at all about the nature of things but only about their labels—that is, whether or not we are combining the names of things according to the stipulations we have laid down about the meanings we have decided to attach to the names. If this is so (and it may be), then reasoning depends on names, names on the imagination, and the imagin-ation perhaps (as I myself hold) on the motion of the bodily organs; and thus the mind would be no more than a motion in certain parts of the organic body.*

Reply

I explained the difference between imagination and the pure concept of the mind at this point, when I listed, using the example of the wax, the things we imagine in it and those we conceive by the mind alone. But I have also explained elsewhere the difference between how we understand something, say, a pentagon, and how we imagine the same thing.* Besides, in reasoning, there is a coupling not of names, but of the things signified by the names; and I am amazed that anyone can think the contrary. No one doubts that a Frenchman and a German can both reason about the very same things, though the words they conceive are utterly different. And is not the Philosopher condemning himself out of his own mouth when he speaks of the stipulations we lay down about the meanings of words? For if he admits that words mean something, why can he not accept that our reasonings are about the thing that is signified, rather than about the words alone? But as far as his conclusion that the mind is motion is concerned, he might just as well conclude at the same time that the earth is the sky, or anything he likes.

Objection V
On the Third Meditation: Of God

Some of these thoughts are apparently images of things, and to these alone the name 'idea' is properly applied: for instance, when I think of a human being, or a chimera, or the heavens, or an angel, or God. (pp. 26–7).

When I think of a human being, I recognize an idea, or an image composed of shape and colour, about which I may ask myself whether it is the likeness of a human being or not. The same applies when I think of the heavens. When I think of a chimera, I recognize an idea, or an image, about which I can ask myself whether or not it is the likeness of some animal that does not exist, but that could exist, or that existed at some earlier time.

But when someone is thinking of an angel, there comes to his mind sometimes the image of a flame, sometimes that of a beautiful boy with wings, about which I think I can be certain that it is not the likeness of an angel, and therefore that this is not the idea of an angel. But believing 180 that there are immaterial and invisible creatures that wait upon God, we attach the name 'angel' to this thing we believe or suppose exists, although the idea, by means of which I imagine an angel, is put together from the ideas of visible things.

The same is true of the holy name of God of whom we have no image or idea; and therefore we are forbidden to worship God in the form of an image, in case we should think we can conceive him who is beyond our conception.

It seems, then, that there is no idea of God in us. But just as a person born blind, who has often come close to the fire and felt himself grow hot, recognizes that there is something by which he is heated, and hearing it called a 'fire', concludes that fire exists, yet does not know what shape or colour it is, nor has any idea or image of fire arising in his mind; so man, realizing that there must be some cause of his images or ideas, and that this cause too must have another cause prior to it, and so on, is finally led to an end-point, or to the supposition of some eternal cause that, since it never began to be, can have no cause prior to itself. He necessarily concludes that something eternal exists.* Yet he has no idea that he could call the idea of this eternal being, but gives this thing he believes in or acknowledges the name or label 'God'.

Now, since it is from this supposition, that we have the idea of God in our soul, that M. Descartes proceeds to prove the theorem that God (that is, a supremely wise and powerful creator of the world) exists, he should have given a better explanation of this idea of God, and deduced from it not only God's existence but his creation of the world as well.

Reply 181

Here he intends the term 'idea' to be taken purely in the sense of the images of material things that are depicted in the bodily imagination. On this basis, it is easy for him to prove that there can be no proper idea of an angel or of God. And yet throughout my work and especially here, I make clear that I take the term 'idea' to signify everything that is directly perceived by the mind.* This means that, because, when I will or fear, I perceive at the same time that I am willing or fearing, willing and fearing count for me as ideas. And I used this term 'ideas', because it had already been very commonly used by philosophers to denote the forms of perception of the divine mind, although we recognize that there is no imagination in God; and I had no more suitable term to hand. But I think I have sufficiently explained the idea of God to all who will take the trouble to bear in mind the sense in which I use it; as for those, on the other hand, who prefer to understand my terms in a different sense from me, I could never do enough to satisfy them. The concluding remarks he adds about the creation of the world are entirely irrelevant.

Objection VI

But others have certain other forms as well; thus, when I will, or fear, or affirm, or deny, I am always in fact apprehending some thing as the subject of this thought, but I am including something further within the thought than the mere likeness of the thing; and of thoughts of this kind some are called volitions, or affects, whereas others are called judgements (p. 27).

182   *When someone wills or fears, he has, to be sure, an image of the thing he fears and of the action he wills; but what he is further including within his thought is not made clear. Even if fear is a thought, I do not see what else it can be than the thought of the thing the person fears. For what is the fear of a charging lion, but the idea of a charging lion, plus the effect (which such an idea produces in the heart) by which the person in fear is impelled to the animal motion we call flight? But this motion of flight is not a thought. Hence we can only conclude that there is no other thought involved in fear beyond that which consists in the likeness of the thing. The same applies to the will.*

Besides, affirmation and negation do not occur without words and labels. This is why brute beasts cannot affirm or deny, even in thought, and therefore cannot judge. Yet a thought may be similar in a human being and in an animal. For when we affirm that a man is running, our thought is no different from that of a dog seeing his master running. Affirmation or negation therefore add nothing to the bare thought itself, except perhaps the thought that the names in which the affirmation consists are the names of the actual thing that is in the person who affirms;

but this adds nothing besides the likeness of the thing to the thought, it merely reproduces that likeness.

Reply

It is a thing directly known that there is a difference between, on the one hand, seeing a lion and at the same time fearing it, and, on the other, simply seeing it. Likewise it is one thing to see a man running, and another to affirm to oneself that one is seeing him, which process occurs without speech. And I can see nothing here that requires an answer.

183

Objection VII

It remains for me only to examine in what fashion I received this idea from God. For I did not derive it from the senses, nor did it ever thrust itself spontaneously on my attention, as do the ideas of sensible things, when the things themselves make an impression on the external sense-organs (or appear to do so). Nor is it a fiction, a creation of my own, for I cannot subtract anything from it, or add anything at all to it. It must therefore be that the idea is innate within me, in the same way as the idea of myself is innate within me (pp. 36–7).

If there is no idea of God (and it has not been proved that there is), and in fact there seems not to be one, this whole investigation collapses. Besides, the idea of myself arises in me (from the point of view of the body) from sight; from the point of view of the soul, there is no idea of the soul at all, but we infer by reason that there is something inside the human body that imparts animal motion to it, and in virtue of which it perceives by the senses and is moved. And this, whatever it is, we call the soul: but we have no idea of it.

Reply

If there is an idea of God (as there manifestly is) this whole objection collapses. And when he adds that the idea of the soul is not given, but it is inferred by reason, this is tantamount to saying that we do not have an image of it represented in our imagination, but that we have what I have called an idea of it.

Objection VIII

184

The other [idea of the sun], however, derives from astronomical reasoning—that is to say, it is derived from some notions innate within me (p. 28).

*There seems to be only one idea of the sun at a given time, whether we
are actually looking at it, or whether we are understanding by a process
of reasoning that its real size is far greater than it appears. For in this
second case, we are dealing not with an idea of the sun, but with an inference on the basis of arguments that the idea of the sun would be many
times greater, if we were viewing it from much closer.*

*It is true that at different times there may be different ideas of the sun,
for instance, if at one time it is viewed with the naked eye and at another
through a telescope. But astronomical reasoning does not make the idea of
the sun bigger or smaller; rather, it shows that the sensible idea of the sun
is deceptive.*

Reply

Here yet again what he says is not an idea of the sun, and yet
describes, is exactly the same as what I call an idea.*

Objection IX

For beyond doubt those ideas that represent substances to me are
something greater, and contain, if I may use the term, more 'objective reality' in themselves, than those that represent merely modes or
accidents. And by the same token the idea by which I conceive a
185 supreme God, eternal, infinite, omniscient, all-powerful, and the
creator of all things that exist beside himself, certainly has more
objective reality in itself than those by which finite substances are
represented (p. 29).

*I have already remarked several times that we have no idea either of
God or of the soul; I would add now, that there is none of substance either.
For substance (considered as matter subject to various accidents and alter-
ations) is inferred by reasoning alone; it is not conceived nor does it represent any idea to us. If this is the case, how can it be asserted that the
ideas that represent substances to me are something greater, and contain
more objective reality, than those that represent accidents to me? Besides
M. Descartes should consider afresh what he means by 'more reality'. Can
there be more or less reality? Or if he thinks that one thing is more of a
thing than another, he should consider how this notion can be explained to
us with the degree of clarity that is required in any demonstration, and
that he himself has achieved elsewhere.*

Reply

I have remarked several times that by 'idea' I mean precisely what is inferred by reason, as well as whatever else is perceived in any way. And I have sufficiently explained how there can be greater or lesser degrees of reality. For instance, a substance is more of a thing than a mode is; and if there are real qualities,* or incomplete substances, they are things in a greater degree than modes, but less than complete substances; and finally if there is an infinite and independent substance, it is more of a thing than finite and dependent substance. And all of this is manifestly known directly.

Objection X
186

And so there remains only the idea of God, in which I must consider whether there is anything that could not derive from myself. By the name 'God' I understand an infinite, independent, supremely intelligent, supremely powerful substance, by which I myself and whatever else exists (if anything else does exist) was created. But certainly all these advantages are so great that, the more carefully I consider them, the less it seems possible that they can be derived from me alone. And so I must conclude that it necessarily follows from all that has been said up to now that God exists (p. 32).

Considering the attributes of God, in order that we may deduce the idea of God from them, and discern whether there is anything in it that could not have derived from ourselves, I find, if I am not mistaken, both that the things we think of in connection with the name of God do not derive from ourselves, and that it is not necessary that they should come from anywhere other than external objects. For by the name of God I mean a 'substance' (that is, I understand that God exists—not by means of an idea, but by a process of reasoning); that is 'infinite' (that is, I cannot conceive or imagine him as having any boundaries or extremities, without being able to imagine others still more remote: from this it follows that the word 'infinite' gives rise to an idea not of the divine infinity, but of my own boundaries or limitations); that is 'independent' (that is, I cannot conceive of a cause by which God has been produced; from which it is clear that the word 'independent' gives rise to no idea in me, beyond my remembrance of my ideas as beginning at different times, and thus as dependent.

187   *Therefore, to say that God is* 'independent' *is to say no more than
that God is one of those things the origin of which I cannot imagine.
Likewise, to say God is* 'infinite', *is the same as saying that he is one of
those things the limits of which we cannot conceive. And thus any idea of
God is shown to be impossible: for what kind of idea can there be without
origin and without limits?*

    'Supremely intelligent.' *Here I ask: By what idea does M. Descartes
understand the intellection of God?*

    'Supremely powerful.' *Likewise, by what idea can we understand his
power, which relates to future things, that is, things that do not exist? It
is certain that I understand power on the basis of an image, or memory,
of past events, by reasoning as follows: he did this, therefore he was able
to do this; therefore the same being will be able to do the same thing again,
that is, he has the power of doing it. Now all of these are ideas that can
have arisen from external objects.*

    'Creator of all that exists.' *I can form a certain image of creation in
my mind based on what I have seen, such as a human being being born or
growing as if from a tiny point into the shape and size it now has. That is
the only idea that can arise in anyone's mind at the word* 'creator'. *But
the fact that we can imagine the world being created is not sufficient proof
that creation took place. Therefore, even if it were proved that some being*
infinite, independent, supremely powerful, &c. *exists, it does not
follow that there exists a creator. Unless someone were to think that from
the fact that there exists something we believe created everything else, we
can validly conclude that the world was therefore created at some time by
that being.*

188   *Besides, when he says that the idea of God and of our soul is innate
within us, I should like to know if the souls of people in a deep dreamless
sleep are thinking. If not, then they have no ideas at that time. Therefore
no idea is innate; for what is innate is always present.*

Reply

None of the properties we ascribe to God can have been modelled on
properties of external objects, since there is nothing in God similar
to the properties of external—that is, bodily—objects. But whatever
we think that is dissimilar to them, clearly derives not from them, but
from a cause of this dissimilarity in our thought.*

    And here I would ask how this philosopher deduces the intellec-
tion of God from external things. Whereas the idea I have of it, I can

readily explain, by saying that by an idea, I mean whatever is the form of some perception. For anyone who understands something perceives that he understands. He therefore has this form, or idea, of intellection, by extending which indefinitely he forms the idea of the divine intellection. The same applies to the rest of God's attributes.*

Since, indeed, I have used the idea of God that we have to demonstrate his existence, and since so much power is contained in this idea that we understand that it is impossible, if God exists, for anything else to exist alongside him, except what was created by him, it plainly follows, from the fact that his existence has been demonstrated, that it has also been demonstrated that the whole world, or in other words every thing other than God, whatever it is, that exists, was created by him.

Finally, when I say that some idea is innate within us, I do not 189 mean that that idea is always present to us—for in that sense certainly there would be no innate ideas; I mean only that we have in ourselves the faculty of producing it.*

Objection XI

The whole force of the argument comes down to this, that I recognize that it cannot be that I should exist, with the nature I possess (that is, having the idea of God within myself), unless in reality God also exists—God, the same being whose idea is within me (p. 37).

Since, therefore, it has not been demonstrated that we have an idea of God, and the Christian religion requires us to believe that God is inconceivable, which means, it seems to me, that we do not have an idea of him, it follows that the existence of God has not been demonstrated, far less his creation [of the world].

Reply

When God is stated to be inconceivable, what this means is that there is no concept that grasps him adequately. But as for how we possess the idea of God, I have said this again and again *ad nauseam*; and nothing at all is asserted here that invalidates my demonstrations.

Objection XII
190
On the Fourth Meditation: Of True and False

And thus I can understand, quite certainly, that error, in so far as it is error, is not something real dependent on God, but purely and simply a deficiency; and therefore that, in order to make mistakes I do not need a special faculty given me by God for this purpose (p. 39).

It is certain that ignorance is nothing but a deficiency, nor do we need any positive faculty to enable us to be ignorant. But this is not so clear as regards error. For it seems that stones and inanimate things cannot make mistakes, purely and simply because they do not have the faculty of reasoning, or of imagining. Hence one is inclined to infer that in order to make mistakes we need the faculty of reasoning, or at least imagining, and both of these are positive faculties, given to all those and only those who make mistakes.

Besides, M. Descartes says this: I realize that they [*sc.* my errors] depend on two simultaneously operative causes, namely, the faculty I possess of acquiring knowledge [*cognoscendi*] and the faculty of choosing, or free will (p. 40). *This seems to contradict the preceding passage. We should also note here that the freedom of the will is assumed without proof, contrary to the opinion of the Calvinists.**

Reply

Even if in order to make mistakes the faculty of reasoning (or rather judging, that is, affirming or denying) is required, it does not follow from the fact that error is a deficiency of this faculty that the deficiency is something real; just as blindness is not something real, even though stones are not said to be blind, purely and simply because they are not capable of vision. And I am amazed that so far I have not found a single valid inference in these objections. Besides, I made no assumptions about freedom here, except what we all experience in ourselves, and what is manifestly known by the natural light. Nor can I understand why this is alleged to be contradictory to what has gone before.*

Even though perhaps that are many people who, when they consider God's foreordaining [of all things], cannot grasp how it can coexist with our freedom, no one, however, when he simply looks at himself, does not realize in his own experience that will and freedom are one and the same thing. And this is not the place to examine other people's opinions about the matter.*

Objection XIII

For example, when I was examining over these last few days, whether anything existed in the world, and realized that, from the very fact that I was examining this point, it clearly followed that I existed, I could not indeed refrain from judging that what I so clearly understood was true. It was not that I was compelled to this by some external force, but that a great illumination of the understanding was followed by a great inclination of the will; and in this way my belief was all the freer and more spontaneous for my being less indifferent (p. 42).

This expression, 'a great illumination of the understanding', is metaphorical, and therefore has no argumentative value. Besides, every- 192 *one who is free from doubt, lays claim to such an illumination, and his inclination of the will to affirm what he has no doubt is true is just as strong as that of someone who really does have knowledge. Besides, not only knowing something to be true, but also believing it or assenting to it, are things that have nothing to do with the will. For if something is proved by valid arguments, or credibly reported, we believe it whether we want to or not. It is true that to affirm and deny, and to defend and refute propositions, are acts of the will. But it does not therefore follow that our internal assent depends on the will.*

Therefore there is no sufficient demonstration of the subsequent conclusion: The privation in which the essence of error consists lies in this wrong use of free choice (p. 43).

Reply

It is entirely pointless to ask whether the expression 'a great illumination' has any argumentative value or not, as long as it has explanatory value, which is certainly does. For no one is unaware that what is meant by an 'illumination of the understanding' is perspicuity of knowledge; and perhaps not all those who think they possess it, possess it in fact. But this does not mean that there is not a very great difference between this illumination and an obstinate opinion formed without an evident perception.

When it is said here that we assent to things we clearly grasp whether we want to or not, that is like saying that we desire what is clearly known to be good whether we want to or not. For the expression 'whether we want to or not' is quite out of place in such matters as this, since it is self-contradictory to say that we want and do not want the same thing.*

Objection XIV
On the Fifth Meditation: Of the Essence of Material Things

For instance, when I imagine a triangle, even if perhaps such a figure does not exist, and has never existed, anywhere at all outside my thought, it nonetheless certainly has a determinate nature, or essence, or form, that is immutable and unchanging, which was not invented by me, and does not depend on my mind. This is clear from the fact that it is possible to demonstrate various properties of the triangle (p. 46).

If a triangle exists nowhere at all, I cannot understand how it can have a nature of any kind; for what is nowhere does not exist; therefore it has no being, or nature of any kind. The triangle in the mind arises from a triangle seen, or from an image based on things seen. However, once we have attached the name 'triangle' to the thing that we think has given rise to the idea of the triangle, then although the triangle itself may cease to exist, the name remains. Likewise, if we have once grasped in our thoughts that the sum of all the angles of the triangle is equal to two right angles, and we attach this other name to the triangle, 'a shape having three angles equal to two right angles', then even if no angle actually existed in the world, the name would still remain, and the corresponding proposition, 'a triangle is a shape having three angles equal to two right angles', would be eternally true. But the nature of the triangle would not be eternal, if it came about that all triangles ceased to exist.

Likewise, the proposition 'man is an animal' will be true for all eternity, since the names are eternal; but if the human race were to perish, then there would no longer be any human nature.

194   *From this it is clear that essence, in so far as it is distinguished from existence, is nothing other than a coupling of names by the word 'is'. Thus essence without existence is a fiction of our own creation. And it seems to be that the relation of the image of a human being in our mind to the actual human being is the same as the relation of essence to existence; or in other words, the relation of the proposition 'Socrates is a human being' to the proposition 'Socrates is, or exists' is the same as the relation of Socrates's essence to his existence. Now the proposition 'Socrates is a human being', uttered at a time when Socrates does not exist, signifies simply a combination of names, and the word 'is' or 'being', involves the underlying image of the unity of a thing referred to by two different names.*

Reply

The distinction between essence and existence is known to everybody; and what is said here about eternal names, instead of concepts and ideas that are eternally true, has been sufficiently refuted already.*

Objection XV
On the Sixth Meditation: Of the Existence of Material Things

For since he has certainly given me no faculty by which I might realize this [*that is to say, that God, by himself or by the intermediary of some creature more noble than bodies, conveys to me the ideas of body*]* to be true, but has, on the contrary, endowed me with a strong propensity to believe that these ideas are conveyed by bodily things, I cannot see how, if they were in fact from some other source, it would be possible to think of him except as a deceiver. And therefore bodily things exist (p. 56).

There is a generally accepted view that doctors commit no sin who 195 *deceive their patients for the good of their health, or fathers who deceive their children for their own good; and that the wrongness of deception consists not in the falsity of what is said, but in the injustice done by deceivers. Therefore M. Descartes should examine whether the proposition 'God cannot in any case deceive us' is universally true; for if it is not universally true, the conclusion does not follow that* therefore bodily things exist.

Reply

It is not necessary to my conclusion that we can in no case be deceived (for I have readily admitted that we are often deceived), only that we are not deceived, when an error on our part would indicate the will on God's part to deceive us, which it is impossible to ascribe to him. Yet another faulty inference.

Final Objection

For now I realize that there is a massive difference between them [*waking and dreaming*], inasmuch as dreams are never combined by my memory with the rest of the actions of my life, as happens with my waking experiences (p. 63).

I would ask whether it is certain that someone dreaming that he is doubting whether he is dreaming or not cannot dream that his dream is connected with ideas of a long chain of past events. If he can, then the

things that in his dream appear to him to be actions carried out in his past
life, can be deemed to be true, just as much as if he were awake. Besides,
196 *since, as M. Descartes himself asserts, all certitude of knowledge and all*
truth depend on the single knowledge of the true God, either an atheist
cannot infer from the memory of his past life that he is awake or someone
can know he is awake without the knowledge of the true God.

Reply

One who is dreaming cannot really connect his dreams with ideas of
past events, although he may dream that he is making the connection.
For who denies that a sleeper may be deceived? Yet when he subsequently awakes he will easily recognize his error.*

   An atheist can certainly infer that he is awake from the memory of
his past life; but he cannot know that this sign is sufficient for him to
be certain he is not mistaken, unless he knows that he was created by
a God that is not a deceiver.

BY MONSIEUR ARNAULD, DOCTOR OF THEOLOGY

Letter from the above to Father Mersenne

*You did not wish, most eminent sir, to confer on me a blessing unearned;
for you require a compensation for this supreme benefit, and a significant
one, since you decided that I should have access to this remarkable work
only on condition that I should disclose my judgements of it. This is indeed
a harsh condition, which the desire of learning some very fine things, has
extorted from me, and from which I would gladly apply for an exemption,*   197
*if the praetor's exception of 'acts compelled by violence or fear' could be
extended to cover 'acts done at the persuasion of pleasure'.**

*For what do you wish for yourself? You do not expect me to pass judge-
ment on this author, whose supreme intellectual power and remarkable
learning you have known for a long time how much I value. Nor are you
unaware of the troublesome commitments by which my time is taken up;*
and, even if you have a higher opinion of my powers than I deserve, it
does not follow that I myself am not conscious of my inadequacy. And yet
what you are putting forward for my examination requires not only an
exceptional intelligence but a mind blest with serenity, so that it can find
space for itself away from the din of all external things. You know full
well that this cannot be achieved except by attentive meditation and by
fixing the mind's eye full on the mind itself. Yet I will nonetheless obey,
if indeed you require me to. Whatever errors I commit, you will be responsible for them, since you are compelling me to write. Although indeed
philosophy could claim that this whole work belongs to her alone, yet
since the author, like the very modest man that he is, has spontaneously
presented himself for the judgement of theologians, I shall play a twofold
role here; and I shall first of all put forward the objections that I think
philosophers could raise against the author's key positions on the nature of
our mind and on God; then indeed I shall explain the reservations a theologian might express about the work as a whole.*

Of the nature of the human mind

What first strikes me here is the fact that M. Descartes adopts as the
starting-point of his whole philosophy what had been previously so*

*adopted by St Augustine, a man of the keenest intellect, altogether
remarkable not only in his theological insights but in his philosophical
insights as well. For in book II, chapter 3 of 'On Free Choice', where*
198 *Alypius is arguing with Evodius, and is about to prove the existence of
God, he says,* I would first of all ask you, so that we may start with
what is supremely evident, whether you yourself exist, or whether
you perhaps fear that you may be deceived even as to this point,
although in fact, if you did not exist, you could not be deceived at
all?* *This is very like what our author says:* But there is some deceiver
or other, supremely powerful and cunning, who is deliberately
deceiving me all the time.—Beyond doubt then, I also exist, if he is
deceiving me (p. 18). *But let us go on, and, what is more relevant, let us
see how from this principle it can be deduced that our mind is separate
from the body.*

*I can doubt whether I have a body, and indeed whether any bodies exist
at all. But it is not possible for me to doubt that I am, or exist, as long as
I am doubting, or thinking.*

*I therefore who doubt and think, am not a body; otherwise, in doubt-
ing the existence of bodies, I would be doubting that of myself.*

*Indeed, even if I obstinately insist that no bodies exist at all, this
position nonetheless remains: I am something, therefore I am not a
body.*

*This is extremely subtle, but someone might raise the same objection as
the author puts to himself: the fact that I doubt the existence of the body,
or deny that the body exists, does not prove that the body does not exist.
For he says:* But all the same it is perhaps still the case, that these very
things I am supposing to be nothing, are nevertheless not distinct
from this 'me' that I know.—Perhaps: I don't know. But this is not
the point at issue at present. I can pass judgement only on those
things that are known to me. I have realized that I exist; I am trying
to find out what this 'I' is, whose existence I have realized. It is
absolutely certain that the knowledge of this 'me', in the precise
sense in question here, does not depend on things of which I do not
yet know whether they exist (p. 20).

199   *But since he himself admits that the argument put forward in the
'Discourse on the Method', enables us only to conclude that whatever is
bodily is excluded from the nature of the mind,* not from the point of
view of the actual truth of the matter (with which in fact I was
not then concerned), but solely from the point of view of my own

perception, so that my meaning was that I was aware of nothing at all that I knew to belong to my essence, except the fact that I was a thinking thing, *it appears from this answer that the argument is still stuck at this same point and therefore that the question remains unanswered that he promised he would solve* (how, from the fact that [he] know[s] nothing else as belonging to [his] essence, it follows that nothing else in fact belongs to it).* *If he has provided this solution, I have been unable (such is my slow-wittedness) to find it anywhere in the Second Meditation. But, as far as I can guess, he tackles the proof of this proposition in the Sixth Meditation, because he judged that it depends on a clear knowledge of God, which he had not yet obtained in the Second Meditation.* *This is how he proves it:* Since I know that whatever I clearly and distinctly understand can be produced by God such as I understand it to be, then if I can clearly and distinctly understand one thing without another, this is sufficient for me to be certain that the one is distinct from the other, since they can at least be produced separately by God. By what power this separation comes about makes no difference to the judgement that the things are distinct. [. . .] Because, on the one hand, I have a clear and distinct idea of myself, in so far as I am a thinking and not an extended thing, and, on the other hand, a distinct idea of the body, in so far as it is only an extended and not a thinking thing, it is certain that I am really distinct from my body, and can exist without it (p. 55).

200

We must linger a little over this point, since, to my mind, the whole difficulty turns on these few words. First of all, indeed, for this syllogism to be true, the major premise *must be understood to apply not to any knowledge, not even to all clear and distinct knowledge, but only to adequate knowledge of the thing. For M. Descartes admits, in his 'First Replies', that only a formal, not a real distinction is required, for one thing to be distinctly conceived as separate from another by an act of abstraction on the part of the understanding conceiving the thing inadequately. Hence he adds in the same place:* On the other hand I have a complete understanding of what body is, by thinking of it purely as having extension, shape, motion, and so forth, and by denying that it has any of the properties that belong to the nature of mind. And on the other hand I understand the mind to be a complete thing, which doubts, understands, wills, and so forth, although I deny that there is anything in it that is contained in the idea of body. Therefore there is a real distinction between the mind and the body (p. 84).*

But in case someone were to question this minor premise, and maintain that your conception of yourself is only an inadequate one, when you conceive yourself* as a thinking and not extended thing, and likewise when you conceive yourself* as an extended, not a thinking, thing, we must see how your position is proved earlier in the work. For I do not think that the issue is so clear that your position has to be assumed as an indemonstrable principle, instead of being proved. And indeed, as far as the first part of the passage goes, that is, when you say that you have a complete

201 understanding of what body is, by thinking of it purely as having extension, shape, motion, and so forth, and by denying that it has any of the properties that belong to the nature of mind, *this is not particularly helpful. For someone claiming that our mind is bodily, would not therefore think that all bodies are mind. They would see the body as standing in the same relationship to the mind, as the genus to the species.* But the genus can be understood without the species, even when we deny of the genus whatever is specific and particular to the species. Hence the logicians' maxim: 'The denial of the species does not entail the denial of the genus.' Thus I can understand shape without understanding any of the attributes that are specific to the circle. It therefore remains to be proved that the mind can be understood completely and adequately without the body.*

I cannot anywhere in the work find an argument capable of proving this, except the one I referred to at the beginning: I can deny that any body, any extended thing, exists, and yet I know for certain that I exist, as long as I deny this, or as long as I am thinking; I am therefore a thinking thing, not a body, and the body does not belong to my knowledge of myself.* *And from this I can see only that it can be inferred that some knowledge of myself can be obtained without the knowledge of the body; but that this knowledge is complete and adequate, so that I can be certain that I am not deceived in excluding the body from my essence—of that I am not yet so clear. I shall make the point clear by an example.*

Let us suppose that someone knows for certain that an angle in a semicircle is a right angle, and hence that a triangle formed from this angle and the diameter of the circle is a right-angled triangle; but that he doubts, and does not yet grasp with certainty (perhaps indeed, deceived by some sophism, he denies) that the square of its base is equal to the squares of the other two sides. Reasoning in the same way as M. Descartes has put forward, it seems he will confirm himself in his incorrect belief. 'While I

clearly and distinctly perceive', he says, 'that this triangle is right-angled,   202
I doubt, on the other hand, whether the square of its base is equal to the
square of the sides. It does not therefore belong to the essence of the tri-
angle that the square of its base should be equal to the square of the sides.

Then, even if I deny that the square of its base is equal to the square of
the other two sides, I still remain certain that it is a right-angled triangle,
and the knowledge remains clear and distinct in my mind that one of its
angles is a right angle; and this being so, not God himself can bring it
about that it is not a right-angled triangle.

Therefore the property about which I doubt, or that can be denied while
leaving the idea intact, does not belong to its essence.

Besides, since I know that whatever I clearly and distinctly understand can be produced by God such as I understand it to be, then if
I can clearly and distinctly understand one thing without another, this
is sufficient for me to be certain that the one is distinct from the other,
since they can at least be produced separately by God. *But I clearly and*
distinctly understand that this triangle is right-angled, even though I do
not understand whether the square of its base is equal to the square of the
other two sides. Therefore God can at least produce a right-angled triangle,
the square of the base of which is not equal to the square of the sides.'

I cannot see how this man can be answered, except by saying that he
does not clearly and distinctly perceive a right-angled triangle. But how
do I know I have a clearer perception of the nature of my mind than he has
of the nature of a triangle? For he is as certain that a triangle in a semi-
circle has one right angle, which is the concept of a right-angled triangle,
as I am that I exist, from the fact that I think.

Therefore just as he is deceived inasmuch as he thinks that it does not
belong to the nature of this triangle, which he clearly and distinctly knows
is right-angled, that the square of its base should be equal to the sum of the   203
squares of the other two sides; so likewise why should I not be deceived
inasmuch as I think that nothing belongs to my nature, which I clearly
and distinctly know to be that of a thinking thing, except my being a
thinking thing—when in fact perhaps it is also part of my nature to be an
extended thing?

And certainly, someone might say, it is not surprising if, when I infer
from the fact that I am thinking that I exist, the idea I form of myself,
whose existence I have thus discovered, represents nothing to my mind
except myself as a thinking thing, since it was derived purely and simply
from my thinking. Hence from this idea it seems impossible to derive any

proof that nothing belongs to the essence of myself beyond what is contained in the idea.

Moreover, this argument the author puts forward seems to prove too much, and to bring us back to the Platonic view (which he, however, rejects) that nothing bodily belongs to our essence, so that man is nothing but a soul, and the body, in fact, is nothing but the vehicle of the soul. That is why the Platonists define him as a soul using a body.

But if you reply that the body is not excluded from my essence absolutely, but only in so far as I am strictly speaking a thinking thing, then there seems to be a risk of someone's suspecting that perhaps my knowledge of myself, in so far as I am a thinking thing, is not the knowledge of a being completely and adequately conceived, but only of one conceived inadequately and by means of an act of abstraction on the part of the understanding.

Hence, just as geometers conceive a line as a length without breadth, and a surface as a combination of length and breadth without depth, even though there can be no length without breadth, and no breadth without depth, so someone might perhaps wonder whether every thinking thing is not also an extended thing, but one in which, alongside the properties it has in common with other extended things (having a shape, being mobile, and so forth), there is a specific faculty of thinking. This would be how it comes about that it can be apprehended, by means of an act of abstraction on the part of the intellect, as possessing only this faculty, although in fact the thinking thing possesses bodily properties as well: just as quantity can be conceived as possessing length alone, although every quantity in fact possesses breadth and depth as well.

What makes the difficulty more acute is the fact that this faculty of thinking seems to be attached to bodily organs, since it can be judged to be dormant in infants and extinct in the mad. This is the most powerful argument of those impious butchers of souls. *

So much for the real distinction between our mind and the body. But since M. Descartes has undertaken to demonstrate the immortality of souls, it is a fair question whether it clearly follows from the fact of this separation. It does not follow at all according to the principles of the established philosophy, since the souls of animals are commonly held to be distinct from their bodies, even though they perish along with them.

I had got to this stage in my answer, and was minded to show how, according to our author's principles, which I thought I could infer from his method of philosophizing, we could readily deduce, from the real distinction between mind and body, that the mind is immortal, when I received a synopsis of the six Meditations by the author himself, which both throws a good deal of light on the work as a whole, and in this context directs exactly the same arguments towards the solution of the question proposed as I myself had been meaning to put forward.

As far as the souls of animals are concerned, he implies quite clearly in 205 *other parts of his work that they have no soul, but only a body configured in a certain way, and endowed with various organs disposed in such a manner that all the activities we see can be accomplished in and through this body.*

But I rather doubt whether this view can carry conviction in readers' minds, unless it is confirmed by extremely solid reasons. For at first sight it appears impossible to believe that in some way, without any involvement of a soul, the light reflected from the body of a wolf onto the eyes of a sheep moves the minute filaments of the optic nerves, and the transmission of this motion to the brain causes the animal spirits* to be dispatched to the nerves in the manner necessary to cause the sheep to take flight.

One thing here I shall add, that I warmly approve M. Descartes's distinction between imagination and thought or understanding, as well as his view that what we grasp by reason is more certain than what presents itself to the bodily senses. For I learned a long time ago from St Augustine ('On the Quantity of the Soul', ch. XV),* that we should have nothing to do with those who convince themselves that the things we perceive by our understanding are less certain than those we perceive by the eyes, which are waging a constant war against rheum. *This is why he also says ('Soliloquies', I. 4)* that he had found the senses, in geometry, to be like a ship*: for when, *he says,* they had carried me to the place for which I was heading, where I took my leave of them, and, now on my own, began to go over these matters with the aid of thought alone, for a long time my legs were unsteady; which is why it seems to me that it is easier to sail on land than to perceive geometrical truths by means of the senses, although they seem to be of some help when we are beginners in that science.

Of God   206

The author's first demonstration of the existence of God, in the Third Meditation, has two parts. First, it shows that God exists, if in fact I have an idea of him; secondly, it shows that I who have such an idea could not exist unless my existence were derived from God.

As to the first part, there is only one thing I cannot agree with: that although M. Descartes has asserted that falsity, strictly speaking, can be found only in judgements, *he nonetheless shortly afterwards admits that* ideas can be false, not formally, but materially, *which seems to me to clash with his own principles* (p. 31).

But I am afraid that in so obscure a matter as this, I may not be able to explain what I mean sufficiently clearly. An example will help. If, our author says, it is true that cold is nothing other than the privation of heat, the idea that represents it to me as something real and positive will be materially false (p. 31).

However, if cold is only a privation, there can be no idea of cold that represents it to me as something positive, and our author is here confusing ideas and judgements.

For what is the idea of cold? Cold itself, in so far as it exists objectively in the intellect. But if cold is a privation, it cannot exist in the intellect through an idea the objective being of which is something positive. Therefore if cold is only a privation, there can never be any positive idea of it, and consequently none that is materially false.

This is confirmed by the same argument by which M. Descartes proves that the idea of an infinite being cannot not be a true idea; for although it can be imagined that no such being exists, it cannot be imagined that its idea represents nothing real to me.

The same can certainly be said of every positive idea. For although it can be imagined that cold, which I suppose to be represented by a positive idea, is not a positive reality, it cannot be imagined that a positive idea represents nothing real and positive to me; for an idea is not called positive in virtue of the existence it possesses as a mode of thinking, but in virtue of the objective existence it contains and represents to our mind. Therefore this idea may not be the idea of cold, but it cannot be false.

But, you will say, the idea is false, precisely because it is not the idea of cold. No: your judgement will be false, if you judge it to be the idea of cold; but the idea itself in you is quite true. Likewise, the idea of God should not be said to be even materially false, although someone can attach it to a thing that is not God, as the idolaters did.

Finally, what does this idea of cold, which you say is materially false, represent to your mind? A privation? Then it is true. A positive entity? Then it is not the idea of cold. And besides, what is the cause of this positive objective being, that, according to you, makes the idea materially false? Myself, *you say,* in so far as I derive from nothing. *Therefore the positive and objective existence of some idea can derive from nothing—which runs counter to M. Descartes's fundamental principles.*

But let us go on to the later part of the demonstration, in which the question is whether I myself, having the idea of an infinite being, can exist from any other cause than an infinite being, and especially whether I can exist of myself (p. 48). *M. Descartes contends that* 208 *I cannot exist of myself, for this reason, that* if I myself gave myself being, I would also give myself all the perfections the ideas of which I am aware of within myself (p. 48). *But the theologian* replies, acutely, that* 'existing of oneself' should be taken not in a positive sense, but in a negative sense, as equivalent to 'not deriving one's existence from any other being' (p. 75). For now indeed, *he says*, if something exists of itself, that is, does not derive its existence from any other being, how could I prove that it contains all attributes in itself and is an infinite being? I will not be satisfied if you say 'Being of itself, it would have easily given itself all these attributes'; for it does not derive its existence from itself as from a cause, nor did it exist before itself, to choose beforehand what it should afterwards be (p. 75).

To refute this argument, M. Descartes contends that 'existing of oneself' should be taken not in a negative but in a positive sense, *and this even where God is concerned; so that God* in a certain sense stands in the same relationship to himself as the efficient cause stands to its effect. *This certainly comes across to me as audacious, indeed as false.*

Therefore I partly agree with M. Descartes, and partly disagree. I confess that I myself could exist of myself only in a positive sense: but I deny that we should say the same of God. Indeed I think the idea of something existing of itself in the positive sense, as if it were caused by itself, is a manifest contradiction. Therefore I reach the same conclusion as our author, but by a quite different path, as follows:

In order to exist of myself, I would have to exist of myself in the posi- 209 tive sense, *and as if I were the effect of myself as a cause. Therefore it cannot be the case that I exist of myself.*

The major premise of this syllogism is proved by the reasons given by our author: namely, that since the parts of time can be separated from one another, it does not follow, from the fact that I exist now, that I shall exist at any future time, unless some cause produces me afresh, so to speak, at each separate moment (p. 35).

As for the minor, that is, 'I cannot exist of myself positively and as if I were the effect of myself as a cause', I think it is so clear by the natural light that it would be a waste of time to try to prove it, which could only mean proving the known by the less well known. Indeed our author seems to recognize its truth, since he did not dare to challenge it openly. For I suggest we should consider these words from his reply to the First Objections:

I did not say that it is impossible that something should be the efficient cause of itself; for even if this is plainly true if the meaning of 'efficient cause' is limited to those causes that precede their effects in time, or that are distinct from them, this limitation does not seem appropriate as regards the present issue [. . .] because the natural light does not dictate that it is of the essence of an efficient cause that it should precede its effect in time (AT 7. 108). *Quite right, as regards the first part of the statement. But why does the latter part fail to add that the same natural light does not dictate that it is of the essence of an efficient cause that it should be distinct from its effect? Is it not because the natural light does not in fact allow us to assert this?**

And surely, since all effects depend upon a cause, and receive their existence from that cause, is it not clear that one and the same being cannot
210 *depend on itself, or receive its existence from itself?*

Besides, every cause is the cause of an effect, and the effect the effect of a cause, so that there is a mutual relationship between the cause and effect. But a mutual relationship requires two parties.

Besides, it would be absurd to conceive that a thing receives existence, and yet also possesses it, before we conceive it to have received it. But this would be the case, if we applied the notions of cause and effect to one and the same thing with respect to itself. For what is the notion of a cause? To give existence. And of an effect? To receive existence. Moreover, the notion of cause is prior in nature to that of effect.

Again, we cannot conceive any thing as a cause giving existence, unless we conceive it as having existence; for no one can give what he does not have. Therefore we first conceive the thing as having existence, before we conceive it as receiving existence; and yet, in the being that receives, receiving comes before having.

This reason could be formulated in another way. No one gives what he does not have. Therefore no one can give himself existence, unless he has this existence already; but if he has it already, what would be the point of his giving it to himself?

Finally, he asserts that it is known by the natural light, that the distinction between conservation and creation exists purely in our thought (p. 35). *But by this same natural light it is known that nothing can create itself; therefore it cannot conserve itself either.*

Finally, moving from the general thesis to the particular thesis concerning God, the thing appears to my mind to be even clearer: that is, God cannot exist of himself in the positive sense, *but only* in the negative sense, *that is,* he does not derive his existence from any other being.

And first of all, this is clear from the reason M. Descartes alleges in order to prove that if a body exists of itself, it must so exist in the positive sense. *For he says:* The different parts of time do not depend on one another. Nor therefore, is the fact that this body is supposed to have existed up to now of itself, that is, without a cause a sufficient reason for its also existing in the future, unless there is some power within it, so to speak, reproducing it continuously (AT 7. 110).

But it is far from being true that this analysis can apply to a supremely perfect or infinite being. Rather, the contrary can be evidently deduced from contrary reasons. For it is intrinsic to the idea of the infinite that its duration should be infinite, that is to say, not confined by any limits; it is rather indivisible, permanent, existing all at once; and it is a mistake, and a mark of the imperfection of our understanding, to conceive of it as containing any 'before' or 'after'.

Hence it plainly follows that we cannot conceive the infinite Being as existing, even for a moment, without conceiving at the same time both that it has existed for ever and that it will exist for ever, as our author elsewhere maintains. Thus, it is futile to ask why it perseveres in being.

Indeed, as Augustine frequently teaches us (and, after the sacred authors, no one has spoken more worthily or more loftily of God), there is no past existence or future existence in God, but only eternal existence. Hence it appears even more clearly that it is simply absurd to ask why God perseveres in being, since this question manifestly presupposes the ideas of 'before' and 'after', 'past' and 'future', which should be excluded from the very notion of the infinite Being.

Besides, God cannot be thought to exist of himself in the positive sense, *if this means he had previously produced himself; for he would then have existed before existing. It could only mean (as the author frequently proclaims) because he actually preserves himself in being.*

But 'preservation' makes no more sense as applied to an infinite being than being produced in the first place. For what is preservation, I ask, but a certain continual reproduction of a thing? Thus all preservation presupposes an initial production; hence the very word 'continuation', like 'preservation', involves a certain potentiality. But the infinite being is the ultimate pure act without any potentiality. *

Let us then conclude that God cannot be conceived as existing of himself in the positive sense, *except on account of the imperfection of our understanding, which conceives God on the model of created things. This can be confirmed by yet another reason.*

When we seek the efficient cause of any thing, we are asking for the reason for its existence, not for its essence. For instance, if I consider a triangle, I shall investigate the efficient cause through which it has come about that this triangle exists. But it would be absurd of me to look for the efficient cause of a triangle's having three angles the sum of which is equal to two right angles. * *And if someone did ask why a triangle has three such angles, the proper answer would not be to adduce an efficient cause, but simply to point out that this is the nature of a triangle. Thus mathematicians, who do not concern themselves with the existence of their objects, never resort to efficient or final causes in their demonstrations. But it belongs no less to the essence of an infinite being that it exists, or indeed, if you like, that it perseveres in being, than it belongs to the essence of a triangle that it has three angles equal to two right angles. Thus, just as the proper answer to someone who asks why a triangle has three angles equal to two right angles is not to cite an efficient cause but to say simply that this is the eternal and unchangeable nature of a triangle; so, if someone*
213 *asks why God exists, or perseveres in being, we should not look, either in God or outside him, for an efficient cause (or for something that acts as an efficient cause, for I am arguing about things, not words): we should simply cite this single reason, that such is the nature of the supremely perfect being.*

Thus when M. Descartes says: The natural light teaches us that no thing exists of which we may not ask why it exists, or, in other words, inquire into its efficient cause; or, if it does not have an efficient cause, ask why it does not (AT 7. 108), *I reply that when someone asks why God exists, we should not answer by citing an efficient cause, but simply by saying that he does so because he is God, or the supreme Being. And if someone asks what is his efficient cause, we should answer that he does not need one. And if they go on to ask why he does not need one, we should reply 'Because he is the infinite being, whose existence is his essence'; for only things in which it is possible to distinguish their actual existence from their essence require an efficient cause.*

On this showing, what he adds in the following words cannot stand up. He says: So true is this, that even if I thought that no thing can stand in the same relation to itself as the efficient cause stands in relation to its effects, yet so far from concluding that there is some first cause, I should in turn inquire the cause of this so-called first cause; and thus I should never arrive at any ultimately first cause (AT 7. 108–9).

On the contrary, if I thought that we must look for the efficient (or quasi-efficient) cause of any thing whatever, I should always look for a cause distinct from the thing itself, since it would be entirely clear to me 214 *that nothing could in any way stand in the same relation to itself as the efficient cause stands in relation to its effect.*

I think, therefore, that our author would be well advised to consider this matter closely and carefully, for I know for certain that one could hardly find a single theologian who would not be scandalized* by the proposition that God exists of himself in the positive sense, *as if he were the cause of himself.*

I have only one final reservation: how can the author avoid arguing in a circle, when he says we know for certain that the things we clearly and distinctly perceive are true, only because God exists (p. 49)?

But we can only be certain God exists, because this is clearly and distinctly perceived by us. Therefore before we can be certain God exists, we must be certain, that whatever is clearly and distinctly perceived by us is true.*

I have forgotten to add one further point, that what M. Descartes affirms as certain, that there can be nothing in himself, in so far as he is a thinking thing, of which he is not conscious (p. 35), *seems to me to be false. By* himself, in so far as he is a thinking thing, *he means nothing other than his mind, in so far as it is distinct from his body. But who does not see that there can be many things in the mind of which the mind is not conscious? The mind of an infant in its mother's womb has the power of thinking; but it is not conscious of it. I pass over a great many similar points.*

On the points that might engage the attention of theologians

To cut short what is already a tedious disquisition, I prefer to be as brief as possible here, and merely point to the issues rather than discussing them in depth.

First of all, I am afraid that some may be scandalized by this rather
215 *free manner of philosophizing, which involves calling all things into
doubt. Indeed the author himself acknowledges in his 'Discourse on the
Method' that this path is a dangerous one for people of ordinary intelligence.* I admit, however, that he has done something to allay these fears
in his synopsis of the First Meditation.*

*Nonetheless I wonder whether this First Meditation should not be pre-
ceded by some sort of short preface, pointing out that we should doubt such
things, not for real, but only so that, by putting aside for a while those
things that leave room* for even minimal and hyperbolical doubt, *as the
author himself calls it elsewhere* (p. 63), *we may be able to find something
so firm and stable that even the most pig-headed person could not doubt it
in the slightest. For this reason I think it would be advisable to replace the
words* since I was still ignorant of the author of my existence *by* since
I was pretending to be ignorant.*

In the Fourth Meditation, Of True and False, *for many reasons
which it would be tedious to rehearse, I would strongly urge the author to
add two clarifications either to the text of the Meditation or to the Synopsis.*

*First, that when he is investigating the cause of error, his concern is
especially with the mistakes we make in judgements of true and false,
rather than in the pursuit of good and evil.*

*For since, first of all, this first issue is sufficient for the purposes and
objects of the author, and what is said here of the cause of error would be
open to grave objections,* if it were applied also to the pursuit of good and
evil, then prudence, if I am not mistaken, dictates this course; so does a
concern for the proper order of exposition, to which our author is so
devoted, which involves leaving out whatever is not relevant to the issue,*
216 *or could offer a handle to objectors. Otherwise, while the reader is wasting his time disputing over inessentials, he may be impeded from perceiving the really important points.*

*The second point to which I should like to draw the author's attention
is that when he says that we should give our assent to nothing except what
we clearly and distinctly know, this applies only to matters that belong to
scientific disciplines and fall under the judgement of the understanding,
and not to those that pertain to faith, and to the conduct of one's life; and
thus that what he is condemning is rashness in forming opinions, not the
conviction of those who believe in obedience to prudence.*

For there are three things, *as St Augustine so wisely points out ('Of
the Utility of Believing', ch. XV) that, though they are close to one*

another, must be carefully distinguished in the human mind: understanding, believing, having opinions.*

To understand, is to grasp something that reason shows us to be certainly true. *To believe*, is to think something is true, under the influence of some weighty authority, even when we cannot grasp it by reason. *Having opinions*, is thinking we know what we do not know.

Having opinions is highly shameful on two counts. First, whoever has convinced himself he knows something already cannot learn it properly (if indeed it can be learnt); secondly, rashness is in itself a sign of an ill-constituted mind.

For what we understand, therefore, we are indebted to *reason*; for what we believe, *to authority*; for the opinions we hold, to *error*. I say this so that we can understand that, when we adhere to our faith even in regard to things we do not yet understand, we cannot be accused of the rashness of those who go by their opinions.

For the people who say that we should believe only what we know are particularly anxious to escape the accusation of having opinions, which, we must admit, is a shameful and highly damaging one. But whoever carefully bears in mind the great difference between thinking one knows something and believing something, under the influence of some authority, that one understands one does not know, will certainly escape the charges of error, ignorance,* or arrogance.

Shortly afterwards, in ch. XII, he adds this:* Much evidence could be adduced to show that human society would collapse altogether if we decided to believe nothing but what we could not know for certain. *So much for Augustine.*

M. Descartes's own prudence will enable him to judge how important it is to make these distinctions, for fear the many people nowadays inclined to impiety might misuse his words in order to subvert the faith.

But what I foresee will be the major stumbling-block to theologians is this: that, according to M. Descartes's doctrines, it seems that the Church's teaching on the most holy mysteries of the altar cannot remain intact.

For we believe by faith that when the substance of bread is taken away from the eucharistic wafer, only the accidents there remain: namely, extension, shape, colour, smell, taste, and other sensible qualities. *

But M. Descartes holds that sensible qualities are nothing but various motions of tiny bodies around us, as a result of which we perceive the various impressions which we then call 'colour', 'flavour', 'smell', and so forth. This leaves shape, extension, and mobility. But the author denies

218 *that these attributes can be conceived without a substance in which to inhere, and therefore that they cannot exist without that substance. He repeats this in the First Replies* (p. 84).

Nor does he acknowledge any distinction between these attributes and the substance except a purely formal one. But this distinction does not seem to be sufficient for the things so distinguished to be separated even by the divine power.

I have no doubt that one so pious as M. Descartes will consider this matter carefully and thoroughly, and judge it worthy of his most urgent attention, lest, while intending to defend the cause of God against the impious, he should appear in any respect to have created a threat to the faith founded by God's authority, and in virtue of which he hopes to attain the immortal life of which he has undertaken to convince his readers.

218   REPLY TO THE FOURTH OBJECTIONS

Letter from the author to the Revd Father Mersenne

I could not have wished for a more perspicacious or more helpful examiner of my work than I find the person to be whose observations you have sent me. For he treats me so humanely, that I readily perceive that he favours both myself and my cause; and nonetheless he has looked so carefully into the aspects of it he attacks, and his insight is so deep, that I may hope that there is nothing in the rest of it that has escaped his eye. Besides, he has been so acute in pointing out what he has judged to be less worthy of approval, that I need not fear that anyone could think that he has concealed anything out of bias in 219 my favour. Therefore I am less troubled by his objections than I am glad that there are not more things that he objects to.

Reply to the first part, on the nature of the human mind

I shall not dwell on my gratitude to M. Arnauld* for bringing the authority of St Augustine to my support, and for formulating my arguments in such a way that he seems to be afraid that they may not appear sufficiently convincing to others.

But first of all I shall say where I begin to prove *how, from the fact that I know nothing else as belonging to my essence,* (that is, to the essence of my mind alone) *except that I am a thinking thing, it follows that nothing else in fact belongs to it* (p. 127). It is where I have proved that God exists—God, I mean, who can bring about all those things I clearly and distinctly know to be possible.

For even if, perhaps, there are many properties in me of which I am not yet aware (as, indeed, in this very place I supposed that I was not yet aware that the mind has the power to move the body, or that it is substantially united to it), nonetheless, because the properties I am aware of are sufficient for me to exist with these alone, I am certain that I could have been created by God without those other properties of which I am not aware, and therefore that these latter do not belong to the essence of the mind.

For it seems to me that none of the properties without which a given thing can exist is included in the essence of that thing; and although the mind is of the essence of a human being, it is not, however, strictly speaking, of the essence of the mind that it should be united to a human body.

But I must also say in what sense I mean that *a real distinction* 220 *cannot be inferred from the fact that one thing can be conceived without another by an act of abstraction based on the intellect's inadequate conception of the thing, but only from the fact that the thing is understood completely, or as a complete thing, in the absence of the other* (p. 127).

For I do not think that an adequate knowledge of the thing is required here, as M. Arnauld assumes; for the distinguishing feature of adequate knowledge is that it contains each and every property contained in the thing known; and therefore only God knows he has adequate* knowledge of all things.

On the other hand, even if a created intellect perhaps does have adequate knowledge of many things, it can never know it has it, except by a particular revelation from God. But for it to have an adequate knowledge of some thing, all that is required is that there should be a match between the power of knowledge possessed by the intellect and the thing itself. And this can easily come about. But for it to know that it has adequate knowledge, or that God has put nothing in the thing but what it knows to be there, its power of knowledge would have to match the infinite power of God; which is clearly impossible.

However, in order for us to know the real distinction between two things, it is not necessary that our knowledge of them should be adequate, unless we can know it to be adequate; but we can never know this, as I just pointed out; therefore it is not necessary for it to be adequate.*

Therefore, when I said, *it is not enough that one thing can be under-*
221 *stood without the other by means of an act of abstraction based on*
the intellect's inadequate conception of the thing (p. 127), I did not think
it could be inferred that we need *adequate* knowledge in order to
recognize a real distinction, only that we must not ourselves have
rendered our knowledge *inadequate* by an abstraction on the part of
the intellect.*

For there is a clear distinction between a given knowledge's being
completely adequate (something we could never know for sure without divine revelation) and its being adequate to this extent, that we
perceive it has not been rendered inadequate by an abstraction on the
part of the intellect.

In the same way, when I said that the thing must be understood
completely, I did not mean that the act of understanding itself had to
be adequate, only that the thing had to be sufficiently understood for
me to know it is complete.

I thought this was clear enough both from what comes before and
from what comes after. For I had just before drawn a distinction
between *complete* and *incomplete entities*, and I had stated that *each* of
two things between which we assert a real distinction, *must be under-*
stood as a being in itself and distinct from any other (p. 84).

Afterwards, moreover, in the same sense as I said that I *completely*
understand what a body is, I immediately added that *I also understood*
the mind to be a complete thing. That is, I was using the words 'to
understand something completely' and 'to understand it as being a
complete thing' in one and the same sense.

But here it would be only fair to ask what I mean by *a complete thing*,
and how I prove that *it is sufficient in order to establish a real distinction,*
that two things should be understood as each complete without the other.

222 My reply to the first point, is that by a *complete thing*, I mean nothing other than a substance endowed with forms or attributes
sufficient for me to recognize it as a substance.

For we do not know substances immediately, as I have elsewhere
remarked, but only because we perceive certain forms or attributes
that cannot exist without inhering in some thing; the thing in which
they inhere being what we call *Substance*.

But if subsequently we wished to strip this same substance of the
attributes on the basis of which we know it, we would destroy all our
knowledge of it; and in that case we could certainly utter various

words about it, but we would not clearly and distinctly perceive the meaning of these words.

I am well aware that certain substances are commonly called *incomplete*. But if they are called incomplete, on the grounds that they cannot exist by themselves, I must admit that there seems to me to be a contradiction between, on the one hand, their being substances, that is, things subsisting by themselves, and, on the other, incomplete, that is, not capable of subsisting by themselves.* However, they can be called incomplete substances in another sense. That is, in so far as they are substances, they have nothing incomplete about them; they are incomplete, purely in so far as they are related to some other substance, with which they compose what is a single entity in itself.

Thus a hand is an incomplete substance, when it is considered in relation to the whole body of which it is part, but a complete substance, when considered by itself. And in exactly the same way, the mind and the body are incomplete substances, when considered in relation to the human being they make up; but, considered by themselves, they are complete.

For in the same way as being extended, being divisible, having a shape, and so forth, are forms or attributes on the basis of which I recognize the substance known as *body*, so understanding, willing, doubting, and so forth are forms on the basis of which I recognize the substance known as *mind*; and I understand that the thinking substance is a complete thing just as clearly as I understand this of the extended substance. 223

And it is impossible to maintain what M. Arnauld adds here, that *perhaps the body stands in the same relationship to the mind, as the genus to the species* (p. 128); for even if the genus can be understood without this or that specific difference, the species cannot in any way be thought without the genus.

For example, we can easily understand the notion of shape, without thinking at all about a circle (although this act of understanding is not distinct, unless it is linked to some specific shape; nor does it relate to a complete thing, unless it also includes bodily nature).* But we cannot understand any specific property of the circle, without also thinking of shape.

But the mind can be perceived distinctly and completely, or at least sufficiently so to be considered a complete thing, without any of those forms or attributes on the basis of which we recognize that body is a substance, as I think I showed sufficiently clearly in the Second Meditation; and the body is understood distinctly and as a complete thing, without those attributes that pertain to the mind.

Here, however, M. Arnauld goes further, arguing that *even if some knowledge of myself can be obtained without the knowledge of the body, it does not therefore follow that this knowledge is complete and adequate, so that I can be certain that I am not deceived in excluding the body from* 224 *my essence* (p. 128). And he makes his point clear by the example of a triangle inscribed in a semicircle, which we can clearly and distinctly understand is right-angled, even if we do not know, or even if we deny, that the square of its base is equal to the sum of the squares of the sides. Yet from that it would not be legitimate to infer that a triangle can exist without the square of its base equalling the sum of the squares of the sides.

But this example differs in many respects from the point at issue.

For, first of all, although perhaps we could accept that in the concrete* a triangle is a substance having a triangular shape, certainly the property of having a base of which the square is equal to the sum of the squares of the sides, is not a substance. Hence neither of the two properties can be understood as a complete thing, in the way in which mind and body are understood. Nor indeed can they be called 'things', in the sense in which I used the word 'thing' when saying that *it is sufficient that I can understand one thing* (that is, a complete thing) *without the other* (p. 55). This becomes clear in the words that follow: *Moreover, I find in myself faculties*, etc. (p. 56). For I did not say that those faculties were things, but took care to distinguish them from things or substances.*

Secondly, although we can clearly and distinctly understand that the triangle in the semicircle is right-angled, without realizing that the square of its base is equal to the sum of the squares of the sides, we cannot, however, in the same way, clearly understand a triangle 225 the square of the base of which is equal to the sum of the sides, without at the same time realizing that it is right-angled. Yet we clearly and distinctly perceive both the mind without the body, and the body without the mind.

Thirdly, even if it were possible for there to be a concept of a triangle inscribed in a semicircle that did not contain the equality of the square of the base and the sum of the squares of the sides, there could never be such a concept in which the triangle was understood without a certain proportion between the square of the base and the sum of the squares of the sides. And hence, as long as we do not know what the proportion is, we cannot rule out any particular proportion, unless we clearly understand that it does not belong to the triangle; and this could never be the case as regards the proportion of equality. But certainly nothing is contained in the concept of body that belongs to the mind, and nothing in the concept of the mind that belongs to the body.

Therefore, although I said, *it is sufficient for me to be able clearly and distinctly to understand one thing without another*, it would not be legitimate to formulate the minor premise *that I clearly and distinctly understand that this triangle is right-angled, even though I doubt or deny that the square of the base is equal to the sum of the other two sides* (pp. 128–9). First, because the proportion between the square of the base and the squares of the sides is not a complete thing. Secondly, because this proportion of equality can be clearly conceived only in a right-angled triangle. Thirdly, because no triangle can in fact be distinctly understood, if the proportion between the squares of the sides and that of the base is denied.

But now I need to say how it is that *if I can clearly and distinctly* 226 *understand one thing without another, this is sufficient for me to be certain that the one is excluded by the other.*

Now the very notion of substance is this: that it can exist by itself, that is without the aid of any other substance; and no one has ever perceived two substances by means of two distinct concepts without judging that they are distinct in reality.

Therefore, if I were not seeking a certainty greater than the common variety, I would have been content with showing, in the Second Meditation, that the mind is understood as a subsistent thing, even though no properties at all that belong to the body are ascribed to it; and that, by the same token, the body is also understood as a subsistent thing, even though no properties at all that belong to the mind are ascribed to it. And I would have added nothing further in order to demonstrate the real distinction between mind and body, because we commonly judge that all things stand in the same relationship with respect to the truth as they stand in with respect to our perception. But the hyperbolic doubts I put forward in the First Meditation included this one, that I could not be certain that things exist in truth as we perceive them, as long as I supposed myself ignorant of the author of my being. Hence everything I wrote in the Third, Fourth, and Fifth Meditations, about God and truth, leads up to the conclusion that the mind is really distinct from the body, which I finally established in the Sixth Meditation.

227   And yet, M. Arnauld says, *I can understand a triangle inscribed in a semicircle without knowing that the square of its base is equal to the sum of the squares of the sides* (p. 129). To be sure, this triangle can indeed be understood, without our thinking about the proportion that obtains between the squares of its base and sides. But we cannot understand this proportion as needing to be denied of the triangle. As regards the mind, on the other hand, we not only understand it as existing without the body, but we also understand that we can deny of it all properties that pertain to the body. For it is of the nature of substances, that they mutually exclude one another.

What M. Arnauld goes on to say, that *it is not surprising if, when I infer from the fact that I am thinking that I exist, the idea I form of myself in this way, represents me only as a thinking thing* (p. 129), does not affect my argument. For in the same way when I examine the nature of body, I find nothing at all in it that smacks of thought. And there can be no greater proof of the distinction between two things, than the fact that, to whichever of them we turn our attention, we discover nothing at all in it that is not distinct from the other.

Nor do I see why this argument is said to *prove too much* (p. 130). For, if we are to show that one thing is really distinct from another, the least we have to be able to say is that they can be separated by the divine power. And I think I have taken sufficient care to forestall the

228   conclusion that *man is* nothing but *a soul using a body* (p. 130). For in this same Sixth Meditation in which I dealt with the distinction between mind and body, I also proved that the mind is substantially united with the body. And I advanced reasons in support of this view than which, to the best of my recollection, I have never encountered any stronger in all my reading.

Someone who calls a human being's arm a substance really distinct from the rest of the body would not therefore be denying that it belongs to the nature of a whole human being; nor does one who says that the same arm belongs to the nature of a whole human being therefore give any occasion for supposing that it cannot subsist by itself. By the same token, I do not myself think that I have proved too much, in showing that the mind can exist without the body, or too little, in saying that it is substantially united to the body, because this substantial union does not prevent our holding a clear and distinct concept of the mind alone as a complete thing. Therefore there is a great difference between this concept and that of a surface or a line (p. 130), which cannot be understood as complete things in this way, except by attributing depth to them as well as length and breadth.

Finally, the fact that the *faculty of thinking is dormant in infants, and in the mad* not indeed *extinct* but out of order (p. 130), is no reason to conclude that it is so closely attached to the organs of the body that it cannot exist without them. For from the fact that we experience that it is often impeded by them, it by no means follows that it is produced by them; which there is not even the slightest reason for thinking.

However, I do not deny that this close conjunction of the mind with the body that we constantly experience by our senses is the   229 reason why we do not realize its real distinction from the body except by attentive meditation. But, in my opinion, those who frequently go over in their minds the points made in the Second Meditation, will readily convince themselves that the mind is not distinguished from the body by a mere fiction, or an intellectual abstraction, but known as a distinct thing, because it is indeed distinct in reality.

I say nothing in reply to the points M. Arnauld has added here about the soul's immortality, because they do not affect my argument. But as for the souls of animals, even though this is not the place to go into the question, and I could add nothing to the account I gave in the fifth part of *A Discourse on the Method*,* without giving a full-scale exposition of physics, I shall not leave the matter aside altogether. The key point to grasp, to my mind, is that no motions can take place, whether in animals' bodies or ours, unless these bodies contain absolutely all the organs or instruments by means of which the same motions could also be produced in a machine. So true is this, that not even in ourselves does the mind move the external limbs directly: it only directs the animal spirits that flow from the heart through the brain into the muscles, and determines them to specific movements, since of themselves the spirits are applied with equal facility to many different actions.* Indeed, most of the movements that occur in us do not depend on the mind at all: for instance, the beating of the heart, the digestion of food, nutrition, breathing when we are asleep, and even, when we are awake, walking, singing,   230 and so forth, when these take place without the mind's attention. And when a person falling thrusts out their hands to protect their head, they certainly do this without any guidance from the reason, purely because the sight of their impending impact is transmitted as far as the brain, and sends animal spirits to the nerves, in such a way as is required to produce this movement, even without the mind's consent—just as would occur in a machine. And since we experience this for certain within ourselves, why should we be at all surprised if *the light reflected from the body of a wolf onto the eyes of a sheep* (p. 131) has the same power to produce the motion of flight in the sheep?

Now indeed, if we wish to use reason in order to distinguish whether some of the motions of animals are like those that are performed in us with the help of the mind, or only like those that depend on the flow of animal spirits and the disposition of our organs, we have to consider the differences that are found between the two kinds of movement. I explained these in the fifth part of the *Discourse on Method*, and I do not think any others are to be found. It will then readily appear that all actions performed by animals are like only those that occur in us without any help from the mind. By this we are forced to conclude that we know no source of movement in them, besides the disposition of their organs and the continuous flows of animal spirits that are produced by the heat of the heart, which thins out the blood. At the same time, we shall realize that nothing previously gave us any reason to imagine any other source of movement in them except this: that, failing to distinguish these two 231 sources of movement, when we observed that the first source, which depends purely on the animal spirits and the organs, is found in animals as well as in ourselves, we unthinkingly decided that the other source, which involves mind and thought, was also in them. And certainly the convictions we have thus formed in our early years, however clearly they are later shown by arguments to be false, are not easily uprooted from our opinions, unless we give prolonged and repeated consideration to these arguments.

Reply to the other part, Of God

Up to now, I have sought to refute the arguments of M. Arnauld, and to stand up against his attack. But from now on, like one faced with a stronger opponent, I will not fight back against him, but rather seek to evade his blows.

There are only three points at issue in this part, and they can readily be conceded, in the sense in which he understands them. But I intended my words to bear another sense, which also seems to me to be true.

The first point is that *certain ideas are materially false* (p. 132): by which I mean, that they are such as offer the judgement material for error. But he, considering ideas in the formal sense, holds that there can be no falsity in them.

The second is that God exists of himself, *positively and as if he were the cause of himself* (p. 133). Here, I meant only this: that the reason why God requires no efficient cause for his existence is founded on a positive reality, namely, God's immensity, than which nothing can 232 be more positive. But he proves that God is not produced by himself or conserved by some positive influence on the part of an efficient cause. To this I completely subscribe.

The third and last is that *nothing can be in our minds of which we are not conscious* (p. 137). I meant this to apply to the mind's operations; he denies it applies to its faculties.

But I shall go into these points more carefully one by one. First, where he says, *if cold is only a privation, there can be no idea that represents it to me as something positive* (p. 132), it is clear that he is talking only of ideas in the *formal* sense. For since ideas themselves are certain forms, and are composed of nothing material, whenever they are considered as representations of something, they are being taken not in the *material* but in the *formal* sense. But if they were considered not as representing this or that, but simply in so far as they are operations of the intellect, it could indeed be said that they are being taken in the material sense. But in this case the truth or falsity of their objects would not come into consideration. I do not therefore think that they can be said to be materially false in any sense other than that I have explained. For whether cold is a positive thing or a privation does not affect my idea of it, but the idea remains in me, the same as it has always been.* And I say that this idea offers me material for error, if indeed cold is a privation and does not possess so much reality as heat; because, when I consider the ideas both of cold and of heat in so far as I have received them both from the senses, I am not aware of one as representing a greater degree of reality to me than the other. 233

Nor indeed did I *confuse ideas and judgements* (p. 132). For I said that *material* falsity could be found in the former, but only *formal* falsity in the latter.

When, however, M. Arnauld states that *the idea of cold is cold itself, in so far as it exists objectively in the intellect* (p. 132), I think a distinction needs to be drawn. It often happens with obscure and confused ideas, among which those of heat and cold should be counted, that we refer them to something other than that of which they are really the idea. Thus, if cold is only a privation, the idea of cold is not cold itself, in so far as it exists objectively in the intellect, but something else for which this privation is mistaken. In fact, it is a certain sensation having no existence outside the intellect.

But this cannot apply to the idea of God, at least not to the clear and distinct idea of him, because it cannot be said to be referring to something to which it does not conform. But, as regards the confused ideas of the gods imagined by idolaters, I do not see why they too cannot be considered materially false, inasmuch as they provide the material for their false judgements about them. Although, to be sure, it seems that those ideas that give no or very little occasion to the judgement to fall into error, are not so validly termed materially false as those that give great occasion; for that some give greater occasion than others, it is easy to show by giving examples. For the occasion is less in the case of confused ideas produced by the imagination at the whim of the mind (such as the ideas of false gods) than it is in the case of the confused ideas arising from the senses, like the ideas of colour and cold—if, that is, it is true, as I have said, that they represent nothing real. But the occasion is greatest in the case of the ideas that arise from the sensitive appetite. For example the idea of thirst in a person suffering from dropsy really does offer him material for error—does it not?—when it gives him occasion to judge that drink would do him good, when in fact it would be bad for him.

But M. Arnauld asks what is represented to me by the idea of cold that I have claimed to be materially false. *For if*, he says, *it represents a privation, then it is true; if it represents a positive entity, then it is not the idea of cold* (p. 132). Well and good: but I call it materially false purely for this reason: that, since it is obscure and confused, I cannot discern whether it is representing to me some positive entity existing outside my senses, or not. Therefore it gives me an occasion to judge that there is a positive entity out there, although perhaps in fact there is only a privation.

Nor, therefore, is there any reason to ask the question *what is the cause of this positive objective being, that according to me makes the idea materially false* (p. 132)? Because I do not say that its material falsity is caused by some positive entity, but only by the obscurity that does, however, have some positive being as its subject, namely, the faculty of sensation itself.

And indeed this positive being exists in me, in so far as I am myself a true thing. But the obscurity, which alone gives me occasion to judge that this idea of the sensation of cold represents some object 235 existing outside myself, and called 'coldness', has no real cause, but arises purely from the fact that my nature is not perfect in all respects.

Nor does this at all affect my fundamental principles. But I would be inclined to fear that, since I have never devoted very much of my time to reading books by philosophers, I was failing to follow their customary manner of speaking, when I called ideas that offer the judgement material for error 'materially false', were it not for the fact that I find the word used in the same sense by the first author whose work I dipped into to check this: namely, Francisco Suárez,* in his *Metaphysical Disputations*, IX. ii. 4.

But let us proceed to the point M. Arnauld finds especial fault with, even though to me it seems the least open to criticism, I mean, when I said that *it is legitimate for us to think of God as standing in a certain sense in the same relationship to himself as the efficient cause stands to its effect* (p. 133). For in these very words I denied what M. Arnauld finds *audacious* and *false*: that is, that God is the efficient cause of himself, because when I said that *in a certain sense he stands in the same relationship* I was making clear that I did not think the relationship was exactly the same. And by putting at the beginning the words *it is altogether legitimate for us to think*, I was making clear that I was explaining the matter in this way only on account of the imperfection of the human intellect. And I confirmed this throughout the rest of the text. For immediately at the start of the discussion, when I say that *nothing exists into the efficient cause of which we cannot inquire*, I added, *or, if it has no efficient cause, we can ask why it does not* 236 *need one* (AT 7. 108). These words make it plain enough that I thought something does exist that needs no efficient cause. But what could that something be, if not God? I said, shortly after, that *in God there is so much and such inexhaustible power that he neither needed the help of any other being in order to exist, nor needs any now in order to be preserved, and thus he is, in a certain sense, the cause of himself* (AT 7. 109). Here the expression *cause of himself* is by no means to be taken as meaning 'efficient cause': it means simply that the inexhaustible power of God is the cause or reason why he requires no cause. And since this inexhaustible power, or the immensity of his essence, is as *positive* as anything could be, this is why I said that there is a *positive* reason or cause why God does not need a cause. But the same could not be said of any finite being, however perfect in its own kind. If such a being were said to exist 'of itself', this could only be in the *negative* sense since no reason deriving from its positive nature could be adduced to explain why it needed no efficient cause.

In the same way, whenever elsewhere in my work I have put forward this comparison between the formal cause, or the reason derived from God's essence on account of which he needs no cause to exist or to be preserved, and the efficient cause without which finite things cannot exist, I have always done so in such words as will make quite clear that I regard the formal cause as different from the efficient cause.* And I have never anywhere said that God preserves himself in being by some positive influence, in the way that created things are preserved by him in being, but only that the immensity of his power, or essence, on account of which he needs no preserver, is a positive thing.

Therefore I can wholeheartedly accept all M. Arnauld says in proving that God is not the efficient cause of himself, and that he does not preserve himself by any positive influence or by continually reproducing himself. This, but this only, he proves by his arguments. But I hope he will not disagree that the immensity of the divine power, on account of which God needs no cause for his existence, is a *positive* reality in him; and that there is nothing *positive* of this kind that we can attribute to any other thing, in virtue of which it would need no efficient cause for its existence. This is all I meant, when I said that nothing can be understood as existing *of itself* save *in the negative sense*, apart from God himself. Nor did I need to give any further explanation in order to resolve the difficulty that has been here raised.

But since M. Arnauld here warns me so seriously that *one could hardly find a single theologian who would not be scandalized by the proposition that God exists of himself in the positive sense, as if he were the cause of himself* (p. 137), I will explain in somewhat more detail why it seems to me that this way of putting it is so helpful, and even so necessary, when discussing this question; and why there is not the slightest reason for scandal.

I know that Latin theologians do not use the word *cause* when talking about God, when they are dealing with the procession of the persons of the Most Holy Trinity, and that, where the Greeks used the words 'cause' (*aition*) and 'principle' (*archên*) with equal readiness, the Latins prefer to use only the word 'principle', as being the most general term.* This they do so as not to give anyone occasion for 238 thinking the Son is inferior to the Father. But where there can be no such risk of error, and we are dealing with God not as a Trinity, but simply as a unity, I cannot see why the word 'cause' is so much to be avoided, especially in a context where it seems both very helpful and virtually necessary to use it.

But the word could not possibly be more helpful than in the demonstration of the existence of God; or more necessary, if, without it, the demonstration could not be made clear.

And that the consideration of the efficient cause is the first and most important means, if not the only means, we have of proving the existence of God*—this, I think, is obvious to everyone. But we cannot follow it through with the proper care unless we give our minds permission to investigate the efficient cause of all things, even God himself. For why should we make an exception of God, if we have not yet proved he exists? Therefore we must ask of every thing, whether it exists *of itself* or *from another being*; and in fact by this means we can conclude that God exists, even without making explicit what it means for something to exist *of itself*. For everyone who follows the guidance of the natural light alone, will at this point spontaneously form for themselves a concept covering both the formal and the efficient cause, according to which what exists *from another being* exists through the other being's activity as an efficient cause; whereas, on the other hand, what exists *of itself*, exists in virtue of a formal cause, that is, because its essence is such that it requires no efficient cause. I did not therefore make this explicit in my Meditations, 239 but passed over it as something known directly.

But when those who are accustomed to judge that nothing can be the efficient cause of itself, and to draw a careful distinction between the efficient and the formal cause, find someone investigating whether anything exists *of itself*, it can easily happen, that, thinking only of the efficient cause in the strict sense, they suppose that the expression *to exist of oneself* should not be understood as meaning *to exist on account of a cause*, but only *in the negative sense*, as meaning *to exist without a cause*; so that they think that something exists of which we are not supposed to inquire why it exists.* But if this interpretation of the expression *to exist of oneself* were allowed, we would be unable to resort to any causal argument for the existence of God, as has been proved by the author of the First Objections. Therefore the interpretation must be disallowed.*

But to reply to it appropriately, I think it necessary to show that between the *efficient cause* in the strict sense and the *absence of cause*, there is an intermediate term, namely the *positive essence of a thing*. The concept of the efficient cause can be extended to include this in the same way as in geometry we customarily extend the concept of a circular line as great as we can imagine so that it coincides with the concept of a straight line, or the concept of a straight-sided polygon with an indefinite number of sides, so that it coincides with the concept of a circle. I do not think that this can be better explained in any other way than I myself explained it when I said

240 *the sense of the term 'efficient cause' should not in this context be restricted to those causes that exist before their effects in time, or that are different from them; first, because this would be superfluous since everybody knows that one and the same thing cannot be prior to itself in time, or different from itself; secondly, because one of these conditions can be removed from the concept, with the notion of an efficient cause nonetheless remaining intact* (AT 7. 108).

That temporal priority is not essential to it is apparent from the fact that something enjoys the status of a cause only for so long as it is producing its effect, as has already been pointed out.

But from the fact that the other condition cannot also be removed, we must infer only that this [*sc.* the essence of a thing] is not an efficient cause in the strict sense; which I agree is true. But we cannot conclude that it is in no way a positive cause, capable of being compared by analogy to an efficient cause. And this is all that is required for this purpose. For by the same natural light by which I perceive that I would have given myself all the perfections of which I have some idea in myself, if I had actually given myself existence, I perceive that nothing can give itself existence in the way we mean when using the term 'efficient cause' in the strict sense it usually bears. For otherwise one and the same being, in so far as it gives itself being, would be different from itself, in so far as it receives it. But same and not-same, or different, are contradictories.

Therefore when we are asking if anything can give itself existence, we should understand this as equivalent to asking whether there is any thing of which the nature or essence is such, that it does not need an efficient cause in order to exist.

And when we add, *if there is something of this kind, it would give itself all the perfections of which there is some idea in itself, if indeed it does not possess them yet* (p. 133), what is meant is that it has to be the case that it possesses in actuality all the perfections it knows, because 241 we perceive by the natural light that a being whose essence is so immense that it requires no efficient cause in order to exist, does not need one either in order to possess all the perfections it knows, and that its own essence gives it, in eminent form, everything we can conceive as being given to other things by an efficient cause.

And the words, *if it does not yet possess them, it would give itself them*, are there simply to assist the explanation, since by the same natural light we perceive that such a being cannot now have the power and will to give itself something new, but that its essence is such that from all eternity it has possessed everything that we, now, can think it would give itself, if it did not yet have it.

Nonetheless, all these ways of speaking, derived from an analogy with efficient causality, are extremely necessary in order so to direct the natural light that we can realize all this quite clearly. This is just the same as when we find in Archimedes the demonstration of several properties of the sphere and other curvilinear figures by means of a comparison with rectilinear figures, without which these things would have been virtually impossible to grasp. And in the same way as these demonstrations are not to be criticized, even though they involve considering the sphere as a polyhedron, so I think that I am not open to criticism here, for using the analogy of efficient causality to explain properties of the formal cause, that is, the very essence of God.

Nor is there any risk of error here, since the only property specific to the efficient cause, and that we cannot predicate of the formal 242 cause, involves a blatant self-contradiction, and no one could believe it: I mean, that something could be different from itself, or at the one and the same time, the same and not the same.*

And we must note here that when we ascribe to God the dignity of being a cause we do so in such a way as not thereby to impute to him the indignity of being an effect. For, in the same way as, when theologians say that the Father is the *principle* of the Son, they do not therefore concede that the Son is therefore *principiated*; so, although I have admitted that God can in some sense be said to be *the cause of himself*, I have nowhere termed him in the same way an *effect of himself*, and this is because the effect is usually subordinated to the cause, the efficient cause especially, and is less noble than it, although often it is more noble than other causes.*

Besides when I here identify the whole essence of a thing as its formal cause, I am merely following in the footsteps of Aristotle. For in *Posterior Analytics*, II. 11, having omitted the material cause, the first cause he names is the *aitian to ti ên einai*, or, as Latin-language philosophers generally term it, the *formal cause*; and he extends the sense of this term to cover all essences of things.* This is because he is not there dealing with the causes of composite beings existing in nature (and the same is true of myself here), but more generally of the causes from which some knowledge may be sought.

But to show that in the case under discussion, it would have been difficult to refrain from applying the term 'cause' to God, there can be no better proof than this: although M. Arnauld has sought to reach the same goal as myself, but by another path, he has not at all fulfilled his aim—at least, so it seems to me. For he has shown at 243 great length that God is not the efficient cause of himself, since it is essential to the concept of an efficient cause that it should be distinct from its effect; and therefore that he does not exist of himself *in a positive sense*, meaning by this expression *on account of a positive influence exerted by a cause*; and also that he does not actually preserve himself in being, taking *preservation* here in the sense of 'the continuous production of a thing'. All of this I freely acknowledge. He goes on to argue that God should not be said to be the efficient cause of himself, *because*, he says, *when we investigate the efficient cause of any given thing, we are looking for a reason for its existence, but not at all for the reason of its essence; but it is no less of the essence of an infinite being to exist than it is of the essence of a triangle to have three angles equal to two right angles; therefore we can no more use the notion of an efficient cause to answer the question why God exists than we can to answer the question why the three angles of a triangle are equal to two right angles* (p. 136). But this syllogism could readily be turned back on him like this: even if we do not look for an efficient cause of a thing's having a certain essence, we can nonetheless look for the efficient cause of its existence;

but in God there is no distinction between essence and existence. Therefore we can look for an efficient cause in connection with God.

But to reconcile these two positions, what we should say is this: if someone is enquiring why God exists, we should not indeed reply to them by adducing an efficient cause in the strict sense, but only with reference to his very essence, or formal cause—and for the very reason that existence and essence are not distinguished from another in God, this formal cause bears a marked analogy to an efficient cause, and can therefore be termed a quasi-efficient cause.

Finally, he adds that, *if someone inquires about the efficient cause of God, we should answer that he does not need one. And if they go on to ask* 244 *why he does not need one, we should reply 'Because he is the infinite being, whose existence is his essence'; for only things in which it is possible to distinguish their actual existence from their essence require an efficient cause* (pp. 136–7). As a result, he argues that what I myself had said cannot stand up: namely, *if I thought that no thing can stand in the same relation to itself as the efficient cause stands in relation to its effects, I should never arrive at any ultimately first cause* (p. 137). But it seems to me that, so far from collapsing, my position is not in the slightest shaken or weakened. And the principal force not only of my own demonstration but of any demonstration whatever that aims to prove the existence of God by tracing effects to their cause depends on it. And in fact almost all theologians contend that no other kind of demonstration, beside the argument from effects to cause, is possible.

Therefore, so far from throwing light on the demonstration of God's existence, by refusing to allow us to think of him as standing in a relation to himself analogous to that between the efficient cause and its effect, he in fact makes it more difficult for readers to follow the argument, especially at the end, where he concludes: *if I thought that we must look for the efficient (or quasi-efficient) cause of any thing whatever, I should always look for a cause distinct from the thing itself* (p. 137). For how could those who do not yet know God investigate the efficient cause of other things in such a way that they can rise to the knowledge of God, if they did not think that we can ask for the efficient cause of every thing? And how, I ask, could they end their search at God, considered as the first cause, if they thought that the cause of any thing 245 must be looked for in something different from that thing?

What M. Arnauld has done here may, it seems to me, be explained by a comparison. Suppose that, speaking of those properties he had demonstrated to belong to the sphere by analogy with rectilinear figures inscribed within a sphere, Archimedes had said: 'If I thought that a sphere could not be considered as a rectilinear or quasi-rectilinear figure with an infinite number of sides, I would give no credence to this demonstration because it holds good not of the sphere considered as a curvilinear figure but only in so far as it is considered as a rectilinear figure with an infinite number of sides.' It is as if, reading these words, M. Arnauld, not wishing the sphere to be called by that name, and yet wishing to hang on to Archimedes's demonstration, were to say: 'If I thought that this conclusion should be understood as applying to a rectilinear figure with an infinite number of sides, I would not admit that it could be applied to the circle, because I know clearly and for a certainty that the circle is not at all a rectilinear figure.'* Now, obviously, in saying this he would not be doing the same as Archimedes: on the contrary, he would certainly be placing obstacles to his own and other people's proper understanding of the demonstration.

I have gone into this issue, perhaps, at rather more length than was necessary, in order to show that it is a major concern with me to ensure that not the slightest thing can be found in my writings with which theologians can justifiably find fault.

Finally, that I did not argue in a circle when I said that *we can be certain that what we clearly and distinctly perceive is true, only if God* 246 *exists, and we can be certain that God exists, only because we clearly perceive it* (p. 137), is already made sufficiently clear in the Second Replies, §§3–4 (p. 92), where I distinguished between what we clearly perceive in actual fact and what we remember we once clearly perceived. For first of all, we are certain that God exists, since we reflect on the reasons by which his existence is proved; but subsequently it is sufficient for us to remember that we have clearly perceived something, in order to be certain it is true; and this would not be sufficient, unless we knew that God exists and does not deceive us.

Moreover, *that there can be nothing in the mind, in so far as it is a thinking thing, of which it is not conscious* (p. 137), seems to me to be self-evident, because we understand there to be nothing in the mind, considered from this point of view, that is not a thought, or dependent on thought; for otherwise, it would not belong to the mind, inasmuch as it is a thinking thing; and there can be no thought in us of which, at the moment at which it is in us, we are not conscious.

Hence I do not doubt that the mind, as soon as it is infused into the body of an infant, begins to think, and is at the same time conscious of its thinking, even if afterwards it does not remember what it has thought, because the forms of these thoughts do not remain in the memory.

But it is important to note that whereas, as far as the acts or operations of our mind are concerned, we are always actually conscious of them, as regards its faculties or powers, this is not always true, except in potentiality. What this means is that, when we apply ourselves to make use of some faculty, we are always, if that faculty does indeed exist in the mind, actually conscious of it; and therefore we can deny   247 that it exists in the mind, if we cannot become conscious of it.*

On the points that might engage the attention of theologians

I have combated M. Arnauld's first arguments, and attempted to parry his second ones. With the arguments that follow I agree altogether, apart from the closing one, and here I hope it will not be difficult to get him to agree with me.

Therefore, that the points contained in the First Meditation, and even the rest as well, are not suitable for everyone or within the capacity of everyone's mind (p. 138), I frankly admit; and wherever the occasion has arisen, I have borne witness to this, and will do so in future. This was the only reason why I did not discuss the same points in the *Discourse on Method*, which was written in French, but held them over for these Meditations, which I have given advance warning are to be read only by the intelligent and learned.* Nor should it be said that I would have done better to refrain from writing things that a great many people should refrain from reading; for I think they are so necessary, that without them, I am convinced that nothing firm and stable can ever be established in philosophy. And although fire and iron cannot be handled by the careless or by children without danger, yet they are so useful to our lives that no one thinks that we should do without them on that account.

That in the Fourth Meditation I was discussing only *the mistakes*   248 *we make in judgements of true and false, rather than in the pursuit of good and evil* (p. 138); and that, when I have asserted that *we should give our assent to nothing except what we clearly know*, I have always made an exception for *matters that pertain to faith and to the conduct of one's life* (p. 138), is clear from the whole context of the Meditations; and

I stated it explicitly in my reply to the Second Objections, §5 (pp. 96–7). I also made this clear in advance in the Synopsis; so that I may thus bear witness to the esteem I have for M. Arnauld's judgement and to the seriousness with which I take his advice.*

There remains the sacrament of the Eucharist, with which M. Arnauld judges that my opinions are not compatible, because he says, that *we believe by faith that when the substance of bread is taken away from the eucharistic wafer, only the accidents there remain*; he thinks, however, that I *admit no real accidents, but only modes that cannot be conceived without a substance in which to inhere, and therefore that cannot exist without that substance* (pp. 139–40).

I could evade this objection very easily by pointing out that up to now I have never denied the existence of real accidents; for although I did not invoke them in the *Dioptrics* and the *Meteorology** to explain the matters I was there dealing with, I nonetheless said in so many words that I do not deny their existence. In these
249 Meditations, indeed, I supposed that they were not yet known to me, but not that they therefore did not exist; for the analytic method of composition I was following allows us to make suppositions on occasion that are not sufficiently investigated at that point. This was clear from the First Meditation, in which I made many assumptions that were subsequently refuted in later ones.* And in fact I did not want here to establish a definite position on the nature of accidents, but was only tentatively putting forward what appeared to be the case on first viewing. And finally, from the fact that I said that modes cannot be understood without some substance in which to inhere, it should not be inferred that I denied that they can be separated from that substance by the divine power, for I plainly declare and fully believe that God can do many things that we cannot understand.

But, to deal with the matter in a fashion more befitting a gentleman,* I shall not conceal my conviction that there is nothing at all by which our senses can be affected besides the surface that forms the boundaries of the body that is perceived by them. For contact takes place with the surface alone. And no sense is affected except by contact: I am not alone in saying this, but nearly all philosophers, including Aristotle himself, say the same. Thus, for example, bread or wine is not perceived, except in so far as its surface makes contact with the sense-organ, either immediately or via the medium of the air and other bodies, as I hold to be the case, or, as most philosophers would have it, via the medium of intentional species.*

But it is important to note that this surface is not to be simply equated with the bodies' external shape that we can touch with our fingers, but that we must also take into account all the tiny gaps that 250 are found among the particles of flour of which the bread is formed, and among the particles of spirit, water, vinegar and dregs or tartar of which wine is made up, and likewise between the little parts of other bodies. For certainly, since these particles have different shapes and movements, whenever they are joined together, however closely, they always leave many gaps between them, which are not vacuums, but filled with air or other matter. Thus, with the naked eye we can see that in bread there are quite sizeable gaps of this kind, which can be filled not only with air but also with water, or wine, or other liquids. Now since the bread still remains the same, even though the air or other matter contained in these pores is changed, it is clear that these do not belong to its substance as such. Therefore its surface is not the one that encloses the whole loaf of bread in a very small space, but the one that is immediately in contact with all the individual particles.

We must also note that this surface can be moved not only in its entirety, as when the whole loaf is transported from one place to another, but also in part, when some particles of the bread are agitated by the air or other bodies entering its pores. So much so, that if any bodies are of such a nature that some or all of their parts are continually in motion (which I think applies to many of the parts of the bread and all the parts of the wine), we should understand also that their surface is in a kind of continual movement.

Finally, we must note that by the surface of the bread, or the wine, or any other body, I do not here mean any part of the substance or even of the quantity of the body in question, nor even a part of the 251 surrounding bodies, but only *the boundary that is conceived as a medium term between the individual particles of the body and the bodies that surround it, and that has no existence except in a modal sense.*

Now, since contact takes place only at this boundary, and nothing is perceived except by contact, it is plain, from the simple fact that the substances of bread and wine are said to be changed into the substance of something else in such a way that this new substance is contained altogether within the same boundaries as the other substances

were contained in before, or that it exists in precisely the same place
as the bread and wine existed before (or rather, since their boundaries are in constant motion, in the same place as they would be existing if they were still present), it necessarily follows that the new
substance must affect all our senses in exactly the same way as the
bread and wine would affect them, if no transubstantiation had taken
place.

Beside the Church teaches (Council of Trent, session 13, canons 2
and 4) that *the conversion takes place of the whole substance of the bread
into the substance of the body of Our Lord Jesus Christ, the appearance
of bread remaining all the while.** Here I cannot see what can be meant
by 'the appearance of bread', apart from the surface interposed
between the individual particles it comprises and the bodies surrounding them.

For as has already been said, contact takes place only at this
surface; and as Aristotle himself concedes, not only the sense particularly called 'touch', but the other senses as well perceive by touch*
(*De anima*, III. 13).

252   And there is no one who thinks that 'appearance' here means anything other than, specifically, what is required in order for the senses
to be affected. Moreover, there is no one who believes that the bread
is converted into Christ's body, who does not think at the same time
that this body of Christ is fully contained within the same surface as
the bread would be contained within, if it were still present; even if
it is not there exactly as if it were in a place, but *in sacramental fashion, and existing in a way that, even if we can scarcely express it in words,
we can grasp, with a mind enlightened by faith, as being possible to GOD,
and that we must believe most faithfully.** All these points are so easily
and plainly explicable according to my principles, that I have no
reason here to be afraid of scandalizing orthodox theologians—on
the contrary, I trust that they will be very grateful to me, for putting
forward views in physics that are far more compatible with theology
than those that are commonly held. For certainly the Church has never
taught anywhere*—at least, to my knowledge—that the residual
appearances of bread and wine in the Sacrament of the Eucharist are
real accidents that, when the substance in which they inhered has
been removed, continue by a miracle to exist on their own.

But since, we may suppose, the first theologians who tried to
253   explain this issue in philosophical terms, were so firmly convinced

that the accidents that affect our senses were something real and distinct from the substance that they did not even realize that anyone could ever doubt it, they supposed without any examination and without good reason, that the appearance of the bread took the form of real accidents of this sort. And they were then in a position where they had to explain how these could exist without a subject. In this business they found so many difficulties that this alone should have led them to realize (like travellers when they have wandered into a rugged and trackless waste) that they had strayed from the true path.

For, first, they seem to contradict themselves (at least those who admit that all sense-perception is based on contact), when they suppose that, in order for objects to affect our senses, something more is required than their surfaces, disposed in various ways—since it is self-evident that surface is by itself sufficient for contact to take place. But if there are any who do not admit sense-perception is based on contact, they can say nothing about this question that has the slightest appearance of truth.

Finally, the human mind cannot think that the accidents of the bread are real and nonetheless that they exist without their substance, without at the same time conceiving them as if they were substances; so much so, that it seems self-contradictory to hold that the whole substance of the bread is changed, as the Church believes, and at the same time that something real, that was previously in the bread, remains; because nothing real can be understood to remain except what subsists, and although it is *called* an accident, is nonetheless conceived as a substance. Therefore in practice this is tantamount to saying that the whole substance of the bread is indeed changed, but that nonetheless the part of its substance that is called 254 a real accident remains. And if this is not self-contradictory on the level of words, it is certainly so on that of concepts.

And this seems to be a principal reason why many people have parted company with the Roman Church about this issue.* For who would deny that where our choice is free, and no theological or indeed philosophical reason compels us to embrace any particular opinion, that we should make a point of adopting those opinions that give no opportunity or pretext to others for swerving away from the truth of faith? But that the belief in real accidents does not fit well with theological considerations, I believe I have shown here pretty plainly; and that it also clashes with philosophical considerations,

I hope to prove clearly in the treatise on the principles of philosophy I am now working on.* There I shall show how colour, taste, weight, and all the other qualities that affect the senses depend only on the outermost surface of bodies.*

Finally, we cannot postulate the existence of real accidents without complicating the miracle of transubstantiation—which alone can be inferred from the words of consecration*—by the pointless addition of a further and incomprehensible miracle, in virtue of which these real accidents exist, in the absence of the substance of bread, yet without, at the same time, becoming substances themselves. But this is contrary not only to human reason, but also to an axiom of theologians, who say that these words of consecration bring about nothing but what they signify; and who are reluctant to ascribe to a miracle what can be explained by natural reasons. But all these difficulties are altogether eliminated by my explanation of the matter.

255 For, according to my explanation, no miracle is needed for the conservation of the accidents after the removal of the substance—so much so, that on the contrary they cannot be removed without a new miracle (one, that is, that would change their dimensions). There are accounts of this happening sometimes, when in the place of the consecrated wafer, living flesh or a child has appeared in the hands of the priest; but it has never been believed that this has happened by the cessation of a miracle, but by an altogether new miracle.*

Besides, there is nothing difficult or incomprehensible in God's being able—after all, he is the creator of all things—to change one substance into another, in such a way that this latter substance remains entirely within the same surface as the earlier one was contained in. Nor is there anything more in keeping with reason, or more commonly accepted among philosophers, than the doctrine that not only all sensation, but generally all action by one body upon another, takes place by means of contact, and that this contact can occur only on the surface. From this it evidently follows that one and the same surface, however much the substance underlying it is changed, must always act and be acted on in the same way.*

And therefore, if I may write this without causing offence, I venture to hope that a time will come one day, when the belief in real accidents is banished by theologians as contrary to reason, and incomprehensible, and dangerous from the point of view of faith, and my view is accepted instead, as certain and indubitable. I thought it would be wrong for me to conceal this here, so that, to the best of my ability, I may forestall the calumnies of those who, since they wish to seem more learned than other people, cannot endure anyone putting forward a view in some scientific matter that they cannot pretend they were aware of already. And often they rage against it all the more vio- 256 lently the truer and more significant they think it is; and what they cannot refute by argument, they claim, quite groundlessly that it is contrary to holy scripture and to the truths of faith. Indeed they are impious in this respect, that they wish to use the authority of the Church to overthrow the truth. But I appeal from them to pious and orthodox theologians, to whose judgements and censures I very freely submit.

FIFTH OBJECTIONS

On the First Meditation

257 *There is not much to detain me in the First Meditation: for I approve your intention of stripping every prejudice away from your mind. One thing alone I do not clearly grasp: why it is you did not think it sufficient simply and succinctly to declare your previous knowledge uncertain, so that you could subsequently pick out the beliefs that turned out to be true,*
258 *instead of declaring them all false, and thus not so much divesting your-self of an old prejudice, as espousing a new one. And note how you found it necessary, in order to convince yourself of this, to imagine a deceiving God, or some deluding evil genius, when it would have seemed sufficient to invoke the darkness of the human mind, and the mere weakness of our nature. Besides, you pretend that you are dreaming, so as to call every-thing into doubt, and consider everything that happens as a delusion. But can you really compel yourself for this reason to believe that you are not awake, and to consider whatever exists or occurs in your presence as uncer-tain and false? Whatever you say, no one will be convinced that you are convinced that nothing you have ever known is true, and that you have been perpetually deceived by your senses, or by dreams, or by God, or by an evil spirit. Would it not have been more worthy both of a philosopher's sincerity and of the love of truth, to state matters as they are, in good faith and straightforwardly, than (as one might object to you) to resort to con-trivances, go in for conjuring tricks, and follow roundabout paths? But since you decided on this approach I will contend with you no further.*

On the Second Meditation

1. [258–60] You still seem to be under a delusion, but you affirm your existence, since it is you that is deluded.* But why all the effort to estab-lish something of which you were already certain, and which could, anyway, have been inferred from any of your actions, since we know by the natural light that whatever acts, exists?

You say, seriously, that you do not sufficiently understand what you are. This is what you should have been investigating directly, instead of putting forward elaborate hypotheses.

In your examination of human nature, you ascribed nutrition, motion, sensation, and thought to the soul: but does not this call into question your distinction between soul and body? Your imagining the soul as something like a wind, or fire, or air, is a striking point, which should be borne in mind. The features you ascribed to bodies you could still ascribe to them today, though not all of them apply to all bodies, except that one cannot see how you know that bodies cannot move themselves, as if their every movement derived from an incorporeal source.

2. [260–1] You find none of the properties of a body in yourself.

At this point you are not considering yourself as a whole human being, 260 *but as an inner and secret part,* * *such as you thought the soul to be. But I ask of you, O soul,* * *or whatever it is you wish to be known as, whether you have yet corrected the view you had of yourself, when you imagined yourself like a wind or something of the kind diffused throughout your body? You certainly have not. So why could you not still be a wind, or rather a very fine vapour that is distilled by the heat of the heart from the very purest part of the blood, or from somewhere else, or produced by some other cause, and diffused through the limbs bringing them life, seeing with the eyes, hearing with the ears, thinking with the brain, and performing all the other functions that are commonly ascribed to you? If this is so, why could you not have the same shape as the body as a whole, as the air has the same shape as the vessel that contains it? Why* 261 *should we not think of you as surrounded by the same container as the body or by the body's outer skin? As occupying space, or at least the parts of space not filled by the solid body or its parts? Indeed the solid body has tiny pores, through which you yourself would be diffused, in such a way, that where your parts are, its parts are not, in the same way as, when water and wine are mixed, where there are parts of one, there are no parts of the other, although the eye cannot distinguish them.*

Why do you think the soul incapable of occupying space or of motion? How can you say in the light of this that there is nothing in you that pertains to the nature of body?

3. [261–3] You say that nutrition and motion, ascribed to the soul, do not pertain to you. But there are bodies in which nutrition does not take place, and a soul on the lines just described could be nourished by a subtle substance. Anyway, you, the soul, grow and decay with the body, and if you move the body, you must move along with it. When you say you do not have a body, you must be joking: but if you are serious, you have to prove you have no body that you inform, and that you are not the type of being that is nourished and moves.

You say you do not have sensations: but you do, and if, as you say, sensation requires a body, well, you do have one: in fact, you are possibly a subtle body, operating through the sense-organs.

You have had false sensations in dreams, without the sense-organs being involved, but you have not found all your sensations false, and you have used your sense-organs in the past.

You do certainly think, but you have to prove that no kind of body, however subtle, can think, before you can know you are not a body. You would have to prove that animals have incorporeal souls, since they can think, and that the solid body* contributes nothing to the process of thinking (though in fact you have never thought without it), if you are to show you think independently of it. In that case, you could not be affected by vapours that affect the brain.

4. [263–5] You reduce the soul, the principle of life, to the mind, whose function is purely to think. But do you mean to say that the mind is thinking continuously?* How can this apply to people in a stupor, or to a baby in the womb?

You say you are not something corporeal: an air dispersed through the body, or a wind, or fire, or vapour, or breath. Yet you admit that perhaps these things may not be distinct from you. Why do you, then, assume they are, without proof?

5. [265–6] You think you do not know yourself by means of the imagination. But if you were a body, is not that how you would know yourself? What do you encounter when you contemplate yourself, but the image of a subtle substance pervading the body or at least the brain? You say that what you can grasp by the imagination has nothing to do with your knowledge of yourself. How can you say this when you have just said you do not know whether the imagination belongs to your essence or not?

6. [266–8] To say you are a thinking thing tells us nothing new, and gives us no knowledge of the kind of substance you are, how it is united to the body, and how it works.

We cannot distinguish intellection from imagination, as if they were distinct faculties or capacities. You yourself confess that you seem to know bodies by the senses and the imagination more clearly than you know the part of yourself you claim to know without the help of the imagination— a mysterious entity the nature of which you do not know. All our knowledge is developed from what we know by the senses, and the existence of bodies outside us is just as certain as our own existence. There is nothing surprising in our knowing other things better than ourselves. The eye sees other things, but not itself.

7. [268–71] You describe yourself as a thinking thing, and define this as including sensation. But you said the opposite earlier. Perhaps you mean

that sensation begins in the sense-organs, and the mind then takes over. But since animals have sensation, don't they have thought, and therefore, on your principles, minds? Any differences between us and the animals are purely of degree. To prove yourself incorporeal, you would have to point to some thinking that does not depend on the brain. But you cannot. There is no reason to assert that sensation and passion work differently in animals and in ourselves, and they are not altogether without choice, reason, or language.

8. [271–3] You distinguish the substance of the wax from its accidents, and hold that we know the substance by the intellect, not by sensation or imagination. But everyone accepts that we can abstract the concept of the wax and its substance from the concept of its accidents. However, this does not mean that we have a clear idea of the substance beneath the accidents. Our idea of substance, such as it is, involves the imagination.

Your judging that you see people passing because you see their hats and coats is not an act of pure intellection, because a dog can make the same judgement, although you think it has no mind.

9. [273–7] You do not gain in knowledge of what you are from your knowledge of the wax: it only confirms the fact of your existence, which is not in doubt. You say you have no sense-organs, but what you say about your experience of the wax's accidents, as visible and tactile, contradicts this. The Meditation has not proved the mind is better known than the body. Knowing that you are not a bodily entity like wind or air (if we grant you know this) is merely negative knowledge. Knowing you are a thinking thing is nugatory.

For who doubts that you are a thinking thing? What is hidden from us, 276 *what we are looking for, is your inner substance, the characteristic property of which is to think. Therefore, what you should have been investigating and deciding was not that you are a thinking thing, but what kind of thing you are that thinks. If we were asking you to give us a knowledge of wine that goes beyond the common, it would not be enough for you to say wine is a liquid extracted from grapes, white or red, sweet, intoxicating, and so forth: would you not try to investigate and discover its internal substance in whatever way you could, showing it to be a combination of spirits, phlegm,* tartar,* and other parts, mixed together in the correct proportions? By the same token, since the aim is to obtain a knowledge of yourself greater than the common, greater, that is, than you have had up* 277 *to now, you surely see that it is not enough to keep harping on about being a thing that thinks, doubts, understands, and so forth; but that it is your duty to examine yourself, by some quasi-chemical procedure, so that you can both discover and reveal to us your internal substance. If you can*

*achieve this, we ourselves shall examine whether or not you are better
known than the body, which is so fully displayed by anatomy, chemistry,
and by so many other arts, so many sense-perceptions and so many observations and experiments.**

On the Third Meditation

1. [277-9] You offer clear and distinct perception as the criterion of truth.
But great minds, surely capable of clear and distinct perception, have
declared that the truth is hidden from us. As the sceptics argue, a clear and
distinct perception simply relates to how things appear to each of us.
I clearly and distinctly perceive the taste of melon to be pleasing, so it is
true it appears to me as pleasing. That does not prove the pleasant taste is
in the melon itself: melons tasted different to me when I was younger, and
different people disagree about their taste. Even of mathematics we may
clearly and distinctly perceive something, and then later clearly and distinctly perceive the opposite. Everyone thinks they clearly and distinctly
perceive their opinions to be true: some people would die for their beliefs,
though they see others ready to die for the contrary beliefs. In fact you
yourself, by your own confession, accepted things as certain and obvious
that you then came to doubt. Since you say you might be deceived about
such propositions as $2+3=5$, your criterion is useless until you have
proved that God exists and cannot be a deceiver. The rule itself could in
fact be a source of error.* What you need to provide is some way of showing us whether we are in error or not, on those occasions we think we
clearly and distinctly perceive something.

2. [279-82] You distinguish innate, adventitious, and factitious ideas. But
all ideas seem to be adventitious, derived from things existing outside the
mind, and affecting our senses. The mind has, or is, the faculty of working on these by abstraction, combination, division, and so forth. Certainly
there is no distinction between factitious and adventitious ideas: the idea
of a giant is simply an expanded idea of a human being. So-called innate
ideas are also adventitious. You place the idea of a thing in this category,
but this general idea is simply an abstraction from ideas of particular
things. You say you have an innate understanding of truth. But truth is the
conformity of a judgement to the thing to which the judgement refers. It
is a relation. So it is nothing distinct from the thing and the related idea.
The idea of truth is the idea of a thing, in so far as it conforms to the thing,
or represents it as it is. So if the idea of the thing is adventitious, so must
the idea of truth be.

   The allegedly innate idea of thought might have been formed by analogy
with other actions, like sight or taste. What you need to show is that the
idea of the mind or soul is innate.

3. [282–4] You say that you do not perceive the earth, the sky, the stars, merely ideas of them: they may not exist. If you really think that, why do you walk on the earth, raise your eyes towards the sun, and so forth? If a blind person has no idea of colour or a deaf person of sound, is this not because the external bodies cannot produce the appropriate impression on them, because the ways to their minds are blocked? You say you have two ideas of the sun, one of it as small, which derives from the senses, and a truer one of it as huge, derived from innate ideas. But they are both like the sun, only one is more like it than the other. The idea of the sun as large has been formed from the initial sensory perception (expanded to allow for distance), not from innate ideas. This is clear because a person born blind would not have it.

And in fact we cannot really form an idea of the sun that does justice to its actual size: our only real idea of the sun is the common-or-garden one deriving from the senses.

4. [284–8] We say that external objects exist formally and really in themselves, objectively and by representation in the mind. So when you speak of the objective reality of an idea, you must mean its conformity to the thing of which it is the idea,* its containing nothing, by representation, that is not in the thing.

The objective reality of an idea is not to be measured by the formal reality the thing itself contains, but by the degree of our knowledge of the thing. Thus an idea of a person based on careful and thorough examination is a perfect idea, whereas an imperfect idea is one based on a superficial and fleeting impression.

Thus we can have a distinct and adequate idea of accidents, but only a confused idea of the underlying substance. It cannot then be argued that the idea of substance contains more objective reality than the idea of its accidents, when any reality it contains comes from the ideas of the accidents themselves [dimensions, shape, colour, etc.].

Is not your idea of God as supreme, eternal, infinite, all-powerful creator simply based on what you have heard of him?

You say there is more reality in the idea of the infinite God than in the idea of a finite thing. But: [i] the human intellect is not capable of conceiving infinity, so we have no representative idea of God. 'Infinite' is a term we do not understand applied to a thing we do not understand; [ii] The perfections attributed to God are all amplified versions of things we admire in human beings. An idea representing them would have no more objective reality than that of the finite things on which it is based. God cannot be adequately represented by any idea of ours and any idea we form of him by analogy contains no reality we do not perceive in other things.

5. [288–91] You use the principle that there must be as much in the cause as in the effect to infer that there must be at least as much formal reality in the cause of the idea as there is objective reality in the idea itself. This is too great a leap.

The causal principle really applies to the material cause, not the efficient cause,* which can be of a very different nature to the effect and cannot be said to give its own reality to the effect: thus a house derives its reality from the architect, but the architect is not giving it any of his own reality.

If you have an idea of me, the cause of the reality it contains is simply myself, insofar as I emit 'species' that impact upon your eye* and so make their way to your intellect. The same applies to all external bodies: the reality contained in the idea of them derives simply from them.

You distinguish between the formal and the objective reality of an idea. The cause of the formal reality of the idea of me is simply the subtle substance emitted by me and causing your sight of me. The cause of its objective reality is simply the likeness of your idea to me, the arrangement of its parts in such a way as to create this likeness. But this is not something real, and hence standing in need of explanation, but simply a relationship between the parts of the idea and between the idea and me.

6. [291–4] You argue that if there is an idea in you of which the objective reality is so great that you cannot contain it either eminently or formally, you cannot be the cause of that idea, so something besides yourself must exist. But you are not in any case the cause of your ideas of things: the things themselves are. In any case, we do not need an argument to prove that other things beside ourselves exist.

You say there is no difficulty about your idea of yourself and that you might be the source of your idea of bodily things. In fact you have either no idea of yourself or a very confused and imperfect one, as observed apropos of the previous Meditation.

A thing cannot act on itself (the sight does not see itself, nor the intellect understand itself, and the hand cannot beat itself). For knowledge to take place the thing must act on the cognitive faculty by transmitting species of itself. But the cognitive faculty cannot get outside itself to do this. Thus knowledge of self is impossible, without some kind of mediating agent like the mirror that enables the eye to see itself: but what would this agent be? Anyway, such knowledge could never be direct, only reflexive.

How could you have an idea of God, except, as suggested above, by hearsay? The same applies to your idea of angels. You could have no idea of animals if you had never seen any. (Thus all ideas come to us from outside.) It is not at all clear how your idea of bodily things could have been derived from yourself, if you know yourself only as an incorporeal substance.

7. [294–7] You argue that your idea of God alone cannot be derived from you, and thus that God necessarily exists. But the idea comes from the people around you! You can say that nothing exists but yourself as a pure mind—but then where did you get the words to say so? Seriously speaking, you must have got them from other people, and, if the words, the ideas as well. The perfections you attribute to God are perfections observed in human beings and in other things, grasped, put together, and expanded by the mind.

You say you could not have derived the idea of an infinite substance from yourself, because, though you are a substance, you are not infinite. But you have no real idea of an infinite substance, which is beyond human comprehension. Anyway, the idea of an infinite substance could have been formed from other ideas in the manner just described. Otherwise, you would have to say that ancient philosophers' idea of an infinity of worlds must have derived from an actually existing infinity of worlds. Your so-called idea of the infinite does not represent the infinite as it is, only by the negation of the finite. It is not enough to say you perceive more reality in the infinite than in the finite, when you do not perceive infinite reality, only an amplified version of finite reality.

You do not claim to grasp the infinite fully, only to have a clear and distinct idea of some of its properties. But knowing a part of the infinite is not to know it, any more than you can know a human being by the tip of a single hair.

8. [297–300] You say your consciousness of imperfection would be impossible without the idea of a more perfect being. But these ideas simply represent the facts of your limitation. And that we lack something does not prove that something more perfect than us exists. We may feel the lack of bread without its being more perfect than us. Your idea of perfection may have come from the universe as a whole, which you see is more perfect than its parts, and your sense of imperfection from your consciousness that you are only a part of the whole, or from your experience of other people superior to you.

You argue that your idea of God cannot derive from perfections latent in yourself and capable of being developed, since the idea of God implies total perfection, requiring no development. But though the properties we perceive in an idea must be in the idea, this does not imply they are in the thing to which the idea relates.*

Your judgements about God's perfections arise from ignorance and are based on assumptions. They are on a par with ancient philosophers' ideas of an infinite number of universes: these do not prove that an infinity of universes exists.

9. [300-4] You argue that you yourself could not exist unless a perfect being existed. But there was no need to prove that your existence does not derive from yourself, or that you have not always existed. You argue that your own existence from moment to moment must have a cause. But many things, including yourself, are generated and produced in such a way that they do not need the continuing activity of their cause in order to go on existing: they can exist even when their cause has disappeared. Your idea that the moments of time are not interconnected is incredible, but it is also irrelevant to the question of your production or reproduction. A river flowing past a rock comprises separate parts of water: but this has nothing to do with the continued existence of the rock. Your existence in one moment does not guarantee your existence in the next: true, but only because you may be destroyed by an external cause or an internal deficiency. You do not need to be created afresh every moment.

The identity of creation and conservation is something you have not proved. Your continued existence is an effect of your natural constitution, though this is not proof against external or internal destructive agencies. You depend on some other being for your existence only inasmuch as you were produced at some time in the past. You exist because you were produced by your parents, and they by theirs, and this process could have gone back in time to infinity. For, although an infinite regress is impossible in subordinated causes, where each cannot act without the activity of a prior cause—as when a stone is driven by a stick moved by somebody's hand—it is possible in series where each member can continue to exist and act, even when the cause that has produced it has perished.* You argue that your idea of God as a unity requires a unitary cause: but it could have been developed from your experience of different perfections in different individuals. You could then have conceived these perfections as existing in an ultimate degree, beyond what is possible for human nature, and so formed the idea of a being possessing them all. Then you could have investigated whether such a being exists. You could have found arguments indicating it exists more probably than not. Then you could have removed from it whatever implies limitation, such as body.* Your conclusion that God exists is true, but you have not demonstrated it.

10. [304-7] Your idea of God could be partly derived from the senses, and partly your own construction: there is no need to think it innate.

What do you mean when you say that the idea of God is imprinted in you as the mark of your maker? How do you recognize this mark? But if the mark is not distinct from the object itself, does this mean you are the idea of God? Are you then simply a mode of thinking? the mark itself and the subject in which it is made? That he made you in his image and likeness is something believable by faith: but by the yardstick of human reason, it seems to imply an anthropomorphic view of God. What likeness can there be between you, the created, and the creator, any more than between a house and a builder? You perceive the likeness through your awareness of yourself as incomplete and dependent: this is a proof of unlikeness. If the idea of God were innate, it would be universal, and all would have the same idea of him and the same beliefs about him. But they do not.

On the Fourth Meditation

1. [307–10] You do not want to make God responsible for our errors, though your explanation in terms of our 'participation in nothingness' is obscure, and does not show why God could not have given us a faculty of judgement immune to error, even if limited.

You are right to say you do not understand the reasons for everything God does. But you say you have a true idea of God as omniscient, omnipotent, and wholly good, yet you see that some of his works are imperfect. This seems to imply he lacked the power or the will to make them better.

Your rejection of final causes in physics is theologically dangerous, since the best proof of God's wisdom, power, providence, and indeed existence is the order and interrelationship of parts in plants, animals, and the human body: we cannot explain these except by a first cause working for a purpose. It cannot be wrong to investigate his purposes when these are manifest, as here.

Your idea of God may be an alternative route to the knowledge of him for you, but other people are not so fortunate as to possess it. In any case, that idea comes from the knowledge of material things. What idea of God do you suppose you would have achieved if all your life you had closed your eyes and blocked up your ears, and ignored the other senses?*

2. [310–14] You explain the imperfection of human knowledge as contributing to the perfection of the universe. But would the universe not be more perfect if all its parts were so—just as it would be better for a state for all the citizens to be good? You say God was not obliged to allot you a prominent and perfect role in the world, but what would we say of a ruler who allocated some of his subjects shameful or wicked occupations? The question is not whether God should have given you greater powers of knowledge than you have, but why the powers he has given you are subject to error. You say that error is in the operation of the faculty, not in the faculty itself: but the faculty was created subject to error, and God cooperates in the act of error.

3. [314–17] Why assert that the will has no boundaries, but that the intellect does? Surely their scope is equal: the will cannot be moved towards

something if the intellect has not first perceived it. In fact, of the two, the intellect has the greater range: we can understand things without choice or judgement resulting. You say the will is infinite, but the intellect, according to you, can attain an infinite object. Error does not arise from the greater range of the will, compared to that of the intellect, but because the intellect does not perceive well, and so the will does not judge well.

You cannot seriously claim to doubt the existence of external things, and if you could think of no reason why they should, or should not exist, you would not be able to pass judgement on the matter—your will would remain indifferent.

You are exaggerating the will's indifference.* The knowledge that the reasons for a point of view are merely conjectural, although probable, may lead you to adopt it with hesitation, but could not lead you to take up the contrary view, unless there were equal or more conjectural reasons on that side.

You cannot support this by appealing to your own experience of considering as false what you had once believed quite true, because you cannot honestly claim to have been convinced that what your senses told you was false.

Error, then, does not consist in the misuse of your free will but in the non-correspondence of the judgement with the thing judged, which the intellect has apprehended as other than it is.* The will is determined by the intellect, and its judgement will be more or less definite as the intellect's perception is more or less clear. We are less able to avoid error than to avoid persevering in error, which we can achieve by concentrating on obtaining clearer knowledge.

4. [317–18] You say you will attain the truth provided you sufficiently distinguish what you understand perfectly from what you apprehend more confusedly and obscurely. This is true, but we didn't need the whole of the preceding Meditation to find that out. What you need to provide is a method of knowing when our clear and distinct understanding that something is so is to be relied on, since we can be mistaken even when we think we understand something perfectly clearly and distinctly.

On the Fifth Meditation

1. [318–22] All you say of the essence of material things is that they have extension, number, shape, place, motion, and duration. You say there are eternal and unchangeable natures or essences, about which there are eternal truths. But it is difficult to believe in any eternal and unchangeable essence except that of God. If there were no human beings, there would be no human nature, and 'a rose is a flower' would not be true if there were no roses.

There is no eternal human nature independent of God, no universal 'human nature' instantiated in particular beings. There is nothing in an individual human being but what is singular. From the observation of similar natures in different individuals, the intellect abstracts a common concept applicable to them all: this is 'universal human nature'. But it does not exist prior to individual human beings, or prior to the intellect's act of abstraction.

You cannot say, for example, 'a human being is an animal' was true before there were human beings, and is thus eternally true. It can only mean 'if there ever is a human being, it will necessarily be an animal'. 'A human being is an animal' means 'human beings exist, and are animals'.*

The same applies to your example of the triangle. The triangle in the mind serves as a yardstick for applying the name 'triangle': but it has no reality outside the intellect, which formed it as a concept on the basis of sense-perceptions of material triangles. The properties of a material triangle or an individual human being are not borrowed from the universals 'triangle' or 'human nature'.

You say your idea of a triangle is independent of sense-perception: but could you have formed it without sight and touch? Your ideas of bodies you have never perceived were formed from those you have.

2. [322–6] You argue from the essence of God to his existence. But you cannot treat existence as a property among others.

For you are right in comparing essence with essence, but thereafter you 322 *are not comparing either existence with existence or a property with a property, but existence with a property. Hence it seems you should have said, either that, for example, omnipotence can no more be separated* 323 *from God's existence than having angles equal to two right angles can be separated from the essence of a triangle; or, indeed, that God's existence can no more be separated from his essence, than the existence of a triangle from its essence. Both these comparisons would have been valid, and not only the first, but also the second, would have been accepted, although you would not as a result have demonstrated that God necessarily exists, because the triangle does not necessarily exist either, even though its essence and existence cannot be separated in reality, however much they are separated by the mind, or considered separately, as the divine essence and existence can also be.*

Then you should bear in mind that you include existence among the divine perfections, yet do not include it among the perfections of the triangle or the mountain, although it would be no less fair to call it a perfection in them, each in their own way. But the truth is that existence is a

*perfection neither in God nor in any other thing: it is that without which
there are no perfections.* *

*Indeed what does not exist has neither perfections nor imperfections;
and what exists and has several perfections does not have existence as a
specific perfection among the others, but as that in which both itself and
its perfections are existent, and without which the thing is said not to exist
and the perfections not to be possessed.* * *Hence existence is not said to exist
in a thing in the same way as its perfections do, and, moreover, if the thing
lacks existence, it is not said to be imperfect [or deprived of perfection] so
much as non-existent.*

*Hence, just as in listing the perfections of the triangle you did not
include existence, or conclude that the triangle exists; so, in listing the perfections of God, you should not have included existence, so as to conclude
that God exists, unless you were begging the question.* *

You say existence and essence can be distinguished in everything besides
God. But this is not so in reality (if Plato ceased to exist, so would his
essence). The distinction can be drawn only in thought, but then it applies
to God as well.

You say that the objection, 'I can think of a mountain with a valley and
a horse with wings, but it does not follow that they exist, and I can think
of God as existing without its following that he exists' is based on a
sophism. Yes, because it is contradictory to think of God as existing and
not existing. But you have made things too easy for yourself. You have to
explain why we can think of a winged horse as not existing, but why we
cannot think of an omniscient and omnipotent God as not existing.

As you say, we are free to think of a horse with or without wings; but
we are equally free to think of God as having all perfections, without
regard to whether he exists or not. And if you insist that unless he has existence, he is not fully perfect, I could say the same of the winged horse
Pegasus: he would not be a perfect winged horse unless he had existence
as well as wings.*

You need to show that the ideas of God and of existence are compatible
in the first place.* You ought to prove your assertions that there cannot be
more than one God and that God has existed and will exist for all eternity.

3. [326-8] You say there can be no true knowledge without the knowledge of God. Can you seriously mean this? Were you not equally sure of
the truth of geometrical proofs, before you began to argue for God's existence? They gain our assent by their own force, and cannot be shaken by
the idea of the evil genius—just as you were convinced 'I think therefore
I am', despite the evil genius, even though you did not yet know God
existed. The proof God exists is less evident than those of geometry

(for everyone accepts the latter and some challenge the former), so how can the latter depend on the former? Atheists can be convinced by geometrical proofs; and believers' acceptance of them does not depend on their belief in a non-deceiving God. The ancient mathematicians were certain of their demonstrations, without ever thinking of God.

On the Sixth Meditation

1. [328–32] Material things, you say, can exist in so far as they are the object of pure mathematics. But pure mathematical entities such as points, lines, and surfaces, do not exist in reality. You are wrong to distinguish intellection from imagination. Both are actions of a single faculty, and any difference between them is of degree.

You say imagination, unlike intellection, involves an effort to make a body appear as if present. Thus you can understand a chiliogon without any effort of imagination. But some effort of imagination is involved, even though you can't form a distinct picture of it; and simply understanding what the word 'chiliogon' means is not, as you seem to imply, the same as understanding, without imagination, the figure itself.

It would be all right if you called it both 'imagination' and 'intellection' when you know a figure distinctly and with an effort on the part of the senses, and 'intellection' alone when you conceive a figure confusedly and with little or no effort.* But there is only one kind of internal knowledge, by means of which you grasp figures with greater or lesser degrees of distinctness and effort. Imagination in fact shades imperceptibly into intellection. And by associating effort and distinctness with the imagination, your distinction in fact degrades intellection.

If there is just the one faculty, with its differences of degree, you cannot say that imagination is not essential to your essence.

You say that in the act of imagination the mind is directing itself to bodies, and in that of intellection to itself and the ideas it has within itself. But the mind cannot direct itself to itself or to any idea, without also directing itself to something corporeal, or represented by a corporeal idea. Ideas of geometrical figures are corporeal, and those of the immaterial beings we believe in,* like God, angels, and the human soul, are also quasi-corporeal, derived from the human form and other subtle and imperceptible things like air. When you say you conjecture that some bodies probably exist, you can't be serious.*

2. [332–4] You discuss the reliability of the senses, and the reasons you came to doubt it. The senses faithfully reproduce things as they appear, and as they have to appear, given the relationships between the sense-organ, the object, and the medium. The errors are really in the judgement or mind, when it overlooks, for example, the factor of distance.

However, we can be certain, for example, that a tower seen from close up is square, even if it looks round from a distance. The amputee's illusion is due precisely to the loss of a limb: it is no reason to cast doubt on a healthy person's perception of pain in an injured limb. We are not always dreaming, and when we are awake we cannot doubt that we are awake and not dreaming. Our nature is subject to error but also capable of grasping truth, beyond doubt. And we cannot doubt that things appear to us as they do. Reason may be at odds with sense-perception, but the faculties can help one another, as when the right hand comes to the aid of the left when necessary.

3. [334–7] You conclude that you cannot accept all that the senses tell you, but that you cannot doubt it all either. But you have probably always believed this, so what have you found out that's new?

You say that whatever you clearly and distinctly conceive can be produced by God as you conceive it; therefore, your clear and distinct perception of one thing without another proves that the two are really distinct, because God could make them exist separately. You should first have proved that God exists, and that he can do whatever you can understand. You can understand two properties of a triangle separately: does that mean God could create a triangle with only one of those properties?

You conclude that, since you are aware of nothing but thinking as belonging to your essence, your essence is simply that of a thinking thing. This has already been commented on apropos of the Second Meditation.*

You conclude that, though closely linked to your body, you are really separate from it, and can exist without it.

335   *Because this is the hinge on which the whole difficulty turns, we need to linger here a little, so that it becomes clear how you deal with it. The first issue is the distinction between yourself and your body. But which body do*
336   *you mean? It must be the solid body consisting of your limbs to which your words apply. [. . .]*

And yet, O mind, the difficulty is not about that body. It would be, if I were objecting, as most philosophers would do, that you are the 'entelechy', the perfection, the form, the species, and, to use the common term, a mode, of the body. Certainly, these philosophers will no more acknowledge that you are distinct and separable from this body than shape or any other mode; and this is true whether you are the whole soul, or if you are also the* nous dunamei, nous pathêtikos, *'possible intellect' or 'passive intellect', as they term it. But I am willing to deal more generously with you, by considering you, indeed, purely as* nous poiêtikos, *the 'active intellect', and indeed as* chôriston, *'separable', even though in a different sense than they would admit.**

For they viewed this intellect as common to all human beings (if not to all things), and as enabling the possible intellect to function, in the same manner and by the same necessity as light enables the eye to see (hence they were in the habit of comparing it with the light of the sun, and hence to consider it as an external agent): but I will rather consider you, as you yourself would like to be considered, as a special kind of intellect, in command of the body.

I repeat that the difficulty is not whether or not you are separable from this body (which is why just now I suggested that there was no need to bring in the power of God, by virtue of which those things are separable that you understand separately), but about the body you yourself are: as if you yourself might be a subtle body, diffused through the solid body, or residing in some part of it. Besides, you have not yet proved convincingly that you are something purely incorporeal. And when in the Second 337 *Meditation you proclaimed that* you were not a wind, not a fire, not a vapour, not a breath, *I pointed out to you quite plainly that you had proclaimed this without proof.*

You *said there* But I am not discussing this at present. *But you haven't discussed it anywhere else, or given any reason to prove that you are not this kind of body. My hope was that you would give it here. But if you are discussing or proving anything, it is that you are not the solid body, which, as I have already said, is not the point at issue.*

4. [337–43] You appeal to your clear and distinct ideas of yourself as a thinking non-extended thing, and of the body as non-thinking and non-extended. But you have not proved that thinking is incompatible with the nature of body, especially subtle body. Anyway, how could you have an idea of body if you are without extension?

I ask you, how do you think that the species or idea of a body that is 337 *extended can be received by you, an unextended subject?* For if such a species proceeds from the body, it is certainly corporeal, and has various parts, and is therefore extended; or if its impression comes from elsewhere,* 338 *because it still has to be representing an extended body, it still has to have parts, and therefore it has to be extended. Otherwise, if it has no parts, how can it represent parts? If it has no extension, how can it represent an extended thing? [. . .]*

Then, as far as your idea of yourself is concerned, there is nothing to add to what I have already said, especially about the Second Meditation. For I showed there that, so far from having a clear and distinct idea of yourself, you seem to have none at all.* Indeed, although you recognize that

you think, you still do not know what kind of thing you, who think, are;
so much so that, since only the operation of thinking is known to you,
you know nothing of what is most important, the substance, that is, that
carries out the operation. To use an analogy: you could be said to be like
a blind man who, feeling heat, and being informed that this comes from
the sun, thinks that he has a clear and distinct idea of the sun, inasmuch
as, if he were asked what the sun is, he could reply that it is a heating
thing.

Knowing, as you claim, that you are not just a thinking, but a non-
extended thing, is not enough.

339 *In order to have a clear and distinct idea, or what comes to the same thing,*
a true and adequate idea of something, is it not necessary to know the
thing itself positively, and, so to speak, affirmatively, and is it enough to
know that it is not some other thing? Or would we say that someone has a
clear and distinct idea of Bucephalus,* if all he knows is that Bucephalus
is not a fly?

How can you, the mind, be united to the body—the whole body, or some
part of it, that is, the brain—without being extended?

If you are not a body, how can you impart motion to a body, when
motion can be transmitted only by contact? (You have said bodies cannot
move themselves.)

The burden of proof is still on you to demonstrate that you are non-
extended and hence incorporeal. You cannot argue from the generally-
accepted view that man is composed of body and soul: this might mean
that he is composed of two bodies, a solid and a subtle one, the latter being
known as the soul. Anyway, we speak of animals as composed of body and
soul, though you seem to deny them a soul as well as a mind like yours. We
can grant that you are distinct from the solid body, but not that you are not
a subtle body.

You conclude that you can exist without the body. Yes, as a subtle
bodily substance you could exist without the solid body, as the smell of an
apple can remain in the air, though you would no longer be a thinking
thing, a mind, or a soul.

343 *I say all this, not as one who doubts the conclusion you are aiming*
at, but as one who is not convinced of the force of the arguments you have
set out.

5. [343–5] You are right to speak of yourself as closely conjoined with
your body. But how is this possible, if you are incorporeal, non-extended,
and indivisible? Doesn't union require contact, and is there contact except
between bodies?

You speak of feeling pain: how could you, if you are incorporeal and non-extended? Pain involves a separation of parts.

In a word, there is a general difficulty that refuses to go away: how what 345 *is incorporeal can communicate with what is corporeal, and what relationship can be established between the two.*

6. [345–6] (Gassendi sums up rapidly the concluding arguments, seeming to imply that Descartes has taken a very roundabout way to come to some very banal conclusions. He urges Descartes to regard their disagreement as a difference of opinion similar to differences of taste, and professes his affection and admiration for him.)

THE AUTHOR'S REPLY TO THE FIFTH OBJECTIONS

[347–8] Descartes thanks Gassendi for his dissertation, and Mersenne for getting him to write it. He then goes on to criticize Gassendi's approach:

Although, however, you have made use not so much of philosophical 347 arguments to refute my opinions, as of various rhetorical techniques to evade them, this too is gratifying to me, for this reason, that I infer that no arguments can be easily brought against me, apart from those contained in the previous sets of objections from other writers, which 348 you have read. And indeed, if there were any, they would not have escaped your intelligence and diligence, and I judge that your intention here was simply to point out to me how those people whose minds are so immersed in their senses that they recoil from metaphysical arguments,* might evade them; and therefore you were giving me an opportunity to come to grips with them. Hence I will here be replying not to you, a most penetrating philosopher, but as if I were dealing with one of these carnal characters.

On the Objections to the First Meditation

You say you *approve* my *intention of stripping every prejudice away from* my *mind*, as, indeed, no one could find fault with it. But you would have wished me to do it *simply and succinctly*, that is, carelessly. As if it were so easy to free ourselves of all the errors we have absorbed since childhood; and as if we could be too careful about doing what everyone agrees has to be done. But I expect you wanted to indicate that most people admit, as far as words go, that prejudices should be avoided, but nonetheless continually fail to avoid them, because they will not make the necessary intellectual effort for this purpose, and think that none of the things they once accepted as true should be ranked as prejudices. Certainly you are playing here the role of such people to perfection, 349 and you have failed to say nothing that might have been said by them; but at the same time you say nothing that smacks of a philosopher. When you say there is no need to *imagine a deceiving God* or *pretend we are dreaming* (p. 166), and so forth, a philosopher would have thought he had to give a reason why these cannot be called into question; or, if he had no reason (and there is none), he would not have said what you say. Nor would he have added that *it would have seemed sufficient here to invoke the darkness of the human mind, and the mere weakness of our nature* (p. 166). For it does not help us to correct our errors, to say that we go astray because our mind is dark or our nature weak. That would be simply like saying that we go astray because we are prone to error; and it is obviously more useful to consider all the points in which we can happen to be mistaken, as I did, in case we rashly give our assent to them. Nor would a philosopher have said that in *treating everything doubtful as false, I was not so much divesting myself of an old prejudice, as espousing a new one* (p. 166): or else he would have tried first of all to prove that this supposition could lead to error. But you, on the contrary, state a little later, that I cannot *really compel myself to consider as uncertain and false the things I have supposed to be false* (p. 166): that is, you say I cannot espouse this new prejudice you were afraid of my espousing. And a philosopher would not have been taken aback by this kind of supposition, any more than by our bending a curved stick back in the opposite direction to make it straight, as we sometimes do. For he knows that it can often be useful to assume that 350 what is false is true, in order to throw light on the truth: as when astronomers imagine an equator, or the zodiac, or other circles in the heavens, or when geometers add new lines to given shapes. Philosophers often do the same. Anyone who calls this *resorting to contrivances, going in for conjuring tricks, and following roundabout paths* and to say it is *unworthy both of a philosopher's sincerity and of the love of truth* (p. 166) is giving proof that he is neither living up to the sincerity of a philosopher nor making use of any argument, only rhetorical flavouring.*

On the Objections to the Second Meditation

350 1. You continue here making use of rhetorical pretences instead of reasoning: for you pretend that I am joking, when I am perfectly serious;*

and you take seriously, as if I were really saying and endorsing it, what I simply put forward, in a tentative spirit and according to the common opinion of other people, so that I might later investigate it further. For when I said that *all the testimony of the senses should be treated as uncertain, indeed as false* (p. 17), this was perfectly serious, and is so essential to the understanding of my Meditations that whoever is unwilling or unable to accept it, is incapable of raising any objection worthy of a reply. But you must bear in mind the distinction I have insisted on in various places, between the conduct of life and the inves- 351 tigation of the truth. For when it is a question of managing one's life, it would certainly be completely foolish not to believe in the senses, and there has never been anything but ridicule for the sceptics who neglected human interests to such an extent that their friends had to look after them to stop them hurling themselves over precipices; and therefore I have pointed out elsewhere that *no one in their right mind has ever seriously doubted such things* (p. 12). But, when we are inves- tigating what can be known with total certainty by the human mind, it is wholly alien from reason to refuse to reject them seriously, as doubtful, and indeed as false, in order to discover that other things that cannot be so rejected are, for this very reason, more certain, and in fact better known to us.

On the other hand, when I said that I did not yet understand who it is that thinks, you took me to be speaking seriously, which you could not do in good faith, since I explained this very point; and the same applies to my saying that I did not doubt in what the nature of bodies consists, and that I credited them with no power of moving themselves, and that I imagined myself as a soul that was like a wind, or a fire, and so forth—in all of which statements I was simply reproducing the common opinion, so that I might show them in due course to be false.

You misleadingly state that my attribution of motion, sensation, and nutri- tion to the soul does not square with my distinction between soul and body.* But I later expressly attribute nutrition to the body alone, and movement and sensation principally to the body, and only their mental aspects to the soul.

Your own misunderstandings disprove your claim I could have proved my existence more simply.

When you say *I could have inferred it from any other of my actions* 352 (p. 166), you are very wide of the mark, since I am completely cer- tain of none of my actions (I am talking of metaphysical certainty,* which is the only kind at issue here), apart from thinking. For instance, the inference 'I am walking, therefore I am' is not legitimate, except in so far as the consciousness of walking is a thought. The inference is certain purely as regards this thought, not as regards the motion of the body, since in dreams when I seem to myself to be walking the body is none the less not moving. Thus, from the fact that I think I am walking, I can validly infer the existence of the mind that thinks this, but not of the body that is walking. And the same applies to other actions.

2. Henceforth you question me, no longer as a whole human being, but, by a delightful prosopopoeia, as a separate soul; by which you seem to be warning me that these objections were put forward, not by the mind of a subtle philosopher, but by the flesh alone. I ask you, therefore, O flesh,* or whatever else you wish to be called, whether you have so little dealing with the mind that you failed to notice when I did correct the commonplace illusion whereby what thinks is imagined to be like a wind or some such body? I certainly corrected it when I showed that we can suppose that no wind or any other body exists in the world, and that none the less everything from which I recognize myself as a thinking thing remains. And therefore all your subsequent questions, *why therefore I could not still be a wind, why I could not occupy space, why I am not moved by various motions*, and so forth, are so pointless as to need no reply.

3. And what you add is no more convincing: *if I am some subtle body, why could I not receive nourishment*, and so forth. For I am denying that I am a body. So—to deal with the matter once and for all—because you use the same style virtually all the time, and do not challenge my arguments, but, by glossing over them as if they were non-existent, or by restating them in incomplete and mutilated form, you heap up various difficulties that are commonly raised by the ignorant against my conclusions, or others like them—or even unlike them—and that are either irrelevant, or have been already eliminated or resolved by me in their proper place, it is not worth my while troubling to answer your questions one by one: for this would mean repeating things a hundred times over that I have already written. But I will just briefly deal with those points that, it seems, could detain readers who are not completely incompetent. And as for those who pay less attention to the strength of an argument than to a flood

of words, I do not care enough for their approval to want to waste words for the sake of extorting it.

Therefore, I shall first point out here that what you say *that the mind grows and decays with the body* is not credible, and you give no proof of it. For, from the fact that it does not function so perfectly in the body of a child as in that of an adult, and that its actions can often be hampered by wine and other bodily causes, it follows only that, so long as it is attached to the body, it uses it as an instrument for those operations with which it is occupied most of the time, but not that it is rendered more or less perfect by the body. And your inference here is no sounder than if you were to infer that, from the fact that a craftsman does not do his work well whenever he uses a faulty tool, he derives his skill from the quality of the tool.*

Even though we do not always experience our senses deceiving us, the fact that we sometimes do is sufficient reason for doubting them. The point about error is that we are not always aware of it as such.

If we do not accept a view, because we do not know it is true, this does not mean we have to prove it false. We have only to be very careful not to admit anything as true that we cannot prove.

Thus, when I discover that I am a thinking substance and form a clear and distinct concept of this thinking substance, containing nothing that belongs to the concept of a bodily substance, this is quite sufficient for me to assert that, in so far as I know myself, I am nothing other than a thinking thing; and this is all I asserted in the Second Meditation, which we are currently dealing with. Nor should I have accepted that this thinking substance is some kind of body—agile, pure, subtle, and so forth—since I had no reason to convince me of this. And if you have such a reason, it is up to you to show it, not to require me to prove that something is false that I rejected for this reason alone, that it was unknown to me. [. . .] When you say that *I need to prove that animals' souls are incorporeal and that the solid body contributes nothing to our thoughts*, you show that you are not only ignorant of where the burden of proof lies, but of what each person has to prove. For I think neither that animals' souls are incorporeal, nor that the solid body contributes nothing to thinking;* only that this is not at all the proper place to consider these issues.

4. [355–7] We cannot change established terminology, but we can modify how it is used. The first human beings did not, perhaps, distinguish the underlying principle* of the functions we have in common with animals

<aside>354</aside>
<aside>355</aside>

(nutrition, growth, etc.) and that do not involve thought from the under-lying source of thought itself, and so called both of them the 'soul'. Then they realized that thought was a special case, and called the thinking part of us the 'mind', which they believed was the dominant part of the soul. Realizing that nutrition and thought should not be predicated of the same agent, I find 'soul' an ambiguous term, and thus tend to speak of the 'mind' instead: but this is coextensive with the soul, not a part of it.

356   *You hesitate as to whether I believe the soul is always thinking.* But why should it not be always thinking, since it is a thinking substance? Why is it surprising that we do not remember the thoughts we had in our mother's womb, or in a stupor, and so forth, when we cannot even remember most of the thoughts we none the less know we have 357 had in adulthood, when in good health and awake? For us to remem-ber the thoughts the mind has had, while it has been attached to the body, some kind of trace of them has to be imprinted on the brain, and the mind remembers by directing itself to these, or applying itself to these. Why is it surprising if the brain of an infant or a person in a stupor is unfit to receive those traces?

It is true that for all I know at this point the mind and the body may not in fact be distinct. But I am not assuming that they are. It is because I do not know the truth of the matter that I concentrate wholly on the mind, and then, in the Sixth Meditation, I prove it is distinct from the body. You are the one making unfounded assumptions.

5. [357] As to the imagination I am not contradicting myself. I can say that something does not belong to my knowledge of myself while still being uncertain whether it belongs to me.

6. [358] These are not objections deserving a reply.

7. [358] Animals are irrelevant at this point. The mind that meditates experiences itself thinking within itself. It has no such experience of whether animals think or not. This has to be investigated from their behaviour, reasoning *a posteriori* from effects to causes. You do not fairly represent my position.

358   For I have often adduced a criterion whereby the mind can be rec-ognized as distinct from the body: namely that its whole nature con-sists in thinking, whereas the whole nature of a body consists in its being an extended thing, and that there is nothing whatever in common between thought and extension. I have also frequently shown quite clearly that the mind can operate independently of the brain; for certainly the brain can be of no use in pure intellection,

only in imagination or sensation. And although, when the imagination or the senses are making a powerful impact on us (as happens when the brain is disturbed), the mind cannot easily apply itself to understanding anything else, we none the less know by frequent experience that, when our imagination is less active, we can understand something quite distinct from what we are imagining. Thus, when, while we are asleep, we realize that we are dreaming, the imagination has to be active in order for us to dream, but our awareness of dream-   359
ing requires the intellect alone.

8. [359] You do not understand what you are trying to criticize. I did not abstract the concept of the wax from that of its accidents. I wanted to show how the substance is manifested by the accidents, and to show how the reflexive and distinct perception of it differs from everyday confused perception.

What proof have you that a dog judges in the same way as we do? I believe it has no mind, and nothing similar to the properties of mind.*

9. [359–61] You say that the consideration of the wax proves I exist, but not what I am. But the two go together.

And I cannot see what further you expect from it, unless it were to   359
say what colour the human mind is, and what smell and taste it has; or of what salt, sulphur, and mercury it is composed; for you want us to examine it, as we would examine wine, *by some chemical procedure*.*
This is certainly worthy of you, O flesh, and of all those who, since   360
they cannot conceive anything except in very confused fashion, do not know the proper questions to ask about any particular thing. But as for myself I have never thought that anything else is needed, in order to manifest a substance, apart from its various attributes, so that, the more attributes we know belong to any substance, the more perfectly we understand its nature. And, just as we can distinguish many and various attributes in the wax (one, that it is white; another, that it is hard; another, that it can become liquid), so there are an equal number in the mind as well, first, that it has the power of knowing the whiteness of the wax; next, that it has the power of knowing its hardness, and then the conversion of its hardness into liquidity; for someone might know its hardness, who does not there-fore know its whiteness (I mean someone born blind), and so forth. And the same applies to the rest. From this it can be clearly inferred that there is nothing else of which we know so many attributes as we do of our mind: for however many attributes are known in any other

thing, there must be an equivalent number in the mind, inasmuch as it knows them. Thus its nature is better known than that of any other thing. Finally in passing you criticize me because, *although I admitted nothing in myself but a mind, I nonetheless speak of the wax I see and touch, which I could not do without eyes and hands*. But you should have realized what I took care to point out, that I was not talking about the sight and touch that require the involvement of bodily organs, but simply of the thought of seeing and touching;* and that the organs are not essential to this, we know by the nightly experience of our dreams.

On the Objections to the Third Meditation

1. [361–2] Finally, an argument! You say that the criterion of clarity and distinctness cannot be true, because great minds, whom we would suppose capable of clear and distinct perception, have believed the truth of things is hidden. But arguments from authority cut no ice here: the mind withdrawn from bodily things cannot be swayed by authority, since it does not even know that other human beings have existed. Arguments from sceptics or people who die for their false beliefs prove nothing, because it can never be proved that they clearly and distinctly perceive what they assert. You are right to say we need a method for distinguishing whether we are mistaken or not, when we think we clearly perceive something: but this is what I have provided, by, first, eliminating prejudices and, then, sorting out confused ideas from clear ones.

2. [362] You say all ideas are adventitious, and none factitious or produced by us. You might as well say a sculptor does not make statues, because he does not make the marble he uses, or that you are not uttering these objections, because you did not make up the words you use but had to borrow them from other people.

My knowledge of the idea 'thing' is from my experience of myself as a thinking thing, not from that of other kinds of thing. Likewise the idea of truth was not derived from things outside me.

3. [363–4] Your argument for the existence of external things is begging the question because it assumes they exist. How do you know a blind person has no idea of colour? And supposing what you say is true, could we not just as well say that their mind has no faculty of forming that idea as that they cannot form it because they have no eyes?

When you say that astronomy gives us no idea of the sun, you are equating 'idea' with 'mental image': but I have made clear that they are not the same.

4. [364-5] The same applies when you say we have no true idea of substance. It is perceived by the intellect, not the imagination.

The idea of substance is not patterned on that of its accidents; nor does the former derive its reality from the latter. The reverse is true in both cases.

If our idea of God simply comes from the people we have heard speak of him, where did they get it from? If from themselves, so can we. If from God, he exists.

You say we cannot grasp an infinite being and do not understand the term 'infinite'. You fail to distinguish the level of intellection proportionate to our limited understanding (and we do understand the infinite in this way) from an adequate concept of a thing (such as we perhaps do not possess of anything). We do not understand the infinite by the negation of limits, since limitation contains the negation of the infinite.

The idea of God *does* contain more objective reality than that of finite things. Even if it were formed by amplifying human perfections, the result is a higher degree of perfection than is found in humans. How could we amplify our ideas of created perfection so as to conceive something greater than ourselves if we did not already have the idea of something greater— God? You keep confusing intellection and imagination, as if our idea of him were the image of him as a massive human being.

5. [366] Some of what you say, as if you were disagreeing with me, I agree with. But I cannot agree that the axiom *there is nothing in the effect that has not previously existed in the cause* refers to the material cause, instead of the efficient cause. For the perfection of the form must exist in the efficient cause, not the material.*

6. [366-7] Your assertion of the existence of material things is mere prejudice, else you would have offered a proof here.

Your argument about ideas needs no reply, because you keep restricting the term 'idea' to mental images of things, but I extend it to cover every object of thought.

Your examples of the impossibility of reflexive action are faulty. It is not the eye that sees the mirror rather than itself, but the mind that sees the eye, and the mirror, and itself. Besides, some things can move themselves.*

I do not say that *ideas of material things are derived from the mind*. I afterwards show that they frequently derive from bodies (which is why they prove the existence of bodies). I argue that we cannot use the causal principle to prove that they *cannot* have come from the mind.

7. [367-8] I have refuted all this already. I do not claim that my idea of the infinite is comprehensive: the infinite is by definition incomprehensible.

But my idea represents not part of the infinite but the infinite as a whole, so far as a human idea can grasp it. Likewise an ordinary person's idea of a triangle simply as a three-sided figure is an idea of the triangle as a whole, even though it does not contain many properties that would be contained in a geometer's idea.

8. [368–9] Even though we do not know everything that is in God, whatever we do know in him is nonetheless true.

The bread analogy does not work. The inference from someone's desire of bread is not that bread is more perfect than them, but that to need bread is less perfect than not to need it. I do not infer from the fact that something exists in an idea that it exists in reality, except when no other cause can be ascribed to an idea than the thing itself existing in reality. And this, I have proved, applies to God alone, not to a plurality of worlds or anything else.

9. [369–71] All metaphysicians recognize, what the uneducated overlook, that causes are of two types: some (relative to becoming) only bring their effects into being (as an architect makes a house), and their influence is then no longer necessary; others (relative to being) are required in order for their effects to remain in being (as light cannot continue to exist in the absence of the sun). God is cause of created things in this latter sense, and they exist by his continued influence.*

Time in the abstract must be continuous: but the time of an existing thing is composed of separable moments, else the thing could never cease to exist.

We have no power of self-preservation. If we had, we would be independent like God, and we could not cease to exist without God choosing to annihilate us.*

You say there can be an infinite regress of causes, but you refute yourself when you concede that this cannot be so when the causes are subordinated one to another, as applies here, where we are dealing with causes relative to being, not becoming.

The process you describe of conceiving human perfections as raised to a level transcending human nature could not occur, I say, if we had not been made by God; whose existence I have demonstrated, only you have continually failed to grasp my arguments.

10. [371–4] You object to my saying that nothing can be added to or taken away from the idea of God, forgetting what philosophers commonly say, that the essences of things are indivisible: change the idea of a thing's essence in any way, and it becomes the idea of another thing. Once the idea of the true God has been formed, we may discover new perfections in him, but these make the idea more distinct and explicit, without adding to it,

since the newly-discovered perfections were already contained in it by implication. The analogy with the idea of a triangle holds good.

As regards the idea of God being like the maker's mark imprinted in us: if I say 'Only Apelles* could have painted a picture this good: the skill is like a signature', I do not mean either that the 'signature' is something distinct from the work itself, or that the picture is identical with Apelles' skill, as if it contained no material element.

The dissimilarities between human nature and divine nature do not prevent us from saying we are made in his image. An image does not have to resemble the original in every respect. Our imperfect power of thought is a representation of God's supreme power of thought. God's creation has more in common with procreation than with building, and anyway a craftsman can make an object resembling himself: a sculptor could produce a self-portrait.

You quote me misleadingly. I said incompleteness and dependence were signs of *dis*similarity, through which I perceive my inferiority to God. My aspiration towards the greater perfections that exist in God is a sign of some similarity to him.

We all have an idea of God, as we all have an idea of a triangle, though not everyone has the same understanding of it, and many reason incorrectly about it.

On the Objections to the Fourth Meditation

1. [374–5] I have explained what idea we have of nothing—it is a negative idea—and how we participate in non-being—we are not the supreme being, and many things are lacking to us.

I do not say some of God's works are imperfect, only that, considered in isolation, and not as parts of the whole universe, they may appear so.

As to final causes, we can indeed know and glorify God by considering how the parts of a plant or an animal work together. But we know him then as an efficient, not as a final cause, since this does not involve asking for what purpose he made everything as he did.

Although in ethics, where it is often legitimate to make use of conjectures, it is sometimes pious to consider what purpose we may conjecture God has in mind in his government of the universe, certainly this is pointless in physics, where everything has to be based on the most solid reasons. Nor can it be imagined that some of God's purposes are more plainly visible than others: for all are hidden in the same way in the inscrutable abyss of his wisdom. 375

What you cite as a mystery* only comprehensible by an appeal to God's purposes is something perfectly well understood without it.

The mind could have formed the ideas of God and itself without sensory input, and even more clearly and easily. The senses are a hindrance here.

2. [376] Our being subject to error is not a positive imperfection, as you take it, but the negation of a higher degree of perfection. And this variation in degrees of perfection contributes to the good of the whole of created being. The analogy with the state does not hold. The wickedness of the citizens is a positive reality, in relation to the state; the imperfection of man is not such, in relation to the universe.

It is totally false to suppose that God destines us to evil deeds,* and endows us with imperfections, or that he has given us a faulty cognitive faculty.

3. [376–8] That the will's range goes beyond the intellect's is shown from your view that the mind is a subtle body, and therefore an extended as well as a thinking thing. You do not understand what you are saying yet you want to go on saying it.

True, we will nothing without a degree of understanding. But the contribution of the two is not equal. We can will many things about something of which we know very little.

377   Although what you go on to deny as regards the indifference of the will is perfectly clear in itself, I do not intend to set about proving it for you. It is the kind of thing a person has to experience in himself, rather than being convinced by arguments; but you, O flesh, seem to pay no attention to what the mind experiences in itself. Then do not be free, if you do not want to be; but for my part I will certainly rejoice in my freedom, since, first, I experience it in myself, and, secondly, it is challenged by you with no arguments, but merely with bare denials. Perhaps others will be more convinced by what I say, because I am asserting what I have myself experienced, and what anyone can experience in himself, than you are, who deny what they accept for the sole reason that you perhaps have never experienced it.

378   Although it could also be deduced from what you say that you have experienced this very thing. For when denying that *we can take care to avoid error*, because you do not accept that the will can be moved towards any object to which it is not determined by the intellect, you concede at the same time that *we can take care to avoid persevering in error* (p. 176). Which is entirely impossible unless we have what you say we do not have: the freedom of the will to move itself in either direction, without being determined by the intellect. For if the intellect has once determined the will to utter some false judgement, I ask you this question: when the will first begins to make an

effort not to persevere in its error, by what is it being determined to do so? If by itself, then it can be moved towards some object, without being impelled towards it by the intellect. You said this was impossible, and this is the only point at issue. But if it is determined by the intellect, the will itself is not making an effort. Rather, all that is happening is that, just as before it was moved towards the falsity put before it by the intellect, so it now just happens to be being moved towards the truth,* because the intellect puts before it what is true. But, besides, I would like to know how you conceive the nature of falsity, and how you think it can be the object of the intellect. For I understand falsity as nothing more than the privation of truth, and thus am convinced it is self-contradictory to speak of the intellect apprehending what is false in the guise of what is true; but this would have to be the case if it ever determined the will to embrace what is false.

4. [378-9] You suggest this Meditation has not achieved much. In the Preface I pointed out that I did not expect readers to benefit from the work who argued about individual points, without grasping how the arguments hang together. And I *have* given a method for distinguishing what we truly clearly perceive from what we only think we clearly perceive: but readers who do not try to get rid of their prejudices will not easily recognize it.

On the Objections to the Fifth Meditation

1. [379–82] When you say this is all I have to say about the issue [the essence of material things], you are ignoring the coherence of my text.

The coherence is, I think, so great that the proof of every point draws 379 on everything that has gone before, and most of what follows: so much so that you cannot in good faith give a full account of my position on a particular question, unless you go through everything I have written about all the others.*

You object to the idea of anything being immutable and eternal apart from God. You would be right if I were saying this of a thing's existence, or if its immutability were supposed to be independent of God. But I do not think that the essences of things, or mathematical truths, are independent of God: but that they are immutable and eternal because God so wished them to be.*

Your criticism of 'universals'* applies to the scholastic logicians' idea of them, not to mine. The ideas of essences that are clearly and distinctly known, for example, a triangle, are not deduced from particular things. You concede this implicitly in a later objection when you say that the objects of pure mathematics (point, line, surface) do not exist in reality. In other words no mathematical triangle has ever existed, and consequently the idea of such a figure was not derived from actually existing things.* You would say these essences are false because they do not conform to the nature of things. But that is only your preconceived idea of the nature of things. Geometrical truths can be rigorously proved, and they are always true, and can thus be termed immutable and eternal. They may not conform to your idea of the nature of things, or the atomistic theory of Democritus and Epicurus, but they do conform to the fundamental nature of things created by God. There are indeed no substances like geometrical figures (having length without breadth, or breadth without depth), but geometrical shapes are not considered as substances but as the boundaries within which substances are contained.

The ideas of geometrical figures do not originate in sense-perception, as everyone believes. We have never seen a really straight line and the drawings of triangles we saw in childhood could never have given us the geometrical concept of a triangle, if we did not interpret them in the light of our prior idea of a true triangle: just as our prior idea of the human face enables us to see a set of lines on paper as a face rather than a set of lines.

382   2. Here I cannot see what kind of thing you think existence is, or why you think it cannot be called a property in the same way as
383   omnipotence can, as long as you take the term 'property' in the sense of any attribute, or as referring to anything that can be predicated of a thing, which is exactly how it should be taken here. But indeed, necessary existence is in reality* a property in God in the strictest possible sense of the term, because it belongs to him alone, and is part of an essence in him alone. And therefore the existence of a triangle cannot be compared with the existence of God, because existence in God clearly has a different relationship to essence than it does in the triangle.

Nor is it begging the question to *include existence when listing the things that belong to the essence of God*, any more than it is begging the question to list 'having three angles the sum of which is equal to two right angles' among the properties of a triangle.

Nor is it true that *existence and essence can be thought separately in God*, just as they can in the triangle, because God is his being,* and the triangle is not. But I do not deny that *possible* existence is a perfection in the idea of a triangle, as necessary existence is a perfection in the idea of God; and it makes the idea of a triangle superior to the ideas of those chimeras* that we suppose to be incapable of existing.

I have answered your other points sufficiently already. You are completely wrong to say that God's existence is not demonstrated, as we can demonstrate that the sum of the angles of a triangle is equal to two right angles: in fact the demonstration of God is simpler and clearer.

3. [384] You forget that the sceptics did doubt even geometrical demonstrations, and I say they would not have done so if they had known God as he is. That one thing is better known than another has nothing to do with whether it seems true to more people. What matters is which of them appears prior in the order of knowledge, more evident, and more certain to those who have a proper knowledge of both of them.

On the Objections to the Sixth Meditation

1. [384–5] I have already (p. 196) dealt with your denial that material things exist in so far as they are the object of pure mathematics.

The understanding of the chiliogon is not confused, or limited to the meaning of the name, otherwise we could not demonstrate many properties of the figure, as we can. That we can understand it simultaneously as a whole but not imagine it simultaneously as a whole shows that the faculties of intellection and understanding are different in kind, not in degree. In intellection the mind alone is at work; in imagination it contemplates the shape of a body. Geometrical shapes are corporeal, but their ideas, when grasped by the intellect operating without the imagination, are not.

The ideas of God, angels, and the human mind are not corporeal or quasi-corporeal. Someone who imagines God or the mind is imagining what cannot be imagined: they conjure up a bodily idea, and then falsely label it 'God' or 'mind'. The true idea of the mind contains only thought and its attributes, none of which are corporeal.

2. [385–6] You are still sunk in prejudice, when you say we should not suspect falsity in things in which we have never detected it, like close-up perception and the certainty, when we are awake, of being awake. You have no reason to think you are aware of all possible sources of error. When you say we cannot doubt that things appear as they appear, this is exactly what I said in the Second Meditation. But that has nothing to do with whether they really exist outside our minds.

3. [386–7] You keep on saying I have not proved things I have proved, or that I have only discussed the solid body, not the subtle body, when what I say applies to every kind of body, solid or subtle. I showed in the Second Meditation that the mind can be understood as an existing substance, even if we understand wind, fire, vapour, breath, or any other kind of body, however subtle, as non-existent. I was not there discussing whether the mind is *really* distinct from all bodies: but here I do discuss it, and I have

shown that it is distinct. You keep on confusing two questions: what can be understood? what actually exists? This shows a fundamental misunderstanding.*

4. [387–9] You ask *how I think that the species or idea of a body that is extended can be received by me, an unextended subject?* The mind does not receive any corporeal species.* Pure intellection, whether of a corporeal or of an incorporeal substance, occurs without corporeal species. Imagination, dealing with only corporeal things, needs a 'species' in the sense of a body to which the mind applies itself. But this is not received into the mind.

A blind man can have a clear idea of the sun as a source of heat, even if not as a source of light. Besides the analogy does not apply. Knowledge of the thinking thing is far more extensive than knowledge of any other kind of thing.*

Saying 'the mind is not extended' is not intended to show what the mind is, but to point to the error of those who think it is extended, just as it would be worth pointing out that 'Bucephalus is not music'* if anyone said he was.

The mind is united to the whole of the body, but this does not mean it is extended throughout the body. Nor does its power to move the body prove it must be a body.

5. [389–90] You keep repeating the same points. You do not challenge my arguments, but simply raise doubts about my conclusions, all of which originate from your insistence on thinking with the imagination about what cannot be imagined. The fusion of mind and body cannot be compared to that of two bodies. The mind can understand parts of bodies without having parts in itself. You seem to think that whatever the mind understands is somehow in it:* in that case, when it understands the size of the earth, it would have to be bigger than the earth in order to contain it.

6. What you say here does not contradict me at all, and your verbosity is a clue to the reader to discount your arguments.

(In conclusion Descartes throws off the fiction of the mind as arguing with the flesh, and pays tribute to the real Gassendi as a philosopher and a man of integrity, and hopes that he will not be offended by the philosophical frankness Descartes has made use of in replying to his objections. Descartes is delighted to find that in so long a critique there are no substantial counter-arguments to his own, and no objections to his conclusions to which he could not easily reply.)

SIXTH OBJECTIONS

[412–19] These objections remain, after a careful reading of the Meditations and the foregoing objections and replies.

1. The Cogito is uncertain. For to be certain you think, and therefore exist, you would have to know what thought and existence are. You do not. So you do not know what 'I think' and 'I exist' mean. To know you are thinking, you would have to know you know, and in fact know you know you know, and so on till infinity. So you cannot know whether you exist or even whether you are thinking.

2. Your belief you are thinking may be erroneous. Your 'thoughts' might be bodily motions, involving subtle matter. No one can follow your argument to the contrary. Can you make it clear, to attentive and perspicacious readers, that thought cannot be reduced to bodily motion?

3. Some Fathers of the Church thought that angels and the rational soul could be corporeal, and that soul was transmitted from father to son. This seems to suggest they believed that thought was therefore virtually indistinguishable from bodily motion. Animals like dogs and monkeys, in whom we acknowledge no soul distinct from the body, are able to think. Dogs bark in their sleep, as if dreaming; they know, when awake, that they are running, and, when dreaming, that they are barking. Perhaps they think we cannot think! You cannot see their inner workings any more than they can yours. Great men past and present have believed animals can reason. We do not believe all their operations can be explained mechanically, without sensation, life, and a soul. Anyway, some would say, if animals' behaviour can be explained mechanically, so can humans' be: the difference between their reason and ours is only of degree.

4. An atheist can experience total certainty, when he judges according to your rule,* for example, of mathematical propositions. How could you prove he does not enjoy such certainty?

5. You say God cannot deceive. But some theologians imply that he can. They think that the damned clearly perceived they are being tortured by fire, when no actual fire is present. Could not God similarly deceive us by continual illusions into believing that the external world and our bodies exist? He would be doing us no wrong in this: he might be aiming to lower our pride, or punishing our sins, actual or original, or acting for reasons hidden from us. Various passages of scripture cast doubt on our capacity for knowledge.

6. You treat indifference of the will as an imperfection, a state that disappears whenever the mind has a clear perception of what to believe or how to act. But the faith teaches us that God enjoys indifference: he could have created a different world from this or innumerable worlds or no world at all. Thus, a supremely clear perception of everything, such as he has, is compatible with indifference. The essence of freedom must be the same in God and in us: therefore we too possess liberty of indifference.

7. You say all our sensations take place on surfaces. We do not understand this. We do not see how there can be no real accidents, capable, by divine aid of existing without a substance, as in the Eucharist.* You may make these points clear in your Physics, although it is doubtful if you will argue people into abandoning long-established beliefs.

8. As regards the Fifth Replies: how can geometrical or metaphysical truths be immutable and eternal, yet not independent of God? Could he have made it so that there was no such thing as a triangle? Could he have made it true that 2×4 is not 8, or that a triangle does not have three sides? Either these truths depend wholly on the human intellect, or on actually existing things; or they are independent, and could not have been changed even by God.

9. You say the intellect is more reliable than the senses. But any certainty the intellect enjoys must derive from the senses (if they are in good order). The intellect does not tell us a stick that looks bent in the water is straight: it is touch that does that. What the senses, when in good order, constantly report offers the greatest certainty of which we are capable.*

We need some kind of criterion for knowing when we understand one thing without another so clearly that it is certain they can exist separately; in other words, we need to know how we can be certain that the distinction is not purely produced by the intellect, but derives from the things themselves. For instance, suppose we think of God's immensity, without thinking of his justice; or of his existence, without thinking of the three persons of the Trinity. We have a complete perception of God's immensity or his existence. But these perceptions are inadequate. Otherwise an unbeliever, relying on the idea of God as a unity, could deny that there are three persons in one God. But is not this the same logic as you apply,* when denying that the body has mind or thought?

Appendix

[419–21] **Further points for clarification:**

1. How I know for certain that I have a clear idea of my soul.
2. How I know for certain that this idea is quite distinct from any other thing.
3. How I know for certain that it has no corporeal element whatever.

Further objections by other philosophers and geometers:

We simply cannot accept your insistence that thought cannot be a bodily function. Some bodies, experience shows, can think, others not. You have got to the point where you seem unable to realize that the properties and operations of the soul depend on bodily motions.

We can clearly and distinctly perceive mathematical truths, but your arguments do not give us the same kind of clear conviction that the soul is distinct from the body or that God exists. This is not because we have failed to meditate along with you: we have read your work very carefully, we have a lifetime's experience of metaphysical argument, and we have made the effort to lift ourselves above the body. We do not know what can be performed by bodies in motion. Nor do you or anyone know with what attributes God may endow a subject. So how do you know that God has not endowed some bodies with the ability to think?*

SIXTH REPLIES

1. It is certainly true that *no one can be certain he is thinking, or that* 422 *he exists, unless he knows what thought is, and what existence is.* But reflexive knowledge or knowledge acquired by means of demonstration is not required for this; still less, the knowledge of reflexive knowledge, by which he knows that he knows, and again that he knows that he knows that he knows, and so on to infinity; we could not have this kind of knowledge about anything. It is altogether enough that he should know it by the internal kind of knowledge that always precedes the reflexive kind, and that, as regards thought and existence, is so innate in all human beings that, although perhaps if we were sunk in prejudice, and attentive more to words than their meaning, we could imagine that we do not have it, we cannot really not have it. So when someone is aware that he is thinking, and that it follows that he exists, although perhaps he has never asked what thought is, or what existence is, he cannot, however, be without sufficient knowledge of both to satisfy himself of this point.

2. Nor, when someone is aware that he is thinking, and understands what being moved means, can it happen that he thinks *he is deceived and is not thinking but only being moved.* For since he has a completely different idea or notion of thought than of bodily motion, 423 he must understand one of them as distinct from the other: even if, on account of the habit of attributing several various properties,

between which no connection is known to exist, to a single subject, he may happen to wonder whether he is one and the same being that thinks and that moves from one place to another; or even to affirm that he is. And we should note that there are two ways in which things of which we have different ideas may be taken as one and the same thing: i. in respect of unity and identity of nature; ii. in respect of unity of composition. Thus, for example, the idea we have of shape is different from the idea we have of motion; the idea we have of intellection is different from the idea we have of volition; likewise we have different ideas of bone and flesh, and of thought and an extended thing. Nonetheless, we clearly perceive that a substance of which shape is a property has also the property of being capable of motion, so that a thing that has shape and a thing that is mobile are one and the same, in respect of unity of nature; and that likewise a thinking thing and a willing thing are one and the same, in respect of unity of nature. However, we do not perceive the same of a thing we are considering in the form of bone, and a thing we are considering in the form of flesh.* Therefore, we cannot take them to be one and the same in respect of unity of nature, only in respect of unity of composition: that is, inasmuch as one and the same animal has bones and flesh. Now here the question is, whether we perceive a thinking thing and an extended thing to be one and the same in respect of unity of nature (which would mean finding some affinity or connection between thought and extension, such as we found between shape and motion, or intellect and volition); or rather whether they are to be said to be one and the same only in respect of unity of composition, inasmuch as they are found in the same human being, just as bones and flesh are found in the same animal. I affirm the latter, because I realize that there is an utter distinction or diversity between the nature of an extended thing and that of a thinking thing, just as much as there is between bones and flesh.

424

There is an appeal to authority here, in the claim that no one can understand my arguments. In fact several people claim to have done so. One witness who after sailing to America claimed to have seen the Antipodes* would deserve to be believed more than a thousand people who say the Antipodes do not exist simply because they do not know they do. Likewise, one person who claims to have understood an argument properly is of more weight than a thousand who say without proof that no one can understand it. Being unable to understand something oneself is no grounds for concluding that no one else can understand it.

I am certain that thought cannot be reduced to bodily motion, but I cannot 425 answer for other people, however attentive and in their opinion perspicacious, if they think only in terms of the imagination, instead of the intellect.

3. This view of souls and angels as corporeal has been rejected by the Church, and by all philosophers, so there is no need to bother with it. Supposing the soul were transmitted by one's parents, this would not make it corporeal.

If I conceded that dogs and monkeys could think, it would not follow 426 that the human mind was one with the body, but that minds and bodies were distinct in the animals also.

But in fact I have not simply asserted, as is here assumed, that animals do not have thought:* I have proved it by very solid reasons, which no one has yet refuted. And it is those who claim that *dogs know that they are running when they are awake, and even when they are asleep that they are barking*, as if they had access to their hearts, who are doing so without proof. And even if they add *that they do not believe that the actions of animals can be explained without sensation, life, and a soul* (which, as I read it, means without thought: for I have never denied that animals have what is commonly called life, or a bodily soul, or organic senses)* *by mechanical means, and would wager any stake in support of their belief that this is an utterly impossible and ridiculous idea*, this does not count as an argument.

People used to laugh at the belief in the Antipodes: but such laughter is no proof of falsity.

If there are people who believe human beings can be explained purely mechanically, this proves only that there are some very confused human 427 beings out there.

Some people conceive everything in such confused fashion, and cling so tenaciously to their existing opinions, which they understand purely verbally, that, rather than changing them, they will deny of themselves what they cannot help constantly experiencing in themselves. For there is no way we do not constantly experience in ourselves that we think.

Anyone who denies he thinks must be clinging to the belief that human beings and beasts operate in the same way. Therefore:

When it is proved to him that beasts do not think, he prefers to strip himself, as well, of thinking, of which he cannot not be conscious in himself [*sibi conscius*], than change his opinion that he operates in the same way as the beasts.

Such people are few, many fewer than those who take the more reasonable line* that, if thought cannot be distinguished from bodily motion, it must be found in the beasts as well as in us, and the differences between us and them are only of degree.

428   4. The less powerful the supposed source of the atheist's being, the more reason he will have to doubt, since his nature may be so imperfect he will be in error even when something appears most evident to him. Only the recognition of a truthful God can rid him of this doubt.

5. God cannot deceive us. The form of deception is a privation, thus incompatible with the supreme being. We could not believe in God's revelation, if we thought he might deceive us.

[428–31] Descartes proceeds to answer specific objections (the suffering of the damned, the evidence of scripture passages) but only in so far as they might be held to affect his own positions. He points out that he does not profess to be a theologian, but is content to repeat what others have said.

431   6. As for the freedom of the will, its nature is very different in God and in us. For it is self-contradictory to say that God's will has
432   not been from all eternity indifferent to everything that has come to pass or will ever come to pass, because we can imagine nothing good, nothing true, nothing that is to be believed, or done, or not done, of which the idea existed in the divine will before its nature was determined by the divine will to be what it is. Nor am I speaking here of priority in time: there was no kind of priority in respect of order, or nature, or of the reasoning reason, as they call it, such that this idea of good impelled God to choose one alternative rather than the other.* For example, he did not will to create the world in time because he saw that this would be better than creating it from all eternity. Nor did he will the three angles of a triangle to be equal to two right angles because he saw that they had to be this way, and so on. On the contrary, because he willed to create the world in time, this is better than if it had been created from all eternity. And because he wanted the three angles of a triangle to be necessarily equal to two right angles, this is now true, and cannot be otherwise than true. The same applies to everything else. And this does not mean we cannot say that the merits of the saints are the cause of their obtaining eternal life;* for they do not cause this in the sense of determining God to will something, they are only the cause of the effect of which God willed from all eternity that they should be the cause.

And thus God's supreme indifference is the supreme indication of his omnipotence. But as to human beings, since they find the nature of all that is good and true already determined by God, and their will cannot be moved towards anything else, it is obvious that they embrace the true and the good all the more willingly, and therefore all the more freely, the more clearly they see it; and they are never indifferent, except when they do not know what is better or truer, or 433 at least when they do not see it so clearly that there is no room for doubt about it. And thus the indifference pertaining to the human will is quite different from that belonging to the divine will. Nor is it relevant to say that the essences of things are indivisible: for, firstly, no essence can belong univocally to God and to the creature; and, finally, indifference does not pertain to the essence of human freedom, since we are free, not only when ignorance of what is right renders us indifferent, but also and especially when clear perception impels us to pursue something.*

7. I conceive the surface by which I think our senses are affected in exactly the same way as all mathematicians and philosophers usually conceive (or at least ought to conceive) the surface they distinguish from the body itself, and which they suppose to be without any depth at all. But the name 'surface' is used by mathematicians in two ways. They use it both for a body considered purely as having length and breadth, and without depth, even if they are not denying it has depth; and also for a mode of a body, that is, when it is said to be without depth. And therefore to avoid ambiguity I said I was speaking of the [latter] kind of surface that, being only a mode, cannot be part of a body; for a body is a substance, and a mode cannot be a part of a substance. But I did not deny that it was the outer edge of the body. On the contrary it can be very accurately called the outer edge of both the body contained and of the container: in the same way as two bodies are said to be contiguous of which the outer edges are 434 simultaneously present. For certainly, when two bodies touch each other, there is one and the same outer edge of both, which is part of neither, but the same mode of both, which can even remain if these two bodies are removed, provided other bodies take their places which are exactly of the same size and shape. Now the kind of place that the Aristotelians say is the surface of a surrounding body can be understood only as equivalent to this surface that is not a substance, but a mode. For the place of a tower is not changed, even if the air

around it is changed, or another body takes the place of the tower, and therefore the surface, which term is here used as equivalent to place, is not a part of the surrounding air or of the tower.

To demolish the belief in real accidents, I think there is no need to call for other reasons than those I have already advanced. For, first, since all sensations function by touch, nothing but the surface of bodies can be perceived by the senses. But if there are real accidents, they must be something different from this surface, which is a mode. Therefore, if they exist, they cannot be perceived by the senses. But they were thought to exist only because it was thought they were perceived by the senses. Moreover, the idea of 'real accidents' is self-contradictory, because whatever is real can exist separately from any other subject. But whatever can exist separately in this way is a substance, not an accident. It makes no difference to say that real accidents cannot be separated from their subjects naturally, but only 435 by the divine power. For what is produced naturally is produced purely by the ordinary power of God, which does not differ at all from his extraordinary power, and does not add anything else to things. Therefore if everything that can naturally exist without a subject is a substance, whatever can exist without a subject through some extraordinary manifestation of the divine power, should be called a substance. Certainly, I admit that one substance can accidentally modify another.* But when this happens, it is not the substance itself that has the form of an accident, but only the mode resulting from the change. Thus, when a garment accidentally modifies a person, the accident is not the garment itself but only 'being dressed'. But the main reason that led philosophers to posit real accidents was that they thought that without them sense perception could not be explained; and this is why I promised to give a detailed account in my Physics with respect to each of the senses in turn.* [. . .]

8. When we consider the immensity of God, it is manifest that there can be nothing at all that does not depend on him: not only any subsistent being, but no order, no law, no reason of truth and goodness. Otherwise, as has just been pointed out, he would not have been fully indifferent with regard to creating what he created. For if any essence [*ratio*] of goodness had existed prior to his act of preordaining, that would have determined him to do what is best. On the 436 contrary, it is because he determined himself to make the things that now exist, that they are, as Genesis says, 'very good'.* That is, the

essence of their goodness depends on his having decided to make
them as they are. And there is no need to ask what kind of causal
relationship is involved in the dependence of this goodness, and of
other truths, both mathematical and metaphysical, on God: for since
the list of different kinds of cause* was put together by people who
perhaps had never thought of this form of causality, it would be
hardly surprising, if they had not found a name for it. But they did
in fact: for we can talk of an efficient cause here, in the same way as
the king is the efficient cause of the law, even though the law itself
has no physical existence, but only, as they say, a moral existence.
Nor is there any need to ask how God could have made it true from
all eternity that 2 × 4 does not equal 8: for I confess we cannot understand this. Yet, since for other reasons I rightly understand that there
can be nothing in any category of being that does not depend on
God, and that he could easily have created certain things in such
a way that we human beings cannot understand that they could be
otherwise than they are,* it would be contrary to all reason to doubt
what we do rightly understand, just because there is something here
that we do not understand and that we are not aware of having to
understand. Therefore we should not think that *the eternal truths
depend wholly on the human intellect, or on actually existing things*: they
depend on God alone, who created them from all eternity, as the
supreme lawgiver.

9. To have an accurate idea of the certitude of sense-perception,
we need to distinguish three levels within it. The first is a matter
purely of the bodily organ's being affected by external objects, and
this can be nothing other than the motion of the particles of this 437
organ, and the change of shape and place resulting from this motion.
The second contains everything that immediately results in the mind
on account of its being united to the bodily organ that is affected in
this way. Of this kind are perceptions of pain, arousal, thirst, hunger,
colours, sound, flavour, smell, heat, cold, and so forth, which arise,
as was stated in the Sixth Meditation, from the union and virtual
fusion of the mind and the body. The third level includes all the
judgements that, on the occasion of motions in the bodily organs, we
have been accustomed to make since childhood about things existing
outside us.

For instance, when I see a stick, we should not think that some
'intentional species' fly from the stick into the eye,* but only that the

rays of light reflected from the stick stimulate certain motions in the optic nerve, and, via the optic nerve, in the brain as well, as I explained in considerable detail in the *Dioptrics*. It is in this cerebral motion that the first level of sensation, which we have in common with the beasts, consists. But from it follows the second, which covers only the perception of colour and light reflected from the stick, and arises from the fact that the mind is so intimately conjoined with the brain that it is affected by the motions taking place within the brain. And this would be all we should include in sense-perception, if we were trying to distinguish it properly from intellection. For when I judge, from this sensation of colour by which I am affected, that the stick, existing outside me, is coloured, and when I estimate its size, shape, and distance from the extension and the boundaries of this colour and from the relation of its position to the parts of the brain, even though these activities are commonly ascribed to the senses, for 438 which reason I included them here in the third level of sensation, it is nonetheless clear that they depend on the intellect alone. And I proved in the *Dioptrics* that size, distance, and shape are perceived by reasoning alone, deducing them from one another.* The only difference is this: the judgements we make now, on the basis of some new observation, we attribute to the intellect; but the judgements we first formed, or the conclusions we first reached from reasoning, in childhood, about things that affected our senses, although made in exactly the same way as now, we ascribe to the senses. This is because in these cases habit has made the judging and reasoning so rapid (or, rather, causes us to remember judgements once made by us about similar things), that we fail to distinguish such judgements from pure sense perception.

From this it is clear that when we say that *the certainty of the intellect is far greater than that of the senses,** it means only that those judgements that we form when we have reached maturity on the basis of new observations, are more certain than those we formed in our earliest infancy, and without thinking about them. This is undoubtedly true. For it is clear that we are not dealing here with the first and second levels of sensation, because there can be no falsity in them. So when it is said *that the stick appears broken in the water on account of refraction*, this is tantamount to saying that it appears to us in a way that would lead a child to judge it is broken, and that would 439 even lead us, on the basis of the prejudices to which we have grown accustomed since childhood, to form the same judgement. But what you add here, that *this mistake is not corrected by the intellect, but by touch*, I cannot agree to, because even if we judge the stick to be straight by means of touch, that is, by means of the same kind of judgement to which we have grown accustomed since childhood and which is therefore called *sensation*, this is not, however, sufficient for correcting the visual error. We need, further, to take the trouble to find a reason to show us that in this case we should trust to the judgement based on touch rather than the judgement based on sight. And since this reason has not been in us ever since childhood, it must be attributed not to sensation, but to the intellect alone. And therefore this very example shows that only the intellect can correct the errors of the senses; nor can any example be found of error due to trusting the operations of the mind rather than the senses.

10. Since the remaining points are put forward as doubts rather than objections, I do not have so much confidence in myself as to venture to undertake to give a sufficient explanation of points on which, as I see, several highly learned and intelligent men are still in doubt. But nonetheless, I wish to do the best I can for my cause, and will therefore frankly say by what means it has come about that I have freed myself altogether from my doubts. For in this way, if the same means are useful to other people, I shall be very pleased; but if not, I shall at least not feel myself to be guilty of rashness.

When I first, for the reasons set out in these Meditations, con- 440 cluded that the human mind was really distinct from the body, and was better known than the body, and so forth, I was indeed forced to assent to these views: for I could discover nothing in them that was incoherent or that was not inferred from evident principles, according to the rules of logic. But I admit that I was not fully convinced, and my experience was almost the same as that of astronomers, who, when they have proved by reasoning that the sun is several times larger than the earth, cannot help judging, while they are looking at it, that it is smaller. However, having proceeded further, and, still relying on the same fundamental principles, moved on to the consideration of physical things, I realized, first, by attending to the ideas or notions of all sorts of things that I found within myself, and by carefully distinguishing them from one another, so that all my judgements would fully agree with the things themselves, that nothing at all belongs to the essence of body, except this: that it is a thing having length, breadth, and depth, plus the capacity to take on different shapes and to move in various ways; and that these shapes and motions are only modes that no power can make to exist without the body itself; but that colours, smells, tastes, and so forth, were only various sensations existing in my thought, and differing just as much from bodies as pain differs from the shape and motion of the weapon that inflicts pain; and finally that weight, hardness, and the power of heating, attracting, purging, and all the other qualities we experience in bodies, consist solely in motion or the privation of motion, and in the configuration and position of parts.

441   These opinions were very different from those I had previously held on these points, and so I began to consider the causes of my earlier beliefs. And I discovered that the key factor was that from my childhood on I had formed judgements about various natural things, inasmuch as these contributed to preserve the life I was just embarking on, and that I had later clung to these opinions I had formed at that stage. And since at that age my mind used the bodily organs less correctly, and, being more firmly attached to them, thought nothing without their aid, it was aware of things only confusedly; and, although it was conscious in itself of its own nature, and had within itself an idea of thought, as well as one of extension, yet because it could not understand anything without imagining something at the same time, it took understanding and imagining to be one and the same, and related all the notions it had of intellectual things to the body. And since in my subsequent life I had never emancipated myself from these prejudices, I knew nothing at all sufficiently distinctly, and nothing that I did not suppose to be corporeal—even though I often formed such ideas or concepts of the things I supposed to be corporeal as related more to minds than to bodies.

For example, when I conceived weight as some kind of real quality present within solid bodies, even though I called it a *quality*, inasmuch as I related it to the bodies in which it was present, yet because I added the word 'real' I was in fact thinking it was a substance: just as a garment, considered in itself, is a substance, even though, when 442 considered in relation to the person wearing it, it is a quality. And likewise the mind also, even though it is in reality a substance, can be called a quality of the body to which it is attached. And even though I imagined weight to be distributed all through the body that is heavy, I did not believe it had the kind of extension that constitutes the nature of bodies. For the true extension of a body is such that all its parts are impossible to penetrate. And I thought that there was the same weight in a piece of wood ten feet long as in a mass of gold or some other metal one foot long. In fact I thought that the same quantity could be contracted within a mathematical point. Indeed, even when the weight was thus distributed equally throughout the body, I saw it could exert its whole force in any part of it, because by whatever part of itself it is attached to a rope, it pulled on the rope with its whole weight, in exactly the same way as if the weight were distributed only in the part in contact with the rope, and not in the other parts. And indeed even today I understand the mind to be coextensive with the body in just this way, wholly present in the whole, and wholly present in any one part. But that the idea I had of weight was partly derived from the idea I had of mind appears above all from this: I thought that weight carried bodies downwards towards the centre of the earth, as if it contained some knowledge in itself of the centre. For this certainly cannot happen without knowledge, nor can there be any knowledge except in a mind. On the other hand, I ascribed several other properties to weight that cannot be understood of the mind in this way: such as divisibility, measurability, and so on.

But once I had sufficiently reflected on all this, and drawn a care- 443 ful distinction between the idea of the mind and the ideas of body and bodily motion, and had realized that all the other ideas of real qualities and substantial forms* I had previously held had been formed and invented by me, by running these different ideas [of mind and body] together, I easily liberated myself from all the doubts that are here put forward. For, first of all, I did not doubt that I had *a clear idea of my mind*, inasmuch as I was intimately conscious of it in myself;* and that *this idea was totally different from the ideas of other things, and contained nothing corporeal*, because when I had investigated the true ideas of other things, and seemed to myself to have acquired a knowledge of them in general, I found nothing at all in them that did not differ radically from the idea of the mind. And I found there to be a far greater distinction between things that, however attentively I thought of both, nonetheless appeared as distinct, such as mind and body, than there is between things of which, indeed, we can understand one without thinking of the other, but of which we see, when we are thinking of both, that one cannot exist without the other. For instance, we can certainly understand the immensity of God even though we are not considering his justice. But it is completely impossible, when we are considering both, to think him to be immense and yet not just. And indeed the existence of God can be truly known, even if one is ignorant of the persons of the Most Holy Trinity,* inasmuch as these cannot be perceived except by a mind enlightened by faith. Even so, when they are perceived, I deny that we can understand there to be a real distinction between them in respect of the divine essence, although one does exist in respect of relationships.

444

And finally I ceased to fear that perhaps I had succumbed to pre-conceptions or error in my analysis, when, from the fact that I saw that *there are some bodies that do not think*, or rather clearly understood that some bodies can exist without thought, I preferred to argue that thought did not belong to the nature of bodies, rather than concluding, from the fact that I saw that *certain other bodies, namely human ones, that do think*, that thought is a mode of bodies. For in fact I have never seen or perceived that human bodies think, but only that the same human beings have both thought and a body. I realized that this comes about through the combination of a thinking thing with a bodily thing for this reason: by examining the thinking thing separately, I could discover nothing in it that belonged to a body, and likewise could discover no thought in the nature of bodies, considered separately. But on the other hand, by examining all the modes both of body and mind, I could discover none at all of which the concept did not depend on the concept of the thing of which it was a mode. And from the fact that we often see two particular things together we cannot rightly conclude that they are one and the same; whereas from the fact that we sometimes discover one of them without the other, we can infer with certainty that they are distinct. Nor should the power of God deter us from making this inference: for it is no less repugnant to the understanding that two things that we clearly perceive as distinct should be intrinsically and without composition one and the same, than that things that are in no way distinct should be separated; and therefore, if God endowed certain bodies with the power of thought* (as he has indeed endowed human bodies), this power can be separated from them, and thus is nonetheless really distinct from them.

445

Nor is it any wonder that in the past, before I had liberated myself from the prejudices of the senses, I rightly perceived that $2+3=5$ and that when equals are subtracted from equals, the remainder is equal, and many things of that kind, although at that point I did not think that the *soul of man is distinct from his body*. For I am well aware that the reason why, when I was still altogether a child, I never made any false judgements about generally accepted propositions is that I was not then familiar with these, and children do not learn to count to two and three before they are capable of judging whether they make five or not. On the other hand, from earliest infancy I conceived mind and body (I mean, the mind and the body of which I was confusedly aware of being composed) in some sense as one thing; and it happens in virtually all imperfect knowledge that many things are apprehended as if they were one and the same that subsequently have to be distinguished by more careful examination.

Descartes professes himself surprised at the objectors' suggestion that if he were to reread his work in the same analytical spirit as he would read the works of an adversary he would be less convinced that everyone should agree with his arguments, since the objectors have not shown any flaw in these. He is less struck by the fact that learned men withhold assent from his conclusions than by their failure to refute his assumptions and inferences. The refusal to accept the conclusions may be due to their holding long-standing and deep-rooted alternative views. 446

Nor can I see any possible reason why neither these men nor any others, to the best of my knowledge, have up to now found any fault in my arguments, except that the arguments themselves are altogether true and certain, particularly since they do not start from any obscure or unknown principles, but from an initial radical doubt of everything, and then are gradually deduced from the notions that appear most evident and most certain of all to a mind free of prejudices: from this it follows that there can be no errors at all in them that could not be easily spotted by anyone of average intelligence. 447 And hence it seems to me at this point that I can fairly conclude not that my writings are undermined by the authority of these most learned men, who, having read them several times over, cannot yet assent to them, but that, on the contrary, they are confirmed by the authority of the same men, since, after such long and careful examination, they have pointed out no errors or faulty reasoning in the course of my demonstrations.

SEVENTH OBJECTIONS

WITH NOTES BY THE AUTHOR, OR DISSERTATION ON FIRST PHILOSOPHY

Preamble by Bourdin

[451] (A) I agree to your request for comments on your method, (B) provided it does not involve discussion of any writings on the subject: instead, you will question me about the difficulties involved in the search for a new method.

Notes by Descartes

[452–4] (A) I never asked him for comments on my method, only for a copy of his attack on the *Meditations*. I did ask other Jesuits to examine my writings. I would have thought that the author of this dissertation was acting as a spokesman for the Society of Jesus, but I cannot think that the Society's views could be represented by a text composed of quibbles, sophisms, abuse, and verbosity. The positions he challenges are figments of his own imagination: he distorts my views beyond all recognition.

(B) Your refusal to engage in textual discussion is simply a stratagem to enable you to attack my *Meditations* without drawing readers' attention to them by attacking them openly. You have produced a distorted image of me, a mask, by clumsily stitching together fragments of my *Meditations*.

Bourdin: Question 1: Whether and in what way doubtful things should be considered as false

[454–9] You ask if your rule 'Whatever is open to the slightest doubt should be considered as false' is a sound method of investigating truth. This involves three questions:

1. What does 'open to the slightest doubt' mean?
2. What does 'considered as false' mean?
3. How far should this 'considering as false' extend?

(§1) (C) You distinguish between doubts based on valid reasons (e.g. about the existence of the external world) and doubts relying on the evil genius hypothesis (e.g. about mathematical truths).

(D) Nothing is exempt from the latter kind of doubt, until we are certain there is a God.

(§2) (E): To treat a doubtful proposition as false, is to believe and affirm the contrary as true. So if it is not certain $2 + 3 = 5$, I am supposed to say $2 + 3 \neq 5$. If it is not certain I am not dreaming, I should affirm 'I am dreaming'. Likewise, if what appears clear and certain to one who doubts whether he is dreaming or waking may not be clear and certain, I should affirm that it is false and obscure.

(F) You would say that some things are so certain, that they cannot appear doubtful even to those who are dreaming or mad. But since they can feel certain about things that are in fact absurd, why should things that are certain in fact not appear to them as false and doubtful? There can be no certainty that what appears certain to one doubting whether he is dreaming or waking is in fact certain:* on your showing, it should be considered as false.

(§3) I am supposed to convince myself $2 + 3 \neq 5$ and that this has to be certainly true. But you can't mean to suggest it is certainly true. So it must be as doubtful as $2 + 3 = 5$. Therefore, I should treat it as false, that is, affirm that $2 + 3 = 5$. Again, if I am uncertain whether bodies exist, I have to treat 'bodies exist' as false, and affirm 'bodies do not exist'. But since this is uncertain, I have to treat it as false, and say 'bodies exist' again. So they exist and do not exist, and

(G) I am going round in circles.

Although now you tell me that I am supposed to treat both alternatives as false and unreliable.

To answer the three questions above:

1. We can doubt everything, especially material things, as long as we have no foundations of knowledge besides those we had previously.

2. To consider something as false is altogether to reverse one's inclination to believe it, and to pretend one's opinion about it is false.

3. What is doubtful should be considered as false to this extent, that its opposite is also considered as doubtful and false.

Descartes: Notes on Question 1

[460-2] (C) His attempt to summarize my approach to doubt suggests that I think we have good reasons to doubt the existence of the external world, and omits the crucial point that my doubts are metaphysical, and have nothing to do with practical life. Bourdin thus gives the unwary reader the impression that I am so mad as to doubt, in ordinary life, whether the earth exists, and whether I have a body.

(D) I do not say 'nothing' is exempt from hyperbolical doubt. I have often explained that we cannot doubt what we clearly perceive when we are attending to it. Doubt creeps in when we are no longer attending to it, until we know that whatever we clearly perceive is true.* I doubted everything in the First Meditation, because I supposed I was not attending to any clear perception. Bourdin implies that because I have once doubted everything I can henceforth never be certain of anything.

(E) My method involves treating doubtful propositions with no more respect than ones that are plainly false. No sensible person could really imagine it involves trying to believe the opposite of every doubtful proposition.

461 (F) He could indeed have concluded from my writings that whatever is clearly and distinctly perceived by someone is true, even though the someone may at the same time be doubting whether he is dreaming or waking—even though, if you like, he is dreaming or delirious: because nothing can be clearly and distinctly perceived, whoever is doing the perceiving, that is not such as it is perceived, in other words, that is not
462 true.* But because only the prudent correctly distinguish between what is so perceived, and what only seems or appears to be, I would not be surprised at this good man's here confusing the two.

(G) I said that we should have no greater regard for things that are doubtful than we would if they were altogether false, so that my thought could be withdrawn from them completely, but not so as to affirm one thing one minute and the contrary the next.

His summary of my position at the end of this question [points 1 to 3] contains none of the absurdities he attributes to me, so he was not serious when he attributed them to me.

Bourdin: Answer to Question 1

[462–3] 1. If you mean only that, when seeking for certainty, we should not rely on positions that are not certain, this is right, but there is nothing new here: all philosophers would say the same.

2. If you mean we should not even give any consideration to doubtful positions, this comes to much the same thing and every beginner in philosophy is taught it.

3. If you mean we should treat doubtful positions as false, and treat the contrary positions as secure foundations, you are wrong, because one cannot achieve certainty by starting from doubtful propositions,* or treat doubtful propositions as certain.

4. Anyone who tries this method on a specific issue (e.g. whether bodies exist) will end up going round in circles. (H)

Descartes: Notes on Bourdin's Answer

[464–6] Concerning points 1 and 2 he agrees with me, but accuses me of banality. Concerning 3 and 4 he attacks an opinion he wants people to think is mine, but which no one in their right mind could hold. He is trying to get people to think that my ideas are ludicrous or banal. I am not interested in novelty for its own sake: my opinions are old, because they have always been valid. If he really thought my opinions so absurd, why would he bother refuting them?

(H) It is a complete misreading to think that my principles involve asserting the contrary of what is found to be doubtful.

When I said in the First Meditation that I wanted to attempt for 465 some time to persuade myself of the opposite of my previous rashly formed beliefs, I immediately added that the reason I wanted this was so that, having, so to speak, balanced the weight of prejudice on either side, I would not incline to one view more than to its opposite: I was not intending to take one or other view to be true, or to establish it as a foundation for certain knowledge.

(Descartes casts doubt on Bourdin's honesty in attributing this view to him.)

I marvel at the force of his imagination, because, although he is 466 fighting only against this idle chimera conjured up out of his own brain, he has adopted exactly the same stance and always used the same words, as if he had me for an adversary, ready to fight back face to face.

Bourdin: Question 2: Whether the renunciation of all doubtful beliefs is the right philosophical method

[466–7] (I) (Bourdin represents Descartes as summarizing his method. He then proposes testing the method, and asks Descartes to guide him through it, using the metaphor of a series of explorations. The titles of each section are Bourdin's.)

Bourdin: §1. The approach to the method is opened up*

[468–72] (K)* I am supposed to say that no earth, or bodies, or minds exist, and

(L) to reject all my former beliefs. All, without exception?

(M) But why should I doubt them? What are your reasons for requiring this? You say: the senses deceive us sometimes; sometimes we are dreaming; some people are mad, and think they see what is not there. But these are doubtful views, and your rule suggests we should accept as true only what is certain, what we can prove.

(N) In fact, since they are doubtful, by your rule, you should assert the opposite: 'the senses never deceive us', and so on. How can you so confidently assert that you sometimes dream? Not knowing whether you are waking or dreaming is no proof you do in fact dream: you may be being deceived by the evil genius into thinking you do. The evil-genius hypothesis poses difficulties you cannot overcome.

(O) The evil genius may be making you doubt propositions that are certain, so as to land you in difficulties you will never get out of. Before renouncing any beliefs, you should have found some certain criterion to indicate which beliefs ought to be renounced.

(P) Rejecting one's former opinions is a very serious matter.

(Q) You say that doubt will not lead to danger or error (p. 16). Is this itself beyond doubt? You are asking people to give up old certainties (2 + 3 = 5), because the genius might be deceiving them,

(R) and telling them to accept the shaky rule that doubt can never land them in error—yet might the genius not be deceiving them here too?

(S) I would be afraid of being too distrustful if I were to give up old truths*—do you have no similar fear?

(T) Do you really reject, as old beliefs, such propositions as; 'I have a clear and distinct idea of God'; 'Whatever I clearly and distinctly perceive is true'?;

(V) 'Thought, nutrition, and sensation have nothing to do with the body, only with the mind.' Do you really affirm the opposite of these?

(Bourdin then affects to remember that he has promised to submit to Descartes's guidance, and agrees to continue the journey.)

Descartes: Notes on §1

[473–7] (I) The summary has me rejecting all I knew as doubtful: but that would be self-contradictory. I rejected everything I *thought* I knew.

(K) Bourdin fails to see that at the start 'mind' is included among the objects of doubt, but that I later discover that a thinking thing exists, which I call a mind, so that I can say at that stage that the mind exists.

(L) He keeps pointlessly hammering away at the word 'all'.

473 [He reacts as if] I should regard the things I denied at one stage because I found them doubtful as for ever needing to be denied, as if it were impossible for them subsequently to be rendered evident and certain for me. And it should be noted that he himself everywhere treats doubt and certainty not as relationships between our knowledge and objects, but as permanently inhering properties of the objects, so that what we have once discovered to be doubtful can never subsequently be rendered certain.*

(M) A reason for doubting may itself be open to doubt, and yet valid, as long as we have not found a certain reason to set it aside.

(N) I assert nothing in the First Meditation: I merely put forward doubts.

(O) Again, Bourdin is considering doubt and certainty as qualities of propositions. If a proposition is presented to me by the evil genius as doubtful, it is doubtful. It looks as if the evil genius is disturbing Bourdin's thought processes.

(P) In the Fourth Replies and the preface to the Meditations, as well as in the *Discourse on the Method*, I made clear that I do not think that rejecting all one's former opinions is a fit exercise for everyone.*

(Q) When I said there was no danger in doubt, I meant from the point of view of practical life.*

(R) There is nothing shaky in my position: one who doubts does not affirm or deny, and therefore cannot err.

(S) He doesn't give reasons why we should avoid being too distrustful. His fear of being too distrustful is an index that he is not certain of his position (he does not *know* we should not be distrustful), so that he should, logically, take up a position of distrust.

(T) He fails to see that rejecting opinions applies only to those that have not yet been clearly and distinctly perceived, unlike the propositions he mentions here. He is trying to insinuate I have doubts about God—but I have always made clear that doctrines of faith and morals are excepted from this renunciation of opinions. Clear and distinct perception puts an end to doubt and scepticism—but the best preparation for it is to renounce one's former opinions.

(V) I make it perfectly clear that nutrition is in fact a purely bodily function: when I ascribed it to the soul in the Second Meditation (p. 19), I was speaking with the voice of common opinion. This error alone shows he does not understand the Meditations.

Bourdin: §2. An entry to the method is prepared

[477-9] (X) You begin by affirming your existence.*

(Y) You talk about conceiving your existence in your mind (p. 18)—but hadn't you rejected the idea of 'mind'? You go over your old beliefs about yourself, but what is the point of this if you have rejected them as doubtful? Can what is doubtful give access to what is certain?

(Z) You say you believed you were a human being—hadn't you rejected this? How would you answer a Pythagorean, who would say you were once a rooster?* When you ask what a human being is (p. 18), you are presumably speaking of the concept of human being we have now rejected—a composite of soul and body.

Descartes: Notes on §2

[480-2] (X) This shows he admits I am right to start my philosophy with the knowledge of my own existence, though elsewhere he talks of me as beginning by rejecting all doubtful opinions.

(Y) To 'conceive with the mind' here means simply to think. I am not working with a pre-existing concept of the mind as a part of the human being. Believing doubtfulness is a quality of propositions, Bourdin fails to see that I could legitimately doubt the concept of mind at one stage, and revive it at another, when it becomes the object of a clear perception, just as he fails to see that I do not imply that what I doubt at one stage must be forever rejected as false.

(Z) Descartes explains his attitude to his prior beliefs:

481 Suppose he had a basket full of apples,* and was afraid that some of the apples might be rotten, and wanted to remove them, so that they did not spread their rottenness to the others, how would he do this? Would he not first of all empty the basket altogether, and then, examining the apples one after the other, put back only those he could see were unaffected, and throw the rest away? By the same token, then, those who have never philosophized properly have various opinions in their mind, and since they began to accumulate these in childhood, they are rightly afraid that most of them will be false, and try to separate these from the rest, in case they all become uncertain from being jumbled up together. And there is no better way to achieve this than to reject them all together and at the same time as uncertain or false; and then, going through them one after the other, to take back only those they discover to be true and indubitable. And thus I was not wrong to reject everything to start with; then, realizing that nothing was known by me more certainly and evidently than that I, since I thought, existed, I was not wrong to assert this first of all. And finally I was not wrong to investigate subsequently what I had once thought I was, not so as to readopt all my former beliefs, but so as to readopt any I perceived to be true, reject any I perceived to be false, and set aside for later examination any I perceived to be uncertain.

The rest of the objection is irrelevant. I was simply considering my former beliefs, which coincide with those spontaneously formed by most other people.

Bourdin: §3. What is a body?

[482–4] (Aa) What conception of body are you talking about? The old, now supposedly faulty, one, which you sum up (p. 19)? What about more recent philosophers' views? There are definitions of body that make it capable of sensation (found in dogs), thought (found in monkeys), and imagination (found in mules). You are entitled to define it in your own way, but your definition is only partial, and leaves many disputed points unresolved.

Descartes: Notes on §3

[484] (Aa) Descartes protests that he is sticking to the accepted sense of the words 'mind' and 'body'.

Bourdin: §4. What is the soul?

[485–6] (Bb) Your investigation of the soul (p. 19) seems to rely on established beliefs about it. But philosophers disagree massively about the soul: some think it a kind of subtle body dispersed through the solid body and performing the functions of sensation, imagination, and thought. It is not enough to protest that this is an impious atheistic view.

(Cc) Since you aim to prove that the soul is incorporeal and spiritual, you should not take for granted that it is, but have a proper debate with the rival views of the nature of body, soul, and mind.

Descartes: Notes on §4

[487] (Bb) This is not my approach at all.*

(Cc) I did not take it for granted that the soul is spiritual. What is asserted (the corporeality of the soul) without supporting reasons requires no answer. I did not begin with the words 'body', 'soul', 'mind', and then discuss how to apply them. I distinguished two really distinct kinds of substance, thinking and extended, and called one 'mind', the other 'body', but the terms are unimportant.

Bourdin: §5. An entry into the method is attempted

[488–90] The Cogito is unshakeable.

(Dd) So now I ask *what* I am. I must be one of the things I thought I was. I thought I was a human being comprising a body and a mind.

(Ee) I cannot be a body: I think I can see or touch myself, but this is obviously false because I have renounced my former beliefs.

(Ff) So I am a mind, a thinking thing.

(Gg) But hadn't I rejected all these former beliefs about what I was?

(Hh) You seem to be saying, though, that I am either a body or a mind. So if there is something in me I once believed a property of body, I am a body.* But I thought thinking was a bodily function. Therefore I am a body!

(Ii) If you tell me 'thought is a mental function', why did you not tell me to stick to this belief when I was getting rid of all my other ones? But why should we obey you, simply because you say so? Aren't you simply assuming what you are supposed to be proving? What about the philosophers who hold that the animals think, and that thought, in them and in us, is the property of an extended, not a spiritual soul? How would you convince them?

Descartes: Notes on §5

[491–2] (Dd) I never said that I must be one of the things I once thought I was,

(Ee) or that I drew conclusions by putting things in doubt. I say the contrary when I admit that the body, whose existence I call into question, might indeed be identical with me (p. 20).

(Ff) I never asked 'Am I a mind?' I begin with the discovery of myself as a thinking thing, which then provides a content for the concept of 'mind'.

(Gg) I never assumed that any of my former beliefs was true: I examine them to see if they are.

(Hh) I never said 'I am either a body or a mind'.

(Ii) Nor have I assumed that mind is incorporeal. I demonstrate that it is, in the Sixth Meditation.

Henceforth I will no longer engage in the tedious task of pointing out his errors. It is embarrassing to see him play the clown in this way, passing himself off as apprehensive, slow-witted, unintelligent.*

Bourdin: §6. Another attempt to enter is made

[493–7] (Kk) You discuss what you believed in the past. But shouldn't you doubt that you ever believed these things, or that there was a past in which you believed them? Besides, the Cogito now seems doubtful: am I dreaming I am thinking? Can I make a distinction between thinking and dreaming? Or might I simply be dreaming that such a distinction exists? It looks as if thinking and dreaming are one and the same: so you are offering a method for dreaming.

Why do you not state your presupposition that (Ll) 'I am one of those things I once believed I was', or 'I am what I once believed I was'? Unless you do, you might be wasting your time examining what you once thought you were, because you might be something different from that. In which case this approach will get us no further.

Try another approach: 'I am either a mind or a body.' But how do you know you are either a mind or a body, since you have rejected both these concepts? You might be something else altogether. Try again: 'I am either a body or a non-body.'* You still have to assume that your prior idea of body was correct and exhaustive.

(Mm) Otherwise you are in the same position as the peasant who, seeing a wolf for the first time and trying to fit it into the list of animals he knows, concludes, first, that it is a donkey, and, then, that it is not an animal. It could be that you are basing your argument on an inadequate conception of body, which omits what could be in fact bodily functions such as thought, sensation, imagination.

Bourdin: §7. A third attempt to enter is made

[498–502] (Nn) You cannot say you are thinking, only that you are dreaming you are thinking. You are merely dreaming that the perception of your existence is clear and evident. What is absolutely certain and evident is one thing, what appears certain another, and the perception of your existence only appears to you certain and evident.

You are certain of your existence only in the present: you can learn nothing by turning back to the past because you are not certain of its existence.

(Oo) You argue that you have thought away everything, and no body or mind exists, in fact nothing exists (antecedent). Therefore, if you exist, you are not a body (consequent). But the argument cuts both ways: it also proves you are not a mind. Again, the antecedent is flawed, because you have to be there to say 'nothing exists'. The result is a logical paradox, such as 'I am lying'. So the antecedent and the consequent undermine each other.

Perhaps you mean you are not certain of being a *particular* body, mind, or thing. But you have an *indeterminate* certainty, immune to doubt, of being a body, or a mind, or some other thing.

(Pp) Your approach to self-knowledge is flawed. It cannot be derived from your previous knowledge, which you have renounced. So it must be based on what you do not yet know (which is absurd).

How can you move from saying you have no determinate knowledge of yourself to later affirming that you have such knowledge? The distinction between determinate and indeterminate knowledge is crucial and you have overlooked it.*

Bourdin: §8. A fourth attempt is made, and given up in despair

[503–7] (Qq) You said nothing exists: therefore you do not.

(Bourdin then gives a summary of Descartes's argument for his existence as a thinking thing.)

But you could have said all this at the start, without going through the circuitous route via universal rejection of prior beliefs.

(Rr) You now say you have a clear and distinct notion of thinking substance. Where did you get that from, or were you keeping it up your sleeve up to now? What do you mean by having a clear and distinct concept of thinking substance? Apparently, it is clear because you know certainly that thinking substance exists, and distinct, because you know nothing else. This thinking substance is not bodily or spiritual, or anything else.

But you fail to realize that we cannot infer the existence of anything from our own knowledge of it.* You overlook crucial distinctions between determinate and indeterminate, distinct and confused, explicit and implicit. Your argument proves too much, and therefore proves nothing. It could be reformulated to prove the thinking substance is a body: I am a thinking thing, I do not know if minds exist, therefore no minds exist, therefore my knowledge of my existence does not depend on my mind, therefore I am not a mind, therefore I am a body.

Bourdin: §9. A retreat is executed in the traditional form

[507–8] (Ss) (Bourdin bears out this last point by putting (what he takes to be) the argument into syllogistic form.)

> No thing that is such that we can doubt whether it exists or not, actually exists.
> All bodies are such that we can doubt whether they exist or not.
> Therefore no bodies actually exist.

> No bodies actually exist.
> Therefore nothing actually existing is a body. [. . .]
> I (the thinking substance) actually exist.
> Therefore I (the thinking substance) am not a body.

But we could perfectly well substitute 'mind' for 'body' in this argument, and it would then prove I am not a mind. The argument is formally valid, so the point of departure, the major premise, must be wrong.

(Tt) In fact the major premise, 'No thing that is such that we can doubt whether it exists or not, actually exists', is far too doubtful to serve as a foundation.

Descartes: Notes on §§6–9

[509–26] Much of what Bourdin says is frivolous,* especially what he says about dreams.

509   (Kk) I expressly pointed out that when I was speaking of abandoned beliefs, I was not dealing with what existed, but only with appearances, so that, in asking what I had once thought I was, I was only asking what at the current time it seemed to me that I had once thought. And when I said that I was thinking, I did not consider whether I was thinking while awake or in my dreams.

(Ll) The assumptions he thinks I should have stated are ridiculous: he must still be joking. It made perfect sense to examine former beliefs about my nature, even if they were incorrect, to see if they could throw any light on my nature now.

(Mm) Again, with his anecdote, Bourdin is acting the fool. My denial that the thinking substance is a body was not based on the supposition that my former ideas about bodies were correct, but on the incompatibility of extended substance and thought.

(Nn) As regards dreaming, I refer the reader back to my answer to point F: what is clearly and distinctly perceived is true, whatever the state of the perceiver.

(Oo) The rest of Bourdin's argument is directed against an imaginary opponent, a figment of his own brain.* He fails to understand the method of withdrawing assent from even true beliefs (the analogy of the apples is used again) and has become obsessed with the idea that everything is supposed to be rejected.*

(Pp) Bourdin fails to see (a) that:

There is no reason why someone should not learn from the things he 514 once knew, because, even if he had rejected them while they were doubtful, he could go back to them, once they had turned out to be true; and besides, even if it were conceded that nothing can be learned from things known in the past, at least there is another way lying wide open, via what is not yet known, but will be known by study and attention. But our author here conjures up an imaginary opponent, who not only concedes that the first way is blocked, but even closes off the second way himself by the few words: *I do not know that these things exist.* As if no knowledge of the existence of things could ever be acquired, and as if not knowing whether something exists prevented our having any knowledge of its essence.

(b) That his own distinction between determinate and indeterminate knowledge backfires on him.

By meditation and attention we can bring it about that what at the 515 moment we know only indeterminately and confusedly, we presently perceive clearly and determinately.

(Qq) (Descartes does not think this point worthy of a serious reply: again Bourdin is refuting imaginary positions.)

(Rr) He has overlooked the process by which I formed the clear and distinct perception of myself, listing the various properties of the thinking thing as well as other properties that do not belong to it, so as to distinguish the two. I say that the thinking thing is not a body, but not that it is not spiritual. He does not understand 'clear' and 'distinct'. Clear conception is not the same thing as certain knowledge: we can have certain knowledge of what we do not clearly understand (revealed religious truths or points we have clearly understood in the past). Knowledge of one thing can be distinct even if we have knowledge of many others.

519   Besides, his statement that *we cannot validly infer from knowledge to*
520   *being* is downright false. For even if it does not follow, from the fact that we know the essence of some thing, that the thing exists; and nor does it follow from the fact that we think we know something that it exists, if there is a possibility of our being mistaken, *the inference from knowledge to being is* perfectly *valid*, because it simply cannot be the case that we know something unless it is in fact as we know it: that is, either existent, if we perceive it to exist, or possessing such and such a nature, if only its nature is known to us.

He has given no proof that there is any thinking substance that is divisible.* Such a notion is incomprehensible, and harmful to the Christian religion, because it blurs the distinction between soul and body. The terms he says I ignore (determinately, indeterminately; distinctly, confusedly; explicitly, implicitly) are meaningless here.* It is not necessarily the case that to prove too much is to prove nothing, because the more we can prove the better, as long as it is properly proved. He keeps incorrectly asserting that I have rejected the existence of mind.

By putting my argument in syllogistic form, he is trying to contrast the syllogism, as a reliable method of reasoning, with mine. But I do use syllogism when it is appropriate.*

(Ss) Bourdin's syllogistic formulation of his argument is based on an absurd major premise, itself based on a total misunderstanding of the method of doubt set out in the First Meditation. I there explained I was *deliberately imagining* my prior opinions, however probable, to be false: it is not that I actually believed them to be false and asserted their contraries to be true. What is intended as an antidote to prejudice is treated by Bourdin as if it were meant as a metaphysical foundation, and at times what he says shows he realizes this.

The minor premise (every body/mind is such that we can doubt whether it exists) is also not a representation of my views. It is presented as timeless.* In fact, I discovered at the start of the Second Meditation, that a thinking thing (a 'mind') exists, and, in the Sixth, that bodies exist too.

(Tt) Descartes objects to Bourdin's misrepresentations of his position and his tactic of trying to bully his readers into agreement by mere repetition; he objects to his arrogant schoolmasterly tone, but decides that perhaps Bourdin is not altogether in his right mind.

Bourdin: Reply to Question 2

[527–35] 1. The starting point of the method is flawed. It lacks clear and evident principles to start from. It rejects old principles, but can only substitute their contraries, replacing the certain by the doubtful.

2. The means are defective. All traditional forms of argument, such as the syllogism, are rejected, no new forms put in their place.

3. The end-result is defective. The method has blocked all the avenues to truth: i. you are dreaming so your thoughts are worthless; ii. you should have begun by looking for propositions immune to doubt instead of doubting everything; iii. you treat the contrary of every proposition open to the slightest doubt as a fundamental principle: but you can build nothing on such principles.

4. *The method sins by excess. That is, it labours to achieve more than the* 530 *laws of prudence require of it, more than any mortal could demand of it. Some indeed request the existence of God and the immortality of the human mind to be demonstrated to them; but assuredly no one has been found up to now who has not been satisfied by knowing that God exists, and that the world is governed by him, and that human souls are spiritual and immortal with the same certainty as he knows $2 + 3 = 5$ or that 'I have a head', 'I have a body', so that to seek for some greater degree of certainty is a waste of effort. Besides just as in the practical sphere and the* 531 *conduct of life, there are definite limits to our certainty, which are how-ever quite sufficient for everyone to govern himself prudently and safely, so in the realms of meditation and speculation there are also definite limits. He who has reached these is certain, and certain to such an extent that he is entitled, putting no hope in or condemning any attempt to go beyond them, to remain prudently and in tranquillity within the limits of the precepts 'thus far, and no further', 'nothing in excess'. [. . .]*

5. *It sins by defect. That is, pruning more ruthlessly than necessary,* it still gathers no fruit. I call on you yourself as sole witness to and judge of this. What have you achieved by all this splendid display? What have you gained by this solemn renunciation of your former views, so wide-ranging and high-minded that you do not spare even yourself, but leave intact only this hackneyed refrain: I think, I am, I am a thinking thing? This, I say, which is so familiar even to the common herd that no one, since the creation of the world, has ever been found who doubted it even frivolously, let alone seriously took it upon himself to prove to himself that he was, that he existed, that he was a thinking thing.*

6. It has the universal faults: it blames everyone else for over-confident assertions and then makes similar assertions itself.

7. It has faults peculiar to itself, asserting positions ('I do not have a head', 'bodies do not exist', 'minds do not exist') that no one else would accept.

8. It sins by imprudence. Not realizing that the propositions ('there are no bodies') with which it replaces those it doubts are themselves doubtful, it imprudently relies on them.

9. It sins prudently, that is, knowingly, by depriving itself of everything necessary in the search for truth.

10. It sins by commission, going back to the old positions it had supposedly rejected.

11. It sins by omission, failing to provide proof for its key assumptions (e.g. the unreliability of the senses).

12. It has nothing new, or nothing good, and much that is superfluous. (Bourdin aims to show that anything Descartes says that is true is not new, and what he says that is new is false.)

If he is saying that he thinks, that is, that he understands, wills, imagines, perceives by the senses; and thinks in such a way that he intuits and considers this thinking by means of a reflexive act; so that he thinks, or knows and considers himself to be thinking (and this is what it really means to 534 *be conscious, and to have a consciousness of some act); and that this is truly the characteristic property of a faculty or thing that exists in a realm that is above matter, and that is purely spiritual; and that for this reason he is a mind or spirit; he will be saying what he has not yet said, and what he should have said, and what I was waiting for him to say, and what I have again and again wanted to suggest when I saw him labouring in vain to give birth: he will be indeed be saying something good, but nothing new, since we once learned this from our own teachers, and they from theirs, and so on, I should think, until we get back to Adam.*

But the rest of the work contains so much that is showy and superfluous, especially the renunciation of old opinions.

To say that only human beings have thought, imagination, and sensation is new, but entirely false, and you give no proof of it.

No doubt, you will work further on your method and remove all its current flaws.

Bourdin: Question 3: Can a new method be developed?

[535] (Only the title exists, and Bourdin either did not write any further or did not send his material to Descartes.)

Descartes: Notes [on Answer to Question 2]

[536–7] It would be enough to quote this judgement of my method to show its absurdity, except that the author's position in the world lends it authority, so I would ask readers to bear in mind that he has produced not the slightest argument against me, but merely distorted my positions.

I have proclaimed everywhere in my writings that I have followed 536 the example of architects in this respect: that, in order to construct solid buildings, in places where the rock, or clay, or any other firm 537 kind of soil is covered over with a surface of sand, they first of all dig trenches, and clear away all the sand and whatever else is resting on or mixed up with the sand, so as then to lay the foundations on solid earth. In the same way, I first cleared away everything doubtful, like the sand; and then realizing that I could not doubt that at least the doubting or thinking substance existed, I used this as the rock on which I set the foundations of my philosophy.

(Descartes then [537–56] goes through Bourdin's twelve-point Answer to Question 2, which had listed all the defects of the method, and translates them into criticisms levelled by the builder at the architect.)

Descartes: On the Answer to Question 2, §4

[In response to the claim that speculation should be content to 548 remain within limits beyond which it cannot go:] It is entirely false, when it comes to establishing a foundation for philosophy, that there are such limits to doubt, falling short of supreme certainty, within which we can remain prudently and in tranquillity. For since the truth consists in an indivisible point, it can happen that what we do not recognize to be supremely certain, however probable it appears, is utterly false. And surely he would not be a prudent philosopher who laid foundations for the whole of this science of his that he knew might perhaps be false. And indeed what answer could he make to the sceptics who push doubt beyond all limits? By what reason can he refute them? He will write them off as hopeless cases, or deserving of condemnation. All very well and good, to be sure: but in the meantime will they not write him off as well?* And we should not think that their sect died out a long time ago. It is thriving today as well as it ever did, and virtually everyone who thinks themselves more intelligent than ordinary people, finding nothing in the estab- 549 lished philosophy to satisfy them, and seeing no other that is truer, is fleeing to scepticism. And these are above all the ones who demand demonstrations of God's existence and of the immortality of the human mind. So much so that in what he says here our author is setting a very bad example, especially since he is a reputed scholar: for it shows that he does not think the errors of sceptical atheists can be refuted, and he is thus doing all he can to shore up and reinforce their position. In fact all the sceptics of today do not doubt *in practice* that they have a head, that $2 + 3 = 5$, and so forth. But they say that they are only treating these things *as if* they were true, because that is how they appear, but that they do not believe in them for certain, because there are no certain reasons impelling them to do so. And because the existence of God and the immortality of the human mind do not appear to them to be true in the same way, they think that therefore they should not even be treated in practice as if true, unless first proved by reasons more certain than any of those we have for accepting all appearances.* Now since these points have been so proved by me, and, to the best of my knowledge, by no one before me, it seems to me impossible to imagine a greater and more unworthy calumny than this of our author's, when, throughout his whole dissertation, he hammers away constantly at the point—entirely his own invention— that I have fallen into the error that is the sole point of departure of the sceptical sect, namely excessive doubt.

Descartes: On the Answer to Question 2, §12, subsection 5*

559 Again, when he says that, in order for a substance to be purely spiritual and to exist in a realm above matter (so as to deserve, he thinks, to be called a mind) it is not sufficient for it to be a thinking substance, but that, over and above this, it has to be thinking, by a reflexive act, that it is thinking, or to have a consciousness of its thought, he is under the same illusion as the builder, when he says that a skilled architect has to consider, by a reflexive act, that he possesses this skill, before he can be an architect. For even if no one is an architect who has not often considered, or at least, may have considered, that he possesses skill in building, it manifest that this consideration is not essential in order to be an architect. No more is a similar consideration or reflection required in order for a thinking substance to be raised above the level of matter. In fact the first thought, by which we become aware of something, differs no more from the second thought by which we become aware that we have become aware of it, than this second

thought from the third thought by which we become aware that we have become aware that we have become aware of it. And if the first kind of thinking is attributed to a corporeal thing, there is not the slightest reason for not attributing the second as well. For this reason we must note that our author's error is far more dangerous than the builder's: for by suppressing the true and most readily intelligible distinction between corporeal and incorporeal things, namely that the latter think and the former do not, and substituting another distinction, which can in no way appear essential, namely that the latter consider they are thinking, and the former do not consider it, he does all he can to block the understanding of the real distinction between 560 the human mind and the body.*

EXPLANATORY NOTES

LETTER TO THE SORBONNE

3 *how have they been so slow to find its Master?*: Wisdom 13: 8–9. The Book of Wisdom is accepted by Roman Catholics as canonical, though not by Protestants (who class it in the Apocrypha) or Jews. The translation quoted is that of the New Jerusalem Bible.

plain in them: the New Jerusalem translation has 'plain to them', but the Vulgate, which Descartes quotes, has *in illis* ('in them'). Descartes seems to be hinting that St Paul is authorizing his method of seeking to prove God's existence from our own minds rather than the external world.

4 *Council of the Lateran*: the Fifth Lateran Council of the Church sat from 1512 to 1517.

demonstrations: rigorous proofs yielding certain knowledge.

so clear and precise an order: the translation here follows the French text F, with its emphasis on the order of the exposition (the rhetorical art of 'disposition' or arrangement): the Latin text L is less explicit ('expound them so carefully and clearly').

5 *argue on both sides of any question*: Descartes is pointing to the scholastic habit of investigating philosophical questions by disputations, in which contrary views are asserted; a habit persisting in humanist rhetoric, which urged the necessity of being able to argue on either side of a question.

PREFACE TO THE READER

7 *so kind as to point it out to me*: see *Discourse*, 61, AT 6. 75.

8 *two quite long writings*: see AT 3. 296, 300.

SYNOPSIS

11 *the idea we possess of God can have only God as its cause*: see First Replies, p. 79.

12 *I am not at all dealing with sin*: in fact the reference to sin remains in the text of the Fourth Meditation (p. 42). Descartes is responding to an objection by the theologian Antoine Arnauld. See Fourth Objections and Replies, pp. 138, 159–60, and the letter to Mersenne of 18 March 1641, AT 3. 334–5.

FIRST MEDITATION

13 *from childhood onwards*: the importance of childhood in the formation of false beliefs ('prejudices') is stressed in the *Principles of Philosophy* (I. 47, 71).

14 *black bile*: Descartes, perhaps ironically, cites the conventional explanation of melancholy madness, based on the theory of the four humours of the body (blood, black bile, choler (yellow bile), phlegm).

Let us then suppose: Descartes shifts pronouns here from first-person singular to plural, as if to draw the reader into his mental experiment.

15 *to exist just as they do now*: the question whether God could annihilate the physical world, and yet leave us 'perceiving' it as we do now, had been raised by the Franciscan philosopher-theologian William of Ockham (*c*.1285–1347). It later becomes a key element in Malebranche's formulation of his theory of perception.

16 *that is certain*: F's addition, 'in the sciences', may be prompted by the concern to avoid the suspicion that Descartes's doubt extends to the doctrines of Christianity.

not with action but only with the attainment of knowledge: Descartes always strictly distinguishes between the necessities of practical life, where we may have to commit ourselves resolutely to a doubtful course of action, and the pursuit of knowledge, where we must reject all that is doubtful. See *Discourse*, 22–3, AT 6. 24–5; Second Replies, §5, pp. 96–7; Fifth Replies, II. 1, p. 185.

has devoted all his efforts to deceiving me: Jorge Secada suggests that the conception of the deceiving spirit comes from the scholastic metaphysician Francisco Suárez (*Cartesian Metaphysics* (Cambridge: Cambridge University Press, 2000), 44). Steven Nadler connects it suggestively with the theme of magical deception in Cervantes's *Don Quixote* ('Descartes's Demon and the Madness of Don Quixote', *JHI*, 58/1 (Jan. 1997), 41–55).

17 *as falsely believing that I have all these*: strikingly, Descartes omits arithmetical truths from this description of the deceiver's possible activity. The same applies to the summary of his doubts at the beginning of the Second Meditation.

to discover any truth: F here adds, 'it is at least in my power to suspend my judgement': an allusion to the principle of the Pyrrhonist sceptics that since, on any question, the balance of argument or evidence will be equal, we should opt for neither alternative.

SECOND MEDITATION

17 *Archimedes*: Greek mathematician and inventor, *c*.287–212 BC.

18 *I can finally decide*: the use of 'decide' here (L *statuendum*) hints at the doctrine of the Fourth Meditation that judgement is an act of the will, as well as the intellect.

what in fact this 'I' is that now necessarily exists: F and L differ here, in that L turns the pronoun *ego* ('I') into a noun, qualified by the demonstrative adjective *ille* (this). F simply treats 'I' as a pronoun. Further on 'this me that I know' (*eo me quem novi*) is rendered by F simply as 'me, whom

I know'. 'Necessarily' here means 'certainly': the implication is not that the Meditator's existence is intrinsically necessary (as God's will turn out to be). Descartes's use of pronouns as nouns is carefully analysed by Terence Cave, *Pré-Histoires: Textes troublés au seuil de la modernité* (Geneva: Droz, 1999), 11–19, 111–27.

18 *rational animal*: a standard definition of 'human being', derived ultimately from Aristotle. Unlike Aristotle, Descartes does not hold that definition in itself contributes to knowledge.

19 *these actions indeed I attributed to the soul*: the Meditator's apparently spontaneous preconceptions are in fact those of Aristotelian psychology, in which the soul is what makes something a living thing. On this basis, all distinctive functions of living things, such as nutrition and motion, must be ascribed to the soul.

20 *nonetheless I am still something*: F, 'I find that I am still certain that I am something'.

not distinct from this 'me' that I know: the Meditator is not talking about what exists as such, but about what he knows to exist. He does not yet think he has proved the real distinction between mind and body. What he means is that, *as far as he knows at the moment*, he is a pure mind.

21 *let us, once again, slacken its reins . . . back to obedience*: the Meditator, that is, is voluntarily relapsing into his familiar belief in the reality of bodies in order to analyse our experience of sense-perception.

22 *modes*: attributes, qualities, or modifications of a substance: see *Principles*, I. 56 for more exact distinctions between these terms.

23 *which could be covering automata*: F is more elaborate, 'which could be covering spectres, or artificial human beings moved by springs'.

'common sense': in scholastic terminology, the 'common sense' is the faculty that correlates the perceptions of the five external senses; the imagination is the storehouse that preserves the 'forms' perceived by the external senses and the common sense (see e.g. Aquinas, *Summa theologiae*, Ia, q. 78, a. 4). Descartes runs the two together.

the lowest animals: strictly speaking, the Meditator does not know at this stage that animals exist: this is a concession to common-sense views, the more legitimate in that he will conclude that they do exist, along with the rest of the physical world. But the passage suggests that animals do have some kind of sensation.

THIRD MEDITATION

26 *I seem unable ever to be certain of any other at all*: there is debate among specialists as to whether Descartes implies here that the propositions just mentioned, including the Cogito itself, are not certain, until we have proof of a veracious God. See e.g. Edwin Curley, 'The Cogito', *BGDM*, 40–1; Secada, *Cartesian Metaphysics*, 43–4. Others take a different view.

Anthony Kenny, *Descartes*, 182–6, gives a very nuanced analysis, as does Van Cleve, 'Foundationalism and the Cartesian Circle', 111–14.

images of things: L, 'imagines rerum'; F, 'images des choses'. But Descartes does not think that all ideas are mental pictures (as if the idea of God were a picture of a giant old man with a white beard and a deep voice). He makes this very clear in his reply to Hobbes apropos of this passage (Third Objections, §5, pp. 113–14). The point is that these ideas are representative of something.

27 *the subject of this thought*: the thing thought about, not the thinker.

adventitious: glossed by F as 'originating outside me'.

hearing a noise, seeing the sun, feeling the heat of a fire: this passage shows clearly that for Descartes the term 'idea' has a far broader meaning than 'concept'. 'To have an idea of heat' can mean, simply, to feel heat.

28 *some natural light*: the metaphor of light for knowledge goes back to Plato, and was much used by Augustine. Descartes introduces the notion of the natural light, a fundamental intuition of truth, of which he makes much use in this Meditation, rather abruptly, without explaining how far we are supposed to be able to trust it. See the article 'Intuition', in John Cottingham, *A Descartes Dictionary* (Oxford: Blackwell, 1993), 94–6.

when it was a matter of choosing the good: F adds, 'when it was a matter of choosing between virtues and vices, and that they have inclined me to evil as often as to good'. The assimilation of belief to ethical choice makes sense in the light of the Fourth Meditation's identification of judgement as an act of the will rather than the reason.

without any assistance from external things: the resistance of sensations to my will was proffered as an indication that things actually exist outside me. But, Descartes points out, I have inclinations that equally resist my will (F, 'ne s'accordent pas . . . avec ma volonté'), yet are inside me. The source of sensations too, therefore, might be internal.

the one that seems to have flowed directly from the sun itself: in the prevalent Aristotelian theories of perception, our ideas of sensible objects come from the object's transmitting 'species', likenesses of itself, to the perceiver. In this case the supposed 'likeness' is, in fact, nothing like the sun. Descartes, it has been argued, presents a distorted picture of the 'species' theory. See Gary Hatfield, 'The Cognitive Faculties', in *CHSCP* ii. 956–9.

29 *eminently*: see Definition IV, p. 103. God does not contain matter formally (actually), since he is immaterial. But he is said to contain it eminently, in that he can produce it.

30 *it requires no other formal reality outside itself*: the 'formal' reality of the idea (its existence as a modification of my thinking) derives from my thinking it (from my formal reality as a thinking substance). In this sense I am a sufficient explanation of the existence of my ideas. But this is not enough to explain the 'objective' reality of the idea: the fact that it is an idea of this object rather than that.

30 *no difficulty here*: the Meditator's actual existence is a sufficient explanation for his idea of himself (which contains exactly as much objective
reality as he possesses of formal reality).

32 *why they might not derive from myself*: in the Sixth Meditation, the
Meditator decides that he could not in fact have himself produced his
ideas of sensible things, for reasons already available to him (sensations
are not under the control of our will, and there is no intellectual dimension to their production, as distinct from their reception). But at this
stage, lacking the knowledge of a truthful God, and unsure of the value of
clear and distinct ideas as a criterion of truth, he cannot put these arguments forward with assurance.

that they can be derived from me alone: F is a little more precise, 'that the
idea I have of them can be derived from me alone'.

33 *I could recognize my own shortcomings*: in other words, the discovery of
God's existence is a kind of unfolding of the primary insight of the
Cogito.

I can neither comprehend, nor even perhaps apprehend: Descartes develops a
tactile metaphor, contrasting *comprehendere* (lit. to grasp, here 'comprehend') with *attingere* (lit. to touch, here 'apprehend'). To comprehend
something would be to have a complete idea of it; to apprehend it to have
a partial yet true idea of it. The same doublet recurs below towards the
end of the Meditation.

been brought into actuality: for Aristotle actuality involves the fulfilling of
a potentiality. If someone is actually being a builder, this is because he has
a potentiality or capacity to build: *Metaphysics*, IX. iii. 1–4 (1046^6–1047^a),
IX. vi. 2–4 (1048^a–1048^b). Descartes wants to forestall an objection
based on this distinction, viz. that my idea of the divine perfections might
be explained, without recourse to God, by supposing that I myself possess these perfections in potentiality.

34 *whether I, who have this idea, could exist if no such being existed*: the second
variety of the causal argument is thus not a totally independent argument,
but is designed to help the Meditator withstand the pressure of customary sense-dominated modes of thinking.

35 *the distinction between conservation and creation exists purely in our thought*:
more literally: 'conservation differs from creation purely in the reason'
(L), 'from the point of view of our way of thinking' (F). On the different
kinds of distinction—real, modal, and (as here) 'of reason', see *Principles*,
I. 60–2.

this 'I': L, 'ego ille'; F has simply 'moi' (myself).

36 *infinite regress*: a series of causes stretching back to infinity.

37 *created in his image and likeness*: Descartes is alluding to Gen. 1: 27, where
God is said to have made man in his own image and likeness. This image
is not, as it were, a label attached to and hence distinct from the object: it
is the nature of man himself, as an entity created with the idea of God.

FOURTH MEDITATION

39 *not a pure negation but a privation*: 'negation' usually denotes a form of proposition not a quality of an object. Descartes uses it here to denote a pure absence, as distinct from 'privation', which here has the sense of the absence of some property in an entity capable of possessing it. Thus the inability to fly would be, in a human being, a pure negation; but an inability to think would be a privation. Descartes uses the distinction later to explain how, from another point of view, error is a negation rather than a privation. Privation has a more general explanatory function in Aristotelian physics: see W. D. Ross, *Aristotle*, 3rd rev. edn (London: Methuen, 1937), 63–6, and, on the early modern period, Roger Ariew and Alan Gabbey, 'The Scholastic Background', in *CHSCP* i. 429–32.

40 *by considering the purposes of things*: the final cause of a thing in Aristotelian philosophy is the purpose or good to which it conduces (*Metaphysics*, I. iii. 1 (983ᵃ)): so one could ask, for instance, why fish have scales, what purpose they serve or what good they are to them. Descartes's mechanistic philosophy of nature has no room for final causes: but he does not deny that they are relevant in ethics (see below, p.193, also *Principles*, III. 2–3; to Hyperaspistes, §10, AT 3. 431). Moreover, the relation between the human body and mind admits of analysis in terms of final causes: the purpose of our senses is to preserve the union of soul and body (Sixth Meditation, p. 62).

41 *we are not being determined in that direction by any external force*: cf. F: 'in order to affirm or deny, pursue or avoid the things the intellect proposes to us we are acting in such a way that we do not feel that any external force is compelling us to do so.' F does not quite convey the idea that volition intrinsically involves movement (cf. L 'feramur', lit. we are carried) towards or away from an object.

to be moved in either direction: cf. F, 'in order for me to be free it is not necessary that I should be indifferent as regards the choice between two contraries'. F uses the technical term 'indifferent' which occurs later in L, and which Descartes understands as the absence of an inner impulsion in one direction or other. F's use of 'contraries', though, is questionable. Scholastic terminology distinguished 'liberty of contradiction' or of 'exercise' (I am free to perform a given action, or not to perform it) from 'liberty of contrariety' or of 'specification' (I am free to choose either of two contraries, say, good and bad). L makes clear that Descartes understands freedom first and foremost in terms of contradiction (to do or not to do), though his reference to 'being moved in either direction' might suggest a choice between contrary alternatives. F makes the reference to contraries explicit. There were theological dimensions in the distinction that Descartes probably did not want opened up. See Robert Sleigh, Jr., Vere Chappell, and Michael Della Rocca, 'Determinism and Human Freedom', in *CHSCP* ii. 1195–1216.

because God so disposes my innermost thoughts: a reference to the action of divine grace, mentioned in the next sentence.

41 *a shortfall in my knowledge, or a certain negation*: 'shortfall' (L *defectum*),
I take to be synonymous with 'privation', so that the distinction between
'privation' and 'negation' comes into play again. That is, it would be a
shortfall or privation in my knowledge, when I am capable of knowing the
truth, but fail to grasp it on account of e.g. intellectual laziness; a negation
when the knowledge is beyond human reach and consequently there are
no reasons on one side or the other.

42 *even to matters I do not understand*: the will is indifferent in matters we do
not properly understand because no strong perception of truth exists to
attract it to one view or the other.

how I come to sin: the theologian Antoine Arnauld objected to the reference to sin here: see Fourth Objections and Replies, pp. 138, 159–60.

the thinking nature that is within me, or rather that I myself am: cf. F, 'this
nature that thinks that is in me, or rather in virtue of which I am what
I am'. This passage confirms that Descartes does not yet claim to know if
the mind is distinct from the body.

43 *the operation in so far as that depends on him*: an erroneous act of judgement, like a correct act of judgement, depends on God to the extent that
he preserves the judger in his or her existence and faculties (this is the
'cooperation' referred to below). But God is not responsible for the error
as such.

44 *it should be classed, purely and simply, as a negation*: here the privation/
negation distinction seems to function as follows. Privation, in the Aristotelian
sense, to which Descartes specifically adverts here, is not a complete
nothing: it is the absence of a specific form (the presence of the form of
steam implies the privation of the form of water). It might then be held to
require a positive cause (in this example, heat). If error is a privation,
then, it might be supposed that God is somehow responsible for making
it come to pass. That is why, from this point of view, Descartes regards it
not as, strictly speaking, a privation, but a negation, a pure absence.

FIFTH MEDITATION

46 *clearly*: F adds 'and distinctly'.

47 *the idea of a valley*: we could of course imagine a mountain rising sheerly
from a plain. Lawrence Nolan and Alan Nelson suggest it makes more
sense to understand Descartes as saying that we cannot separate the idea
of an upslope from that of a downslope ('Proofs for the Existence of God',
BGDM 104–21 (p. 120)); and this is in fact how Descartes glosses it (to
Gibieuf, 19 Jan. 1642, AT 3. 476–7).

48 *the original supposition was not itself necessary*: the objection is that,
although existence follows from the nature of God, conceived as a
supremely perfect being, the original conception is not necessary, and
might in fact be intrinsically flawed (like the idea that all quadrilaterals

can be inscribed in a circle). The Meditator replies that the concept of God, being clear and distinct, cannot be taken for an arbitrary or flawed supposition.

51 *the whole of this bodily nature which is the object of pure mathematics*: cf. F, 'bodily nature, in so far as it can be the object of geometrical demonstrations, in which the existence of things is not taken into account'. So far the Meditator has no reason for believing that bodies exist: but, like the geometer, he can bracket this out, and consider simply the properties they would have, supposing they did exist.

SIXTH MEDITATION

52 *myriogon*: a figure of ten thousand sides.

from me: cf. F, 'from my mind'.

it understands itself: cf. F, 'it has produced by itself'. Imagination may be directed at objects initially either conceived by the intellect or perceived by the senses.

pure mathematics: cf. F, 'geometry'.

53 *emphatic*: L, 'expressae'; F, 'expresses'. Descartes wants a word that will do justice to the vividness and intensity, and in their own way clarity and distinctness of sensations (after all, the sensations of heat or bitterness are very different from those of cold or sweetness), without leaving room for confusion between this and the clarity and distinctness of intellectual perceptions.

formed: L, 'effingebam'; F, 'feindre': these terms are usually associated by Descartes with the work of the imagination.

from myself: cf. F, 'from my mind'.

54 *that I had not previously had in the senses*: on this allusion to a standard doctrine of scholasticism see Introduction, pp. xx–xxi.

appeared from close up as square: the example of the square tower that looks round from a distance is found in Lucretius, *De rerum natura*, IV. 501–2: the passage is quoted in Montaigne, 'Apologie de Raimond Sebond', *Essais*, II. 12, VS 591.

55 *or at least was pretending to be so*: Descartes, responding to a suggestion by Arnauld (p. 138), is making clear that the method of doubt does not imply abandoning one's religious faith in God, but simply discounting it for the purpose of philosophical investigation.

it is certain that I am really distinct from my body: cf. F, 'it is certain that *this self* [ce moi], *that is to say my soul, by which I am what I am*, is entirely and truly distinct from my body'. The words in italics occur also in *A Discourse on the Method* (IV. 29, AT 6. 33). Descartes does not claim here to prove the immortality of the soul, since God could always annihilate it if he so chose, simply that there is no reason to believe that the soul perishes just because the body has to.

56 *for they contain a certain degree of intellection in their formal concept*: cf. F, 'For in the notion we have of these faculties, or (to use the scholastic term) in their formal concept, they include some kind of understanding'. The intellectual element in sense-perception and imagination was established in the Second Meditation.

as modes are from a thing: cf. F, 'I conceive that they are distinct from me as shapes, movements and the other modes or accidents of bodies are distinct from the bodies themselves that underlie them'.

cannot . . . exist in myself: F adds, 'in so far as I am purely a thing that thinks'.

often even against my will: although there is an intellectual element in the experience of sensation, inasmuch as I can become conscious of the sensation as such rather than its (apparent) object, the production of sensations is not an act of intellection. Since sensation is not under the control of the will, then it cannot be understood in terms of the mind's key operations of understanding and willing. It therefore presupposes a body.

as I have already pointed out above: in the Third Meditation, pp. 29–34.

57 *pure mathematics*: cf. F, 'speculative geometry'.

as a pilot is present in a ship: Descartes is aware that his conception of the soul, in which it is not, as in Aristotle, the form of the body, but an independent substance, will be read and criticized as a mere restatement of Platonism. Summarizing the Platonic view, Aquinas uses Aristotle's analogy (*De anima*, II. i. 8–9 (413ª)) of the pilot in the ship, who occupies it, but is not part of it. Descartes mentions the analogy, as he does in the *Discourse* (V. 48, AT 6. 59), to distance himself from the Platonic conception, and to show that he himself is not vulnerable to the Aristotelian critique. See *Discourse*, 78 (p. 48 n.) and *Discours de la méthode*, ed. Étienne Gilson, 6th edn. (Paris: Vrin, 1987 [1925]), 430–1.

58 *a vacuum*: Descartes, here in agreement with Aristotle, held that completely empty space was impossible (see *Principles*, II. 16–18). The experiments of Torricelli (1644) and then Pascal (1646–7) cast doubt on this view. See Daniel C. Fouke, 'Pascal's Physics', in Nicholas Hammond (ed.), *The Cambridge Companion to Pascal* (Cambridge: Cambridge University Press, 2003), 75–101.

and so on and so forth: the qualities we perceive in sensation are, for Descartes, simply effects of movements in bodies (*Principles*, IV. 198): e.g. 'heat' is an aspect of our perception, not, as in Aristotle's physics, a fundamental active quality inhering in matter.

it has a tendency to fall downwards: F refers instead to 'the quality it has of being heavy'.

59 *the star is no bigger than the torch*: cf. F, 'there is no real or natural faculty in me inclining me to believe that the star is no bigger than the blaze of the torch'.

for signifying to the mind: the conception of sense-perceptions as signs is put forward in *Le Monde*, ch. I, using the analogy of language (AT 11. 4–5).

corrupted: the implied target here is Aristotle, who speaks of disease as a privation or degeneration (for which 'corruption' is an equivalent term), contrary to the body's nature (*Metaphysics*, VIII. v. 2 (1044ᵇ)).

60 *denomination*: shorthand for 'extrinsic denomination', a technical term used below. It here means a term, in this case, 'nature', the application of which has no foundation in the thing to which it is applied, but purely in the way we consider it. That is, when we say that the feeling of thirst in a sufferer from dropsy is natural, in the sense that it results from physiological mechanisms, our use of 'natural' is grounded in the nature of the body as a machine. But if we call it unnatural, because thirst 'naturally' indicates the body's need to drink, we are imposing a normative concept of nature from outside the body itself, and this will be an extrinsic denomination. See also First Objections, p. 74 and note.

a genuine error of nature: the teleological perspective, considering not how a given effect is produced but what purpose it serves, and which, contrary to Aristotle, is irrelevant to the purely physical realm, is relevant on the level of soul–body union.

61 *in which the 'common sense' is said to reside*: on the 'common sense' see above, note to p. 23. The particular part of the brain in question is identified as the pineal gland in *The Passions of the Soul*, §§31–2.

observations: see note to p. 170.

physics: the study of processes inside the body belongs to physics in the traditional sense of the philosophy of nature.

62 *it could have represented something else altogether*: Descartes's point is that we do not directly experience the physiological process involved in sensation (the transmission of a movement along the nerves to the brain) that we know scientifically takes place, although God could have created us in a such a way that we did experience it. Instead, we experience, in this case, a pain that appears to be located directly in and confined to the foot. But although this experience obscures the intrinsic mechanism of sensation, it is particularly suited to serve the function of sensation: to prompt us to take, as soon as possible, whatever actions are necessary to preserve the body.

64 *we must acknowledge the frailties of our nature*: Descartes's conclusion reaffirms the distinction between practical life and speculation, and the final reference to the frailties of our nature strikes a reassuring religious note.

FIRST OBJECTIONS AND REPLIES

74 *Euripus*: the strait between Boeotia and Euboea in Greece, famous in the ancient world for its turbulence. The allusion is fairly conventional, but shows the influence of humanism in Caterus' scholastic milieu.

74 *the thing itself that is thought, insofar as it exists objectively in the intellect*: in the scholastic view upheld by Caterus, there is no need for ideas as mediating entities between real objects and the mind. The thing itself is present in the mind in virtue of its form, divested of its matter. Hence the question of the reality of our ideas, as distinct from that of the reality of their objects, does not arise.

determining the act of the intellect in the manner of an object: 'determine' (L *terminare*, F *terminer*) does not have the sense of 'causing' or 'producing': what is meant is that the object makes the thought a thought of that object. Caterus' point is that this relationship of being thought about is not something real, needing to be explained by the causal principle—any more than my being seen by someone is something real, apart from their act of vision. The relationship in both cases is external to the object, which is why Caterus calls it an 'extrinsic denomination' (see above, p. 60 and note, and following note below). The only kinds of reality involved are (1) the actual reality of the thing and (2) the reality of the act by which the thing is thought or known. We do not need to bring in (3), the 'reality' supposedly contained in the idea of the object.

extrinsic denomination: when I am seen by someone, the predicate 'being seen' is not in me: rather, the predicate 'seeing' is in the seer. My being seen is not something real in me, so to speak of me 'being seen' is to apply a denomination extrinsic to me. See Stephen Menn, 'The Greatest Stumbling Block: Descartes' Denial of Real Qualities', in Roger Ariew and Marjorie Grene (eds.), *Descartes and his Contemporaries: Meditations Objections, and Replies* (Chicago and London: University of Chicago Press), 182–207 (pp. 190–1).

no part of the thing: F, 'and adds nothing real to the thing'.

75 *ens rationis*: lit. a 'being of reason': in Scholastic philosophy, a purely conceptual or abstract entity, without real existence. Caterus here uses 'imagined' (L 'fictum', F 'feint') and 'conceived' as synonymous, whereas in the Sixth Meditation Descartes carefully distinguishes them.

76 *Duns Scotus*: John Duns Scotus (c.1266–1308), theologian and philosopher, of the Franciscan Order, known as the 'Subtle Doctor'; probably from Scotland, although in Descartes's time he was commonly thought to be Irish. He differed from Aquinas in certain important respects, and his thought exerted considerable influence in the early seventeenth century. See Roger Ariew, *Descartes and the Last Scholastics* (Ithaca and London: Cornell University Press, 1999), 39–57.

The idea is the thing itself that is thought about, in so far as it exists objectively in the intellect: not an exact quotation but a paraphrase of what he says in the Third Meditation, p. 30.

the theologian represents himself as understanding: Descartes courteously refrains from accusing Caterus of misunderstanding—thereby, perhaps, maliciously emphasizing the misunderstanding.

78 *complexity*: L, 'artificium'; F, 'artifice', normally bearing the sense of workmanship or skill. 'Complexity' has been chosen because, like 'artificium' here, it can denote a quality both of the actual machine (e.g. the multiplicity of components) and of the intellectual operation required to conceive it. This passage is important as an explanation of the difficult concept of objective reality. It is important to note the exact scope, and hence the limitations, of the analogy. Descartes's point is that the power of the intellect in general cannot explain the particular content, the particular complexity, of the idea embodied in this machine (the concept, say, of harnessing steam or electricity as a motive force). The specific conceptual content of the idea requires an explanation: it cannot come from nothing. The same applies to the specific ontological content of the idea of God. But the analogy cannot be taken too far. As Descartes admits, an actually ('formally') existing cause outside the intellect (a real steam locomotive that the person holding the idea has seen) is only one possible cause of the idea. The idea might have been invented by the individual using his or her specific knowledge or intelligence. In the case of the idea of God, however, Descartes denies it could have been invented, and only a formally existing God can provide the explanation of the existence of the idea of a supremely perfect being.

79 *By this answer it seems he meant to show*: again, Descartes professes to believe that Caterus is voicing objections without subscribing to them.

80 *there can be nothing in me of which I am in no way aware*: this should not be taken as implying that Descartes believes in the mind's transparency or that he leaves no room for any concept of unconscious or subconscious thoughts. He denies that he can possess any faculty of which he is not aware, and any thoughts of which he could not become aware. The issue is raised again in the Fourth Objections. See above, Introduction, pp. xxxviii–xxxix.

we must first understand what it is: Descartes's 'essentialism' here breaks with the dominant scholastic tradition, in which we must enquire whether something exists before we can ask what it is (Secada, *Cartesian Metaphysics*, 1–26).

and therefore that it is God: Descartes is implicitly criticizing St Thomas, whose investigation of God's nature follows the proof of his existence. Descartes's own proof from the idea of the perfect takes us straight to God, as the supremely perfect being, the traditional proofs establishing the existence only of a first mover, a first cause, a self-existent being, without immediately showing that this is God.

81 *we have to distinguish between possible and necessary existence*: Leibniz was in fact to argue that the failing of this proof, as presented by Descartes, is that it fails to consider the possibility that the idea of God is contradictory, and not that of a possible being. Once it has been shown that the idea is not contradictory, then, indeed, the proof is valid. See *Discourse on Metaphysics*, §23, *A Specimen of Discoveries about Marvellous Secrets of a General Nature*, and *Monadology*, §45, in Leibniz, *Philosophical Writings*,

ed. G. H. R. Parkinson, trans. Mary Morris and G. H. R. Parkinson, Everyman University Library (London: Dent, 1973 [1934]), 32–3, 76, 186. This passage is perhaps Descartes's fullest approach to anticipating this objection; see also Second Replies, §6 (pp. 97–8).

83 *when we consider its immense power*: this shows that Descartes's formulation of the argument from God's essence depends not so much on the idea of existence as one perfection among others as on its being a function of power. In the Fourth Replies he identifies the divine power with the divine essence (pp. 151–2).

only two ways of proving the existence of God: Descartes tacitly signals his dissent from Aquinas, who advances five proofs of God. Descartes discards the first, from motion to mover, and the fifth, from the evidence of purpose in the universe to a supreme guiding intelligence; he can be seen as fusing together, in his own fashion, the second, from causality to a first cause, the third, from contingent being to necessary being, and the fourth, from degrees of perfection to the supremely perfect being. He adds the argument, rejected by Aquinas, from God's essence to his existence. This passage helps explain why this argument is postponed to the Fifth Meditation, instead of being included in the Third.

84 *modal distinction*: in Descartes's terminology, a modal distinction is one between a mode and the substance in which it inheres, or between two modes of one and the same substance (*Principles*, I. 61). Thus there is a modal distinction between a just person and his or her justice, or between God's justice and his mercy, though neither could justice exist without the just person, nor could God's justice exist in separation from his mercy.

SECOND OBJECTIONS AND REPLIES

85 *Flies and plants are produced by the sun, the rain, and the earth, which are lifeless*: the belief that living things could be generated from non-living matter was still widely accepted in the seventeenth century.

Savages such as the Canadians and the Hurons do not possess it: travellers to the New World reported that the inhabitants did not possess an idea of God, contrary to the belief, voiced influentially in Cicero's *De natura deorum* (*Of the Nature of the Gods*) that belief in the gods is universal and indeed natural to mankind (I. xvi. 43, II. xii. 12; though doubt is cast on this argument in I. xxiii. 62–4, III. iv. 11).

generic unity: the unity of the members of a genus, such as 'human beings'.

your conclusion was not certain: compare the classic objection that Descartes's claim that certainty depends on the knowledge of God involves him in arguing in a circle. It occurs in the Fourth Objections.

86 *there are biblical texts to the contrary*: the particular references are to Jonah 3: 4, where God announces through the mouth of the prophet that Nineveh will be destroyed in forty days, when in fact he spares the town when the

citizens repent; and to Exodus, where there are frequent references to the Lord hardening Pharaoh's heart (e.g. 7: 3, 9: 12, 10: 2, 10: 20, 10: 27) so that he fails to heed the warning signs and refuses to let the Israelites depart from Egypt.

they do not have a clear and distinct knowledge of its truth: in other words, Descartes's theory is inimical to faith, since it encourages us to disbelieve the mysteries we do not understand. 'Turks' here, as often in early modern usage, is used as equivalent to 'Muslims'.

although you claimed you would be proving this: the title of the first edition of the Meditations (selected by Mersenne: Descartes to Mersenne, 11 Nov. 1640, AT 3. 239) does indeed state that they demonstrate the existence of God and the immortality of the soul. The title of the second edition removes the mention of immortality: it is the distinction between mind and body that is claimed to be demonstrated.

87 *absolutely nothing in it except what he knew*: Descartes here as elsewhere is careful to distinguish accurate knowledge, which he says we can attain, from absolute knowledge.

Academics: like the Sceptics, the Academics challenged claims to absolute knowledge, but some of them at least accepted that we can regard some views as more probable than others—which the radical Pyrrhonist sceptics denied.

89 *requiring a really existent cause*: this point is discussed much more fully in the First Replies.

90 *along with me*: F adds: 'But I cannot drive it into the minds of those who read my Meditations like a romance (*roman*), merely to pass the time, and without paying close attention.' Whereas *roman* in modern French is equivalent to 'novel' (and thus normally implies a certain degree of realism), in the seventeenth century it commonly refers to 'romances', fictions remote from the reader's experience. In fact, Descartes himself suggests that the reader of the *Principles* should read it for the first time like a 'roman', before rereading it more attentively (Letter from the Author to the Translator, AT 9B. 11–12). But the *Principles* are a textbook, not a series of meditations, requiring quite different reading habits.

91 *The same applies to the rest of God's individual attributes*: the question whether, when properties such as goodness or knowledge are predicated of God and of finite beings, they are predicated in a different sense (equivocally) or in the same sense (univocally) was much discussed by medieval philosophers and theologians (Aquinas's solution is that they are predicated analogically: *Summa theologiae*, Ia, q. 13, a. 5).

nothing more than a fiction: in the Third Meditation (p. 37) the idea of God is stated to be inscribed within me as 'the mark by which the craftsman makes himself known in his handiwork': i.e. in understanding ourselves to be limited and dependent beings, who can aspire indefinitely to greater things, we understand the difference between ourselves and

God, who actually enjoys in infinite measure what we can only indefinitely aspire to. Descartes draws out some of the implications of the earlier passage here, as regards the question of univocity: we realize that knowledge or power in us (finite though indefinitely augmentable) cannot be the same as God's infinite knowledge and power.

91 *denying the name and affirming the thing*: this seems to be a somewhat belated answer to the argument from so-called savages' lack of an idea of God: they have an idea of him, but a very inadequate one.

92 *the reasons on the basis of which we deduced them*: not an exact quotation but a paraphrase: see Fifth Meditation, p. 50.

scientific knowledge: L, 'scientia': knowledge resulting from convincing proofs ('demonstrations'), whereas principles are known directly. Here Descartes is following Aristotle, *Posterior Analytics*, II. xix (100ᵇ). See the Note on the Text and Translation.

known directly [per se notam]: see Note on the Text and Translation, s.v. *per se notum*.

94 *denying him the grace of conversion*: a seventeenth-century theologian would have seen that Descartes is here restating a traditional Catholic interpretation, whereas Calvin had argued that God did positively act on Pharaoh (*Institution de la religion chrétienne*, ed. Jean-Daniel Benoist, 5 vols. (Paris: Vrin, 1957–63), bk. I, ch. 18, bk. II, ch. 4 (i. 257, ii. 75–82).

96 *a light more certain than the whole light of nature*: Descartes's point is that his rule that we should give our assent only to clear and distinct ideas does not rule out belief in the mysteries of the Christian religion such as the Trinity (God is one, but in God there are three persons). These mysteries are indeed obscure. But we give our assent to them in virtue of a supernatural illumination akin to that by which we clearly and distinctly perceive metaphysical truths such as the Cogito and the existence of God.

does not diminish our freedom: not a literal quotation, but cf. p. 41.

98 *implicancy*: F has 'implicance', a neologism corresponding to the Latin term *implicantia*, which is used in L. Its meaning is 'self-contradictoriness'.

99 *a priori*: the expression has caused some difficulty. In modern English-language philosophy, inspired by the usage of Kant, *a priori* denotes a form of argument that does not depend on experience, whereas *a posteriori* argument does. This is not the sense in question here. Clerselier interprets *a priori* in the standard medieval and early modern sense of 'proceeding from cause to effect', and *a posteriori* in the next paragraph as 'proceeding from effect to cause'. But this does not seem very helpful either. Alquié's suggestion (*OP* ii. 582, n. 1) seems plausible: the terms are used in a very general sense, to denote different phases in the process of knowledge. The *a priori* phase is that of the actual discovery of truth, in which the ultimate end-point may be invisible from the starting-point: this is reproduced in the analytic order. Once truth has been discovered, the material is organized, synthetically, in the light of the ultimate truths

discovered, and this backward look over the path traversed is a perspective *a posteriori*. (On the other hand, Descartes says in the next paragraph that the synthetic method makes more use of specific *a priori* arguments than the analytic method. Here he may be using *a priori* in the other sense of 'proceeding from cause to effect'.) See also Henri Gouhier, *La Pensée métaphysique de Descartes* (Paris: Vrin, 1962), 108–11.

100 *a posteriori*: the translation here is based on the reading of *a priori* and *a posteriori* given in the previous note. Literally, L says that 'Synthesis . . . following the opposite path, one sought so to speak *a posteriori*'; F means 'following a quite different path, and so to speak examining causes by their effects'.

even of the reluctant: synthesis, then, unlike analysis, works both for lazy readers and for those reluctant to be convinced, because it does a lot of the work of thinking for them. The translation of this last sentence draws on the fuller version in F.

101 *Meditations, rather than Disputations*: see Introduction, pp. xiii–xv.

less capable of perceiving it: the rest of the discussion is missing from F, which concludes with a brief paragraph indicating Descartes's willingness to set out some of his arguments in synthetic fashion.

104 *Postulates*: in the conventional sense, postulates are basic assumptions, specific to a given science, on which the science is founded, e.g. that it is possible, at least in theory, to draw straight lines and circles: unlike axioms, which are self-evidently true, they are simply proposed for the learner's acceptance, though they may be contrary to his opinion. See Aristotle, *Posterior Analytics*, I. 10 (76^b), and also the discussion in *The Thirteen Books of Euclid's Elements*, ed. and trans. Sir Thomas Heath, 2nd edn. (New York: Dover, 1956), 117–24. Descartes's postulates, however, clash with more than learners' assumptions about a particular science: they call on them to adopt habits of thought that run counter to the grain of all prior experience, above all to learn to distrust their senses and focus instead on their own awareness of their mind. On postulates, see Peter Dear, 'Mersenne's Suggestion: Cartesian Meditation and the Mathematical Model of Knowledge in the Seventeenth Century', in Ariew and Grene (eds.), *Descartes and his Contemporaries*, 44–62 (pp. 47–51), and Daniel Garber, 'Morin and the Second Objections', ibid. 63–82 (pp. 78–80).

105 *theorems rather than axioms*: the difference between an axiom and a theorem is that the former is presented as self-evident, whereas the latter is deduced. Descartes could, therefore, he says, have proved some of the following propositions, which would thus have become theorems, which in fact he presents baldly as axioms. This is in keeping with the remark he has just made that what is directly known to one person, may need proof in order for another to understand it.

THIRD OBJECTIONS

107 *with the author's replies*: Hobbes's objections begin with quotations from the *Meditations* (the page number is added in brackets), on which he then comments; his comments are followed by Descartes's replies.

criterion: Hobbes uses the Greek word *kriterion*, which F renders by 'certain and evident mark'. The impossibility of finding a criterion of truth was one of the key positions of Pyrrhonist scepticism.

phantasms: cf. F, 'images of things'.

the Philosopher: this is how Descartes refers to Hobbes throughout.

metaphysical doubts: hyperbolical doubts (F, 'so wide-ranging and extraordinary').

108 *the subject of any act*: 'act' used here not only in the sense of 'action, operation' but in the sense of 'quality, attribute'.

109 *his method of combining a number of things together*: on Hobbes's method, see p. 112 below.

the Sixth Meditation, in which I prove my view: Descartes has made the same reply to the Second Objections, §1, p. 88.

110 *only in bodily terms*: Descartes is quoting Hobbes's words back at him but substituting 'substance' for 'matter'; to be more precise, he allows the word 'matter' in a 'metaphysical' sense, if it denotes simply the substance, of whatever nature, underlying different acts or qualities, as long as this is not equated with matter in the ordinary sense of 'body'.

Whoever, apart from himself, ever imagined this?: Hobbes argues that thought, as an act, must have a subject. But this subject cannot be thought (which he continues to interpret in the sense of an act of thinking): for all this could mean is that a thought is being thought by another thought, resulting in an endless series: 'I am thinking I am thinking I am thinking . . .'. But if the subject of thought is not thought, it must be a body. Descartes thinks it ridiculous that anyone should imagine that this is what is meant by conceiving thought as the subject of thought: clearly it means that the subject of the *act* of thought is thought in the sense of a *thinking substance*.

only inasmuch as it is the subject of certain acts: this passage shows that Descartes does not suppose the mind to be immediately present to itself.

111 *What is there that can be said to be separate from me?*: the translation given here has been modified from that given in the text of the Second Meditation ('Is there any of them that can be distinguished from my thinking? Is there any that can be said to be separate from me?') in order to bring out Hobbes's objection more clearly. It seems that he thinks that Descartes is still failing to distinguish the subject from its acts, the thinker from thinking. But Descartes is not implying that there is nothing in general apart from his thinking. His question follows on from the previous sentence, in which he is talking about the various activities (doubting, understanding, desiring, and so on) of which he is aware. His point is that

none *of these* cannot be distinguished from his thinking, because they are all forms of thinking (see Alquié's note in *OP* ii. 606, n. 2).

conceiving: Hobbes has 'concipere' (conceive). Descartes's text has 'percipere' (to perceive).

Peripatetics: followers of Aristotle.

112 *a coupling and attachment of names or labels, by means of the word 'is'*: Hobbes here sketches out the conception of reasoning he will develop in *Leviathan*, I. 4–5 (see Thomas Hobbes, *Leviathan*, ed. Richard Tuck (Cambridge: Cambridge University Press, 1996), 24–37).

the same thing: F adds: 'That is, when we imagine a pentagon we need a particular effort of the mind that makes the figure (its five sides and the space they enclose) appear to be present, and this is not required in the act of conceiving.' See Sixth Meditation, AT 7. 72–3, for the distinction between imagination and intellection or 'conceiving'.

113 *something eternal exists*: cf. the argument for the existence of a first cause in *Leviathan*, I. 12, pp. 77–8.

114 *everything that is directly perceived by the mind*: cf. the definition given at the end of the Second Replies, Definition II, pp. 102–3.

116 *I call an idea*: F adds: 'And as long as this philosopher refuses to agree with me about the meaning of words, he can offer none but frivolous objections.'

117 *real qualities*: for Aristotle, heat, cold, wetness, dryness are fundamental entities, exercising a real causal influence. This basic list of what they called 'real qualities' was lengthened by the later scholastics to include all properties (sensible and insensible) of bodies. See Steven Nadler, 'Doctrines of Explanation in Late Scholasticism and in the Mechanical Philosophy', in *CHSCP* i. 513–52 (esp. 514–18). Descartes rejects the concept: see *Le Monde*, V (AT 11. 25–6), but, rather than engage in controversy about it here, he indicates the place that real qualities (assuming they existed) would occupy on the scale of reality. On complete and incomplete substances, see Fourth Objections and Replies below.

118 *in our thought*: F adds, 'that is, God'.

119 *The same applies to the rest of God's attributes*: this might seem problematic, because Descartes appears to be implying that we form the idea of God's attributes by an extension of our ideas derived from finite substance, which would negate the priority of the idea of God argued for elsewhere. He would doubtless reply that it is only the prior idea of the infinite that prompts us to extend our ideas of finite qualities.

the faculty of producing it: producing it, that is, from ourselves, without requiring prompting from external objects. Descartes therefore does not suppose e.g. that a newborn baby has an actual concept of God.

120 *contrary to the opinion of the Calvinists*: Calvin's theology of predestination makes human actions dependent on a divinely established necessity.

120 *contradictory to what has gone before*: the contradiction alleged by Hobbes does not bear, as Descartes supposes, on his reference to free will. Hobbes thinks that Descartes is contradicting himself because he has just said that we do not need to invoke any faculty to explain the existence of error, and is now invoking the faculties of knowing and choosing. But Hobbes has misunderstood Descartes's point, which is that we do not need to invoke a special 'mistake-making' faculty to explain error: he agrees with Hobbes that it derives from a misuse of the same faculty as we use to obtain knowledge, though he adds that the will is also involved. So he is not contradicting himself. In any case, Descartes says, Hobbes has missed the essential point that error, like blindness, is not a positive entity. (If it were, its reality would have to be derived from God, the source of all reality, which would make God responsible for our errors; as he would be, if he had given us a special faculty for making mistakes.)

other people's opinions about the matter: a Calvinist would not deny that some actions are voluntary: X gets drunk and fights because he wants to. But he would deny that such actions are free: X, he would say, is predestined to sin. Descartes's point is that introspection dissolves such distinctions, for it shows that to do what we want and to be free are one and the same.

121 *it is self-contradictory to say that we want and do not want the same thing*: Hobbes is clearly right to argue, what Descartes seems reluctant to acknowledge, that our assent to truth can be reluctant, e.g. when we perceive it clashes with a cherished belief. Descartes's later discussion of freedom in the letters to Mesland of 1645 is more subtle.

123 *sufficiently refuted already*: see the reply to Objection IV above.

conveys to me the ideas of body: the explanatory note in parentheses is taken from F. L has '*whether ideas are conveyed by bodily things*'. F's statement of the point at issue is more accurate.

124 *he will easily recognize his error*: Hobbes's point is that if you make coherence and a sense of continuing identity a sufficient test of the difference between genuine and illusory experience, you have to admit the possibility of dream-experiences that, on this showing, would count as real.

FOURTH OBJECTIONS AND REPLIES

125 *acts done at the persuasion of pleasure*: Arnauld, who had initially trained in the law before devoting himself to theology, invokes a legal analogy: the magistrate ('praetor', a Roman term) does not hold people responsible for acts performed under the influence of violence or fear. If the same applied to acts performed under the influence of pleasure, the pleasure that had kept him reading Descartes's work would excuse him from the responsibility of writing about it.

the troublesome commitments by which my time is taken up: the preparation of the doctorate in theology, which he had not yet been awarded despite the reference to him in the title as a 'doctor'.

M. Descartes: L refers to Descartes throughout not by name but as 'Vir Clarissimus' (this most illustrious man), often abbreviated to 'V.C.'. F usually refers to him by name, and I follow that usage here. But it is worth noting that Arnauld observes the formalities of humanist politeness throughout, and Descartes reciprocates. There is none of the aggression evident in the confrontations with Hobbes, Gassendi, and Bourdin.

if you did not exist, you could not be deceived at all: Augustine, *De libero arbitrio*, II. iii. 7 (*PL* xxxii. 1243). Cf. *The City of God*, XI. 26, where a similar argument appears. Descartes's possible debts to Augustine have been examined afresh in recent scholarship: see e.g. Stephen Menn, *Descartes and Augustine* (Cambridge: Cambridge University Press, 1998).

127 *it follows that nothing else in fact belongs to it*: the passages quoted by Arnauld are in the Preface to the Reader, p. 7.

which he had not yet obtained in the Second Meditation: Arnauld is perfectly correct in this: he is the only one of the objectors who raise this point to grasp the order of Descartes's argumentation here.

major premise: the technical terms 'major' and (below) 'minor premise' appear only in F. The major premise is a general statement, the minor a particular statement that can be subsumed under the general assertion, so as to yield a particular conclusion. Here the major may be summarized as: 'Whatever I clearly and distinctly understand without another thing, is really distinct from that thing.' The minor is: 'I clearly and distinctly understand the mind without the body, and the body without the mind.'

between the mind and the body: Arnauld has slightly simplified the last sentence: he sometimes paraphrases Descartes rather than quoting him verbatim.

128 *when you conceive yourself*: 'that is, your mind' (F).

and likewise when you conceive yourself: 'that is, your body' (F).

as the genus to the species: such people would consider the mind as a particular kind of body, differentiated by its capacity for rational thought. In that case, we could have a complete idea of what is meant by body, which excluded rational thought, since this is specific only to one kind of body; and this idea could not be used to prove the non-identity of mind and body.

my knowledge of myself: not an exact quotation but a summary of Descartes's argument.

130 *butchers of souls*: the impious are called 'butchers of souls' because they deny the existence of the soul: perhaps also because this teaching leads to spiritual death in those who accept it.

131 *animal spirits*: physical, not spiritual, entities: the more subtle and rarefied parts of the blood which, in Descartes's theory, pass through the brain and thence to the nerves and the muscles. They thus allow him to explain the movement of the body without invoking, in Aristotelian fashion, the notion of soul. See *The Passions of the Soul*, §§10–13. The concept derives

from the medical theories of Galen: see Ian Maclean, *Logic, Signs and Nature in the Renaissance: The Case of Learned Medicine* (Cambridge: Cambridge University Press, 2002), 242–4, for an account of different early modern versions of it.

131 *ch. XV*: Arnauld is paraphrasing Augustine, *De quantitate animi*, XV. 25 (*PL* xxxii, 1049–50).

'Soliloquies', I. 4: Arnauld is quoting Augustine, *Soliloquiorum libri duo*, I. iv. 9 (*PL* xxxii, 874).

132 *materially false*: Arnauld thinks that the only authentic idea of cold is the idea that is correct: cold is a privation. The idea of cold as a positive entity is a non-idea, because it is an idea of what is not. Descartes's concept of the material falsity of the idea of cold implies that the idea of cold has some positive content: it represents cold as a positive entity. But if this is so, and Descartes's concept of ideas as containing a certain objective being is valid, then the idea of cold contains a certain objective being, which, like the objective being of all other representative ideas, requires an explanation in terms of some 'formal' (really existing) cause. Descartes either has to specify this cause (which Arnauld thinks he has failed to do) or to admit that an idea's objective reality can derive from nothing, in which case his whole proof of the existence of God collapses.

133 *the theologian*: Caterus, author of the First Objections.

134 *the natural light does not in fact allow us to assert this*: Descartes has discussed two possible restrictions of the term 'efficient cause'. The first would limit it to causes that precede their effects in time; the second to causes distinct from their effects. He then argues that the natural light shows us that the first restriction is inappropriate here. Arnauld shrewdly points out that he says nothing about the second restriction, as if, in fact, it is difficult to sustain the notion of a cause identical to its effect.

136 *without any potentiality*: F is fuller: 'Thus the terms "continuation" and "preservation", denote potentialities rather than acts, and involve a certain capacity or disposition to receive; but the infinite being is an utterly pure act, incapable of possessing such dispositions.' Arnauld here invokes the Aristotelian distinction between act and potentiality. For the purposes of this argument, a potentiality can be understood to denote an entity's capacity to become something other than it currently is (e.g. the capacity of water to become steam). If something is preserved or continued in being, the implication is it has a capacity, or potentiality, of not being. But God is all that he can be and his nature admits of no potentiality. See Aquinas, *Summa theologiae*, Ia, q. 3, a. 1.

the sum of which is equal to two right angles: this is not absurd, however, in the light of Descartes's distinctive doctrine that eternal and necessary truths, such as those of geometry, are true because God has willed them so. He could have decided that the sum of the angles of a triangle would not be equal to two right angles. In other words, God is the efficient cause of such truths: he has made the laws of nature as a king makes the laws of his kingdom (letter to Mersenne, 15 Apr. 1630, AT I, 145–6).

137 *be scandalized*: L, 'offendatur'; F, 'offensent'. Arnauld is not talking about subjective reactions of anxiety or indignation. He means that theologians would find this view 'scandalous' in the sense of providing a stumbling-block (Gk. *skandalon*, L *offendiculum*: see below, p. 139) to others; i.e. it would be, ultimately, a threat to their faith.

whatever is clearly and distinctly perceived by us is true: this is a wonderfully succinct formulation of a classic difficulty in Descartes's system (that it involves arguing in a circle).

138 *for people of ordinary intelligence*: see *Discourse on the Method*, II. 15, AT 6. 15.

since I was pretending to be ignorant: as the text of the Sixth Meditation shows (p. 55), Descartes accepted this suggestion.

grave objections: the 'objections' Arnauld has in mind involve the doctrines of original sin and grace, especially as taught by Augustine and his followers. For if Descartes is right in tracing sin to the same root as error (the faulty use of the judgement), then he is, seemingly, implying it can be avoided by the same method. This would smack of the Pelagian heresy, which holds that all human beings have the power to do God's will, whereas Augustine held that only some human beings, those in receipt of divine grace, possess it. Here Descartes does not act on Arnauld's advice, since the text continues to make mention of sin as well as error.

139 *understanding, believing, having opinions*: Augustine, *De utilitate credendi*, XI. 25 (not 'XV' as Arnauld says), *PL* xlii, 83.

ignorance: L, 'inhumanitatis'. Despite the reading in F ('peu [. . .] d'humanité'), the accusation is presumably of lack of education (cf. L *inhumanus*, which can bear the sense of 'uncultured') rather than lack of humanity.

in ch. XII: Augustine, *De utilitate credendi*, XII. 26 (*PL* xlii, 84).

other sensible qualities: Arnauld's point of reference is the Roman Catholic doctrine of transubstantiation, restated by the Council of Trent (1545–63): when the bread and wine are consecrated, their substance is replaced by that of the body and blood of Christ, although the accidents, or appearances, of bread and wine remain.

140 *M. Arnauld*: as in F; L has 'Vir Clarissimus' (this most distinguished man) throughout.

141 *adequate*: cf. F: 'entire and perfect'.

for it to be adequate: we may have adequate knowledge of some things, but we can never know we do. If we could have (and know we have) adequate knowledge of the things in question, then it would be reasonable to require such knowledge as the basis of the assertion of a real distinction between them. But, because we can never know we have such knowledge, this requirement, Descartes says, is unnecessarily stiff.

142 *by an abstraction on the part of the intellect*: we can establish a formal distinction between two attributes (shape and motion, say) and can think of each in abstraction from a particular body: but if we took this as evidence of a real distinction, as if motion could exist independently of a moving body, or independently of shape, we should, by an intellectual abstraction, be producing an inadequate 'knowledge' of motion. See First Replies, p. 84.

143 *subsisting by themselves*: existing as things in their own right, not as attributes or modifications of some other thing. It does not mean that such things exist independently of God. Spinoza, however, was to suggest that if finite entities cannot exist without an infinite substance, it makes no sense to speak of them as 'existing by themselves' even in the first sense, and consequently that they should be seen not as substances but as modifications of a single substance, God or nature.

bodily nature: L, 'naturam corporis'; F, 'la nature du corps'. Descartes means that the concept of shape is that of a complete thing only when combined with the notion of body.

144 *in the concrete*: as opposed to 'in the abstract'. If we thought of a triangle not as a mathematical idea, but as an object in the real world (a triangular piece of paper, say), Descartes concedes that it could then be thought of as a substance. His point is that, although we can erroneously conceive a property as existing in one and the same substance without another property with which it is necessarily linked, this does not cast doubt on our ability to distinguish two separate substances on the basis of their distinct properties.

things or substances: cf. F, 'I tried to distinguish explicitly between, on the one hand, things, that is, substances, and, on the other, the modes of these things, that is, the faculties of those substances'.

147 *in the fifth part of A Discourse on the Method*: V. 46–8, AT 6. 56–9.

to many different actions: on the relations between the brain, the animal spirits, the nerves, and the muscles, see *The Passions of the Soul*, §§7–16.

149 *the idea remains in me, the same as it has always been*: it seems that the fundamental difference between Arnauld and Descartes is in the understanding of the term 'idea'. Arnauld takes it in the sense of 'concept'. But for Descartes the actual sensation of cold counts as an idea of cold. And when I feel cold, I do not simply feel not-hot: I may feel the cold as an active aggressive force. This might, however, lead me to assume, erroneously, that cold *in itself* is a positive reality, whereas, however I feel it, it can only be understood scientifically as an absence of heat, which is something positive, an effect of certain kinds of motion (see *Principles*, IV. 198). Hence the sensation can be termed materially false. The confused perception of the absence of heat is 'referred to' (experienced as if due to) a positive presence of cold. But if, Descartes goes on to explain, our idea of God is clear and distinct, we know it conforms to its object: it is not a pseudo-idea 'referred' by us incorrectly to something else that is not God

(as would be the case if, thinking we have an idea of God, we conceived him as limited in power or knowledge).

151 *Francisco Suárez*: Spanish theologian and philosopher (1548–1617), a member of the Society of Jesus, whose *Metaphysical Disputations* (1597) enjoyed a European influence.

152 *I regard the formal cause as different from the efficient cause*: 'formal cause', the essence of a thing considered as explaining its attributes, is a scholastic term, derived, as Descartes presently points out, from Aristotle.

153 *as being the most general term*: in the Christian theology of the Trinity, the Son and the Holy Spirit can be said to 'proceed' from the Father (in Latin Christianity the Spirit proceeds from the Father *and* the Son, which the Greeks deny). But the Son and the Spirit are not caused or produced by the Father, in the way that creatures distinct from God are caused or produced (that is, out of nothing). Hence the word 'principle' (in the sense of 'source') is used of the Father, as distinct from 'cause'.

the first and most important means . . . of proving the existence of God: if this is so, why does Descartes put forward the so-called ontological argument for God's existence as well? Alquié suggests that this argument too is, for Descartes, a causal argument: God's essence implying his existence, he can be considered in this sense as the cause of himself (*OP* ii. 681, n. 1).

154 *to inquire why it exists*: Descartes implies that those who follow the natural light alone are better able to grasp his demonstration than those whose minds are cluttered with scholastic concepts.

the interpretation must be disallowed: Descartes's point is that, if 'to exist of itself' means no more than 'to exist without a cause', we are admitting the concept of a being existing without a cause. In that case, we might end up saying that finite creatures, as distinct from God, exist without a cause: they just exist (as Sartre, say, would have it) and no causal connection to a creator need, or can, be traced.

155 *the same and not the same*: Descartes acknowledges that the analogy by which God's essence is considered as if it were the efficient cause of his existence can only go so far: for an efficient cause in the strict sense must be distinct from its effect (as Arnauld has shown, a thing cannot be the efficient cause of itself); and so to make God the efficient cause of himself would be to say that he is distinct from himself. But this is so plainly self-contradictory that we can all see the limits of the analogy.

156 *more noble than other causes*: Descartes is still using hierarchical language. The effect is considered, within scholastic metaphysics, as less 'noble' than the cause, because it depends on it. Hence Descartes is reluctant to speak of God as the 'effect' of himself, though logic would seem to imply that he should. But he is simply, he claims, following the example of theologians, who speak of God the Father as the principle or source of God the Son, but do not speak of the Son as 'principiated' (i.e. standing in the same relationship to a principle as an effect to its cause) less this appear to render him inferior to the Father.

156 *to cover all essences of things*: Aristotle, *Posterior Analytics*, II. 11 (94ª), in *Posterior Analytics*, ed. and trans. Hugh Tredennick, *Topica*, ed. and trans. E. S. Forster, Loeb Classical Library (Cambridge, Mass. and London: Harvard University Press, 1960), 208–9. 'Essence' is indeed the translation there offered for *to ti ên einai*.

158 *not at all a rectilinear figure*: the syntax of both L and F here is so tortuous that the translation is freer than usual. The analogy is as follows. Archimedes has demonstrated properties of the sphere by conceiving it, paradoxically, as a straight-sided figure (albeit with an infinite number of sides). Descartes has demonstrated the existence of God by applying the causal principle (everything that exists must have a cause), with God thus being viewed, paradoxically, as the cause of himself. Arnauld wants to keep the demonstration of God as first cause, but to abandon the concept of God as self-causing. This is like wanting to keep Archimedes' demonstration but treating it as if it applied only to a rectilinear figure with an infinite number of sides, and asserting a distinction between this concept and that of the sphere, on the grounds that a sphere is not rectilinear.

159 *if we cannot become conscious of it*: we know in this way that we have no faculty of reproducing our existence from moment to moment, and thus depend on some other being. See the Third Meditation, p. 35.

read only by the intelligent and learned: see the 'Preface to the Reader', pp. 7–9.

160 *I take his advice*: nonetheless, as noted above, the text of the Fourth Meditation retains the reference to sin as well as error (p. 42).

Dioptrics and the Meteorology: the *Dioptrics* (*La Dioptrique*), on light and vision, and the *Meteorology* (*Les Météores*), about weather, are two of the essays appended to *Discourse on the Method*, as examples of the author's method. The reference is to *Les Météores*, I, AT 6. 239. It seems that Descartes is being a trifle disingenuous here, as he goes on to acknowledge. He says in *Les Météores* that he is not denying the existence of real qualities because he wants to avoid quarrels with philosophers, but he implies that his own mode of explanation, which makes no reference to such qualities, is sufficient and preferable because more economical.

assumptions that were subsequently refuted in later ones: the possible existence of the evil genius is an obvious case in point. On the distinction between analytic and synthetic methods, see Second Replies, pp. 99–102.

more befitting a gentleman: L, 'liberalius'. F has 'avec plus de franchise' (more frankly). 'Liberalis' in Latin means freeborn and often gently or nobly born. The social connotations of the word are part of Descartes's self-presentation: a gentleman should candidly declare his views and not hide behind the letter of his statements.

161 *intentional species*: the orthodox Aristotelian theory of perception held by the late scholastics was that we perceive objects not directly, but via 'intentional species', representations of the qualities (such as colour)

perceived in external objects and in some sense like those qualities. This did not involve the belief that the object emits, as it were, little copies of itself, though Descartes characterizes it as if it did (*La Dioptrique*, I, AT 6. 85). See Gary Hatfield, 'The Cognitive Faculties', *CHSCP* ii. 952–1002 (pp. 957–9). On Descartes's own theory of perception, see *La Dioptrique*.

has no existence except in a modal sense: the surface is not a body or a distinct part of a body in its own right: it exists purely as a modification of a body. Descartes explains his concept of surface in letters to Mersenne (23 June 1641, AT 3. 387) and Mesland (9 Feb. 1645, AT 4. 164).

162 *the appearance of bread remaining all the while*: Descartes is summarizing the decree of the Council of Trent, session 13, canons 2 and 4: *Enchiridion symbolorum, definitionem et declarationum de rebus fidei et morum*, ed. Heinrich Denzinger, rev. Adolf Schönmetzer, 35th edn. (Barcelona, Freiburg-im-Breisgau, Rome, New York: Herder, 1973), paras. 1652, 1654. A full English translation of the decree can be found at: http:// history.hanover.edu/texts/trent/ct13.html.

but the other senses as well perceive by touch: Descartes quotes the text in Greek: 'kai ta alla aisthêtêria haphê aisthanetai' (the other sense organs perceive by contact too) (Aristotle, *De anima*, III. 13, 435ᵃ, in *On the Soul, Parva Naturalia, On Breath*, ed. and trans. W. S. Hett, Loeb Classical Library (Cambridge, Mass: Harvard University Press, and London: Heinemann, 1986 [1936]).

and that we must believe most faithfully: again, Descartes is quoting the decree of the Council of Trent, Session XIII, ch. 1, *Enchiridion symbolorum*, para. 1636.

the Church has never taught anywhere: Descartes insists on the distinction between the doctrine of transubstantiation itself, as defined by the Church, and conventional theological explanations of it. What follows is contained only in the second edition, having being withdrawn, on Mersenne's advice, from the first, so as not to alienate theologians (to Huygens, 26 Apr. 1642, AT 3. 785). It has been noted that at the Council of Trent 'care was taken to avoid any formal definition of transubstantiation in terms of accidents and substance': E. L. Cross and E. A. Livingstone (eds.), *The Oxford Dictionary of the Christian Church*, 3rd edn. revd (Oxford: Oxford University Press, 2005), 570b, s.v. 'Eucharist'.

163 *parted company with the Roman Church about this issue*: Lutherans, for instance, taught that the bread remains, although Christ is really present within it ('consubstantiation' or 'impanation'). Calvinists held that although no change in the bread and wine took place, the faithful received the power or virtue of the Body and Blood of Christ.

164 *the treatise on the principles of philosophy I am now working on*: the *Principles of Philosophy*, published in 1644.

depend only on the outermost surface of bodies: see *Principles*, IV. 191–8.

164 *the words of consecration*: the words of Christ, 'This is my body', 'This is my blood', repeated by the priest in the service of the Mass. Descartes's point is that the words of the consecration make the bread into Christ's body, but cannot be taken to produce any other effect (in this case that the 'accidents' of the bread should exist in the absence of its substance).

an altogether new miracle: the conventional explanation requires, in addition to the miraculous transformation of the substance of bread into that of Christ's body, the miraculous preservation of the accidents of bread in the absence of its substance. On some occasions, it would seem, the body of Christ has actually appeared in the sacrament: the accidents themselves have been replaced by those of Christ's own flesh. In theory, this should have been explained by the cessation of the miraculous preservation of the accidents. In practice, it was taken to be a new miracle. And this spontaneous religious sentiment accords with Descartes's theory. He requires no miracle for the preservation of the accidents, though their exceptional replacement by Christ's flesh would need a miracle. Thus his explanation is both more economical and more in keeping with spontaneous religious sentiment.

must always act and be acted on in the same way: since the surface of the new substance remains our senses will be affected in the same way as by the old one: we shall continue to perceive it with the old appearances (white, round, etc.).

FIFTH OBJECTIONS AND REPLIES

166 *deluded*: *ludificatio* in Latin can mean either 'ridiculing' or 'fooling'. As a summary of Descartes's argument, the latter reading seems more natural: you may be being fooled about everything else by the deceiver, but you, who are being fooled, must exist. Descartes, however, reads Gassendi as saying 'you are persisting in your joke', which sense the Latin words could also bear, and, as we shall see, vehemently objects.

167 *as an inner and secret part*: cf. F: 'the innermost and most secret part of yourself'.

O soul: Gassendi ironically addresses Descartes as 'O soul' ('ô Anima'), since he identifies himself with the soul as distinct from the body. Later (II. 4) he notes that for Descartes 'soul' refers only to the intellectual faculty, the mind ('mens'). Henceforth he addresses him only as 'Mens'.

168 *the solid body*: for Gassendi there is a key distinction between two kinds of body: solid (*crassum*) and subtle (*tenue*). The human body, as a set of limbs and organs, would be an example of the former; air, breath, fire, vapour, of the latter. Whether or not the soul is, as Gassendi suggests, a 'subtle' body, he argues that it needs the help of the solid body in order to think. Descartes thinks the distinction between 'solid' and 'subtle' bodies unimportant when it comes to distinguishing between kinds of substance (thinking and extended).

do you mean to say that the mind is thinking continuously?: Hobbes and Arnauld also raise the question.

169 *phlegm*: in the chemistry of the time, the watery part released from bodies by distillation, from which the alcohol is then extracted (see Alquié's note, *OP* ii. 723, n. 1).

tartar: 'a brownish-red substance consisting mainly of potassium hydrogen tartrate, present in grape juice and deposited during the fermentation of wine' (*Collins English Dictionary*).

170 *observations and experiments*: I follow Ian Maclean, *Discourse*, 73 (p. 26, n. 1) in translating *experimenta* as 'observations and experiments' since the word at this period can bear either sense and the context here does not determine in favour of one or the other. Note Gassendi's assumption that all knowledge conforms to the model of scientific observation of an object.

a source of error: because it might lead us to assert what is false, thinking we clearly and distinctly perceive it to be true. See Alquié, *OP* ii. 726, n. 1.

171 *you must mean its conformity to the thing of which it is the idea*: Gassendi is off target here: the 'objective' reality of an idea, as conceived by Descartes, is not a matter of its accuracy as a representation of a really existing thing. The idea of a thing has a certain quota of 'objective reality', proportionate to the formal reality the thing would have *if it existed*, as a substance (finite or infinite) or an attribute.

172 *the material cause, not the efficient cause*: Gassendi here mobilizes the Aristotelian taxonomy of causes (*Metaphysics*, V. ii. 1–3 (1013^{a-b})). The material cause is the matter from which the effect is made (say, the wood used by a carpenter to make a table). The efficient cause is the agent that brings the effect about (the carpenter himself). He does not here mention the other two kinds of cause: formal (what gives the effect its form—here, the carpenter's idea of a table), and final (that for the sake of which the effect is produced, the purpose the table will fulfil). Final causes are discussed later.

'species' that impact upon your eye: on 'species' see above, note to p. 161.

173 *in the thing to which the idea relates*: Gassendi seems to anticipate here his critique of the 'ontological' argument of the Fifth Meditation.

174 *even when the cause that has produced it has perished*: Descartes agrees: see Fifth Replies, p. 192.

whatever implies limitation, such as body: Gassendi is sketching out what he takes to be a sounder approach to arguing for the existence of God.

175 *you had closed your eyes . . . and ignored the other senses*: an allusion to the opening of the Third Meditation.

176 *the will's indifference*: see Fourth Meditation pp. 41–3 and notes.

which the intellect has apprehended as other than it is: on this passage, see the Introduction, p. xxxix.

177 *human beings exist, and are animals*: thus *all* propositions about essences involve an implicit assertion of existence. In the light of this view, it is not surprising that Gassendi does not accept the ontological argument for God's existence, which holds that the link between essence and existence applies to God alone. See below.

178 *it is that without which there are no perfections*: cf. F, 'it is a form or an act without which there can be no perfections'.

but as that in which both itself and its perfections are existent . . . and the perfections not to be possessed: cf. F, 'but as a form or an act by which the thing itself and its perfections are existent and without which neither it nor its perfections would exist'.

begging the question: (L, *principium petere*), in the technical sense of putting forward a proof that assumes what it purports to prove. Descartes, says Gassendi, is trying to prove God's existence from his perfections: but if he did not exist in the first place, one could not speak of him having any perfections. Gassendi's objection (existence is not a property among others) will be restated by Kant, *Critique of Pure Reason*, 502 (A 594–5/ B 622–3).

unless he had existence as well as wings: a familiar (and faulty) objection to the ontological argument, dating back to Gaunilo, the critic of St Anselm, who first propounded a version of it. The concept of a 'supremely perfect horse' is self-contradictory, since a horse is a finite substance.

compatible in the first place: as noted above (note to p. 81), a similar objection is urged by Leibniz.

179 *confusedly and with little or no effort*: clearly Descartes would not be prepared to accept this reformulation of his position.

those of the immaterial beings we believe in: or, possibly, 'ideas of things believed to be immaterial' (which is closer to F). However, Gassendi is most likely implying not that these beliefs are erroneous (as if God were really a body), but that immaterial beings are objects of religious faith, not philosophical understanding.

you can't be serious: Gassendi thinks it absurd to say we conjecture something to be probably true (that bodies exist) when we know it is true. As usual, he refuses to take Descartes's doubt seriously or to follow his logic.

180 *apropos of the Second Meditation*: Gassendi does not see that the knowledge of myself as a thinking thing has a completely different significance in the Second Meditation and in the Sixth. In the latter it is supported by the knowledge of a non-deceiving God.

'entelechy': Gassendi uses the Greek word *entelecheia*, a term of Aristotle's, which can be translated 'actuality'. He is presupposing the Aristotelian theory of matter and form. Matter, for Aristotle, is by itself pure potentiality or possibility: it can only exist when actualized in some form, that of a branch, say, or a table-leg. Soul is a particular kind of form that actualizes matter as a living body of a particular species.

See Aristotle, *De anima*, II. 1 (412ª–413ª). Gassendi is using 'perfection' in much the same sense as 'actuality', and 'species' and 'form' as more or less synonymous.

though in a different sense than they would admit: Gassendi's critique is two-pronged. First, he mobilizes the Aristotelian model of the soul, still dominant among seventeenth-century scholastic philosophers. If the soul, as in this theory, is what makes the body a living human body, it is not separable from the 'solid' body. This is so whether or not we factor in the Aristotelian concepts of the possible, or passive, intellect and the active intellect. To summarize one of the most difficult areas of Aristotle's philosophy, the active intellect enables the passive intellect to realize its capacity, by uniting it, so to speak, with the object of knowledge. See *De anima*, III. 5 (430ª) and Ross, *Aristotle*, 148–53 (where the term 'reason' is used instead of 'intellect'). Gassendi claims not to be endorsing these philosophers' views. But he is arguably using the rhetorical figure of *preteritio*, where the speaker affects not to say something he nonetheless is saying ('I will say nothing of his disastrous performance as Minister for Social Affairs'). That is to say, he is not so much reaffirming the Aristotelian categories as valid as pointing out that they provide a complex alternative model to Descartes's dualism, which Descartes does not even trouble to discuss. He then passes on to his second critique: Descartes fails to consider that he himself may be a 'subtle' body.

181 *subject*: Gassendi uses 'subject' here, like Descartes himself, to mean anything of which certain attributes are posited.

so far from having a clear and distinct idea of yourself, you seem to have none at all: the objection that we have no clear idea of ourselves will be emphasized by Descartes's most important and original follower, Malebranche.

182 *Bucephalus*: Alexander the Great's horse.

183 *those people whose minds are so immersed in their senses that they recoil from metaphysical arguments*: Descartes will be criticizing the objections harshly, and so to make it seem that he is not criticizing Gassendi, he affects to believe that Gassendi is not speaking for himself, but for a certain category of incompetent readers. He adopts no such subterfuge with Hobbes.

184 *rhetorical flavouring*: the disparaging comparison of rhetoric with cookery goes back to Plato.

when I am perfectly serious: it is possible that Descartes has misunderstood Gassendi's words here. See the notes on the corresponding passage in the Fifth Objections above, p. 166.

185 *my distinction between soul and body*: Gassendi seems to find it difficult to distinguish when Descartes is speaking provisionally and when definitively, and which of his former beliefs he has abandoned and which he would maintain. Here in particular he seems not to realize that Descartes is talking about his former beliefs, corresponding to the general view of scholastic philosophers, and that he has since redistributed various supposed

functions of the soul between soul and body. Thus the physical process of walking or touching now belongs to the body alone, the consciousness of them to the soul. Not all the original beliefs were false, for in the original passage Descartes includes the belief that bodies are incapable of thought. But some of his former beliefs about the nature of bodies (e.g. that they cannot move themselves) turn out to be false (as is plain from the example of the spinning-top: see below).

185 *metaphysical certainty*: absolute certainty, which we aim at in the search for truth, distinguished implicitly from 'moral' certainty, which is sufficient for the conduct of life (it would be ridiculous to distrust our oldest and best friends because we cannot logically prove their friendship is genuine).

186 *O flesh*: Descartes sarcastically copies Gassendi's strategy of addressing him as a separate mind, closely echoing his words. Again he restates the accusation that Gassendi is substituting rhetoric for philosophy. Prosopopoeia is a rhetorical figure, which can operate in two ways: i. the speaker addresses not his or her actual audience but an imaginary or absent listener: thus Gassendi is addressing not René Descartes but his mind; ii. the speaker speaks not in his or her own person, but in someone else's ('if Winston Churchill were alive, he would be saying "You have betrayed everything I fought for"'). Descartes pretends to read Gassendi's discourse as a prosopopoeia in this latter sense as well: this cannot be Gassendi himself talking, he must be speaking for the materially minded and hence metaphysically incompetent reader. See Quintilian, *Institutio oratoria*, ed. and trans. H. E. Butler, 4 vols., Loeb Classical Library (Cambridge, Mass.: Harvard University Press, and London: Heinemann, 1920–2), III. viii. 49–52, VI. i. 25, IX. ii. 29–37, XI. i. 39–41.

187 *the quality of the tool*: it is fair to say that this notion of the soul using the body as a tool or instrument, which has been influential on modern perceptions of Descartes, is hard to square with the account of body–soul union in the Sixth Meditation, the letters to Elisabeth, and *The Passions of the Soul*.

nor that the solid body contributes nothing to thinking: the 'solid body' plays a role in certain kinds of thinking, e.g. sensation.

principle: here in the sense of an underlying source or agency.

189 *nothing similar to the properties of mind*: as Alquié observes, this is a hasty answer to a perfectly serious point (*OP* ii. 802, n. 2).

by some chemical procedure: Gassendi's words were 'by some quasi-chemical procedure' or 'by, so to speak, a chemical procedure'.

190 *the thought of seeing and touching*: 'thought' (L *cogitatio*, F *pensée*) here refers to the conscious experience of seeing, touching, etc.

191 *the efficient cause, not the material*: on the distinction between different kinds of causality, see above, note to p. 172.

some things can move themselves: Descartes's example here is a spinning-top, which once set in motion continues moving.

192 *they exist by his continued influence*: otherwise they would owe their existence to nothing, or to themselves. But a finite being, Descartes argues, cannot be self-existent.

without God choosing to annihilate us: a positive will on God's part to annihilate us would be incompatible with his goodness (Alquié, *OP* ii. 815, n. 2).

193 *Apelles*: a famous Greek painter of the 4th century BC. The second part of the sentence refers to Gassendi's suggestion that if you assert that the mark of God's handiwork (the idea of God) is identical with the work itself, you are implying that you are identical with the idea.

What you cite as a mystery: Gassendi's example is the valves of the heart. Descartes argues that there is nothing mysterious in their workings.

194 *God destines us to evil deeds*: Gassendi did not in fact say that God destines us to evil deeds (a view Descartes would recognize as hardline Calvinism). He accepts that for God to distribute cognitive powers unequally is no more unfair than for a ruler to allocate higher functions to some citizens than to others. But if a ruler allocated some citizens degrading or immoral tasks, we should think him at fault. Likewise, we can wonder why the cognitive powers God has given us are not simply limited but faulty. Descartes conflates the analogy and the reality it is intended to illuminate.

195 *so it now just happens to be being moved towards the truth*: in other words, we are not really involved in correcting our views: we are simply responding blindly to the changes of our understanding. It does seem here that Descartes has bought excessively into the scholastic tendency to reify the different activities of the soul, treating them as separate agencies within the psyche.

everything I have written about all the others: Descartes does not mean that the proof of one point in the argument depends on a later point, because in that case he could well be accused of arguing in a circle: he must mean that the development of the argument throws light retrospectively on its earlier stages.

they are immutable and eternal because God so wished them to be: Descartes's view that the eternal truths are such only because God chose to create them as such is set out in the letters to Mersenne of 15 April 1630 and 6 May 1630 (AT 1. 145–6, 149–50).

'universals': Gassendi was attacking the view (known as 'realism' in one use of this term) upheld by some scholastics that the properties we attribute to particular things exist as 'universal' realities above and beyond particulars and outside the human mind. Thus, Plato is human because he has a share in a universal human nature existing above and beyond individual human beings. Descartes, however, points out that he is not talking of properties in general but of things that are clearly and distinctly known.

196 *not derived from actually existing things*: see Fifth Objections, VI. 1, p. 179.

in reality: L, 'revera', here used with the implication that necessary existence does not belong merely to the abstract idea of God, but to God himself existing in reality; it is a property 'in the strictest possible sense' of being an exclusive property, not one he might share with other beings.

God is his being: what God is, is being (*esse*): his nature is (his) existence. The same cannot be said of anything else.

chimeras: imaginary beings of Greek mythology, part-lion, part-goat, and part-snake.

198 *This shows a fundamental misunderstanding*: Descartes's reply here does not engage with Gassendi's use of Aristotelian theory, in keeping with his tactic of avoiding direct confrontation with Aristotle. He would think the Aristotelian categories confusing and superfluous.

species: on the sense of 'species' here, see above, note to p. 161.

knowledge of any other kind of thing: see above, Fifth Replies, II. 9 (pp. 189–90).

Bucephalus is not music: Descartes misreads Gassendi's 'musca' (fly) as 'musica' (music), and then, in rather surreal fashion, suggests that Gassendi's arguments that the mind must be extended are like arguments for calling a horse music, because of the sounds it makes.

whatever the mind understands is somehow in it: Descartes has got to the root of the matter here, in identifying his target (implicitly) as the Aristotelian view of knowledge in which the object is in the mind, instead of being represented by an idea.

SIXTH OBJECTIONS AND REPLIES

199 *your rule*: the rule that whatever we clearly and distinctly perceive to be true, is true.

200 *the Eucharist*: see Fourth Objections and Replies, pp. 139–40, 160–5, and notes.

of which we are capable: the numbering of the objections stops at this point in the original.

the same logic as you apply: that is to say, we think we can form a clear and distinct idea of God's immensity, without his justice: but they cannot in fact exist separately. Likewise, our clear and distinct idea of a unitary God belies his existence as Three in One. An unbeliever applying your rule ('what I can clearly and distinctly conceive separately from another thing, can exist without that thing') would conclude that God is not essentially Three in One, since he can conceive him as purely unitary. So such clear and distinct ideas of the separateness of two things can be at variance with reality. 'Unbeliever' here (L, 'infidelis'; F, 'infidèle') must mean a believer in one God but not in the Trinity, such as a Jew or a Muslim.

201 *how do you know that God has not endowed some bodies with the ability to think?*: arguments later put forward by Spinoza, *Ethics*, III. 2, scholium; Locke, *An Essay concerning Human Understanding*, ed. Peter H. Nidditch (Oxford: Clarendon Press, 1979 [1975]), IV. 3, pp. 541–2.

202 *in the form of flesh*: we understand that a thing that has bones does not necessarily have flesh, although in many creatures the two are combined.

claimed to have seen the Antipodes: to us this example may look odd, as if Descartes were saying we can believe someone who has been to America and claims to have been to Australia. But 'Antipodes' here is used in its old sense, and probably refers to the inhabitants of a region rather than the region itself. An image of the earth popularized in antiquity by Cicero represented our hemisphere as cut off by an impassable torrid zone from the southern hemisphere inhabited by 'Antipodes' (see C. S. Lewis, *The Discarded Image: An Introduction to Medieval and Renaissance Literature* (Cambridge: Cambridge University Press, 1964), 28, 31, 61). A Church Council of the eighth century denied the existence of the Antipodes, and Descartes alludes to this in a letter to Mersenne of 1634 (AT 1. 288: see *Discourse*, p. xxxvii). Thus it would be perfectly possible to travel to southern America and meet 'Antipodes', but someone who reported doing so would be challenging authorities to the contrary.

203 *animals do not have thought*: 'animals' here renders L *brutis*, and later *belluarum*: strictly speaking, the 'brute beasts', as distinct from human animals.

animals have what is commonly called life, or a bodily soul, or organic senses: this is a crucial passage, for it shows that Descartes does not believe that animals are purely and simply machines, which would imply that they are incapable, for instance, of feeling. See the letter to the Marquess of Newcastle, 23 Nov. 1646, AT 4. 573–6, which credits them with passions such as hope and fear, and even a kind of thought linked to the organs. See also Introduction, p. xxxvii, for recent discussions of the problem. But among the followers of Descartes, Malebranche, for instance, endorses the radical conclusion that animals are incapable of feeling (*Entretiens sur la mort*, I, in *Œuvres*, ed. Geneviève Rodis-Lewis and Germain Malbreil, 2 vols., Bibliothèque de la Pléiade (Paris: Gallimard, 1979–92), ii. 984–5).

204 *those who take the more reasonable line*: Descartes is not implying that this view (such as Gassendi would subscribe to) is intrinsically rational, still less a tenable alternative to his. It is, however, a rational deduction from a faulty initial position, and incorporates a degree of observation, whereas the view that sees humans also as mechanical flies in the facts of our most immediate experience.

to choose one alternative rather than the other: it is not that God sees intellectually that something is good or true, and approves or endorses it by an act of his will: his will makes it good or true. The 'reasoning reason' (L, 'ratio ratiocinata'; F, 'raison raisonnée') is the reason that proceeds by steps, by applying e.g. general laws to particular instances, rather than grasping truth through intuition.

204 *the merits of the saints are the cause of their obtaining eternal life*: Descartes has been arguing that God's will cannot be determined by anything outside himself. But this might be held to imply that human actions cannot contribute to salvation, and that salvation or damnation depends wholly on God's predestination—a Calvinist position. Descartes therefore points out that his theory is entirely compatible with the Catholic belief that human efforts can earn 'merit', that is, that they have a role, subordinate to God's grace, in bringing about salvation.

205 *when clear perception impels us to pursue something*: this view of human freedom develops the line of argument of the Fourth Meditation. Whether Descartes's later writings on freedom (in particular the letters to Mesland of 2 May 1644 and 9 Feb. 1645 (AT 4. 115–18, 173–5) involve a change of view is much debated. See Étienne Gilson, *La Liberté chez Descartes et la théologie* (Paris: Alcan, 1913) and Ferdinand Alquié, *La Découverte métaphysique de l'homme chez Descartes* (Paris: Presses Universitaires de France, 1950), 280–99, who argue that there is a change; and, for the alternative view, Jean Laporte, 'La Liberté selon Descartes', in *Études d'histoire de la philosophie française du XVIIe siècle* (Paris: Vrin, 1951), 37–87, and Anthony Kenny, 'Descartes on the Will', in Cottingham (ed.), *Descartes* (Oxford: Oxford University Press, 1998), 132–59.

206 *can accidentally modify another*: cf. F, 'can be applied to another'. A coat is a substance, yet when a person (also a substance) puts it on, it modifies their substance by endowing it with a new quality or accident. But the coat has not become an accident; rather, it is the means by which the person acquires the accident 'wearing a coat'.

with respect to each of the senses in turn: see *Principles*, IV. 189–95.

as Genesis says, 'very good': Gen. 1: 31.

207 *the list of different kinds of cause*: Descartes is referring to the Aristotelian taxonomy of causes discussed above, note to p. 172.

they could be otherwise than they are: the Aristotelian conception of knowledge includes the requirement that we know that the fact in question cannot be otherwise than it is (*Posterior Analytics*, I. 2 (71^b)). But from Descartes's point of view, we can know in the abstract that e.g. 2×4 might not have been equal to 8, if God had so ordained. Yet this does not, he implies, undermine our claims to knowledge: for we cannot understand 2×4 as not being equal to 8. Within the limits of our understanding, then, we can be said to know that $2 \times 4 = 8$, and that this cannot be otherwise. Thus the essence of the Aristotelian requirement is retained. But one can see why it has been argued that the doctrine of the createdness of the eternal truths bears, in its implications, a certain affinity to Kantianism. See Alquié, *La Découverte*, 87–109, esp. pp. 108–9.

some 'intentional species' fly from the stick into the eye: F explains the term 'intentional species': 'we should not imagine that the stick sends tiny images of itself (what are commonly called "intentional species") flying through the air to the eye.' See above, note to p. 161.

208 *deducing them from one another*: La Dioptrique, VI, AT 6. 130–47; see esp. pp. 140–1.

the certainty of the intellect is far greater than that of the senses: the certainty that derives from the intellect ranges, of course, far wider than the correction of sense-perceptions. Descartes' point is relative to the context of sense-perception.

211 *substantial forms*: in Aristotelian metaphysics all substances are composed of matter and form. So, in any existing thing, e.g. a table, it is the form 'table' that makes it what it is (not a chair), but this could not happen without the matter (wood or metal) through which the form is realized (*Metaphysics*, VII. iii. 2 (1029ª) for the second part). Each substance, then, must have a 'substantial form' that makes it what it is. In the process of change, say, from water to ice, the 'substantial form' of water is superseded by the 'substantial form' of ice, the underlying matter remaining the same. Descartes dispenses with the concept of substantial forms in general but allows that the soul can be referred to as the 'true substantial form of the human being' (to Regius, Jan. 1642, AT 3. 505). (In this particular case, he is, however, urging Regius, his follower, to retain traditional terminology as much as possible so as to defuse attacks by critics: see Desmond M. Clarke, *Descartes: A Biography* (Cambridge: Cambridge University Press, 2006), 218–26.) But different material substances are simply different combinations of matter. On the rejection of substantial forms, see Daniel Garber, 'Descartes' Physics', *CCD*, 286–334 (esp. pp. 287, 301–3), and Desmond M. Clarke, *Descartes's Theory of Mind* (Oxford: Oxford University Press, 2003), 16–23. On real qualities, see above, pp. 160–4.

I did not doubt that I had 'a clear idea of my mind' . . . *conscious of it in myself*: cf. F, 'I no longer doubted that I had a clear idea of my own mind, of which I could not deny that I had knowledge, since it was so present to me and so conjoined with me'.

212 *the Most Holy Trinity*: Descartes is careful to mark his adherence to the orthodox doctrine of the Trinity: the three persons participate equally in the divine essence (each is as much God as the other two), yet differ as to their relationships (the Father, the Son begotten by the Father, and the Holy Spirit who proceeds from both). See above, Fourth Replies, p. 153.

if God endowed certain bodies with the power of thought: Descartes is considering the objection that we cannot set limits to God's power: for all we know, he could endow bodies with the ability to think. Relying on the presupposition that God cannot do what is intrinsically contradictory, Descartes is implying that the only sense in which God can be said to endow bodies with thought is that he combines them with a separate and separable thinking substance.

SEVENTH OBJECTIONS

215 *no certainty that what appears certain . . . is in fact certain*: a recurring
theme of Bourdin's critique, and perhaps the only telling point he makes.
See Alquié, *OP* ii. 955, n. 1–3.

until we know that whatever we clearly perceive is true: Descartes is restating the point he made in answer to the accusation of arguing in a circle
(Second and Fourth Objections and Replies).

216 *in other words, that is not true*: Descartes restates the same point in similar
words on p. 225.

one cannot achieve certainty by starting from doubtful propositions: Bourdin's
objection is sound from the point of view of traditional logic: one cannot
draw a conclusion that is certain from doubtful premises. But in Descartes's
philosophy doubt is not a quality of propositions: it is a mental exercise,
designed to open our minds to the experience of certainty.

217 *The approach to the method is opened up*: Bourdin here actually quotes at
length from the text of the First Meditation (pp. 16–17).

(K): there is no point (J), the letters I and J being equivalent in the Latin
alphabet. Ditto for U and V. The Latin alphabet does not contain W.

218 *old truths*: as examples of such truths, Bourdin cites 'An argument in
Barbara is sound', and 'I am a thing composed of body and soul'.
'Barbara' is the name for the classic form of the syllogism, whereby from
two universal affirmative premises ('All mammals are warm-blooded',
'All human beings are mammals') a universal affirmative conclusion is
drawn ('All human beings are warm-blooded').

can never subsequently be rendered certain: the same point is made at
pp. 219, 220. It is a restatement of what Descartes says at the end of the
Fifth Meditation (pp. 50–1).

219 *a fit exercise for everyone*: Fourth Replies, p. 159; Preface to the Reader,
pp. 8–9; *A Discourse on the Method*, II. 15, AT 6. 15.

from the point of view of practical life: on the distinction between practical
life and the search for truth, see above, note to p. 16.

by affirming your existence: Bourdin proceeds to ironize over Descartes's
reference to Archimedes (p. 17).

once a rooster: Pythagoras, the Greek mathematician and philosopher
(6th century BC), is said to have taught the doctrine of metempsychosis
(the transmigration of souls from one creature, e.g. an animal, to another,
e.g. a human being).

220 *a basket full of apples*: Cf. p. 225, where the image recurs. It has been criticized, since it seems to imply that Descartes can simply examine each of
his former beliefs in isolation and decide whether they are true, whereas
they have in fact to be inserted into a system of deductions from the fundamental certainty of the Cogito, which is therefore something other than

one belief (one apple, so to speak) among others (Alquié, *OP* ii. 982 n.); or because Descartes presupposes without proof that having some false beliefs should prevent my being certain about any (Anthony Kenny, *Descartes: A Study of His Philosophy* (New York: Random House, 1968), 18–19).

221 *This is not my approach at all*: Bourdin seems indeed to be taking Descartes's exposition of his former beliefs as simply a restatement of them as true. See also Dd (pp. 221, 222).

I am a body: Bourdin continues to interpret Descartes's argumentation as simply based on his old beliefs—but if the beliefs were false, as Descartes himself stated, how can they lead to truth? Besides, as in this example, from a former (false) belief, he can reach a quite opposite conclusion to Descartes's.

222 *apprehensive, slow-witted, unintelligent*: this ironic self-depreciation is indeed part of Bourdin's rhetorical strategy. Descartes's theatrical allusion is interesting: he compares Bourdin not to the comic slaves of ancient comedy, but to the low clowns of contemporary theatre. On his discussion of drama, see Henry Phillips, 'Descartes and the Dramatic Experience', *French Studies*, 39 (1985), 408–22.

I am either a body or a non-body: the contraries 'mind' and 'body' cannot provide a foundation for the argument. Bourdin imagines Descartes trying afresh with the contradictories 'body' and 'non-body'.

223 *you have overlooked it*: Bourdin's fundamental point is this. Descartes's argument depends on the contrast between my lack of certainty as to what I am (e.g. a body) and my certainty that I exist. Consequently, he suggests, it collapses if we recognize that we have an *indeterminate* certainty of being something. This is why the indeterminate–determinate distinction is (he thinks) so crucial.

224 *we cannot infer the existence of anything from our own knowledge of it*: Bourdin quotes the scholastic adage *a nosse ad esse non valet consequentia* ('from knowledge to being there is no valid inference'). He here adds a diagram, a logical matrix, of the type known as the 'Porphyrian tree', mapping out the possible variations of thinking substance. It is either corporeal (i.e. having and using a body) or incorporeal. The first division subdivides into extended and divisible substances, like the soul of a horse or a dog, and non-extended indivisible substances, like the mind of Socrates or Plato. The second subdivision contains God and the angels. The point is to suggest that Descartes should have measured his alleged self-knowledge against the categories in the diagram, so as to have a more accurate idea of his own nature.

Much of what Bourdin says is frivolous: Descartes does not take seriously Bourdin's question whether there was in fact a past time in which he held various beliefs. Bourdin makes the same point at Nn (p. 223).

225 *a figment of his own brain*: the passage, too long to quote here, is a splendid satirical portrayal of Bourdin as a stage performer acting out a battle
against an invisible adversary.

that everything is supposed to be rejected: more literally, that nothing is not
supposed to be rejected. That is to say, he fails to see how a preliminary
rejection of all beliefs can lead to later affirmations.

226 *any thinking substance that is divisible*: the reference is to the category of
extended and divisible souls, like that of a horse or a dog, in Bourdin's
diagram (see note to p. 224).

are meaningless here: this is not entirely fair. Bourdin wants Descartes to
acknowledge indeterminate, confused, implicit forms of knowledge, cut-
ting across his too rigid distinction between ignorance or doubt and actual
certainty. However, the very notion of innate ideas, as used by Descartes,
shows that he is well aware that not all knowledge is actual.

I do use syllogism when it is appropriate: for example, the ontological argument for the existence of God has the structure of a syllogism, but it is
noteworthy that in the body of the Fifth Meditation he does not set it out
in an explicitly syllogistic form. He does so in reply to objections, where
the objectors appeal to the syllogistic model to disclose alleged fallacies in
the argument (see First Replies, p. 81; Second Replies, §6, pp. 97–8).

It is presented as timeless: the proposition is in fact only temporarily true,
true, that is, for the duration of the doubting process that takes place in
the First Meditation. The syllogistic form is in fact ill suited to represent
the process of thought over time.

227 *pruning more ruthlessly than necessary*: cf. F, 'seeking to incorporate more
than it can'. The translator (Clerselier) reads L *stringit* (of which the fundamental sense is 'to strip, clip, prune') as meaning something like 'grips'
or 'grasps at': i.e. the method attempts great things but achieves nothing.
I think the context implies the alternative reading given in the translation
here (which draws on the etymological sense of the Latin verb): you make
tremendous efforts to reject what is uncertain, in the hope of achieving
certainty, but nothing results.

229 *will they not write him off as well?*: more literally: 'He will add them to the
list of hopeless or condemned cases: but in the meantime to what list will
they add him?'

230 *reasons more certain than any of those we have for accepting all appearances*:
the sceptics' logic, as reconstructed by Descartes, is this. It certainly
appears to us—we can't help thinking—that e.g. bodies exist, that a
London bus is red, and so forth. So we accept this in practice. But we
have no *certain* reason to believe that appearances correspond to reality.
But since e.g. the existence of God is not so apparent as that of bodies,
we would require even stronger arguments in order to believe in it than
those (by which we are not convinced) in favour of accepting the reality
of appearances.

subsection 5: The subsections here refer to Descartes's rewriting of sec. 12 of Bourdin's critique of the method in his Answer to Question 2 (see p. 228).

231 *to block the understanding of the real distinction between the human mind and the body*: this is an important but difficult passage. It is important to recognize that Descartes is not discussing the nature of thinking in general, but purely what kind of thinking constitutes the difference between immaterial and material substance. From this point of view Bourdin's focus on reflexivity is disastrous, because it implies that immaterial substances can think, albeit non-reflexively, and so undermines the argument for the real distinction between thinking and extended substances. On the other hand, if reflexivity is not essential to thinking, it might, after all, appear that animals can think, since Descartes does not deny that they have sensations, merely that they are aware of their sensations in the same way as we are or can be. The solution would have to be something like this: thought involves a capacity to become aware of itself (the presence of a fire near me causes a physical sensation of heat, such as an animal can have, but of which, as a human, I can become aware ('I'm feeling hot')), without this awareness being the result of a quite distinct reflexive act, a conscious attention to the sensation of heat, of the kind Bourdin seems to require. (For an important treatment of the concept of consciousness in Descartes, see Gordon Baker and Katherine J. Morris, *Descartes' Dualism* (London: Routledge, 1996). In any case, this passage, as Jean-Luc Marion points out (*Questions cartésiennes: méthode et métaphysique* (Paris: Presses Universitaires de France, 1991), 165–6) militates against the view, influentially propagated by Heidegger, that for Descartes thinking is intrinsically reflexive, *cogito* always meaning *cogito me cogitare* ('I am thinking that I am thinking'): that thinking is an act by which I represent myself to myself as thinking. See Martin Heidegger, *Nietzsche*, trans. Frank A. Capuzzi, ed. David Farrell Krell (San Francisco: Harper & Row, 1979–87), vol. 4: *Nihilism* (1982), 106–10.

INDEX

The Oxford World's Classics Website

www.worldsclassics.co.uk

- Browse the full range of Oxford World's Classics online

- Sign up for our monthly e-alert to receive information on new titles

- Read extracts from the Introductions

- Listen to our editors and translators talk about the world's greatest literature with our Oxford World's Classics audio guides

- Join the conversation, follow us on Twitter at OWC_Oxford

- Teachers and lecturers can order inspection copies quickly and simply via our website

www.worldsclassics.co.uk

American Literature

British and Irish Literature

Children's Literature

Classics and Ancient Literature

Colonial Literature

Eastern Literature

European Literature

Gothic Literature

History

Medieval Literature

Oxford English Drama

Poetry

Philosophy

Politics

Religion

The Oxford Shakespeare

A complete list of Oxford World's Classics, including Authors in Context, Oxford English Drama, and the Oxford Shakespeare, is available in the UK from the Marketing Services Department, Oxford University Press, Great Clarendon Street, Oxford OX2 6DP, or visit the website at www.oup.com/uk/worldsclassics.

In the USA, visit www.oup.com/us/owc for a complete title list.

Oxford World's Classics are available from all good bookshops. In case of difficulty, customers in the UK should contact Oxford University Press Bookshop, 116 High Street, Oxford OX1 4BR.

HORACE	The Complete Odes and Epodes
JUVENAL	The Satires
LIVY	The Dawn of the Roman Empire
	Hannibal's War
	The Rise of Rome
MARCUS AURELIUS	The Meditations
OVID	The Love Poems
	Metamorphoses
PETRONIUS	The Satyricon
PLATO	Defence of Socrates, Euthyphro, and Crito
	Gorgias
	Meno and Other Dialogues
	Phaedo
	Republic
	Selected Myths
	Symposium
PLAUTUS	Four Comedies
PLUTARCH	Greek Lives
	Roman Lives
	Selected Essays and Dialogues
PROPERTIUS	The Poems
SOPHOCLES	Antigone, Oedipus the King, and Electra
STATIUS	Thebaid
SUETONIUS	Lives of the Caesars
TACITUS	Agricola and Germany
	The Histories
VIRGIL	The Aeneid
	The Eclogues and Georgics
XENOPHON	The Expedition of Cyrus